years. They have assimilated and synthesized a number of approaches (standard and revisionist) to a series of problems, and have taken into account (when applicable) periodical literature, m i m e o-graphed studies, and theses and dissertations as well as books. The result is a work of vital interest not merely to specialists, but to the general community of Latin Americanists.

Currently a contributing editor to the *Handbook of Latin American Studies,* Dr. ROBERTO ESQUENAZI-MAYO is director of the Institute of Latin American and International Studies, p r o f e s s o r of romance languages and literature and department chairman, University of Nebraska. He received the Cuban National Prize in Literature in 1951 for *Memorias de un estudiante soldado.* He is the author of *Historiography of the War between Mexico and the United States* (1962), has translated the works of Lewis Hanke and Frank Tannenbaum into Spanish, and has contributed to numerous scholarly publications, including *Revista Hispánica Moderna* and *Cuadernos.* He was formerly a correspondent to the United Nations and an editor of the Spanish edition of *Life.*

DR. MICHAEL C. MEYER is professor of history, University of Nebraska. He is the author of *Mexican Rebel: Pascual Orozco and the Mexican Revolution, 1910–1915* and co-editor of *A Bibliography of United States–Latin American Relations since 1810* (1968). His articles have appeared in *The Americas, New Mexico Historical Review,* and *Hispanic American Historical Review.*

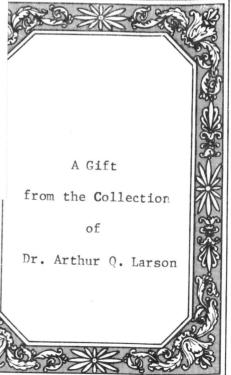

LATIN AMERICAN SCHOLARSHIP

SINCE WORLD WAR II

# LATIN AMERICAN SCHOLARSHIP
# SINCE WORLD WAR II

*Trends in History, Political Science, Literature,*
*Geography, and Economics*

Edited by
ROBERTO ESQUENAZI-MAYO
and
MICHAEL C. MEYER

*98 - 229*

UNIVERSITY OF NEBRASKA PRESS · LINCOLN

# CONTENTS

# LIST OF CONTRIBUTORS

Robert J. Alexander, Professor of Economics and Political Science, Rutgers State University

Martin Carnoy, Assistant Professor of Education and Economics, Stanford University

Joseph T. Criscenti, Associate Professor of History, Boston College

Raymond E. Crist, Research Professor of Geography, University of Florida

Joshua C. Dickinson III, Assistant Professor of Geography, University of Florida

Bernard Gicovate, Chairman, Department of Spanish and Portuguese, Stanford University

Richard Graham, Professor of History, University of Texas

Charles A. Hale, Associate Professor of History, University of Iowa

Luis Leal, Professor of Spanish, University of Illinois

Fábio Lucas, Visiting Professor of Brazilian Literature, University of Minnesota

Wilson Martins, Professor of Romance Languages and Literatures, New York University

Thomas G. Mathews, Research Professor of Social Sciences, University of Puerto Rico

Michael C. Meyer, Professor of History, University of Nebraska

Frederick M. Nunn, Associate Professor of History, Portland State University.

Stephen L. Rozman, Assistant Professor of Political Science, University of Nebraska

Stuart B. Schwartz, Assistant Professor of History, University of Minnesota

John TePaske, Professor of History, Duke University

Roger R. Trask, Associate Professor of History, Macalester College

Frederick C. Turner, Professor of Political Science, University of Connecticut

# INTRODUCTION

During the last twenty-five years Latin American studies in United States colleges and universities may be said to have come of age. New journals have been founded, new courses have been introduced, staffs and faculties have been enlarged, library funds for Latin American acquisitions have been augmented, and increased funds have been made available for graduate and postdoctoral research. Interdisciplinary programs have proliferated both at the small undergraduate liberal arts college and the large state university. In addition to their more traditional academic pursuits, the interdisciplinary programs often have assumed many ancillary functions for government and industry, much as has the university community at large. The results of this clearly demonstrable growth in the Latin American field are manifold, and certainly not least among them has been a tremendous publication explosion which has left even the most dedicated professional at times bewildered and distressed.

The scholar finds it increasingly difficult to keep abreast of publications—even in his own field. It is almost a truism that his knowledge of trends in most of the disciplines, which in an earlier day were considered necessarily supportive, is at best scant. It is easy, perhaps too easy, to single out the publish or perish syndrome as the culprit in the publication explosion; but this generic censure of academia, even if it is justified, does nothing to alert the scholar or the student to what is new and valid or refreshing and stimulating in fields that are inevitably crowded by works of peripheral interest and marginal significance.

The evidence is persuasive that the publication explosion is not solely responsible for the lack of intellectual communication between the disciplines. True as it may be that keeping up with the literature in one's own field is a full-time enterprise, nevertheless, the scholar who haphazardly ventures across the arbitrary disciplinary lines more often than not is quickly discouraged by unfamiliar methodology and terminology and his own scant appreciation for the type of research problem and technique encountered in that strange domain. Retreat to the more comfortable confines of his field of specialization is too often the norm. But to decry exaggerated specialization is not to proffer relief.

To be sure, the Latin Americanist in any field can turn to a number of indispensable bibliographies, some skillfully annotated, such as

the *Handbook of Latin American Studies,* published annually since
1936. A new interdisciplinary journal, the *Latin American Research
Review,* fills an important gap. But these guides are designed primarily as descriptive summaries of projects recently completed or in
progress and as aids to future research. To our knowledge there is
no single volume dedicated to a conceptualization of Latin American
scholarship in the post–World War II period—certainly none which
is designed in part to acquaint the Latin American historian with
the work of the literary critic, the economist with the work of the
geographer, and the political scientist with the efforts of his colleagues
specializing in the Spanish American or Brazilian novel.

As editors we have assembled a group of Latin Americanists—
historians, political scientists, literary critics, geographers, and economists—and asked them to prepare for us a twenty-five-year overview
of the scholarship and literary currents in their fields of specialization.
They bring to their analyses the type of authority that can be acquired
only from active professional concern in the Latin American area
over a number of years. But they have not rendered a simple store
of knowledge; rather they have assimilated and synthesized a number
of approaches (standard and revisionist) to a series of problems. They
have not limited their analyses to book-length publications but, when
applicable, have included pertinent periodical literature, mimeographed studies, and theses and dissertations as well. The results, we
believe, will be of interest not only to other specialists in their particular fields, but to the general community of Latin Americanists and
to advanced graduate students interested in the region.

Our contributors have isolated and examined a number of different
kinds of problems; some are unique to their respective disciplines
while others are shared by two or three or more. All agree, however,
that the years since the end of World War II have been vital and
productive. Tired shibboleths have been discarded as the scholars
of the postwar era began to view reality in a different way. They
began to ask new kinds of questions and to grapple with new answers.
While the academic community would agree that the responses have
not always been adequate, the queries themselves were more suggestive
and more meaningful to a Western Hemisphere generation which
witnessed, as no other, the ultimate dichotomy between the vast po-
tentiality of scientific innovation on one hand and endemic socioeconomic stagnation on the other.

We have tried, insofar as possible, to standardize the format of the essays. Since specific reference footnotes are at best tangential to the general purpose of the analyses, we have, in their place, appended a numbered bibliography at the end of each article. The numbered references found in parentheses in the body of the text direct the reader to the corresponding citation in the bibliography. Only brief substantive footnotes are included in the articles themselves, and these appear only when the information detracts from the argument developed in the text. Each of the four major sections is preceded by a brief introduction.

To be sure, our project is not as comprehensive as we would have desired; a volume twice the size would not have sufficed to exhaust the subject. Some disciplines have been unavoidably omitted, as other pressing commitments prohibited some contributors from completing their manuscripts in time to be included. The lacunae notwithstanding, we believe that with representation from six fields, the resulting volume makes a useful contribution and that instead of increasing compartmentalization, the total effort yields a more integrated view of two and a half centuries of Latin American scholarship. The scholarship, in turn, reveals certain basic truths about Latin American reality in the postwar period and is illustrative of the nature of the problems that complex region is called upon to face in the 1970s.

We wish to thank Mrs. Linda Weber, secretary of the Institute for Latin American and International Studies, Miss Nikki Bruns, and Miss Charlene Pflug for their assistance in helping to prepare the manuscripts. The University of Nebraska has given encouragement and support throughout the undertaking. And finally, we wish to extend our gratitude and thanks to the eighteen specialists who worked with us so closely in producing this work. This is their volume.

ROBERTO ESQUENAZI-MAYO
Director, Institute for Latin American and
International Studies and Chairman of the Department
of Romance Languages and Literatures, University
of Nebraska

MICHAEL C. MEYER
Professor of History, University of Nebraska

# Part One

# HISTORICAL SCHOLARSHIP SINCE WORLD WAR II

# 1. HISTORICAL SCHOLARSHIP SINCE WORLD WAR II

Latin American historiography since World War II has been marked by increased professionalization, experimentation with new methodology, and, in general, a tendency to question many of the cherished historical assumptions of the past. The historian in Latin America, Europe, and the United States has found his task made somewhat easier by improved research guides and bibliographies, reprints of important works, high-quality journals, and comprehensive projects of documentary publication.

The large majority of Latin American historians have chosen to work in the national period, but as Professor TePaske and Professor Schwartz indicate in their essays, the colonial period has attracted much new talent in the last twenty-five years. Indeed, some of the most significant contributions in the colonial historiography of Spanish America and Brazil are of fairly recent vintage. While the period of conquest and exploration of the early sixteenth century and the late eighteenth-century background to independence continue to find devotees, more colonialists than ever before are venturing into the fertile two hundred years between 1550 and 1750. Overviews and syntheses are losing ground to monographic studies, institutional analyses, and biographies, all based on European and Latin American archival resources, some as yet barely tapped.

The national history of Mexico traditionally has attracted the interest of the Latin American historian in the United States, but in recent years, because of a concerted emphasis in graduate training in the 1960s, Brazilian history has challenged Mexico's hitherto dominant position. In both cases the North American scholar has found that his own efforts, when carefully conceived and executed, complement the excellent work being carried forward by professionally oriented scholars within those two countries. It is heartening that the historiographical relationship in both cases has been marked by cooperation rather than rivalry; while the majority of the most significant work continues to be done by Mexicans and Brazilians, the contributions of United States scholars have been substantial and are recognized as such by the national schools in those countries. An illustration of this trend is that Charles Hale was awarded the Prize in History of the Mexican Instituto Nacional de Antropología e Historia for his scholarly and perceptive *Mexican Liberalism in the Age of Mora.*

3

Argentina and Chile both have long-established historical traditions and until recently most of the history not prepared by the nationals of those two countries was the preserve of the European. Since the end of World War II, however, United States historians have ventured into those fields and, as in the cases of Frederick Pike, Robert Burr, Thomas McGann, and James Scobie, have produced works of superior quality. The record in the Andean republics and the Caribbean is less enviable, but even here where meticulous monographic research has scarely outrun the supply of virgin subject matter, sustained progress is discernible to the trained eye.

It is not yet time for the Latin American historian to rest on his laurels. Access to archival collections must be improved so that the lacunae can continue to be filled. Many analyses of earlier periods still await thoughtful reappraisal. But the record of the last two and a half decades is encouraging and portends sustained enrichment of the field in the 1970s.

# SPANISH AMERICA: THE COLONIAL PERIOD

*John TePaske*

Without question the last twenty-five years have been productive ones for historians of colonial Spanish America. The last quarter century has seen the production of a number of important monographs, new methodological approaches and conceptual schemes, elaborate statistical studies, general syntheses, and bibliographical aides. Scholars have begun to ask and to answer vital new questions. New research has begotten more perplexing problems, but in so doing the field has come of age. One might agree with Pierre Chaunu (18, 19) that colonial Spanish American history is no longer a "privileged area of study," as Lucien Febvre argued in 1929, nor is it still a new frontier. The parameters are now too well staked out, and the pioneer trail blazer has given way to the organizer and systematic plodder.

These should have been good years. For over a decade the Spanish Civil War and World War II closed off opportunities for research in the Archivo de Indias, the Elysian Fields for most investigators working in the colonial period. With the end to the conflict in Europe, however, researchers found it possible to complete long-pending projects and to undertake new ones. For scholars and their students in the United States, especially, and for those in Latin America and Europe as well, a greater abundance of scholarships and fellowships has made possible more frequent pilgrimages to *fondos* in Spain and Latin America. Universities have reduced teaching loads and lent support for research. Jet travel has made shorter periods of investigation more feasible and attendance at international conferences more commonplace. New professional groups such as the Latin American Studies Association and the Consejo Latinoamericano de Ciencias Sociales (CLACSO) have grown up to encourage professional interchange and to act as stimuli to research. New journals such as *Historia Mexicana* and the *Latin American Research Review* have provided additional outlets for scholarly production. To be sure, we have not entered a golden age, but the possibilities for further development of Spanish American colonial history seem bright indeed if we are not subverted by undue emphasis upon the contemporary scene or by the presentistic, short-range vision of those who hold the purse strings for scholarly investigation.

5

Perhaps this last statement deserves a bit of gratuitous elaboration. A few years ago Richard Morse (75) referred tongue-in-cheek to a "Latin American Boom," wryly commenting on the sudden discovery of Latin American history as a new field of study. This boom has been attributed to a number of factors: Fidel Castro, the Third World, Ché Guevara, the present generation's boredom or disenchantment with traditional European and United States history, the quest for relevance (however that may be interpreted), and the search for the exotic in another culture. Whatever the reason, the boom has touched us in the colonial period less than our colleagues who labor on the contemporary scene. In terms of student interest or financial support, we are almost stepchildren, not because of the quality of our work but because of the concentration upon the present and the relevant. While we enthusiastically give our students the last word on sixteenth-century Mexican demography or Spanish colonial administration, they sit bored and restless, waiting for an explanation of the Guatemalan affair of 1954, the ouster of *Belaúnde* in Peru, or the *violencia* in Colombia. Foundations, too, have become more enamoured of the scholar working on relevant topics—social change in Venezuela, the military in Chile, entrepreneurship in Honduras—than of us dedicated to seemingly sterile irrelevancies which cannot be used as tools for social reform and economic change.[1]

My task here is to analyze basic trends in research on colonial Spanish America since World War II. I realize that a subjective analysis is dangerous. For one thing we are not cut from the same mold—methodologically, ideologically, or temperamentally. We bring different values, interests, and attitudes to our research and find personal and scholarly fulfillment in remarkably different sorts of endeavor. To claim a special value for one piece of scholarship over another or to ignore one monograph and highlight another is to risk being accused of academic hubris, especially since so much of ourselves is tied up in our research and writing. Thus it should be clear at the outset that this is a *personal* view of basic trends in research over the past quarter century.

Contrasted with the prewar years, post–World War II scholarship

---

1. See, for example, the restriction to the national period for grants given to North American and Latin American scholars cooperating on the same project by the Joint Committee on Latin American Studies of the Social Science Research Council and the American Council of Learned Societies. Such grants are not open to scholars who wish to cooperate on a project for the colonial period.

has taken a number of different directions. One obvious shift has been away from the semiromantic personal history of the exploits of discoverers and conquistadors, priests, viceroys, and the like. To be sure, books like the Bolton biographies of Coronado and Father Kino or the Prescott histories are absolutely basic, but building on these earlier works, scholars have turned to other themes, even for the highly dramatic period of the conquest. As an example, James Lockhart's fine study (58) covering the years 1532–60 in Peru barely mentions the deeds of the Pizarros and Almagro but attempts to find the underpinning for Peruvian society during its formative years. For Chile in the sixteenth century Alvaro Jara's *Guerre et société au Chili* (46) has the subtitle "Essay in Colonial Sociology" and deals far more with the structure and function of Chilean society than with the feats of the Spanish military or the Araucanians. For Mexico, although Robert Padden's beautifully written *The Hummingbird and the Hawk* (82) does not neglect the conquistadors or their Indian antagonists, the work stresses culture change and the Aztec idea of sovereignty. One might cite numerous other examples of the trends away from romantic eulogizing of heroes, martyrs, villains, and patriots and toward more penetrating analysis of colonial society as a whole, but these are sufficient here.

With some exceptions—Salvador de Madariaga being the most notable—historians of the colonial period have stopped jousting directly with the Black Legend. We have forsaken history rooted in moral outrage, either against Spanish atrocities and barbarities in the New World or against accounts which highlighted these excesses at the expense of Spanish contributions or achievements. We have stopped worrying about the perpetuation or debunking of this myth about Spain in America. To be sure, myths are important in giving meaning to life and ratonalizing one's existence or actions and may be constructive or destructive for an individual, society, or nation. On one level they should be perpetuated or debunked, but serious history does neither; it subjects myths to critiques. Thus serious historians have criticized the Black Legend, not directly but indirectly, through empathic, coldly analytical study of colonial life and institutions. Sherburne Cook's and Woodrow Borah's studies (9, 10, 11, 12) of Mexican demographic patterns, Charles Gibson's work (36) on the Aztecs under the Spaniards, and John Tate Lanning's monograph (54) on the Enlightenment in Guatemala are excellent examples of sophisticated scholarship leading to more sensitive understanding of Spain in America, not burdened by moral preconceptions. For the most part Spanish colonial historians have not yet turned to moral criticism, a kind of history which might in the long run make our calling more difficult and more challenging (43). Perhaps this tendency to avoid moral criticism may be the inevitable reaction of our guild against the strong moral overtones surrounding Spanish colonial history in the past, but this kind of history, of which Frank Tannenbaum's thoughtful essay (107) on comparative slavery is a good example, offers many possibilities for the future.

Another recent trend has been to broaden the base of research on colonial institutions and Spanish colonial policy. In the past, analysis or description of colonial practices was based primarily upon what was laid down in royal law. Too often such accounts were accepted as colonial reality rather than the idealization of what crown officials hoped for in the empire. More recently, scholars have blended law and actual practice. In the immediate postwar years Clarence Haring (41) and José María Ots Capdequí (79, 80, 81) were instrumental in helping to broaden the framework of institutional analysis and laid the groundwork for more sophisticated research. One has only to contrast the works of John Lynch (64) and Gisela Morazzini de Pérez Enciso (72) on the intendancy system with that of Lillian Estelle Fisher (32) to see an example of this new sort of scholarship. For Spanish colonial policy one can contrast the work of Father Eugene Korth (53) and Lewis Hanke (40). In his recent work Korth emphasized the reality of the search for justice in Chile and its success and failure; Hanke stressed the idealism inherent in Spanish attitudes toward the Indian, as reflected in law, polemics, debate, and utopian experiments in the New World.

Since World War II borderland history has taken a new direction, not so much in the quality or the type of research being carried on, but in its tendency to split apart from the larger area of Latin American history. In the halcyon days of Herbert E. Bolton at Berkeley the borderlands were intricately tied to Hispanic America and served as a springboard for the study of Latin American history as a whole. Many distinguished Hispanists got their start laboring on a borderland topic, but now the dividing line between borderland expert and Latin American historian seems much sharper than before. Like the Brazilianists, borderland specialists seem to form a coterie with an identity all their own. Some scholars like Arthur Whitaker or France Scholes, who originally made their marks as borderland experts, have since shifted to other endeavors. Others like A. B. Thomas (109, 110) and Abraham Nasatir (77, 78) have continued their research on the fringe areas of the Spanish Empire, and fortunately a new generation is following in their wake—Charles Arnade, Donald Cutter, Odie Faulk, Robert Gold, Richard Greenleaf, Jack D. L. Holmes, Oakah Jones, Jr., Michael Mathes, Max Moorhead, and Luis Navarro, to name a few (49). Perhaps specialization in this case means progress.

Achievements in the last twenty-five years have been many, but in few subfields has more been accomplished than in economic history. Heading the list is the work of Pierre and Huguette Chaunu (18, 19, 20). In twelve volumes these French scholars have put together a welter of statistics, maps, tables, charts, and graphs on Spanish trade with America and the Canaries between 1504 and 1650. Using the *libros de registro* of the Casa de Contratación in Seville, they set down data on some 17,967 Spanish voyages, including the name and type of vessel; the master, the owner, and members of the crew; and the cargo, tonnage, and destination of the ship. They also devised tables on the importation of slaves and the number of slave ships; mercury shipments to the New World; gold, silver, and mercury production; commodity trade statistics for such items as cochineal, indigo, dyewoods, sugar, spices, medicinal plants, and textile fibers; and the type and number of losses incurred by Spanish vessels in the American trade. In sum, simply the compilation of these vast amounts of raw evidence makes this work absolutely basic for the scholar, but Pierre Chaunu went one step further toward synthesis by developing cyclical patterns of boom and depression for the Spanish Empire and for Europe. Unquestionably this is the most impressive work using quantitative data yet to appear in the field of colonial Spanish American history, and the Chaunus promise more for Cádiz and the Atlantic for the period 1650–1800.

These French scholars are not alone in their efforts at quantification. In Spain María Encarnación Rodríguez Vicente (90) recently directed a team of researchers at the Archivo de Indias in a study of the income and outgo from the *caja de Lima* for the entire colonial period.[2] At the Centro de Investigaciones de Historia Americana in Santiago de Chile, Alvaro Jara (46, 47, 48) has taken data from the same *cartas cuentas* used by Rodríguez and analyzed mining production in Peru. Jara has also calculated gold and silver shipments to

---

2. Dr. Rodríguez lacks data for only eight years of the entire colonial period.

Spain on the basis of value rather than weight and has revised Earl Hamilton's earlier estimates of production of precious metals in Peru until 1660. Other scholars have used quantitive data to good advantage but not on such a grand scale as the Chaunus, Jara, or Rodríguez. Walter Howe (44), Roland D. Hussey (45), Clement Motten (76), R. S. Smith (100, 101, 102), and R. C. West (114, 115), in the United States; María Lourdes-Díaz Trechuelo Spinola (63) and Antonio Domínguez Ortiz (27), in Spain; Jean Pierre Berthe (7, 8) and Michèle Colin (22), in France; and Eduardo Arcila Farias (2, 3) and a small coterie at El Colegio de México in Latin America are just a few examples.[3]

Another subfield which has undergone significant development over the past twenty-five years is institutional and administrative history. As already pointed out, Clarence Haring and José María Ots Capdequí were instrumental in increasing our understanding of Spanish colonial institutions, and their carefully wrought descriptive accounts paved the way for more sophisticated analyses. Mario Góngora's work (38) on the establishment of Spanish institutions in the New World is a good example. He has pointed up the basic periods in the formation of institutional life until 1570. Still another provocative work is Richard Morse's brilliant piece in Louis Hartz's *The Founding of New Societies* (73). In it Morse suggests that the Spanish Empire in America be viewed as Max Weber's prototype of the decentralized patrimonial society. Not only has this interpretation helped to eliminate some of the clichés about the centralization of the Spanish Empire in America but it has also helped to demonstrate the continuity between the colonial and national periods. A sociologist, Magali Sarfatti (96), has expanded on Morse's interpretation and applied Weber's conceptual scheme on a grander scale but is less convincing and more pretentious.

Still another attempt at creating a new frame of analysis has come from John Phelan (86) in his book on Quito in the seventeenth century. Like Morse and Sarfatti, Phelan was attracted by Weber's concept of the decentralized patrimonial society and Weber's various types of authority, but Phelan was also intrigued by S. N. Eisenstadt's *The Political Systems of Empire* (28) and added his concept of historical bureaucratic politics to Weber's three categories of

3. Volume 17 of *Historia Mexicana* (January–March 1968) contains five articles on the colonial period based on statistical materials. These articles were researched primarily by scholars at El Colegio de México.

charismatic, traditional, and legal domination. Just where all this leads is still not altogether clear, but Phelan's suggestive ideas may ultimately be crystallized by further application and reinterpretation. (85)

Not all the major contributions in administrative and institutional history have been concerned with devising new ways to view the colonial system or the bureaucracy. Some scholars have studied and analyzed colonial institutions in depth. Among the most important are the works of J. H. Parry (83, 84) on the *audiencia* and the sale of public offices; John Preston Moore (70, 71) and Francisco Xavier Tapia (108) on the *cabildo;* John Lynch (64) and Gisela Morazzini de Pérez Enciso (72) on the intendancy system; María Encarnación Rodríguez (90) on the *consulado;* Guillermo Lohmann Villena (60) on the *corregidor;* and J. Ignacio Rubio Mañé (94), Vincente Rodríguez Casado and Guillermo Lohmann Villena (88) on the viceroy. These and others have given us a deeper understanding of the colonial scene, and without their contributions attempts at new conceptualization would be futile.

Demographic history, an area long dominated by Angel Rosenblat (91, 92, 93), has also been a vital field of research during the last quarter century. In 1935 Rosenblat first laid down the bases for his estimates of the indigenous population of America. Ten years later he followed with his *La población indígena de América desde 1492 hasta la actualidad,* further refined by *La población indígena y el mestizaje en América,* a two-volume work published in 1954. For Rosenblat population estimates could not be ascertained from documentary evidence for the early period; these sources were entirely too scanty. He preferred rather to work backwards from present, known population figures and to make estimates on the basis of what he considered the land could support.

After World War II others entered the field in earnest, and Rosenblat was challenged by a group of scholars at Berkeley, first Lesley Byrd Simpson (99) and Sherburne Cook and then Woodrow Borah and Cook (9, 10, 11, 12). Devoted primarily to Central Mexico, the Berkeley school based its estimates of Indian population on tribute, fiscal, and financial records and came up with these calculations for Central Mexico—25,200,000 in 1519; 16,800,000 in 1548; 2,650,000 in 1568; 1,900,000 in 1580; 1,375,000 in 1595; and 1,075,000 in 1605. These figures contrast sharply with Rosenblat's estimate of a total Indian population for *all* America of 13,385,000 in 1492; 10,827,150 in 1570;

and 10,035,000 in 1650. Both in numbers and the rate of decimation, the two calculations are radically different. In 1967 Rosenblat, in an impassioned defense of his methods, attacked the Berkeley estimates as gross miscalculations of the tribute records and exempted classes. The differences are still unresolved with both sides having their defenders (26, 34).

This work in demographic history has been complemented by other efforts. For Peru the Chilean scholar Rolando Mellafe is attempting to determine demographic patterns for Huánaco in the sixteenth century.[4] Another young researcher, David Cook, has developed population figures for Peru in the sixteenth century.[5] The German historian Günter Vollmer, who has already completed an exhaustive treatment of demographic patterns for Peru in 1792, is now putting his expertise to work on Puebla de los Angeles in New Spain for the entire colonial period.[6] For Venezuela at the end of the eighteenth century Trent Brady and John Lombardi (16) are looking at *mestizaje*. Still others who have been active are Nicolás Sánchez-Albornoz (95) for the River Plate area, Juan Friede (33) for Colombia, and Gonzalo Aguirre Beltrán (1) for the black population of New Spain. In his work on the passengers to the Indies, Peter Boyd-Bowman (13, 14, 15) has introduced still another dimension into demographic research.

Demographic history has been closely related to ethnohistory, social history, the relationship of man to land, historical ecology, and other subfields. Lesley Simpson (99), for example, used demographic data in explaining the rise and decline of the *encomienda* system in New Spain. Charles Gibson (36) relates many changes in New Spain in the sixteenth and seventeenth centuries to the decline in the Indian population. In the same vein, work on land tenure, forced labor, the hacienda system, social change, tribute, and a number of other topics has benefited immeasurably from research on population. The scholarship of Carl Sauer (98), Charles Gibson (36, 37), Mario Góngora (38), Silvio Zavala (116, 117, 118), José Miranda (68,

---

4. Although Mellafe's work has not yet been published, he indicated to me in conversation that his findings for Huánaco would bear out the same pattern found by the Berkeley scholars for Central America.

5. See his article in volume 8 of the *Anuario del Instituto de Investigaciones Históricas* of the Universidad del Litoral in Rosario.

6. Vollmer's excellent dissertation presented at the University of Cologne, "Bevolkerungspolitik und Bevolkerungstrucktur im Vizekonigreich Peru ze Ende de Kolonialzeit, 1741–1821," should be published.

69), Juan Friede (33), Jean Borde (39), Richard Konetzke (51, 52), François Chevalier (21), and others clearly demonstrates this interconnection.

But Hispanists have done more than count or dabble in the social sciences these past twenty-five years. Cultural history has also been vital, particularly the work of two North Americans, John Tate Lanning (54, 55) and Irving Leonard (56, 57). Lanning's work on the colonial university and the Enlightenment has been exceptionally innovative from the standpoint of both methodology and interpretation. Taking one of the few educational institutions in Hispanic America for which the sources are still extant, the University of San Carlos de Guatemala, Lanning has explained its rise and decline, organization, financial and factional trials, and student life. From the information he has given us for Guatemala, we can surmise, at least in part, what university life was like in other areas of the Spanish Empire. For the Enlightenment Lanning again focused on San Carlos, devising a new methodology to ascertain the entrance and acceptance of the ideas of the scientific revolution and the Enlightenment. His approach was to read student theses as a reflection of the change in intellectual currents. His conclusions show a decline in scholasticism, a lively interest in Cartesianism and Newtonianism, a pragmatic and eclectic spirit among teachers and students at San Carlos, and a readiness to accept the latest scientific knowledge from Europe without much lag. As complements to Lanning's work on the Enlightenment, one might consult two excellent books on Spain during the same period by Jean Sarrailh (97) and Richard Herr (42).

With his work in literary history Irving Leonard has been another pioneer. His *Books of the Brave* (57) graphically described the reading habits of Spanish colonials, showed their addiction to the novels of chivalry of the fifteenth and sixteenth centuries, and pointed out the relationship between what colonials read and their value system. In his work on cultural and intellectual life in seventeenth-century Mexico (56), Leonard has dedicated himself to a period sometimes referred to as the "long noonday nap" of the Spanish Empire in America. His analysis of the literary and intellectual achievements of Sor Juana Inés de la Cruz and Carlos de Sigüenza y Góngora and his study of colonial society and colonial entertainments bring a new dimension to our knowledge of the colonial scene. At the same time Leonard has translated the fine synthesis of Mariano Picón Salas (87) on colonial intellectual life, first published in 1944.

Lanning and Leonard are not the only giants in cultural history. Antonello Gerbi's provocative *Dispute over the New World* (35) takes up the lively dispute over the nature of the American environment and whether its effects were debilitating. In art and architecture (for which I have no expertise) a large number of books published over the last quarter century testify to the extensive interest in this area.[7] For Spanish colonial drama much less is available, although one could turn to the books of Irving Leonard (56), J. Luis Trenti Rocanuro (112), and Guillermo Lohmann Villena (59) for some guidelines. For colonial music the work of Robert M. Stevenson (104, 105, 106) stands virtually alone. Colonial science and scientists have also received little attention, although Arthur Steele's excellent study (103) of the Ruiz and Pavón expedition provides a useful model for future endeavors in this area.

Histories and documents on the church and clergy during the colonial period have long been streaming from the presses as testimony to the pious work of dedicated priests and friars in the New World. This outpouring has not diminished. As in the pre–World War II epoch, the various orders have continued to publish documents and monographs on the achievements of their brethren in Spanish America. As might be expected, the Jesuits have led the way, followed by the Franciscans, Dominicans, and Augustinians.[8] Histories of the regular clergy and their missions have thus been oriented toward the friars' feats in converting and civilizing the natives or toward their martyrdom. Still, the sectarian nature of this scholarship has not detracted from its scholarly value. One has only to look at the work of the Franciscan Antonine Tibesar (111) on the *alternativa* in Peru to see how important these contributions can be. Besides those works categorized above, recent scholarship has produced two books of broad scope which have been significant in explaining the larger role of

7. The books on art and architecture constitute a considerable number of volumes. Since I have no specialized knowledge in the field, I am reluctant to list titles and authors. A few names which do stand out are George Kubler, Martín Soria, Harold Wethey, Pál Kelemen, Diego Angulo Iñíguez, Sidney Markman, José de Mesa and Teresa Gisbert, Erwin Walter Palm, Manuel Toussaint, and Enrique Dorta.

8. Titles are too numerous to list here, but I might mention as examples the kind of work being turned out by the various orders—the Jesuit series published in Spain, *Missionalia Hispánica,* and the Franciscan series of documents, monographs, bibliographies, and historical classics published by the Academy of American Franciscan History.

the church in colonial society. The first is by Nancy Farriss (31) on clerical privilege in Mexico in the late eighteenth century; the second is Michael Costeloe's analysis (23) of church wealth in the Archbishopric of Mexico. Both works break out of narrow sectarian or scholastic boundaries to help explain the place of the church in the colonial milieu and provide new substantive material for scholarly reinterpretation.

In the United States recently there has been a strong drive to make black or Afro-American history a new specialty. In this area Hispanists have long had an interest, although much remains to be done. It might be argued too that Latin American historians have been in the vanguard of black history. As already seen, Frank Tannenbaum published his *Slave and Citizen* in 1946 (107) and has since stimulated further research on comparative slavery by United States historians (24, 28). A Hispanist who has attempted to test the Tannenbaum theses more precisely is Herbert Klein (50), who has compared slavery in Cuba and Virginia. Still others have been active as well. An authority on the slave trade in Chile, Rolando Mellafe (66, 67) has written a brief but cogent synthesis on slavery in the Americas which deserves translation. Frederick Bowser, a young historian at Stanford, is currently engaged in a study of slavery in colonial South America which should bring new insights into the black experience there. The book by Gonzalo Aguirre Beltrán (1) on black demography in Mexico has already been mentioned, but others could be added on slavery in Chile, Colombia, and Puerto Rico (113, 30, 25).

For all the accomplishments in Spanish colonial history, one cannot help being struck also by certain areas which have been almost completely neglected. Urban history, for example, a subfield rapidly becoming fashionable among United States historians, has not excited Hispanists, despite the urban boom and the suggestive article by Richard Morse (74) in the *American Historical Review* a few years ago. Except for Las Casiana, which never ceases to intrigue both scholars and polemicists, political theory as it affected colonization and colonial development has received only a smattering of attention. Strangely, especially in view of the strong military tradition of Spain and Spanish America, military history has few devotees. In fact the two works which do come to mind on the military and colonial defense are really marginal to military history (17, 65).

Mining has not attracted much scholarly interest despite its importance for Spain and Spanish America. In his pioneer works Earl

Hamilton estimated gold and silver production fairly accurately, but his analyses were concerned more with the effect of American treasure on the European economy than with mining per se. As one prime example of the void, Potosí cries out for investigation, both of a quantitative and qualitative sort; the same is true of mining in New Spain. Fortunately, a few scholars have set guidelines—Guillermo Lohmann Villena (61) on mercury mining in Huancavelica to the end of the seventeenth century, Robert West (114, 115) on placer mining and the Parral mining district, Modesto Bargallo's *La minería y la metalurgia en la América española* (5), and Walter Howe's study (44) of the mining guild of New Spain. As already pointed out, Alvaro Jara has been active in research on mining production in Peru and hopes to carry out micro studies of individual miners in the viceroyalty.

In one last word I might hazard a tentative prediction as to future trends. In my view the Chaunus—and our colleagues in the physical and natural sciences—have set the tone, at least for a time, toward team research. Attracted by both the social sciences and the computer, scholars will turn more to projects with a grandiose design, demanding the coordinated effort of a number of individuals. Large-scale projects on the colonial economy or colonial society will dwarf investigations by the lone humanist, finding fulfillment and making his contribution in the peaceful bliss of an archive or library. Whether this will be healthy either for the individual scholar or the discipline is open to question, but whatever the trend in the future, we are in an exciting field with a bright future before us.

# BIBLIOGRAPHY

1. Aguirre Beltrán, Gonzalo. *La Población negra de México (1519–1810): Estudio etno-histórico.* Mexico, 1946.

2. Arcila Farias, Eduardo. *Comercio entre Venezuela y México en los siglos XVI y XVII.* Mexico, 1950.

3. ———. *Economía colonial de Venezuela.* Mexico, 1946.

4. Arrom, José Juan. *El teatro de Hispanoamérica en la época colonial.* Havana, 1956.

5. Bargallo, Modesto. *La minería y la metalurgia en la América española durante la época colonial.* Mexico and Buenos Aires, 1955.

6. Bayle, Constantino, S.J. *Los cabildos seculares en la América española.* Madrid, 1952.

7. Berthe, Jean Pierre. "El cultivo del 'pastel' en Nueva España." *Historia Mexicana* 7 (January–March 1960): 340–67.

8. ———. "Las minas del oro del Marqués del Valle en Tehuántepec, 1540–1547." *Historia Mexicana* 8 (July–September 1958): 122–31.

9. Borah, Woodrow, and S. F. Cook. *The Population of Central Mexico in 1548: An Analysis of the Suma de visita de pueblos.* Ibero-Americana, 43. Berkeley and Los Angeles, 1960.

10. ———. *The Indian Population of Central Mexico, 1531–1610.* Berkeley and Los Angeles, 1960.

11. ———. *The Aboriginal Population of Central Mexico on the Eve of the Spanish Conquest.* Berkeley and Los Angeles, 1963.

12. ———. *The Population of the Mixteca Alta, 1520–1960.* Berkeley and Los Angeles, 1968.

13. Boyd-Bowman, Peter. *Indice geobiográfico de 40,000 pobladores de América en el siglo XVI.* Vol. 1. *La época antillana: 1493–1519.* Bogotá, 1964.

14. ———. "La emigración peninsular a América: 1520–1539." *Historia Mexicana* 13 (October–December 1963): 165–92.

15. ———. "Regional Origins of the Earliest Spanish Colonists of America." *PMLA* 71 (December 1956): 1157–72.

16. Brady, Trent, and John Lombardi. "The Application of Computers to the Analysis of Census Data: The Bishopric of Caracas, 1780–1820, a Case Study." Paper read September, 1968, at Bloomington, Indiana.

17. Calderón Quijano, José Antonio. *Historia de las fortificaciones en Nueva España.* Seville, 1953.

18. Chaunu, Pierre. "L'Amérique espagnole colonial: Les grandes lignes de la production historique de 1935 à 1949." *Revue Historique* 204 (July–September 1950): 77–105.

19. ———. "L'Amérique latine: Les grandes lignes de la production historique (1950–1962)." *Revue Historique* 231 (January–March 1964): 153–86.

20. Chaunu, Pierre, and Huguette Chaunu. *Séville et l'Atlantique (1504–1650)*. 11 vols. Paris, 1955–60.

21. Chevalier, François. *Land and Society in Colonial Mexico: The Great Hacienda*. Berkeley, Calif., 1963.

22. Colin, Michèle. *Le Cuzco à la fin du XVIIᵉ et au début du XVIIIᵉ siècle*. Paris, 1966.

23. Costeloe, Michael P. *Church Wealth in Mexico: A study of the "Juzgado de Capellanías" in the Archbishopric of Mexico, 1800–1856*. Cambridge, Eng., 1967.

24. Davis, David B. *The Problem of Slavery in Western Culture*. Ithaca, N.Y., 1966.

25. Díaz Soler, L. M. *Historia de la esclavitud negra en Puerto Rico (1493–1890)*. Madrid, n.d.

26. Diffie, Bailey. Review of Charles Gibson's *Spain in America. American Historical Review* 72 (April 1967): 1068–69.

27. Domínguez Ortiz, Antonio. *Política y Hacienda de Felipe IV*. Madrid, 1960.

28. Eisenstadt, S. N. *The Political Systems of Empires*. New York, 1963.

29. Elkins, Stanley M. *A Problem in American Institutional and Intellectual Life*. Chicago, 1959.

30. Escalante, A. *El negro en Colombia*. Bogotá, 1964.

31. Farriss, N. M. *Crown and Clergy in Colonial Mexico, 1759–1821: The Crisis of Ecclesiastical Privilege*. London, 1968.

32. Fisher, Lillian Estelle. *The Intendant System in Spanish America*. Berkeley, Calif., 1929.

33. Friede, Juan. *Los quimbayas bajo la dominación española*. Bogota, 1963.

34. García Martínez, Bernardo. Review of Angel Rosenblat. *Historia Mexicana* 17 (July–September 1967): 147–52.

35. Gerbi, Antonello. *La disputa del Nuevo Mundo*. Mexico, 1960.

36. Gibson, Charles. *The Aztecs under Spanish Rule*. Stanford, Calif., 1964.

37. ———. *Tlaxcala in the Sixteenth Century*. New Haven, Conn., 1952.

38. Góngora, Mario. *El estado en el derecho indiano: Epoca de fundación, 1492–1570*. Santiago de Chile, 1951.

39. Góngora, Mario, and Jean Borde. *Evolución de la propiedad rural en el Valle del Puangue*. 2 vols. Santiago de Chile, 1956.

40. Hanke, Lewis. *The Spanish Struggle for Justice in the Conquest of America*. Philadelphia, 1949.

41. Haring, Clarence. *The Spanish Empire in America*. New York, 1947.

42. Herr, Richard. *The Eighteenth-Century Revolution in Spain*. Princeton, N.J., 1958.

43. Higham, John. "Beyond Consensus: The Historian as Moral Critic." *American Historical Review* 67 (April 1962): 609–25.

44. Howe, Walter. *The Mining Guild of New Spain and Its Tribunal General, 1770–1821*. Cambridge, Mass., 1949.

45. Hussey, Roland D. *The Caracas Company, 1728–1784: A Study in the History of Spanish Monopolistic Trade*. Cambridge, Mass., 1934.

46. Jara, Alvaro. *Guerre et société au Chili: Essai de sociologie coloniale.* Paris, 1961.

47. ———. "La producción de metales preciosos en el Perú en el siglo XVI." *Boletín de la Universidad de Chile* 44 (November 1963): 58–64.

48. ———. *Tres ensayos sobre economía minera hispanoamericana*. Santiago de Chile, 1966.

49. Jones, Oakah L., Jr. "The Spanish Borderlands: A Selected Reading List." *Journal of the West* 8 (January 1969): 137–42.

50. Klein, Herbert S. *Slavery in the Americas: A Comparative Study of Virginia and Cuba*. Chicago, 1967.

51. Konetzke, Richard, ed. *Colección de documentos para la historia de la formación social de hispanoamérica, 1493–1810*. 3 vols. Madrid, 1953–62.

52. ———. *La emigración española al Río de la Plata durante el siglo XVI*. Madrid, 1952.

53. Korth, Eugene H., S.J. *Spanish Policy in Colonial Chile: The Struggle for Social Justice, 1535–1700*. Stanford, Calif., 1968.

54. Lanning, John Tate. *The Eighteenth-Century Enlightenment in the University of San Carlos de Guatemala*. Ithaca, N.Y., 1956.

55. ———. *The University in the Kingdom of Guatemala*. Ithaca, N.Y., 1955.

56. Leonard, Irving. *Baroque Times in Old Mexico*. Ann Arbor, Mich., 1959.

57. ———. *Books of the Brave*. Cambridge, Mass., 1949.

58. Lockhart, James. *Spanish Peru, 1532–1560: A Colonial Society*. Madison, Wis., 1968.

59. Lohmann Villena, Guillermo. *El arte dramático en Lima durante el virreinato*. Seville, 1945.

60. ———. *El corregidor de indios en el Perú bajo los Austrias*. Madrid, 1957.

61. ———. *Las minas de Huancavelica en los siglos XVI y XVII*. Seville, 1949.

62. ———. *Las relaciones de los virreyes del Perú*. Seville, 1959.

63. Lourdes-Díaz Trechuelo Spinola, María. *La Real Compañía de Filipinas.* Seville, 1965.

64. Lynch, John. *Spanish Colonial Administration, 1782–1810: The Intendant System in the Vice-Royalty of the Rio de la Plata.* Fair Lawn, N.J., 1958.

65. McAlister, Lyle N. *The "Fuero Militar" in New Spain, 1764–1800.* Gainesville, Fla., 1957.

66. Mellafe, Rolando. *La esclavitud en Hispano-América.* Buenos Aires, 1964.

67. ———. *La introducción de la esclavitud negra en Chile: Tráfico y rutas.* Santiago de Chile, 1959.

68. Miranda, José. *España y Nueva España en la época de Felipe II.* Mexico, 1962.

69. ———. *El Tributo indígena en la Nueva España durante el siglo XVI.* Mexico, 1952.

70. Moore, John Preston. *The Cabildo in Peru under the Hapsburgs: A Study in the Origins and Powers of the Town Council in the Viceroyalty of Peru, 1530–1700.* Durham, N.C., 1954.

71. ———. *The Cabildo in Peru under the Bourbons: A Study in the Decline and Resurgence of Local Government in the Audiencia of Lima, 1700–1824.* Durham, N.C., 1966.

72. Morazzini de Pérez Enciso, Gisela. *La intendencia en España y en América.* Caracas, 1966.

73. Morse, Richard. "The Heritage of Latin America." In *The Founding of New Societies,* ed. Louis Hartz, pp. 123–77. New York, 1964.

74. ———. "Some Characteristics of Latin American Urban History." *American Historical Review* 67 (January 1962): 317–38.

75. ———. "Latin American Boom." *Times Literary Supplement,* July 28, 1966, pp. 283–84.

76. Motten, Clement. *Mexican Silver and the Enlightenment.* Philadelphia, 1950.

77. Nasatir, A. P., and N. M. Loomis. *Pedro Vial and the Roads to Santa Fe.* Norman, Okla., 1966.

78. Nasatir, Abraham. *Spanish War Vessels on the Mississippi, 1792–1796.* New Haven, Conn., 1968.

79. Ots Capdequí, José María. *El estado español en las Indias.* Buenos Aires and Mexico, 1957.

80. ———. *Instituciones.* Barcelona, 1958.

81. ———. *Instituciones de gobierno del nuevo reino de Granada durante el siglo XVIII.* Bogotá, 1950.

82. Padden, R. C. *The Hummingbird and the Hawk: Conquest and Sovereignty in the Valley of Mexico, 1503–1541.* Columbus, Ohio, 1967.

83. Parry, J. H. *The Audiencia of New Galicia in the Sixteenth Century: A Study in Spanish Colonial Government.* Cambridge, Eng., 1948.

84. ———. *The Sale of Public Offices in the Spanish Indies under the Hapsburgs.* Ibero-Americana 37. Berkeley and Los Angeles, 1953.

85. Phelan, John L. "Authority and Flexibility in the Spanish Imperial Bureaucracy." *Administrative Science Quarterly* 5 (June 1960): 47–65.

86. ———. *The Kingdom of Quito in the Seventeenth Century: Bureaucratic Politics in the Spanish Empire.* Madison, Wis., 1967.

87. Picón Salas, Mariano. *A Cultural History of Spanish America from Conquest to Independence.* Trans. by Irving Leonard. Berkeley and Los Angeles, 1962.

88. Rodríguez Casado, Vicente, and Guillermo Lohmann Villena, eds. *Joaquín de la Pezuela, virrey del Perú, 1816–1821: Memoria de gobierno.* Seville, 1947.

89. Rodríguez Casado, Vicente, and Florentina Pérez Embid, eds. *Manuel de Amat y Junient, virrey del Perú, 1761–1776: Memoria de gobierno.* Seville, 1947.

90. Rodríguez Vicente, María Encarnación. *El tribunal del Consulado de Lima en la primera mitad del siglo XVII.* Madrid, 1960.

91. Rosenblat, Angel. *La población de América en 1492—viejos y nuevos cálculos.* Mexico, 1967.

92. ———. *La población indígena de América desde 1492 hasta la actualidad.* Buenos Aires, 1945.

93. ———. *La población indígena y el mestizaje en América.* 2 vols. Buenos Aires, 1954.

94. Rubio Mañé, J. Ignacio. *Introducción al estudio de los virreyes de Nueva España.* 4 vols. Mexico, 1955–63.

95. Sánchez-Albornoz, N. "Perfil y proyecciones de la demografía histórica en la Argentina." *Anuario del Instituto de Investigaciones Históricas* 8 (1965): 31–56.

96. Sarfatti, Magali. *Spanish Bureaucratic Patrimonialism in America.* Berkeley, 1966.

97. Sarrailh, Jean. *L'Espagne éclairée de la seconde moitié du XVIII° siècle.* Paris, 1954.

98. Sauer, Carl O. *The Early Spanish Main.* Berkeley, 1966.

99. Simpson, Lesley Byrd. *The Encomienda in New Spain: The Beginning of Spanish Mexico.* Berkeley and Los Angeles, 1950.

100. Smith, Robert S. "Datos estadísticos sobre el comercio de importación en el Perú en los años 1696 y 1699." *Revista Chilena de Historia y Geografía* 113 (1949): 162–77.

101. ———. "Indigo Production and Trade in Colonial Guatemala." *Hispanic American Historical Review* 39 (May 1959): 181–211.

102. ———. "Sales Taxes in New Spain, 1575–1770." *Hispanic American Historical Review* 28 (February 1948): 2–37.

103. Steele, Arthur R. *Flowers for the King: The Expedition of Ruiz and Pavón and the Flora of Peru.* Durham, N.C., 1964.

104. Stevenson, Robert M. *Music in Aztec and Inca Territory.* Berkeley, Calif., 1968.

105. ———. *Music in Mexico: A Historical Survey.* New York, 1952.

106. ———. *The Music of Peru: Aboriginal and Viceregal Epochs.* Washington, D.C., 1960.

107. Tannenbaum, Frank. *Slave and Citizen: The Negro in the Americas.* New York, 1946.

108. Tapia, Francisco Xavier. *El cabildo abierto colonial.* Madrid, 1966.

109. Thomas, Alfred B., ed. *After Coronado: Spanish Exploration Northeast of New Mexico, 1696–1721.* Norman, Okla., 1935.

110. ———. *Forgotten Frontiers: A study of the Spanish Indian Policy of Don Juan Bautista de Anza, Governor of New Mexico, 1777–1787.* Norman, Okla., 1932.

111. Tibesar, Antonine S., O.F.M. "The *Alternativa:* A Study in Spanish-Creole Relationships in Seventeenth-Century Peru." *The Americas* 11 (January 1955): 229–83.

112. Trenti Rocanuro, J. Luis. *El repertorio de la dramática colonial hispanoaméricana.* Buenos Aires, 1950.

113. Vial, Gonzalo. *El africano en el Reino de Chile: Ensayo histórico-jurídico.* Santiago de Chile, 1957.

114. West, Robert. *Colonial Placer Mining in Colombia.* Baton Rouge, La., 1952.

115. ———. *The Mining Community in Northern New Spain: The Parral Mining District.* Berkeley and Los Angeles, 1949.

116. Zavala, Silvio. *Contribución a la historia de las instituciones coloniales en Guatemala.* Mexico, 1945.

117. ———. *Los intereses particulares en la conquista de la Nueva España.* Mexico, 1964.

118. ———. *La libertad de movimiento de los indios de la Nueva España.* Mexico, 1948.

# BRAZIL:
# THE COLONIAL PERIOD

*Stuart B. Schwartz*

Long the domain of the retired lawyer or the avocation of the literate elite, the writing of colonial Brazilian history has since the end of the first Vargas era (1945) come increasingly into the hands of professional academics. To a greater or lesser extent these men employ modern critical techniques of research and analysis, and thus colonial Brazilian historiography has begun to move from dilettantism to professionalism. This is not to say that a great deal of marginalia fails to appear in the pages of the state historical publications, where inflated *discursos* still outweigh the occasional excellent article, but, in general, Brazilian and foreign scholars have made great strides in the description and analysis of the colonial heritage. Progress, of course, has been uneven and certain aspects have received far more attention than others. Legal history, a favorite of the nineteenth-century *bacharéis,* has suffered a decline, while economic studies are all the rage. Such trends reflect the interests of the age and are tied to the concern of Brazilians with their future as well as their past.

Euphoria, however, should not dominate an essay on colonial, Brazilian historiography, for as the carioca historian José Honório Rodrigues (153) somberly indicated in 1967, much Brazilian historical writing is still elitist and antiquarian in approach.[1] But, as the work of Rodrigues himself and others shows, change has taken place. This essay, therefore, will emphasize achievement and progress rather than stagnation and inertia. Futhermore, space and the author's limitations place certain restrictions on the materials cited. The discussion will by necessity be highly selective and will concentrate on recent trends rather than on a comprehensive listing of all books. Moreover, certain fields such as diplomatic, literary, and art history have been omitted.

A good index of the professionalization of historical production in Brazil and of another development, the growth of interest among foreign scholars in colonial Brazilian history, is the increasing number of periodicals that carry articles of importance on the colonial past.

---

1. For a more recent survey see Georg Thomas (180).

The flourishing *Revista de História* (São Paulo: 1950–) stands unquestionably as the most important historical journal in Brazil and it has in many ways supplanted the hallowed but less professional *Revista do Instituto Histórico e Geográfico Brasileiro* (Rio de Janeiro, 1838–). Scholars now must scan the pages of non-Brazilian journals such as *Studia* (Lisbon), *Revista Portuguesa de História* (Coimbra), the *Luso-Brazilian Review* (Madison, Wis.), *Journal of African History* (New York) and *Caravelle* (Toulouse), all of which carry articles of value to colonial historians. The international dispersion of interest evidenced by these publications indicates a growing awareness of the validity of colonial Brazil as a field of serious investigation.

Recent work in other fields of history and the findings and methodology of other disciplines, especially sociology and social anthropology, have extended the perimeters of colonial history. Partly responsible for this development is the comparative perspective, which thus far has been most concerned with race relations and, by extension, slavery. It is no longer odd to see experts on the United States South citing Florestan Fernandes, while the best Brazilian scholars continue to read widely and to absorb foreign scholarship. Most important in this respect is the impact of French scholars and their approach to history. Fernand Braudel both by the example of his magisterial work and by his impact as a teacher at the University of São Paulo in the early 1950s has been a major influence on the vigorous group of young Paulista historians, just as the French sociologist Roger Bastide contributed to the healthy recent developments in Brazilian social science studies.

To find his way through the labyrinth of documents and books on colonial history the researcher must depend on sound bibliographical guides. The area of bibliographical and historiographical writing has since 1945 been dominated by José Honório Rodrigues. His work in this field has been so prolific and so consistently good that his opinions go virtually, and some times unjustifiably, unchallenged. Nevertheless, his guide, *Historiografia e Bibliografia do dominio holandês no Brasil* (157), and his two volumes on sixteenth- and seventeenth-century historiography (155, 156) are indispensable. In *Teoria da história do Brasil* (158) Rodrigues provides much information on various aspects of historical research in his country as well as an intelligent discussion of the philosophy of history in Brazil. Rodrigues is Brazil's principal exponent of history *engagé* and his recent volumes of historiographical essays (154, 159) demonstrate his continuing desire to make Brazilian history relevant to present problems.

Although no other scholar has matched the production of José Honório Rodrigues, other important guides have appeared in the last two decades. Georges Raeders's *Bibliographie franco-brésilienne* (142) complements the standard work of A. L. Garraux (68) on French materials. The composite *Manual bibliográfico de estudos brasileiros* (120) contains sections on the colonial epoch, the *bandeirantes*, and the Dutch in Brazil. Rubens Borba de Morães's *Bibliographia brasiliana* (119) includes with few execptions all books on Brazil and by Brazilians published abroad before 1822. Since there was no printing press operating in the colony before 1808, virtually all contemporary published materials on colonial Brazil are contained in it. E. Bradford Burns provides a handy compilation of historiographical essays in translation in *Perspectives on Brazilian History* (33).

Various scholars since 1945 have contributed to the healthy growth of a corpus of critical editions of chroniclers and colonial documents. José Antônio Gonçalves de Mello, the Pernambucan von Ranke, is a leader in this movement and his efforts are models of judicious scholarship. His facsimile edition (116) of the letters of Duarte Coelho should now replace the older version of Antônio Baião published in 1924. Gonçalves de Mello has also produced an excellent edition of the pithy and prosugar planter, *Diálogos das grandezas do Brasil* (112), and his introduction is a powerful argument on behalf of the New Christian Ambrósio Fernandes Brandão as the author of this work. The most thorough and scholarly effort by the Pernambucan, in this area, however, is his translation and fully annotated edition of Adrien van der Dussen's *Relatório sôbre as capitanias conquistadas* (1639) (113), an indispensable document for the study of economic conditions in Dutch Brazil.

Similar rigor has been used by other historians. The indefatigable Serafim Leite has not rested since the publication of the monumental *História da Companhia de Jesus no Brasil* but instead has continued to publish carefully researched and collated volumes of Jesuit documents such as the complete writings of Father Manuel da Nóbrega, the most astute political observer of sixteenth-century Brazil (96, 97). Also in this tradition is Hélio Vianna's excellent edition of the *Livro que dá razão do estado do Brasil* (184), which leaves little doubt that its author was Sargento-Mór Diogo de Campos Moreno, an opinion also expressed by Engel Sluiter in his earlier but less fully

annotated edition (176). Frédéric Mauro has in his perceptively introduced and meticulously edited volume of seventeenth-century documents provided an excellent companion volume to his *Portugal et
l'Atlantique* (110) and has made materials from the provincial deposi-
tory of Evora readily accessible to scholars.

Although both seventeenth- and eighteenth-century materials have
merited new critical editions, those of the latter century have concentrated on the civilization of Minas Gerais. André Mansuy (108)
has uncovered a description of Brasil at the beginning of the "golden
age" in the National Archive of Paris, while another foreign scholar,
Charles R. Boxer (26, 27), has brought to light a Portuguese pamphlet
of 1764 which illumines our knowledge of attitudes toward slavery
in colonial Brazil through its dialogue between a Brazilian miner and
a lawyer. The two-volume *Resíduos seiscentistas em Minas* (12) is
a serious attempt to provide an analysis of the baroque civilization
of Minas Gerais. The author, Affonso Avila, has based his analysis on
two rare works, *Triumpho eucharistico* (1733) and *Aureo throno
episcopal* (1747), both of which deal with the *mineiro* era of gold and
both of which he has reproduced in facsimile. Although not a documentary publication, reference should be made at this juncture to
M. Rodrigues Lapa's *As "Cartas chilenas"* (94, 95), which despite its
full supporting documentation is still a basically textual argument
on behalf of Tomás Antônio Gonzaga as author of this satirical
description of *mineiro* provincial abuses.

Not all efforts in this area have been of the same caliber. The
recent reissue of Frei Vicente do Salvador's *História do Brasil* (1627)
(166) has added very little to the previous annotations of João Capistrano de Abreu and Rodolfo Garcia (62). Nevertheless, the republication of this work is a most welcome tribute to Brazil's first historian.
The new edition (65) of the 1618 Inquisition visit to Bahia is more
complete than its predecessor, but its lengthy and ostentatiously foot-
noted introduction is mostly irrelevant to the subject. Even these less
successful publications, however, have contributed to the increasing
availability of primary materials concerning the colonial period.[2]

Special mention should also be made of a series of colonial documents published by commercial presses. The series "Cadernos de
História," published by Editôra Obelisco, is designed for the student
and general reader, but its publication of the writings of Pero Lopes

2. At present, José Antonio Gonçalves de Mello is preparing the Confissões of
Pernambuco, 1593–95, for publication.

de Sousa (177), José de Anchieta (6), and Pero de Magalhães Gandavo (67) are inexpensive, handy, and especially useful for didactic purposes. The series "Roteiro do Brasil," of the Companhia Editôra Nacional, on the other hand, is far more sophisticated and promises to make a continuing contribution in this field. For example, Sérgio Buarque de Hollanda's hard-minded introduction to the collected economic essays of Bishop Azeredo Coutinho (81) shows that cleric to be a pragmatic elitist and not quite the humanist that others have portrayed. In a similar vein, Alice P. Canabrava has done a fine introduction to Ancheoni's edition of *Cultura e opulencia* (7) in the same series. Unfortunately for her but luckily for the rest of us, Canabrava's edition has already been superseded by the exhaustive facing-page translation and critical edition of Antonil done by Andrée Mansuy (9). Mlle Mansuy's work is marked by careful reasoning and evidence in regard to authorship and wide supporting research in the Torre do Tombo and even beyond the "Azulejo curtain" in the archive of the Casa de Cadaval.[3]

The National Library of Rio de Janeiro no longer publishes the great "Documentos Históricos" series, but scholars of Luso-Brazilian history find the tradition of unedited document publication continuing albeit in a somewhat disorganized fashion. Many monographs contain documentary appendixes and it is increasingly difficult to control this material or to prevent duplication. Despite these handicaps, printed documents have considerably enriched the possibilities of research. The Centro de Estudos Históricos Ultramarinos (44, 45) of Lisbon merits special praise for its series of published documents which contain much Brazilian material. In Brazil institutions like the Foreign Ministry, the National Library, and the Sugar Institute have all published important collections of historical documents.[4] The manuscripts of the Pedro de Angelis Collection published by the National Library (47, 49) are particularly important for the history of Brazilian-Platine relations. Various centenary celebrations are another source of documentary publications. The availability in print

---

3. The rich collection of Braziliana in the Casa de Cadaval has been ably cataloged (143). The catalog does little but whet scholarly appetites, since few scholars have had Mlle Mansuy's good fortune to gain access to the collection.

4. The Foreign Ministry has published *Livro primeiro do Govêrno do Brasil (1607–1633)* (Rio de Janeiro, 1958), but the companion manuscript volume of the correspondence of Governor Gaspar de Sousa, also in the Foreign Ministry library, is as yet unpublished.

of the minutes of the Câmara of Salvador and the financial portfolios of the Benedictines of Olinda and Salvador (10, 100, 182) have resulted from such commemorations.

Major series of eighteenth-century documents are less common than earlier materials but publications such as the *Anuário do Museu da Inconfidência,* published since 1952, often contain valuable sources. Perhaps most significant is the three-volume edition of the correspondence of Francisco Xavier de Mendonça Furtado, governor of Grão Para and Maranhão and brother of Pombal (117).

As a general survey of colonial history, Varnhagen's nineteenth-century *História geral* is still unsurpassed, but scholars have produced useful and suggestive general works in recent years. The traditional factual-chronological approach is used by Hélio Vianna (183) and Pedro Calmon (35, 51). Vianna's book is concise but dull, while Calmon's multivolume and well-footnoted set follows the outlines of Varnhagen although providing interesting supplementary material, especially on social history. The isles of theory have lured many Brazilian historians to their shores and the interpretive survey of the past is a constant in Brazilian historiography. The still widely-read essays of Capistrano de Abreu (1) were models of this genre. Viana Moog's comparative analysis of the United States and Brazil (118) is filled with highly debatable iconological insight. Far sounder is the perceptive study of the colonial heritage by Sérgio Buarque de Holanda (83) written in 1936 and considerably revised in 1948. Buarque de Holanda is also involved in a new development, the composite topical survey. He is serving as editor of a composite history of Brazil (79) written primarily by Paulista scholars of which the first two volumes are devoted to the colonial period.[5] Like most efforts of this nature it is uneven in quality. Unfortunately, there are few footnotes and the bibliography is highly and irrationally selective, but despite these deficiencies the work is a major synthesis. Of a somewhat different style but also topically arranged is Caio Prado Júnior's synthesis (138), which although based principally on published material of the eighteenth century is a significant attempt at synthesis from the Marxist viewpoint.

The general surveys, chronological, topical, or synthetic, have naturally followed five to ten years behind the cutting edge of re-

---

5. Another such effort is the *História do povo brasileiro* soon to be published by Editôres Culturais.

search, and therefore in the monographic studies rather than in the syntheses the important developments in colonial historiography are best seen. Nowhere is this truer than in the study of economic history.

There was a time when the work of Roberto Simonson (172) so dominated the field of colonial economic history that most other scholars were discouraged from research in this area. Since 1945, however, a wide range of excellent studies in economic history have been produced by Brazilian and foreign scholars. This new economic history falls unevenly into three categories: (1) studies of trade patterns and Brazil's linkage to the Atlantic world, (2) narrower monographs on particular products or aspects of trade, and (3) syntheses of economic history.

The influence of the French school of economic history interested in linkages and the total economic system is readily apparent in the first category. Studies of the origins of capitalism in Portugal, Portuguese economic thought, and Portuguese overseas expansion set the stage for this approach (55, 69, 107). Frédéric Mauro's *Portugal et l'Atlantique* (110), a product of the VI section of the Ecole Practique des Hautes Etudes, uses archival materials from Continental, insular, and overseas Portugal as well as from Brazil and Europe to construct a model monograph on the Portuguese Atlantic. Although Mauro treats a number of problems and commodities, his study is, as Pierre Chaunu (46) has pointed out, an analysis of the great Brazilian sugar cycle (1570–1670) and its impact on the Luso-Brazilian economy. Mauro's statistics leave no doubt that by 1650 Brazil was the keystone of the empire.

A more recent work of the French school is Pierre Verger's study (186, 187) of the slave trade between Bahia and the Bight of Benin.[6] Verger, who had already established himself as an ethnographer of note, has now shed much light on the eighteenth-century slave trade and its interrelation with tobacco agriculture. He has many subthemes. He suggests that the slave uprisings of 1807–35 were really the extension of African religious wars, more antipagan than antiwhite. Moreover, he tries to show that the origins of Brazilian independence lay in the divergence of interests between Brazilian merchants and their metropolitan counterparts. Both hypotheses call for further examination.

---

6. Other works treating relations between Brazil and Africa include Manuel dos Anjos Silva Rebelo's (146) and José Honório Rodrigues's (152).

Interest in Brazil's commercial ties to Africa have been paralleled by attention to connections with Spanish America and Europe. In the latter case, Hermann Kellenbenz (88, 90) has concentrated on the Hamberger and other northern firms and families engaged in trade to the Iberian world. The growth of the sugar trade and the vigorous nature of the maritime economy stimulated important side effects. One, the opening of an active although often clandestine trade between Brazil and the River Plate, has been brilliantly described by Alice P. Canabrava (38). Her dependence on printed sources leaves work still to be done based on the holdings of the Arquivo Histórico Ultramarino of Lisbon and the Archivo General de Indias of Seville, despite the supplementary studies of Ricardo Zorraquín Becú and others (22, 103). The opportunities for wealth open to Portuguese in the Spanish Indies during the Iberian union (1580–1640) drew many of them across the line of Todesillas, and Lewis Hanke (75) has pointed this out. Portuguese contractors and merchants also benefited from the Spanish connection and Walter Rodney (151) has shown how the union allowed the Portuguese to establish predominance on the Guinea coast. Stuart Schwartz (170) has suggested a change in Luso-Spanish political and economic relations in the early 1620s, and the excellent articles of Engel Sluiter (174, 175) and the findings of Kenneth Andrews (8) place this change in the context of European competition and Spain's Continental difficulties.

José Roberto do Amaral Lapa's work (93) on Bahia and the East India trade looks at first glance to be a study of Brazil's contact with the Indian Ocean. It is this, but it is far more a study of the Bahian shipping industry in the eighteenth century. Most eighteenth-century economic history, however, is marked by a resurgence of interest in the achievements and failures of the Marquis of Pombal and their impact on Brazil. The Portuguese scholars Magalhães Godinho (70) and Jorge Borges de Macedo (105) suggested approaches to these topics in the early 1950s and since then studies such as Manuel Nunes Dias's analysis (57) of the Pombaline Companhia Geral do Grão Pará e Maranhão have tested the hypothesis. Nunes Dias has excavated a great deal of material from archival bedrock but his presentation of it is often turgid and his admiration for Pombal occasionally leads him to excesses. To claim, as he does, that Pombal tore down one system to build another or to state that the Methuen Treaty ruined attempts at Portuguese industrialization ignores the convincing arguments of Magalhães Godinho and Borges de Macedo. Nevertheless, studies such as that of Nunes Dias and that of Magalhães Godinho (71) on prices are essential before generalizations can be made.

In the category of monographs on special topics the efforts of Myriam Ellis (59, 60, 61) merit first mention. Her excellent studies of the royal monopolies of salt and the whale fishery are filled with much socioeconomic data. Manuel Nunes Dias has a study on cacao (54) but other important economic activities remain unstudied. Tobacco awaits its historian, and stock raising, so important in the expansion of the colony, is also relatively unexplored. Two studies of the Bahian *sertão*, Poppino's dissertation on Feira de Santana (135, 136) and the minutely detailed description of the cattle *fazenda* of Brejo do Campo Seco by Lycurgo Santos Filho (168) begin, however, to fill the gap. Dauril Alden's writings (2, 3) on the eighteenth-century economic renaissance considerably illumine a period of false euphoria that may have mitigated the ardor for independence.

The sugar agro-industry, keystone of colonial agriculture, remains a topic of considerable interest to historians. José Wanderley de Araújo Pinho's study (133) of a Bahian plantation is one of the only studies in depth of a single plantation over time, but it suffers from a lack of seventeenth-century data. The sociological approach to sugar popularized by Gilberto Freyre has new exponents among scholars like Manuel Diégues Júnior (58) and Fernando de Azevedo (14). Unfortunately, most of these studies use the nineteenth-century plantation as a model and superimpose it on the colonial past. An interesting recent development is studies of the sugar industry in regions where it was a secondary activity. *A cana-de-Açúcar em Minas Gerais* by Miguel Costa Filho (52) describes an industry producing for internal consumption, not European markets. Despite the traditional association of sugar with the northeast, studies in Belgian and Italian materials have underlined sixteenth-century interest in São Paulo as a sugar-producing area (82, 92).[7] Dealing with a later period, Maria Thereza Schorer Petrone's work (131) on the Paulista sugar plantations indicates that despite the secondary nature of sugar in São Paulo, it was that crop that set the mercantile and communications patterns later used by coffee growers.

Surveys of economic history are by necessity limited by monographic progress. Despite the many lacunae that still exist in colonial economic history some interesting surveys have been written. Sergio

---

7. Studies of land grants are also essential to an understanding of the sugar industry. The best study to date is that of Costa Porto (137).

Bagú (17) and Frédéric Mauro (109) have both attempted comparative studies. The colonial chapters of the *História econômica do Brasil* of Caio Prado Júnior (139) remain popular, as the ten editions of this book attest. Celso Furtado's analysis (66) of Brazilian economic history contains a good discussion of the colonial period, especially the seventeenth century. In general, surveys of colonial economic history lag far behind the advances made in more specialized studies.

Certain topics that have long been popular subjects of historical research continue to receive scholarly and sometimes not so scholarly interest. Paulista historians and essayists seem never to tire in their efforts to point out the role of the *bandeiras* in opening up the interior of Brazil. The quality and status of research can be gleaned from Richard Morse's anthology (122). Studies of similar expeditions and territorial penetration originating in Bahia or Maranhão are still far from satisfactory and are often ignored by the Paulista historians. The theme of territorial expansion, however, is an important one in colonial history and there have been several publications that contribute to our knowledge. Affonso d'Escragnolle Taunay's eleven volumes (178) are a feast of information still to be digested. The everyday life of the Paulista in city and *sertão* has been painted by Alcântara Machado (106), using municipal council records and the twenty-three volumes of published wills and testaments. The Portuguese Jaime Cortesão (48, 50) has put forth the suggestive but still tenuous contention that a conscious geopolitical thrust lay behind Paulista expansion.

The stimulating essays of Capistrano de Abreu, the Brazilian "Turner," first underlined the importance of the frontier in his nation's history. Sérgio Buarque de Holandá stands as the man who has in many ways inherited Capistrano's mantle. Beautifully written essays based on a wide reading of Brazilian and European materials distinguish his work. In *Monções* (80) he treated the opening of Goias, the Brazilian Far West, still the least-studied region of colonial Brazil. His essays in *Caminhos e fronteiras* (78) deal with the social and material life of the *sertão* and in *Visão do paraíso* (84) he analyzes in depth the lure of the backlands, the call of the wild and of gold. Taken as a group, these works of a social, psychological, and historical nature mark a milestone in the historiography of colonial expansion.

Nineteenth- and early twentieth-century historians produced good studies of the Dutch period (1630–54). In the last twenty-five years two scholars, one Brazilian the other English, have made significant contributions. José Antônio Gonçalves de Mello (115) has produced an excellent study of the society of Dutch Brazil. In this monograph and in his series of thoroughly researched biographies of important Luso-Brazilians in Dutch Brazil, Gonçalves de Mello eschews over-simplified nationalism and seeks the origins of the rebellion of 1645 in the urban rivalry of Portuguese Olinda and Dutch Recife and in the indebtedness of the sugar planters to the Dutch West India Company (114). C. R. Boxer's *The Dutch in Brazil* (23) concentrates on politico-military events, while his biography of Salvador de Sá (30) is a "life and times" study in the finest tradition of that genre. The work of both authors is noteworthy for their use of Dutch sources along with the traditional Portuguese materials.

Given the legalistic approach of many nineteenth-century historians, it is somewhat surprising to find that Luso-Brazilian historiography still lacks adequate studies of basic social and administrative institutions. Legalistic administrative studies of Portuguese and Brazilian institutions do exist, and although some like Gama Barros' classic (18) are valuable, analyses of the functions, personnel, and actual performance of the institutions remain undone. Probably the best summary of administrative history is Eulalia Lahmeyer Lobo's comparative description (101) of the Spanish and Portuguese colonial systems in the New World.[8] Such works must, however, remain cursory so long as institutions as basic as the Mesa da Conciência and the Conselho Ultramarino are known only through their *regimentos* (statutes). Of the metropolitan organs only the Conselho da India and the Casa dos Contos have received adequate monographic treatment (104, 144).

The situation is approximately the same concerning colonial institutions, although some recent progress has been made. Dauril Alden's fine study (5) contains much information on colonial and metropolitan government, especially the treasury and the colonial governors. The city and urban institutions serve as focal points of interest as historians are beginning to turn away from the generalizations of Oliveira Viana and others about the predominately rural nature of colonial Brazil and are beginning to seek the past in the alleys of Olinda as well as the plantations of the Recôncavo. Richard Morse's essays (123, 124) on urbanization in Latin America contain perceptive insights into the phenomenon in Brazil. More specifically

8. A less satisfactory multivolume work (31) projected for eighteen volumes is currently under way.

Brazilian are Nelson Omegna's *A cidade colonial* (128), Aroldo de Azevedo's *Vilas e cidades do Brasil colonial* (13), and Edmundo Zenha's *O municipio no Brasil* (194), this last being the best of the three. C. R. Boxer's comparative study (28) of Portuguese colonial municipal councils *(câmaras)* is an excellent introduction. Affonso Ruy's two works (162, 163) on the municipal history of Salvador complement Boxer's chapter, but similar studies in depth on other cities have not been done.[9] Various quatrocentennary celebrations such as that of Salvador (1949) and more recently of Rio de Janeiro (1965) usually result in a flurry of historical activity, some of which is valuable. Outside the large coastal cities, however, the problem of sources is a major difficulty. Climate, insects, and neglect have combined to eliminate many important municipal records, and the deficiencies of an interesting study like Antonio Lopes' *Alcântara* (Maranhão) (102) lie in the lack of extant municipal records. The descriptions of municipal archives that have appeared in the *Revista de História* (160, 192) offer a ray of hope and should stimulate studies of secondary colonial population centers.

In 1947 Manuel Cardozo (39) underscored the importance of another basically municipal institution, the religious brotherhood. In the boom towns of Minas Gerais where the regular clergy were prohibited, the brotherhoods were vital social and religious organizations, a situation well-described by Fritz Teixeira de Salles (165). A. J. R. Russell-Wood (161) has used the prestigious brotherhood of the Misericórdia of Bahia as the basis of his wide-ranging study of its relation to the socioeconomic and religious life of the community. His data indicate that the sort of men who in the 1500s had fought for municipal positions were by the 1670s seeking excuses not to serve. This may well indicate a diminution of the municipal power and prestige of the planters parallel to a decline in sugar production and it suggests that pseudomanorialism was a rather late phenomenon and that it may have come as a result of a political defeat of the planters by the merchants.

The Church and the family exercised considerable dominance on colonial life, but with the exception of the brotherhoods little has been done on these institutions. Most religious history has concentrated on the regular clergy, especially the Jesuits, and to a lesser

---

9. The exception is São Paulo, a city which has attracted the interest of historians. See, for example, the interesting essay by Maria Conceição Martins Ribeiro (150).

extent the Franciscans (21, 77, 79, 191). Dom Oscar de Oliveira's study (127) of the tithe has been republished as well as a more specific article by Manuel Cardozo (40), but in general Church-state relations are unstudied: Surveys like Silveira Camargo's (36, 37) are useful, but the role of the secular clergy, the parish as an institution of settlement, and the everyday Catholicism of colonial society need detailed investigation.

The family, like the Church, solidified colonial society and the two reinforced each other (72). Emilio Willems's sociological studies (189, 190) of the Luso-Brazilian family could serve as an excellent point of departure for an examination of the role of "clans," but thus far only L. A. Costa Pinto (134) has tried to develop some kind of model of the family feuds which wracked every region of colonial Brazil.

Catholicism, Roman and Apostolic, combined in colonial Brazil with indigenous and African religious beliefs to form syncretic forms of worship. Maria Issaura Pereira de Queiroz (140) has studied the messianic aspects of syncretic religion within a context of socioeconomic discontent. Roger Bastide (20) and Pierre Verger (188) have described aspects of African religions in Brazil with a concentration on the postcolonial period but with data also useful to the colonial historian.

Many of the works already cited in this essay might also be mentioned under the rubric of social history. Class structure, social stratification, and race relations were all topics of interest before 1945, but some notable advances and changes in approach have been made since that date. Some regions are far better studied than others. Bahia probably leads the list with excellent monographs by Carlos Ott (129) and the anthropologist Thales de Azevedo (15, 16) on the population of the city and its environs. Studies on Rio de Janeiro suffer from the disappearance of that city's municipal records. Minas Gerais, however, runs a close second to Bahia. C. R. Boxer's *The Golden Age of Brazil* (24) deals with the whole colony from 1695 to 1750, but the centrifugal forces engendered by the gold of Minas Gerais stand at the core of his book. The social and religious history of the mining district are ably discussed in José Ferreira Carrato's fine study (43). Other areas lack the same concentration of research, but individual scholars like Gonçalves de Mello (114) in Pernambuco and Artur Ferreira Reis (147, 148) in Amazonas have done singular service in illumining their regional history.

Studies in population, settlement, and demographic change must precede any full understanding of society. To the above-mentioned works of Ott and Azevedo should be added Manuel Nunes Dias' study (56) of eighteenth-century Amazonia and Artur Hehl Neiva (126) on the general population of the colony. Quantitative techniques have been used to good effect by Tarcizio do Rêgo Quirino (141) and Dauril Alden (4). The former has used the Inquisition records of 1591–93 to analyze the colonial population at the end of the sixteenth century and his data are, therefore, limited and subject to a criticism of preselection. Alden, on the other hand, has collated many of the late colonial population counts *(mappas)* for his article, but the deficiencies of data on Minas Gerais, probably the most populous area by the late eighteenth century, keep this essay from being even more important.

A most striking development in colonial social history is the increased interest in the disinherited and marginal groups: the Indian, the Afro-Brazilian, and the New Christian. The problems of these racial and ethnic majorities and minorities have captured the imagination of many scholars. Least easy to identify and thus hardest to study are the crypto-Jewish New Christians. Their history, taken from the loving hands of anti-Semites like Gustavo Barroso, who "exposed" colonial Jews, has been the subject of more scholarly and sane work by Revah (149), Kellenbenz (88, 89, 90), Gonçalves de Mello (115), and especially by Arnold Wiznitzer in his *Jews in Colonial Brazil* (193). Although a certain ethnic myopia sometimes creeps into Wiznitzer's work, it is perhaps a welcome antidote to the unbalanced writing of Barroso and others in the 1930s.[10]

Since the discovery of Brazil the Indian has captured the imagination of scholars and travelers. On European contacts with the Indians both historians and anthropologists have produced important works. Alexander Marchant's *From Barter to Slavery* of 1942 was an important beginning, but the studies of economic anthropologists like Karl Polanyi now indicate that Marchant assumed the Indian to be an "economic man" in the European sense, something that he probably was not. Mathias Kieman (87) and Georg Thomas (181) have studied

10. Revah is a diligent researcher on the Iberian New Christians and as editor of the *Revue des Etudes Juines* has given much space to material about them. Wiznitzer has also published on many aspects of Jewish life in the *Publications of the American Jewish Historical Society* between 1952 and 1956. Conçalves de Mello is planning a history of the Jews in Dutch Brazil to be published in 1970.

Portuguese Indian policy in detail. Most important, however, is Florestan Fernandes's study (64) of the Tupinambá and the effects of European contact on them. Fernandes's meticulous research and the application of anthropological methods to his material is a significant beginning at the writing of Brazilian history from a viewpoint other than that of the conquerors. No one has yet tried a similar study of the Gê tribes, although Julio Cezar Melatti's *Indios e Criadores* (111) on the Krahó of southern Maranhão is a step in that direction. Enslavement, Jesuit control, detribalization had far-reaching effects on colonial society and the tools of anthropology can do much to explain them.

Undoubtedly the place of the African in Brazilian society, his condition under slavery, the opportunities open to him to achieve freedom and to find access to social mobility have generated the greatest interest. It was, of course, the mulatto abolitionist Perdigão Malheiro who in 1866 wrote the first and still useful scholarly study on slavery in Brazil, but the present interest has its origins in the work of Gilberto Freyre and others done in the early 1930s. Since that time there has been a steady flow of materials on Afro-Brazilian themes. Many of these works are produced not by historians but by social scientists, and their analysis of colonial slavery is more often marked by the trenchant phrase of the traveler's account than by the aroma of archival dust. A notable exception is the well-researched monographs of the "São Paulo school," but their studies have been limited thus far to the south, an area of small Afro-Brazilian population in the colonial period. Probably the best historical survey of Brazilian slavery is contained in Mauricio Goulart's now difficult to obtain monograph (74). The sociological and ethnological studies of Pierson (132), Bastide (19), Ramos (143), and Fernandes (63) all have implications or information useful to the historian of colonial Brazil.

African resistance to slavery has been best portrayed in Edison Carneiro's *O quilombo dos Palmares* (41), to which the fine article by R. K. Kent (91) is a welcome supplement on African survivals. Clovis Moura's *Rebeliões da senzala* (125) is a sympathetic but far from satisfactory survey, and in general most studies remain at a somewhat unsophisticated level of analysis. There are very few studies (130) of the *quilombo* or resistance on a regional level and virtually nothing of value exists on urban slavery or resistance.

Despite the extent of monographic deficiencies, the debate on the nature of Brazilian slavery and race relations is fully joined. Freyre's emphasis on Portuguese adaptability and the relative mildness of Brazilian race relations has long been popular in Brazil and Portugal and has found adherents among North American scholars. Historians like Frank Tannenbaum and Stanley Elkins counterbalance the malignity of North American slave treatment with the milder reality of Brazil and they tend to emphasize startling contrasts. C. R. Boxer stirred up a hornet's nest in Portugal when he claimed that the Portuguese were no better (and no worse) than others in their treatment of conquered peoples (29). His position has also been expressed or supported with considerable variation by the North Americans Harris (76) and Davis (53), and by the Brazilians Fernandes (63) and Ianni (85). These men tend to see disheartening sameness rather than startling contrast in North American and Brazilian slavery (121).

Colonial attitudes toward race and slavery have not usually been of interest to intellectual historians but this situation is changing. Sonia Aparecida Siquiera (173) has examined Azeredo Coutinho's opinions on the matter, and the racial attitudes of the seventeenth-century Jesuit Vieira have also been studied (25, 77). Intellectual history in Brazil, however, does not flourish. The Church was in many ways synonymous with colonial intellectual history, and the writings of Nobrega, Vieira, and others constitute important documents on the intellectual life of the colony. Beyond this, a few figures, the poet Gregorio de Mattos, Padre Antonio Vieira, and Bishop Azeredo Coutinho receive most attention to the exclusion of lesser-known individuals or general trends. The one aspect of intellectual history that has generated the most interest is the impact of the Enlightenment, but nobody has yet offered convincing proof that this intellectual movement significantly influenced late colonial political unrest (32, 34, 42).

No series of revolutions brought an end to colonial rule in Brazil, but unrest and revolutionary activity did mark the end of the eighteenth century. The *inconfidência mineira of* 1778 has traditionally been viewed as an independence movement, and although in the nineteenth century Joaquim Norberto de Sousa e Silva (171) played down the revolt and the importance of Tiradentes, defenders of the importance of the movement and its leader rose to the fray (167). Since 1945 various documents concerning the conspiracy have been published but no major work of synthesis has appeared.

The same cannot be said of the Bahian Tailor's revolt of 1798.

There have been important recent works on this uprising which involved many individuals of low social class, including both slaves and freedmen. Affonso Ruy (164) has called this the first social revolution in Brazil, and Luis Henrique Dias Taveres (179) has written a fine analysis of the ideology of the participants (see also 185). These works and the pertinent documents published in 1931 and 1959 now present a fair picture of what may have been the first of a series of urban revolts that extended into the nineteenth century (11, 86).

Recent political events in Brazil have endangered the progress made in colonial historiography. Many of the distinguished scholars cited in this essay have lost their academic positions for personal and political reasons. Foreign scholarship cannot fill the vacuum that this situation may create. It is true that Brazilian historiography remains in many ways deficient and that it still suffers from a heritage of antiquarianism and irrelevance. Nevertheless, Brazilian scholars have overcome great difficulties in the inadequacies of libraries and the lack of funds for research and publication to open new areas of historical investigation. However significant the influence or contributions of foreign scholars, credit for progess in the final analysis must go to the Brazilians themselves as they seek in their past the roots of the present.

# BIBLIOGRAPHY

1. Abreu, João Capistrano de. *Capítulos de historia colonial.* 4th ed. Rio de Janeiro, 1954.

2. Alden, Dauril. "The Growth and Decline of Indigo Production in Colonial Brazil: A Study in Comparative Economic History." *Journal of Economic History* 36 (March 1965): 35–60.

3. ———. "Manoel Luís Vieira: An Entrepreneur in Rio de Janeiro during Brazil's Eighteenth-Century Agricultural Renaissance." *Hispanic American Historical Review* 34 (November 1959): 521–37.

4. ———. "The Population of Brazil in the Late Eighteenth Century: A Preliminary Survey." *Hispanic American Historical Review* 43 (May 1963): 173–205.

5. ———. *Royal Government in Colonial Brazil.* Berkeley, Calif., 1968.

6. Anchieta, José de. *Informação do Brasil e de suas capitanias.* Introduction by Leonardo Arroyo. São Paulo, 1964.

7. Andreoni, João Antônio. *Cultura e opulencia do Brasil.* Introduction by A. P. Canabrava. São Paulo, 1967.

8. Andrews, Kenneth R. *Elizabethan Privateering: English Privateering during the Spanish War, 1585–1603.* Cambridge, Eng., 1963.

9. Antonil, André João. *Cultura e opulencia do Brasil por suas drogas e minas.* Ed. by Andrée Mansuy. Paris, 1968.

10. *Atas da câmara da Bahia, 1625–1700.* 6 vols. Salvador, Braz., 1949–54.

11. "Autos de devassa do levantamento e sedição intentada na Bahia em 1798." *Anais do Arquivo Público da Bahia* 35 (1959).

12. Avila, Affonso. *Resíduos seiscentistas em minas.* 2 vols. Belo Horionte, Braz., 1967.

13. Azevedo, Aroldo de. *Vilas e cidades do Brasil colonial.* São Paulo, 1956.

14. Azevedo, Fernando de. *Canaviais e engenhos na vida política do Brasil.* Rio de Janeiro, 1948.

15. Azevedo, Thales de. *Ensaios de antropologia social.* Salvador, Braz., 1959.

16. ———. *Povoamento da cidade do Salvador.* Salvador, Braz., 1949.

17. Bagú, Sergio. *Economia de la sociedad colonial.* Buenos Aires, 1949.

18. Barros, Henrique da Gama. *História da administração pública em Portugal,* 2d ed. 11 vols. Lisbon, 1945–54.

19. Bastide, Roger. *Les Amériques noires: Le civilisations africaines dans le nouveau monde.* Paris, 1967.

20. ———. *Les religions africaines au Brésil.* Paris, 1960.

21. Bazin, Germain. *L'Architecture religieuse baroque au Brésil.* Paris, 1960.

40

22. Becú, Ricardo Zorraquín. "Orígenes del comercio rioplatense, 1580–1620." *Anuario de Historia Argentina* 1 (1943).

23. Boxer, C. R. *The Dutch in Brazil, 1624–1654.* Oxford, Eng., 1957.

24. ———. *The Golden Age of Brazil, 1695–1750.* Berkeley, Calif., 1962.

25. ———. *A Great Luso-Brazilian Figure, Padre Antonio Vieira, S.J., 1608–1697.* London, 1957.

26. ———. "Negro Slavery in Brazil." *Race* 5 (1964): 38–47.

27. ———. "Nova e curiosa relação." In *Anais do Congresso Comemorativo do Bicentenário da Transferência da Sede do Govêrno do Brasil,* 1: 171–86. 3 vols. Rio de Janeiro, 1963.

28. ———. *Portuguese Society in the Tropics: The Municipal Councils of Goa, Macao, Bahia, and Luanda, 1510–1800.* Madison, Wis., 1965.

29. ———. *Race Relations in the Portuguese Colonial Empire, 1415–1825.* Oxford, Eng., 1963.

30. ———. *Salvador de Sá and the Struggle for Brazil and Angola.* London, 1952.

31. Brazil, Departmento Administrativo do Serviço Público. *História administrativa do Brasil.* 6 vols. 1962–.

32. Burns, E. Bradford. "The Enlightenment in Two Colonial Brazilian Libraries." *Journal of the History of Ideas* 25 (July–September 1964): 430–38.

33. ———. *Perspectives on Brazilian History.* New York, 1967.

34. ———. "The Role of Azeredo Coutinho in the Enlightment of Brazil." *Hispanic American Historical Review* 44 (May 1964): 145–60.

35. Calmon, Pedro. *História do Brasil.* 7 vols. Rio de Janeiro, 1959.

36. Camargo, Paulo Florencio da Silveira. *História eclesiástica do Brasil.* Petrópolis, Braz., 1955.

37. ———. *A igreja na história de São Paulo.* 7 vols. São Paulo, 1952–3.

38. Canabrava, Alice P. *O comércio português no Rio da Prata (1580–1640).* São Paulo, 1944.

39. Cardozo, Manuel. "The Lay Brotherhoods of Colonial Bahia." *Catholic Historical Review* 33 (April 1947): 12–30.

40. ———. "Tithes in Colonial Minas Gerais." *Catholic Historical Review* 38 (July 1952): 175–82.

41. Carneiro, Edison. *O quilombo dos Palmares.* 3d ed. Rio de Janeiro, 1966.

42. Carrato, José Ferreira. *Igreja, iluminismo e escolas mineiras colonials.* São Paulo, 1968.

43. ———. *As Minas Gerais e os primordios de caraça.* São Paulo, 1963.

44. Centro de Estudos Históricos Ultramarinos. *Documentação ultramarina portuguesa.* 4 vols. to date. Lisbon, 1960.

45. ———. *As gavetas de Torre do Tombo.* 5 vols. to date. Lisbon, 1960.

46. Chaunu, Pierre. "Bresil et Atlantique au xviiᵉ siècle." *Annales Economies, Sociétés, Civilisations* 6 (November–December 1961): 1176–1207.

47. Cortesão, Jaime. *Alexandre de Gusmão e o Tratado de Madrid.* 8 vols. Rio de Janeiro, 1950–59.

48. ———. *Introdução à história das bandeiras.* 2 vols. Lisbon, 1964.

49. ———. *Manuscritos da colecção de Angelis.* 5 vols. Rio de Janeiro, 1951–55.

50. ———. *Raposo Tavares e a formação territorial do Brasil.* Rio de Janeiro, 1958.

51. Cortesão, Jaime, and Pedro Calmon. *Brasil.* Historia de América, 26. Barcelona, 1956.

52. Costa Filho, Miguel. *A cana-de-Açúcar em Minas Gerais.* Rio de Janeiro, 1963.

53. Davis, David Brion. *The Problem of Slavery in Western Culture.* Ithaca, N.Y., 1966.

54. Dias, Manuel Nunes. "O cacau luso-brasileiro na economia mundial subsídios para a sua história." *Studia* 8 (July 1961): 7–94.

55. ———. *O capitalismo monârquico português.* 2 vols. Coimbra, Port., 1963–64.

56. ———. "Colonização da Amazonia (1755–1778)." *Revista de História* 72 (1967): 471–90.

57. ———. "Fomento ultramarino e mercantilismo: A Companhia Geral do Grão Pará e Maranhão (1755–1778)." *Revista de História* 66 (1966): 359–428; 67 (1966): 47–120; 68 (1966): 367–416; 69 (1967): 99–148; 71 (1967): 105–66; 73 (1968): 71–114.

58. Diégues Júnior, Manuel. *População e açúcar no nordeste do Brasil.* Rio de Janeiro, 1954.

59. Ellis, Myriam. *Aspectos da pesca da Baleia no Brasil colonial.* São Paulo, 1958.

60. ———. "As feitorias baleeiras meridionais do Brasil colonial." Mimeo. 2 vols. São Paulo, 1966.

61. ———. *O monopólio do sal no estado do Brasil (1631–1801).* São Paulo, 1955.

62. Faria, Francisco Leite de. Review of Frei Vicente do Salvador's "Historia do Brasil." *Studia* 24 (1968): 150–56.

63. Fernandes, Florestan. *A integração do negro na sociedade de classes.* 2 vols. São Paulo, 1965.

64. ———. *Organização social dos Tupinambá.* 2d ed. São Paulo, 1963.

65. França, Eduardo D'Oliveira and Sonia A. Siqueira. "Segunda visitação do Santo Ofício ás partes do Brasil." *Anais do Museu Paulista* 17 (1966).

66. Furtado, Celso. *The Economic Growth of Brazil.* Berkeley, Calif., 1963. Port. ed. *Formação econômica do Brasil.* Rio de Janeiro, 1959.

67. Gandavo, Pero de Magalhães. *História da província Santa Cruz: Tratado da terra do Brasil.* São Paulo, 1964.

68. Garraux, A. L. *Bibliographie brésilienne.* 2d ed. Rio de Janeiro, 1962.

69. Godinho, Vittorino Magalhães. *A econômica dos descobrimentos henrequinos.* Lisbon, 1962.

70. ———. "Portugal as frotas do açúar e as frotas do ouro 1670–1770." *Revista de História* 15 (1953): 69–88.

71. ———. *Prix et monnaies au Portugal, 1750–1850.* Paris, 1955.

72. González, Elda R., and Rolando Mellafe. "La función de la familia en la historia social hispanoamericana colonial." *Anuario del Instituto de Investigaciones Históricas* (1965): 57–71.

73. Goulart, José Alínio. *Brasil do boi e couro.* 2 vols. Rio de Janeiro, 1965–66.

74. Goulart, Mauricio. *A escravidão africana no Brasil.* São Paulo, 1949.

75. Hanke, Lewis. "The Portuguese in Spanish America with Special Reference to the Villa Imperial de Potosí." *Revista do História de América* 61 (June 1961): 1–48.

76. Harris, Marvin. *Patterns of Race in the Americas.* New York, 1964.

77. Maubert, Maxime. *L'Eglise et la défense des "sauvages": Le Père Antoine Vieira au Brésil.* Brussels, 1964.

78. Holanda, Sérgio Buarque de. *Caminhos e fronteiras.* Rio de Janeiro, 1957.

79. ———, ed. *História geral da civilização brasileira.* 5 vols. to date. São Paulo, 1960–.

80. ———. *Monções.* Rio de Janeiro, 1945.

81. ———, ed. *Obras econômicas de J. J. da Cunha de Azeredo Coutinho.* São Paulo, 1966.

82. ———. "Os projectos de colonização e comercio toscanos no Brasil ao tempo do Grão Duque Fernando I (1587–1607)." *Revista de História* 71 (1967): 61–84.

83. ———. *Raíces del Brasil.* Mexico, 1955.

84. ———. *Visão do paraíso: Os motivos edênicos no descobrimento e colonização do Brasil.* Rio de Janeiro, 1959.

85. Ianni, Octavio. *As metamorfoses do escravo.* São Paulo, 1962.

44  LATIN AMERICAN SCHOLARSHIP SINCE WORLD WAR II

86. "A inconfidência da Bahia em 1798: Devassa e Sequestros." *Anais da Biblioteca Nacional de Rio de Janeiro* 43–44 (1929–30): 83–225; 45 (1931): 1–421.

87. Keiman, Mathias C. *The Indian Policy of Portugal in the Amazon Region, 1614–1693.* Washington, D.C., 1954.

88. Kellenbenz, Hermann. "Der Brasilienhandel der Hamburger Portugiesen zu Ende Des 16 und in der Ersten Halfte des 17 Jahrhunderts." In *Actas*, III Congresso Internacional de Estudos Luso-Brasileiros, 2: 277–96.

89. ———. *A participação da Companhia de judeus na conquista holandesa de Pernambuco.* João Pessoa, Braz., 1966.

90. ———. *Unternhmerkräfte im Hamburger Portugal-und Spanienhandel 1590–1625.* Hamburg, 1954.

91. Kent, R. K. "Palmares: An African State in Brazil." *Journal of African History* 6 (1965): 161–75.

92. Laga, Carl. "O engenho de Erasmos em São Vicente." *Estudos Históricos* 1 (1963): 113–43.

93. Lapa, José Roberto do Amaral. *A Bahia e a Carreira da India.* Marília, Braz., 1966.

94. Lapa, M. Rodrigues. *As "Cartas chilenas": Um problema histórico e filológico.* Rio de Janeiro, 1958.

95. ———. *Obras completas de Tomás Antônio Gonzaga.* São Paulo, 1942.

96. Leite, Serafim, ed. *Cartas do Brasil e mais escritos do P. Manuel da Nóbrega (opera omnia).* Coimbra, Port., 1958.

97. ———. *Monumenta Brasiliae.* 4 vols. Rome, 1956–60.

98. ———. *Novas páginas de história do Brasil.* São Paulo, 1965.

99. Lima, M. Oliveira. "A Nova Lusitânia." In *História da colonização Portuguesa no Brasil,* ed. Carlos Malheiro Dias. 3 vols., Oporto, Port., 1921–24.

100. *Livro Velho do Tombo do Mosteiro de São Bento.* Bahia, Braz., 1945.

101. Lobo, Eulalia Maria Lahmeyer. *Processo administrativo ibero-americano.* São Paulo, 1962.

102. Lopes, Antonio. *Alcântara: Subsídios para a história da cidade.* Rio de Janeiro, 1957.

103. Lowery, Martin J. "The Inland Customhouse at Cordoba." *Mid-America* 35 (n.s. 24): 18–36.

104. Luz, Francisco Paulo Mendes da. *O Conselho da India.* Lisbon, 1954.

105. Macedo, Jorge Borges de. "Portugal e a economia pombalina: Temas e hipóteses." *Revista de História* 19 (1954): 81–100.

106. Machado, Alcântara. *Vida e morte do Bandeirante.* São Paulo, 1965.

107. Magalhães, José Calvet de. *Historia do pensamento econômico em Portugal.* Coimbra, Port., 1967.

108. Mansuy, Andrée. "Memoire inédit d'Ambroise Jauffret sur le Brésil à l'epoque de la découverte des mines d'or (1704)." In *Actas,* V Congresso Internacional de Estudes Luso-Brasileiros, 2: 5–42.

109. Mauro, Frédéric. "México y Brasil: Dos economías coloniales comparadas." *Historia Mexicana* 40 (1961): 571–87.

110. ———. *Le Portugal et l'Atlantique au xvii$^e$ siècle (1570–1670): Etudes économique.* Paris, 1960.

111. Melatti, Julio Cezar. *Indios e criadores: A situação dos Krahó na área pastoril do Tocantins.* Rio de Janeiro, 1967.

112. Mello, José Antônio Gonçalves de. *Diálogos das grandezas do Brasil.* 2d ed. complete. Documentos para a Historia do Nordeste, vol. 1. Recife, Braz., 1966.

113. ———, ed. and trans. *Relatório sôbre as capitanias conquistadas no Brasil pelos holandeses (1639).* Série História, vol. 3. Rio de Janeiro, 1947.

114. ———. *Restauradores de Panambuco.* Recife, Braz., 1967.

115. ———. *Tempo dos flamengos: Influência da ocupação holandesa na vida e na cultura do norte do Brasil.* Rio de Janeiro, 1947.

116. ———, and Cleonir Xavier de Albuquerqe, eds. *Cartas de Duarte Coelho a el Rei.* Documentos para a História do Nordeste, vol. 2. Recife, Braz., 1967.

117. Mendonça, Marcos Carneiro de, ed. *A Amazônia na era pombalina.* 3 vols. Rio de Janeiro, 1963.

118. Moog, Clodomir Viana. *Bandeirantes and Pioneers.* New York, 1964.

119. Moraes, Rubens Borba de. *Bibliographia brasiliana.* 2 vols. Rio de Janeiro, 1958.

120. ———, and William Berrien, eds. *Manual bibliográfico de estudos brasileiros.* Rio de Janeiro, 1959.

121. Morner, Magnus. "The History of Race Relations in Latin America: Some Comments on the State of Research." *Latin American Research Review* 1 (Summer 1963): 17–44.

122. Morse, Richard, ed. *The Bandeirantes: The Historical Role of the Brazilian Pathfinders.* New York, 1965.

123. ———. "Latin American Cities: Aspects of Function and Structure." *Comparative Studies of Society and History* 4 (July 1962): 473–93.

124. ———. "Some Characteristics of Latin American Urban History." *American Historical Review* 67 (January 1964): 317–38.

125. Moura, Clovis. *Rebeliões da senzala. (Quilombos, insurreições, guerrilhas)*. São Paulo, 1959.

126. Neiva, Artur Hehl. "Povoamento do Brasil no século xviii." *Revista de História* 10 (1952): 379–88.

127. Oliveira, Oscar de. *Os dízimos eclesiàsticos do Brasil nos períodos da colônia e do império*. Belo Horizonte, Braz., 1964.

128. Omegna, Nelson. *A cidade colonial*. Rio de Janeiro, 1961.

129. Ott, Carlos. *Formação e evolução étnica da Cidade do Salvador*. 2 vols. Bahia, 1955–57.

130. Pedreira, Pedro Thomás. "Os quilimbos baianos." *Revista Brasileira de Geografia* 24 (1962): 79–93.

131. Petrone, Maria Theresa Schorer. *A lavoura canaveira em São Paulo: Expansão e declínio (1765–1851)*. São Paulo, 1968.

132. Pierson, Donald. *Negroes in Brazil: A Study of Race Contact at Bahia*. Carbondale, Ill., 1967. (Originally published in 1942.)

133. Pinho, José Wanderley de Araújo. *História de um engenho do Recôncavo*. Rio de Janeiro, 1946.

134. Pinto, L. A. Costa. *Lutas de famílias no Brasil*. São Paulo, 1949.

135. Poppino, Rollie. "Cattle Industry in Colonial Brazil." *Mid-America* 31 (October 1948): 219–47.

136. ———. *A Feira de Santana*. Salvador, Braz., 1968.

137. Porto, Costa. *Estudo sôbre o sistema sesmarial*. Recife, Braz., 1965.

138. Prado, Caio, Júnior. *The Colonial Background of Modern Brazil*. Berkeley, Calif., 1967.

139. ———. *História econômica do Brasil*. 10th ed. São Paulo, 1967.

140. Queiroz, Maria Issaura Pereira de. *O messianismo no Brasil e no mundo*. São Paulo, 1965.

141. Quirino, Tarcizio do Rêgo. *Os habitantes do Brasil no fim do século xvi*. Recife, Braz., 1966.

142. Raeders, George. *Bibliographie franco-brésilienne (1551–1957)*. Rio de Janeiro, 1960.

143. Ramos, Artur. *A aculturação negra no Brasil*. São Paulo, 1952.

144. Rau, Virginia. *A Casa dos Contos*. Coimbra, Port., 1952.

145. ———, and Maria Fernanda Gomes da Silva. *Os manuscritos do Arquivo da Casa de Cadaval respeitantes ao Brasil*. 2 vols. Coimbra, Port., 1958.

146. Rebelo, Manuel dos Anjos Silva. *Relações entre Angola e Brasil*. Lisbon, 1968.

147. Reis, Artur Ferreira. *Epocas e visões regionais do Brasil*. Manaus, Braz., 1966.

148. ———. *Súmula de história de Amazonas*. Manaus, Braz., 1965.

149. Revah, I. S. "Le plaidoyer en faveur des 'Nouveaux Chrétiens' portugais du licencié Martin Gonzalez de Cellorigo." *Revue des Etudes Juives* 122 (July–December 1963): 279–398.

150. Ribeiro, Maria de Conceição Martins. "Os oficiais da câmara de São Paulo no século xvi." *Anais* 4 (1951): 461–99.

151. Rodney, Walter. "Portuguese Attempts at Monopoly on the Upper Guinea Coast." *Journal of African History* 6 (1965): 307–22.

152. Rodrigues, José Honório. *Brasil and Africa.* Berkeley, Calif., 1965.

153. ———. "Brazilian Historiography: Present Trends and Research Requirements." In *Social Science in Latin America,* ed. Manuel Diégues Júnior and Bryce Wood, pp. 217–40. New York, 1967.

154. ———. *História e historiadores do Brasil.* São Paulo, 1965.

155. ———. *Historiografía del Brasil: Siglo xvi.* Mexico, 1957.

156. ———. *Historiografía del Brasil: Siglo xvii.* Mexico, 1963.

157. ———. *Historiografía e bibliografia do domínio holandês no Brasil.* Rio de Janeiro, 1949.

158. ———. *Teoria da história do Brasil.* 2d ed. rev. 2 vols. São Paulo, 1957.

159. ———. *Vida e história.* Rio de Janeiro, 1966.

160. Rodrigues, Maria Regina da Cunha. "Relação de 134 codices valiosos para uma eventual história local de Santana do Parnaíba (1660–1932)." *Revista de História* 48 (1961): 379–92.

161. Russell-Wood, A. J. R. *Fidalgos and Philanthropists: The Santa Casa da Misericórdia of Bahia, 1550–1755.* Berkeley, Calif., 1968.

162. Ruy, Affonso. *A história da câmara municipal da cidade do Salvador.* Salvador, Braz., 1953.

163. ———. *História política e administrativa da cidade do Salvador.* Salvador, Braz., 1949.

164. ———. *A primeira revolução social brasileira, 1798.* 2d ed. Salvador, Braz., 1951.

165. Salles, Fritz Teixeira de. *Associações religiosas no ciclo do ouro.* Belo Horizonte, Braz., 1963.

166. Salvador, Frei Vicente do. *História do Brasil, 1500–1627.* 5th ed. with notes by Capistrano de Abreu, Rodolfo Garcia, and Frei Venâncio Willeke. São Paulo, 1965.

167. Santos, Lúcio José dos. *Inconfidência mineira.* São Paulo, 1927.

168. Santos Filho, Lucurgo. *Uma comunidade rural do Brasil antigo.* São Paulo, 1956.

169. Sayers, Raymond. *The Negro in Brazilian Literature.* New York, 1956.

170. Schwartz, Stuart B. "Luso-Spanish Relations in Hapsburg Brazil, 1580–1640." *Americas* 25 (July 1968): 33–48.

171. Silva, José Norberto de Sousa e. *História da conjuração mineira*. 2d ed. 2 vols. Rio de Janeiro, 1948. (First published in 1873.)

172. Simonson, Roberto. *História econômica do Brasil, 1550–1820*. 4th ed. São Paulo, 1962.

173. Siquiera, Sonia Aparecida. "A escravidão negra no pensamento do Bispo Azeredo Coutinho." *Revista de História* 56 (1963): 349–56; 57 (1964): 141–98.

174. Sluiter, Engel. "Dutch Maritime Power and the Colonial Status Quo, 1585–1641." *Pacific Historical Review* 11 (1942): 29–41.

175. ———. "Os holandeses no Brasil antes de 1621." *Revista do Instituto Arqueológico, Histórico e Geográfico Pernambucano* 46 (1961): 186–207.

176. ———, ed. "Report on the State of Brazil, 1612." *Hispanic American Historical Review* 29 (1949): 518–62.

177. Sousa, Pero Lopes de. *Diário da navegação*. Introduction by J. P. Leite Cordeiro and notes by Comandante Eugênio de Castro. São Paulo, 1964.

178. Taunay, Affonso d'Escragnolle. *História geral das bandeiras paulistas*. 11 vols. São Paulo, 1925–50.

179. Tavares, Luis Henrique Dias. *Introdução ao estudo das idéias do movimento de 1798*. Salvador, Braz., 1959.

180. Thomas, Georg. "Literaturbericht über die Geschichte Brasiliens." *Historische Zeitschrift* 3 (1969): 546–74.

181. ———. *Die portugiesjsche Indianerpolitik in Brasilien, 1500–1640*. Berlin, 1968.

182. "Tombo do Mosteiro de São Bento de Olinda." *Revista do Instituto Arqueológico Histórico e Geográfico Pernambucano* 41 (1946–47).

183. Vianna, Helio. *História do Brasil*. 2 vols. São Paulo, 1956.

184. ———, ed. *Livro que dá razão do Estado do Brasil (1612)*. Recife, Braz., 1955.

185. Vianna Filho, Luiz. "Homens e causas da revolução baiana de 1798." *Anais do 3° Congresso de Historia Nacional* 4 (1941): 642–63.

186. Verger, Pierre. *Bahia and the West African Trade, 1549–1851*. Ibadan, Nigeria, 1964.

187. ———. *Flux et reflux de la traite des nègres entre le golfe de Bénin et Bahia de todos os santos du xvii<sup>e</sup> au xix<sup>e</sup> siècle*. Paris, 1968.

188. ———. *Notes sur le culte des Orisa et Vodun à Bahia, la Baie de tous les saints, au Brésil et à l'ancienne Côte des esclaves en Afrique*. Dakar, Senegal, 1957.

189. Willems, Emílio. "A Familia portuguesa contemporânea." *Sociologia* 17 (1955): 6–55.

190. ———. "The Structure of the Brazilian Family." *Social Forces* 31 (1953): 339–46.

191. Willeke, Vanancio. "Three Centuries of Missionary Work in Northern Brazil: Franciscan Province of St. Anthony, 1657–1957." *Americas* 15 (October 1958): 129–38.

192. Wilter, José Sebastiaõ. "Arrolamento das fontes históricas de Mogi das Cruzes-Estado de São Paulo." *Revista de História* 57 (1962): 493–502.

193. Wiznitzer, Arnold. *Jews in Colonial Brazil.* New York, 1960.

194. Zenha, Edmundo. *O municipio no Brasil.* São Paulo, 1948.

# BRAZIL:
# THE NATIONAL PERIOD

*Richard Graham*

Brazil has been developing rapidly since 1945 and all aspects of its society have felt the grinding pressures of modern change. New groups have been added to the old sociopolitical mix and old ones have yielded ground only with the utmost reluctance. The resulting conflicts and uncertainties have driven some historians to look at Brazil's past with new questions and evaluate old answers by new criteria.

Many of these authors are dissatisfied with the old Brazilian historiography, characterized as it was by endless recitation of undifferentiated detail, sterile generalizations regarding the heroic deeds of the past, and principal emphasis upon political and military affairs. Although that kind of historical writing still continues to be practiced, it has become less and less typical of Brazil since the end of World War II, first of all, because some of the younger historians found it of little use in understanding the present crises which shaped not only their everyday life but that of the universities in which their professional existence was often rooted; second, and perhaps more important, because many of the new generation considered the old explanations simply unbelievable in the light of what they were learning about class structure, human motivation, international conflict, and the nature of political power. And of course many who were not willing to attack the status quo were also impelled by this intellectual milieu to examine social and economic questions with new interest.

In addition, the growing precision and technical sophistication which characterize all aspects of this newly industrializing society have also heightened interest in the dispassionate "scientific" approach based on the exhaustive use of primary sources that has so deeply marked Western historiography. This is evident not only in the relatively new fields of history of ideas and of science, but also in the older approaches of biography, political and diplomatic studies, and local or regional history.

Meanwhile, the situation within which North American historians of Brazil were working has also been changing. Despite the imaginative and scholarly work of such men as Stanley Stein (115, 116) and Richard Morse (71), the first fifteen years after World War II were characterized by a singular lack of interest in Brazilian history even greater than that for Latin American history in general. After 1960, however, a flood of younger historians rushed to the new historiographical frontier, not in austere covered wagons, but with the ready funds which foundations and government were making somewhat indiscriminately available for the study of Latin America in general and Brazil in particular. The fear of revolution and the desire to find peaceful means of bringing about development stimulated the flow of funds and, to some extent, may even have shaped the interests of these students. Today one may detect a still newer trend toward the development of historians who are skeptical regarding the possibility of achieving genuine progress without revolution and who are especially interested in such issues as imperialism, class struggle, and the techniques by which power has been agglomerated and maintained by a small and flexible Brazilian elite.

A good example of the historian in Brazil who has been swept up by the urge to make his work relevant to his society's immediate problems is José Honório Rodrigues. In the 1940s and 1950s he was making a name for himself with publications on historiography, by perceptive monographic articles (87), and by his dynamic direction of the National Archive in Rio de Janeiro. In the 1960s, however, finding it increasingly difficult to remain aloof from the swirling currents of political strife and social discontent, he decided to use his historical skills—without sacrificing methodological technique—to explore more relevant topics. He studied the nineteenth-century background of electoral reform and voting qualifications at a time when suffrage for illiterates was being hotly debated (86). When Brazil was somewhat ineffectually striving to establish its position as a leader of the "Third World," he published his book (85) which explored at length the historical connections between Brazil and Africa. He then examined the constants of Brazilian policy and found no contradictions between them and the effort to break away from the previously unquestioned preeminence of the United States (88). He has not always managed to remain objective once he gave up detachment, but his attempt has been courageous and invigorating.

Marxist historians have been prominent in Brazil, perhaps because a Marxian analysis often seems so easily applicable in a newly industrializing society like Brazil. Two prominent historians who apply this interpretation to Brazilian history are Caio Prado Júnior and Nelson Werneck Sodré. Aside from this common starting point, there are few similarities between them. Prado is one of the heirs of Brazil's most prominent coffee-planter-turned-railroad-builder-and-banker. His approach is urbane and restrained. In 1945 he published his *História econômica do Brasil* (81), a skillful reinterpretation of the entire texture of the Brazilian past. Utilizing secondary sources, he wove a pattern that set Brazilian historiography on a new path. Only by remembering the disjointed and basically anecdotal quality of much previous historical writing in Brazil—merely a chronological listing of events—can the importance of his work be properly appreciated. Not a digger in archives himself, he made it possible for the writers of detailed monographs to find a conceptual framework within which to place their studies. Many of them did not share his ideological position but found his contribution invaluable. His interpretation may be seriously questioned today from either left or right. He himself subsequently struggled with the realities of recent political developments, faced the failure of the national bourgeoisie to reform as expected, and attempted to explain it by another interpretation of the past (82). But those who dismiss his 1945 work for not living up to our methodological standards have missed its point.

Nelson Werneck Sodré is surely the most prolific Marxist historian in Brazil. An army officer, he has found much time for writing since his dismissal by the rightist leaders of the 1964 coup d'état. In 1939 he published his *Panorama do segundo império* (111), but only the very perceptive reader would have guessed the lengths to which he would later carry his particular viewpoint. In his long list of publications (104, 105, 106, 107, 108, 109, 110, 111, 112) his most important book to date is his *História da burguesia brasileira* (104). In it he began with a forthright exposition of Marxist-Leninist theory, then moved on to apply it to the Brazilian scene. Although infuriating at times—there is nothing urbane or restrained about his writing—the work is extremely important both because of the wealth of data which he brings to bear upon his theme and because of the insights he provides into the nature of the historical process. Although one may disagree with his interpretations, one is the richer for having been exposed to them.

It is a curious reflection of the state of the art that some Brazilians have considered his rather commonplace assertions (112) regarding British interests in the independence of Latin America as bad history because of his emphasis on economic factors, if not actually treasonous because he places inadequate emphasis upon the heroic deeds of the founders.

An incident that reflects the atmosphere within which the historian must work in Brazil is the case of the *História nova*. A government "think-tank," the Instituto Superior de Estudos Brasileiros, had been set up within the Ministry of Education to research major issues in Brazilian life and to recommend policies (16). One of its many activities included proposed revisions of educational materials, and Sodré had been allowed to gather about him a group of students who would prepare a pilot set of supplementary readings to accompany Brazilian history textbooks. Again, it is only by noting the stultifying and mindless compendiums of unrelated historical "facts" which characterize Brazilian texts that the importance of the venture can be gauged. In a series of brief, provocative studies the authors suggested the role that economic power, social conflict, and international pressure had played in Brazil's past (92). They erred precisely in the opposite direction of the prevailing texts; that is, they played rather fast and loose with the facts. But from the students' point of view, these studies would have been a breath of fresh air. Needless to say, the "Establishment" was shocked. Four or five of the studies were barely out when the coup d'état of 1964 took place. Remaining stocks were confiscated and copies are extremely hard to find today. Subsequently, the Editôra Brasiliense, owned by Caio Prado Júnior, published enlarged and revised versions of these books (93), but they too were banned by the the government and the publisher was threatened with imprisonment for his trouble. Sodré was hailed before a military court to answer charges of subversion because of the threat to national security that these studies allegedly posed (106). That the studies were not very good history is obvious; that their circulation was not allowed and students are not exposed to historical controversies may partly explain why bright young men and women are not much attracted to the field.

Among the socioeconomic topics that have attracted the attention of serious scholars, the richest field has been the history of slavery. The works of Gilberto Freyre—not only *The Masters and the Slaves* (44), but also *The Mansions and the Shanties* (45), which deals with the transition to the national period—provided the interpretive foil against which others have sparred. Although he was evidently sensitive to the dehumanizing quality of slavery, he was nevertheless read as defending the institution and the paternalism and loyalty that allegedly characterized it. As one critic put it, "The idealization of slavery, the romantic idea of the suavity and gentleness of slavery in Brazil, the picture of the loyal slave and the benevolent master, friend of the slave—interpretations that ended up prevailing in our literature and our history—were some of the myths forged by a slave society to defend a system which it considered essential" (31).

Stanley Stein (116) was one of the first to seriously question the benevolence of Brazilian slavery. He based his argument on a meticulous examination of records in a coffee-growing county in the province of Rio de Janeiro. Subsequently, sociologists at the University of São Paulo probed the historical background of race prejudice in present-day Brazil and provided further substantiation for the view that slavery was harsh, cruel, and devoid of saving graces (24, 55). More recently, Emília Viotti da Costa (31) has written the most thorough examination yet to appear of slavery and abolition in São Paulo. It is well written and straightforward in its argument and makes impressive and systematic use of local government archives, newspapers, governmental reports, legislative debates, travelers' accounts, and contemporary pamphlets.

The biggest lack so far apparent in this revisionistic literature is in studies of slavery in the northeastern part of the country. That is the area about which Freyre wrote and the region where slavery was most firmly entrenched. Also, the family connections and economic interests of the abolitionists need to be explored if we are to understand their motivation.[1] There are many little-used records that would shed additional light on the slave and free-black population: their location, span of life, and distribution by sex. Many were used by Luiz Delgado (37). And the whole question of the economic role and profitability of slavery needs to be examined as it has been, at least partially, for the United States (see 49, 50, 123).

Surprisingly, there has not yet appeared any well-documented large-scale study of immigration, another aspect of Brazil's labor problem. Costa pays considerable attention to the efforts of coffee planters in São Paulo to attract immigrants before 1888 and one regrets that she did not bring her talents to bear in completing that story for the period immediately after the abolition of slavery. There have been some studies of particular aspects of this topic (6, 20, 30, 53, 119, 126), but we await a major study.[2]

---

1. I understand this is being done by Rebecca Baird, a graduate student at Stanford University.

2. Michael Hall, of the University of North Carolina, is currently studying Italian immigration to Brazil.

Economic history has been more developed for the colonial era than for the national one. Celso Furtado (46), however, covered both periods and raised an entire set of questions not usually considered by the conventional historian. Maria Teresa Schorer Petrone (94) has done a magnificent job with the manuscript records available in São Paulo, examining all aspects of sugar agriculture there from 1765 to 1851. Stein's study of the cotton textile industry has already been referred to, and further contributions have been made by Alice P. Cannabrava (22, 23). Although there have been some other studies such as Nelson Lage Mascarenhas's biography (66) of his entrepreneurial father, not as much has been done on strictly economic history as one could have expected.[3]

Two titles that include a fairly broad range of economic, social, and intellectual topics are Gilberto Freyre's *Ordem e progresso* (43) and my own *Britain and the Onset of Modernization in Brazil, 1851–1914* (51). Freyre's *Ordem e progresso* is probably the most poorly organized of all his works. One may also question whether the conceptual framework which was so effective in the earlier works is large enough or effective enough a vehicle for the events of the late nineteenth and early twentieth centuries. Nevertheless, the information he presents (sometimes frustratingly imprecise as to source) is basic to an understanding of the period. As for my book, I think its quality had best be evaluated by others—probably by Freyre, who has written on the same topic!—and I need only say that it deals primarily with the nineteenth century and uses the British presence as a thread with which to explore the labyrinth of modern change in Brazil: not only economic development but the attempts through liberalism, Spencerianism, laissez faire economics, the "gospel of work," and even Protestantism to break the bonds exerted upon the individual by a traditional society.

The history of ideas has drawn some attention since World War II, but there has been no really significant breakthrough in which the roots of "Brazilian-ness" would be explored through the course of intellectual history. True, João Cruz Costa, in his *History of Ideas in Brazil* (32), perceptively links the economic and social developments of the past to intellectual currents. The most significant author here has been Roque Spencer Maciel de Barros. His *A ilustração brasileira*

---

3. The sugar economy of northeastern Brazil is being examined by Peter Eisenberg, a graduate student at Columbia University.

*e a idéia de universidade* (12) is, unfortunately, rather turgid, but it is an insightful examination of nineteenth-century currents of thought and their meaning within the national experience. The proposed creation of a university, its connection to church or state, its monopolistic or free-enterprise nature, and its inner structure and curriculum touched upon so many points of discord within a society in transition that the entire project was postponed into the twentieth century.

A major weakness of these studies is their "Whig" interpretation. Historians in Brazil as elsewhere are more interested in the victors than in the vanquished, more interested in those who advanced progress than in those who held it back. Yet, given the relatively little progress that has taken place, there is a real need for an examination of the intellectual roots of conservatism. A somewhat better balance than usual is achieved in the excellent *História das idéias políticas no Brasil* by Nelson Saldanha (91). In a systematic study of the political ideas of his countrymen he points out the weight of conservative thought throughout Brazil's history. He is especially strong on the nineteenth century and the book is thoroughly based on the sources, which are cited with precision. It does not come up to José Luis Romero's *History of Argentine Political Thought* (89) principally because the political theorists of Brazil have not been up to the Argentine standard. It still remains true that until we have a fuller understanding of the ideology of the old societal structure we will have an inadequate grasp of the Brazilian past (but see 68).

Nor has the history of the church attracted as much attention as one would have expected in view of the close alliance between it and the conservative society. The old issue of church and state no longer excites the younger historians as much as it did Sister Mary C. Thornton some twenty years ago (118). Unfortunately, George Boehrer's untimely death in 1967 prevented his carrying through on the study promised by his article "The Church and the Overthrow of the Brazilian Monarchy" (15). The position of the Catholic church on the issues being debated during the two decades before World War II is being studied by Margaret Todaro of the University of Southern California. Perhaps she will be able to elucidate the mechanism through which a conservative church laid the intellectual bases for the present ferment within its structure and its thought.

Also important in this connection is the history of science, still in its infancy in Brazil. How was it possible for leaders to accept man-over-nature as an intellectual premise while doing so little to exercise the scientific spirit? Fernando de Azevedo has edited a collection entitled *As ciências no Brasil* (8), which, when combined with his famous but badly translated *Brazilian Culture* (7), suggests a surprisingly rich field for further examination. See, for instance, the recently published notes of the self-taught Freire Alemão (35). Perhaps the present investigation of Donald Cooper of Ohio State University into government attempts to control yellow fever and other epidemics will shed some light on relationships between scientific ideas and scientific practices.

Among the more traditional historiographical approaches there have also been significant developments in Brazil. With reference to biography, for instance, there have been two tendencies. One has concentrated on an exaggerated debunking of old heroes, and the other has been characterized by methodological thoroughness and interpretive effort. The best example of the former tendency is Raimundo Magalhães Júnior's study of Rui Barbosa (62). In the light of the adulation that has been heaped upon the curious figure, it is indeed refreshing to read this author's biting comments and snide innuendos. But one must conclude that although a reconsideration is long overdue, Magalhães has merely set the stage for someone else's cool evaluation. His similar effort on Deodoro da Fonseca (60) is more successful, probably because the panegyrics against which he reacted have not been so numerous.

Magalhães's work must be contrasted with the proliferation of Barbosana that accompanied the anti-Vargas sentiments so widely expressed after 1945. Barbosa's liberalism stood in sharp contrast to the policies of the just overthrown dictatorship and one may suspect that his cooperation with the coffee oligarchs also made him an attractive figure to those hurt by Vargas' policies. The 1949 centennial of Rui also contributed to the spate of such studies (9, 13, 48, 63, 122, 125).[4] The lengths to which the publication of Barbosa's works (10) are being carried can be contrasted with the restraint exercised in the publication of the selected works plus a bibliography of the more moderate Joaquim Nabuco (17, 73, 124). It is not that Barbosa's

---

4. It is important to note that Oliveira Vianna, whose works in the 1920s and 1930s may be connected to the use of Vargas, was very critical of Rui Barbosa. Before Magalhães's work, Barbosa's own secretary had begun to reel at the praise heaped upon his former employer (125). One should also note the broader perspective contributed by Francisco Clementino de San Tiago Dantas (36).

complete works are not potentially useful, but only that this publishing effort reflects a misguided sense of priorities when so much historically important material remains unpublished.

The emperor Pedro II is surely the next figure to require a thorough reexamination. Alberto Rangel's study (83) of Pedro's much vaunted education was a start in this direction. And some studies have placed an exaggerated emphasis upon the recently discovered set of letters he exchanged with the Countess de Barral (61, 77; see also 72). But although these could be interpreted as denying his heretofore glorified marital fidelity, what really needs to be done is an evaluation of the degree to which he did or did not advance economic progress, social change, and political development—always in the light of what he had to work with.

Other figures need to be similarly removed from their pedestals. Mauá, for instance, has for too long been the subject of uncriticai praise. Anyda Marchant's recent biography (64) is a useful presentation in English, but is totally uncritical and fails to analyze the reasons for his rise. The theory of entrepreneurship in underdeveloped areas profits little from her study. As for his financial collapse, she accepts the explanations he himself presented; needless to say, he never pointed to his own weaknesses. Although there had been earlier criticisms of Mauá (84), they equally failed to deal with these issues. Especially lacking has been any awareness of the changing circumstances which characterized the Brazil in which he operated, before and after 1865. Thus other entrepreneurs survived and the government was relatively friendly toward industrialists precisely at the time of Mauá's decline.[5]

Besides the debunking tendency, the other trend in biographical writing is the development of more precise techniques. Reference has already been made to works by Luiz Vianna Filho, an active politician, who, for all that, writes biography with sophistication and skill, relying on the sources although not always citing them. But another author who deserves even more praise is Octavio Tarquinio de Sousa, whose studies of Brazilian leaders at the time of independence (113)—especially Pedro I and José Bonifácio—are thoroughly researched and well balanced. One wishes he had paid more attention

---

5. Another figure who needs to be critically reevaluated is the Duke of Caxias, in both his political and military roles; and, speaking of military history, the Paraguayan War needs to be studied from the standpoint of recruitment practices, logistical and transportation problems, health affairs, economic effect, and cost and financing.

to the economic and social issues with which these figures dealt, but his studies are nevertheless of key importance.

Another sort of biographical work has opened up an entirely new historiographical possibility. It is Luís Martins's *O patriarca e o bacharel* (65). In it the author uses psychological insights and a restrained but vigorous imagination to examine the lives of several leaders active during the period of transition from monarchy to republic at the end of the nineteenth century. Using unorthodox sources, including family photograph albums, he delicately traces the inner crises of the men who overthrew an old regime, for which they were immediately nostalgic.

One direction in which the post-1945 historiography has been moving is toward a greater interest in the First Republic (1889–1930). It is difficult to speak of it as a trend, however, since books on it have been scattered more or less evenly over the past twenty-five years. As is natural for a newly explored field, the first emphasis has been primarily biographical. I have in mind, for instance, the filial (but informative) studies by Raja Gabaglia (47) and Generoso Ponce Filho (79), Costa Portó's *Pinheiro Machado e seu tempo: Tentativa de interpretação* (80), Affonso Arinos de Melo Franco's masterful *Um estadista da republica* (42), Lauro Romero's biography *Clovis Bevilacqua* (90), the biographies of Nilo Peçanha by Brigido Tinoco (120) and Artur Bernardes by Paulo Amora (2), and, finally, Barbosa Lima Sobrinho's study of Alberto Tôrres (57).

There have also been a few attempts at a more complex analysis of the politics of the First Republic. The nonhistorian Victor Nunes Leal has had a profound influence on the understanding of the political process in Brazil, past and present, through his book *Coronelismo, enxada, e voto* (56). Biographies of several *coronéis* have also appeared, for instance, the rather poor one of Horácio de Matos (29). Joseph Love of the University of Illinois is about to publish his description of the inner workings of a state political machine (Rio Grande do Sul) along with a perceptive analysis of the relationship between it and the national political system. More studies of this nature are needed.

The phenomenon of *tenentismo* and its expression through the "long march" of Luís Carlos Prestes's column in 1924–27 have received some attention. Robert J. Alexander (1) and John Wirth (128) have both written articles on the subject, although neither has attempted to systematically explore the meaning of these events. Neil

Macaulay of the University of Florida is preparing a detailed narrative of the column's march with particular attention to the military causes of its failure. Hélio Silva has prepared two long volumes (99, 100) on these events which will prove highly useful to the historian because of their lengthy quotations from extensive private papers, although his citations are erratic and analysis is totally lacking. Memoirs (41) and biographies of *tenentes* have also appeared, such as João Alberto de Barros's (11) and Glauco Carneiro's study of Siqueira Campos (25).

The overthrow of the Getúlio Vargas dictatorship in 1945 led to a flood of anti-Vargas publications, few of them of much value (see, for example, 38). Yet any work on this period represents a significant development, for a glance at Brazilian textbooks usually shows that whereas approximately two-thirds of the pages are devoted to the colonial period, practically none deal with the post-1930 era. The Vargas question has continued very much alive in the political life of Brazil up to the present day, and it is not surprising that there is also historical interest. But the majority of works that have appeared have been by participants in the events and lack either objectivity or breadth of vision. An exception to this narrow point of view is Paulo Nogueira Filho's *Ideais e lutas de um burguês progressista* (75).

So far the major study of Vargas is by John W. F. Dulles (39). Although it deserves appreciation in view of the unavailability in English of information on the subject, it is very narrowly political. It deals neither with those societal forces and issues that explain politics nor with the economic and social programs Vargas pursued. And the author does not even devote sufficient attention to the techniques of political action: it is primarily a chronological summary of the events and is based on interviews, some newspapers, and secondary sources. The later volumes of Hélio Silva's "Ciclo de Vargas" (95, 96, 97, 98) are also useful but they suffer from the lack of analytical effort already noted. Few works so far have attempted an interpretation: Edgard Caronés's *Revoluções do Brasil contemporâneo, 1922–1938* (26) is an exception. Fortunately, there are a number of young American scholars working on this period, for instance, John Wirth, Robert Levine, and Stanley Hilton; and we may expect our understanding of the Vargas phenomenon to be sharply revised in the near future.

Diplomatic history has received a good bit of attention in the literature, but unfortunately it has not been studied with much acumen. One especially mourns the failure to examine Brazil's foreign policy as the expression of economic and social forces at work within the country, as Thomas F. McGann (67) did for Argentina. The volumes on the baron of Rio Branco and his diplomacy are a case in point. There have been studies by Cassiano Ricardo (27), Lewis Tambs (117), Aluizo Napoleão (74), and E. Bradford Burns (19). But although Burns includes a chapter on the coffee export economy, none of these studies raises the specific question of how the coffee oligarchs were connected to the rapprochement with the United States. None of them studies the reciprocity treaties of the early twentieth century that gutted large sectors of the Brazilian industrial park. None of them asks what the long-range effects of this policy have been, in the light of United States' subsequent predominance in Brazilian affairs and Brazil's imperialist image in Spanish America. The same points could be made with only a little less validity regarding studies of Brazilian policy in the River Plate (101, 102, 103, 114).

One very encouraging development during the last quarter century has been the growth of local and regional history. Although a great deal of it suffers from amateurish technique and narrow emphasis, there have been several studies that emerged as first-rate. Furthermore, the mere growth of such interests around the country will inevitably produce a better national historiography. One of the leading forces encouraging this development has been the *Revista de história*. It has fostered the systematic survey of local archival resources, and many Brazilian history teachers have for the first time become aware of the possibility of applying their training wherever they are. And the amateurs have also been encouraged to pay more attention to the canons of historical scholarship at least regarding citations (see, for example, 59).

One local theme that is an especially rich vein is comprised of regional revolts that occurred during the first half of the nineteenth century. Beginning with Ernesto Cruz's *Nos bastidores da cabanagem* (34), there have been a number of such studies. One of the latest and best is by Manuel Correia de Andrade (3).

The arid *sertão* has produced a colorful past of badmen, religious fanatics, and political in-fighters. The amateur historian, and more recently the professional one as well, have been attracted to this story. There have been Marxist studies like Rui Facó's (40) and studies of particular parts of the *sertão* like that by Walfrido Moraes (69). Padre Cícero has attracted a good deal of attention as an individual (4,

70); from the promise of Ralph della Cava's article (28) on the political and religious ramifications of that man's rule, we have reason
to expect analysis to be forthcoming as well.

Local and regional history now deserves a systematic annotated
bibliography which includes many entries for books that in themselves
are not particularly good but that can be useful to the historian
attempting to piece together the larger story. Minas Gerais has already
attracted a specific study of its historiography (76)—not to mention
a very detailed history of the state by a reputable historian (121)—
and similar essays for other areas need to be carried out. The coordination of already existing local and regional histories would do much
to advance historical writing in Brazil.

As for the publication of the sources of history, there has been some
progress but not as much as one would hope for. Even the collection,
organization, and opening of private and public papers has not occurred on the scale which is needed. The systematic publication of
the correspondence of such men as Rui Barbosa and Epitácio Pessoa
would probably be more profitable at this stage than that of their
complete works (10, 78). Among public archives the best organized
is still the Foreign Office one (18) with the possible exception of the
Museu Imperial. The publication of records in the "Documentos
históricos" series has only once wandered into the post-independence
period (on the Revolution of 1817) and must be speeded up. The state
archive of Pernambuco has been surprisingly graced with good leadership; one evidence of this fact is the catalog of the papers of the
Barão de Lucena (5), a leading political figure at the end of the empire
and beginning of the republic. Despite a biography based on these
papers (52), little has been done to use them for the history of
economic affairs in which he was so deeply embroiled or for the
wheeling and dealing that characterized his political style.

On the other hand, one of the best indications of the increasing
sophistication of Brazilian historiography is the *Revista de história,* a
quarterly published since 1950 at the University of São Paulo. It is
not concerned solely with Brazilian history and although the articles
published in it on ancient, medieval, and modern European history
may not be of the highest quality—I am not competent to judge—they
give the profession a sense of their authors' participation in the world-
wide community of historians. The articles on Brazilian history are
often very good, and the journal also carries documents, professional
news, proceedings of conferences, and reviews, although all too few

of the latter. If one may know the state of a profession by its journal, then the Brazilian historians are well on the way to maturity.[6]

The new techniques being exemplified by the *paulista* historians need to be extended throughout the country. José Antônio Gonsalves de Mello Neto has done a good deal to train a new group of young historians in Recife, but their concern has been almost entirely with the colonial period and thus their work lies outside the scope of this essay. Surprisingly little has been done in Rio de Janeiro, the chief archival center with a national scope where so many items of local interest must also be researched. Aside from individually productive historians like the aforementioned Rodrigues, there is no school of vigorous historical research there dealing with the period since independence. What is needed is a research institute and center for graduate training that could combine the archival resources of that city with the expertise—on a visiting basis—of the *paulistas*. The results might then rival the historical productivity of the Colegio de Mexico group.

Looking over the historical writing that has emerged since World War II on Brazil during the national period, it is clear that although there have been some studies on the history of ideas, of science, and of religion, these have remained relatively neglected fields. Biography, on the other hand, continues to be enormously popular among Brazilian historians, whether for the purpose of cutting past heroes down to size or as an opportunity to exercise new methodological skills in the use of sources. With reference to periods, the First Republic and the Vargas era are in for increasing examination; although what has emerged so far is not entirely satisfactory, a goodly number of fresh approaches may be on the verge of publication. Local and regional histories both for these periods and for the nineteenth century are increasing both quantitatively and qualitatively. The major trend, however, has been toward greater concentration on social topics. Special attention has been paid and continues to be paid to the history of slavery. Economic historians have not been as prolific, but they have produced some major studies. On the whole the record so far is encouraging.

The outlook for the future, however, is problematical. The current regime in Brazil is not supplying sufficent funds for higher education,

---

6. Another measure of how far Brazilian historiography has come is the generally good quality of the contributions to the multiauthored *História geral da civilização brasileira* (54).

books, and libraries. Furthermore, it is suspicious of any history that does not glorify past heroes and of independent thinkers in general. Finally, it is unlikely to foster that national commitment that could lead Brazilians to seek their identity and self-awareness in their past. One can only hope that, despite all this, historical studies in Brazil may continue to prosper and multiply.

# BIBLIOGRAPHY

1. Alexander, Robert J. "Brazilian 'Tenentismo,'" *Hispanic American Historical Review* 36 (1956): 229–42.
2. Amora, Paulo. *Bernardes, o estadista de Minas na república*. São Paulo, 1964.
3. Andrade, Manuel Correia de. *A guerra dos cabanos*. Coleção Temas Brasileiros, vol. 7. Rio de Janeiro, 1965.
4. Anselmo, Octacílio. *Padre Cícero, mito e realidade*. Retratos do Brasil, vol. 66. Rio de Janeiro, 1968.
5. Arquivo Público Estadual de Pernambuco. *Arquivo do Barão de Lucena: Catálogo*. Recife, Braz., 1956.
6. Auler, Guilherme. *A companhia de operários, 1839–1843: Subsídios para o estudo da emigração germânica no Brasil*. Recife, Braz., 1959.
7. Azevedo, Fernando de, ed. *Brazilian Culture: An Introduction to the Study of Culture in Brazil*. New York, 1950.
8. ———. *As ciências no Brasil*. 2 vols. São Paulo, 1955.
9. Baleeiro, Aliomar. *Rui, um estadista no ministerio da fazenda*. Rio de Janeiro, 1952.
10. Barbosa, Rui. *Obras completas*. 2 vols. Rio de Janeiro, 1942–.
11. Barros, João Alberto de. *1ª parte: A marcha da coluna*. Rio de Janeiro, 1953.
12. Barros, Roque Spencer Maciel de. *A ilustração brasileira e a idéia de universidade*. São Paulo, 1959.
13. Bastos, Humberto. *Ruy Barbosa, ministro da independência econômica do Brasil*. Rio de Janeiro, 1949.
14. Besouchet, Lídia. *Mauá e seu tempo*. São Paulo, 1942.
15. Boehrer, George. "The Church and the Overthrow of the Brazilian Monarchy." *Hispanic American Historical Review* 48 (1968): 380–401.
16. Bonilla, Frank. "A National Ideology for Development: Brazil." In *Expectant Peoples: Nationalism and Development,* ed. by Kalman H. Silvert, pp. 232–64. New York, 1963.
17. Braga, Osvaldo Melo. *Bibliografia de Joaquim Nabuco*. Coleção B-1, Bibliografia, vol. 8. Rio de Janeiro, 1952.
18. Brazil, Ministério das Relações Exteriores. *Arquivo histórico do Itamaraty. Parte I—Correspondência*. Rio de Janeiro, 1952.
19. Burns, E. Bradford. *The Unwritten Alliance: Rio Branco and Brazilian-American Relations*. New York, 1966.
20. Cabral, Oswaldo R. *Brusque: Subsídios para a história de uma colônia nos tempos do império*. São Paulo, 1958.

21. Cândido, Antônio. *Formação da literatura brasileira (momentos decisivos)*. 2 vols. São Paulo, 1959.

22. Cannabrava, Alice. P. *Desenvolvimento da cultura do algodão na província de São Paulo (1861–1875)*. São Paulo, 1951.

23. ——. "Manufaturas e indústria no período de D. João VI no Brasil." In *Uma experiência pioneira de intercâmbio cultural*, ed. by Luiz Pilla. Pôrto Alegre, Braz., 1963.

24. Cardoso, Fernando Henrique. *Capitalismo e escravidão no Brasil meridional: O Negro na sociedade escravocrata do Rio Grande do Sul*. Corpo e Alma do Brasil, vol. 8. São Paulo, 1962.

25. Carneiro, Glauco. *O revolucionário Siqueira Campos*. 2 vols. Rio de Janeiro, 1966.

26. Caronés, Edgard. *Revoluções do Brasil contemporâneo, 1922–1938*. Coleçao Buriti, vol. 11. São Paulo, 1965.

27. Cassiano, Ricardo. *O tratado de Petrópolis*. 2 vols. Rio de Janeiro, 1954.

28. Cava, Ralph della. "Brazilian Messianism and National Institutions: A Reappraisal of Canudos and Joaseiro." *Hispanic American Historical Review* 48 (1968): 402–20.

29. Chagas, Americo. *O chefe Horácio de Matos*. São Paulo, 1961.

30. Costa, Emilia Viotti da. *Lauro Muller: Ensaio biobibliográfico*. Rio de Janeiro, 1953.

31. ——. *Da senzala à colónia*. Corpo e Alma do Brasil, vol. 19. São Paulo, 1966.

32. Costa, João Cruz. *A History of Ideas in Brazil: The Development of Philosophy in Brazil and the Evolution of National History*. Trans. by Suzette Macedo. Berkeley and Los Angeles, 1964.

33. Costa, João Frank da. *Joaquim Nabuco e a politica exterior do Brasil*. Rio de Janeiro, 1968.

34. Cruz, Ernest. *Nos bastidores da cabanagem*. Belém, Braz., 1946.

35. Damasceno, Darcy, and Waldir da Cunha, eds. *Os manuscritos do botânico Freire Alemão*. Anais da Biblioteca Nacional, vol. 81. Rio de Janeiro, 1964.

36. Dantas, Francisco Clementino de San Tiago. *Dois momentos de Rui Barbosa* 2d ed. Rio de Janeiro, 1951.

37. Delgado, Luiz. *Escravos em Olinda sob a Lei Rio Branco*. Recife, Braz., 1967.

38. Duarte, Paulo. *Palmares pelo avêsso*. Coleção Eguassú, vol. 5. São Paulo, 1947.

39. Dulles, John W. F. *Vargas of Brazil: A Political Biography*. Austin, Tex., 1967.

40. Facó, Rui. *Cangaceiros e fanáticos: Gênese e lutas.* Retratos do Brasil, vol. 15. Rio de Janeiro, 1963.

41. Fontoura, João Neves da. *Memórias.* 2 vols. Pôrto Alegre, Braz., 1958–63.

42. Franco, Affonso Arinos de Melo. *Um estadista da república (Afrânio de Melo Franco e seu tempo).* Coleção Documentos Brasileiros, No. 85. 3 vols. Rio de Janeiro, 1955.

43. Freyre, Gilberto. *Introdução à história da sociedade patriarcal no Brasil, III: Ordem e progresso. Processo de desintegração das sociedades patriarcal e semi-patriarcal no Brasil sob o regime de trabalho livre: Aspectos de um quase meio século de transição do trabalho escravo para o trabalho livre; e da monarquia para a república.* 2 vols. Rio de Janeiro, 1959.

44. ———. *The Masters and the Slaves (Casa-grande e senzala): A Study in the Development of Brazilian Civilization.* Trans. by Samuel Putnam. New York, 1956.

45. ———. *The Mansions and the Shanties (Sobrados e mucambos): The Making of Modern Brazil.* Trans. by Harriet de Onís. New York, 1963.

46. Furtado, Celso. *The Economic Growth of Brazil: A Survey from Colonial to Modern Times.* Trans. by Ricardo W. de Aguiar and Eric Charles Drysdale. Berkeley and Los Angeles, 1963.

47. Gabaglia, Laurita Pessôa Raja. *Epitácio Pessôa, 1865–1942.* Coleção Documentos Brasileiros, No. 67. 2 vols. Rio de Janeiro, 1951.

48. Gonçalves, Silo. *A águia de Haia: Biografia de Rui Barbosa.* Rio de Janeiro, 1947.

49. Goulart, Maurício. *Escravidão africana no Brasil (das origens à extinção do tráfico).* São Paulo, 1949.

50. Gouveia, Maurílio. *História da escravidão.* Rio de Janeiro, 1955.

51. Graham, Richard. *Britain and the Onset of Modernization in Brazil, 1851–1914.* Cambridge Latin American Studies, vol. 4. Cambridge, Eng., 1968.

52. Guerra, Flávio. *Lucena, um estadista de Pernambuco.* Recife, Braz., 1958.

53. Guimarães, Ary Machado. *Contenuem benvindos: A valiosa contribução do italiano para o desenvolvimento do Brasil.* Rio de Janeiro, 1962.

54. Holanda, Sérgio Buarque de, ed. *História geral da civilização brasileira.* São Paulo, 1963–.

55. Ianni, Octavio. *As metamorphoses do escravo: Apogeu e crise da escravatura no Brasil meridional.* Corpo e Alma do Brasil, vol. 7. São Paulo, 1962.

56. Leal, Victor Nunes. *Coronelismo, enxada, e voto.* Rio de Janeiro, 1949.

57. Lima Sobrinho, Barbosa. *Presença de Alberto Tôrres (Sua vida e pensamento)*. Retratos do Brasil, vol. 62. Rio de Janeiro, 1968.

58. Lins, Ivan Monteiro de Barros. *História do positivismo no Brasil*. Brasiliana, No. 322. São Paulo, 1964.

59. Lopes, Antônio. *Alcântara: Subsídios para a história da cidade*. Rio de Janeiro, 1957.

60. Magalhães, Raimundo, Júnior. *Deodoro: A espada contra o império*. Brasiliana, vol. 12. 2 vols. São Paulo, 1957.

61. ———, ed. *D. Pedro II e a condessa de Barral, através da correspondência íntima do imperador*. Rio de Janeiro, 1956.

62. ———. *Rui, o homen e o mito*. Retratos do Brasil, vol. 27. Rio de Janeiro, 1964.

63. Mangabeira, João. *Rui, o estadista da república*, Coleção Documentos Brasileiros, No. 40. Rio de Janeiro, 1943.

64. Marchant, Anyda. *Viscount Mauá and the Empire of Brazil: A Biography of Irineu Evangelista de Sousa (1813–1889)*. Berkeley and Los Angeles, 1965.

65. Martins, Luís. *O patriarca e o bacharel*. São Paulo, 1953.

66. Mascarenhas, Nelson Lage. *Bernardo Mascarenhas: O surto industrial de Minas Gerais*. Rio de Janeiro, 1955.

67. McGann, Thomas F. *Argentina, the United States and the Inter-American System*. Cambridge, Mass., 1957.

68. Mercadante, Paulo. *A conciência conservadora no Brasil: Contribuição ao estudo da formação brasileria*. Rio de Janeiro, 1965.

69. Moraes, Walfrido. *Jagunços e heróis: A civilização do diamante nas lavras da Bahia*. Retratos do Brasil, vol. 14. Rio de Janeiro, 1963.

70. Morel, Edmar. *Padre Cícero: O santo do Juàzeiro*. 2d ed. Retratos do Brasil, vol 43. Rio de Janeiro, 1966.

71. Morse, Richard M. *From Community to Metropolis: A Biography of São Paulo, Brazil*. Gainesville, Fla., 1958.

72. ———. "Some Themes of Brazilian History." *South Atlantic Quarterly*, 61 (1962): 159–82.

73. Nabuco, Joaquim. *Obras completas*. 14 vols. São Paulo, 1949.

74. Napoleão, Aluizo. *Rio-Branco e as relações entre o Brasil e os Estados Unidos*. Rio de Janeiro, 1947.

75. Nogueira Filho, Paulo. *Ideais e lutas de um burguês progressista*. 4 vols. São Paulo and Rio de Janeiro, 1958–66.

76. Oiliam José. *Historiografia mineira, esboço*. Coleção Estudos Brasileiros, vol. 2. Belo Horizonte, Braz., 1959.

77. Pedro II. *Abrindo um cofre: Cartas de Dom Pedro II à condessa de Barral*. Ed. by Alcindo Sodré. Rio de Janeiro, 1956.

78. Pessosa, Epitácio. *Obras completas*. Rio de Janeiro, 1955–.

79. Ponce Filho, Generoso. *Generoso Ponce, um chefe*. Rio de Janeiro, 1952.

80. Portó, Costa. *Pinheiro Machado e seu tempo: Tentativa de interpretação*. Rio de Janeiro, 1951.

81. Prado, Caio, Júnior. *História econômica do Brasil*. São Paulo, 1945.

82. ———. *A revolção brasileira*. São Paulo, 1966.

83. Rangel, Alberto. *A educação do príncipe: Esboço histórico e crítico sôbre o ensino de D. Pedro II*. Rio de Janeiro, 1945.

84. Rebello, E. de Castro. *Mauá, restaurando a verdade*. Rio de Janeiro, 1932.

85. Rodrigues, José Honório. *Brazil and Africa*. Trans. by Richard A. Mazzara and Sam Hileman. Berkeley and Los Angeles, 1965.

86. ———. *Conciliação e reforma no Brasil: Um desafio histórico-político*. Retratos do Brasil, vol 32. Rio de Janeiro, 1965.

87. ———. *Notícia de vária história*. Rio de Janeiro, 1951.

88. ———. "Uma política externa própria e independente." *Política externa independente* (May 1965): 15–39.

89. Romero, José Luis. *A History of Argentine Political Thought*. Trans. by Thomas F. McGann. Stanford, Calif., 1963.

90. Romero, Lauro. *Clovis Bevilacqua*. Rio de Janeiro, 1956.

91. Saldanha, Nelson. *História das idéias políticas no Brasil*. Recife, Braz., 1968.

92. Santos, Joel Rufino dos, et al. *O descobrimento do Brasil. As invasões holandesas. A expansão territorial. Independência de 1822. Da independência à república*. Coleção História Nova, vols. 1, 3, 4, 6, 7. Rio de Janeiro, 1964.

93. ———. *História nova do Brasil*. Vol. 4, *Abolição, advento da república, florianismo*. São Paulo, 1964.

94. Schorer Petrone, Maria Teresa. *A lavoura canavieirâ em São Paulo: Expansão e declínio. (1765–1851)*. Corpo e Alma do Brasil, vol. 21. São Paulo, 1968.

95. Silva, Hélio. *1930: A revolução traída*. Rio de Janeiro, 1966.

96. ———. *1931: Os tenentes no poder*. Rio de Janeiro, 1966.

97. ———. *1932: A guerra paulista*. Rio de Janeiro, 1967.

98. ———. *1933: A crise do tenentismo*. Rio de Janeiro, 1968.

99. ———. *1922: Sangue na areia de Copacabana*. Rio de Janeiro, 1964.

100. ———. *1926: A Grande Marcha*. Rio de Janeiro, 1965.

101. Soares, Alvaro Teixeria. *Diplomacia do império no Rio da Prata até 1865*. Rio de Janeiro, 1955.

102. ———. *O drama da tríplice aliança, 1865–1876*. Rio de Janeiro, 1956.

103. ———. *O gigante e o rio: Ação de Mauá no Uruguai e Argentina, 1851–1878*. Rio de Janeiro, 1957.

104. Sodré, Nelson Werneck. *História da burguesia brasileira*. Retratos do Brasil, vol. 22. Rio de Janeiro, 1964.

105. ———. *História da literatura brasileira: Seus fundamentos econômicos*. 4th ed. Coleção Vera Cruz, vol. 60. Rio de Janeiro, 1938.

106. ———. "História da *História nova*." *Revista civilização brasileira*, no. 3 (July 1965): 27–40.

107. ———. *A ideologia do colonialismo: Seus reflexos no pensamento brasileiro*. 2d ed. Retratos do Brasil, vol. 31. Rio de Janeiro, 1965.

108. ———. *Introdução à revolução brasileira*. 2d ed. Retratos do Brasil, vol. 16. Rio de Janeiro, 1963.

109. ———. *Memórias de um soldado*. Retratos do Brasil, vol. 60 Rio de Janeiro, 1967.

110. ———. *A Military History of Brazil*. Washington, D.C., 1967.

111. ———. *Panorama do segundo império*. Brasiliana, no. 170. 1939.

112. ———. *As razões da indepêndencia*. Retratos do Brasil, vol. 39. Rio de Janeiro, 1965.

113. Sousa, Octavio Tarquinio de. *História dos fundadores do império do Brasil*. 10 vols. Rio de Janeiro, 1957.

114. Souza, José Antônio Soares de. *Honório Hermeto no Rio da Prata: Missão especial de 1851–1852*. Brasiliana, no. 297. 1959

115. Stein, Stanley J. *The Brazilian Cotton Manufacture: Textile Enterprise in an Underdeveloped Area, 1850–1950*. Cambridge, Mass., 1957.

116. ———. *Vassouras, a Brazilian Coffee County, 1850–1900*. Cambridge, Mass., 1957.

117. Tambs, Lewis. "Rubber, Rebels, and Rio Branco: The Contest for the Acre." *Hispanic American Historical Review* 46 (1966): 254–73.

118. Thornton, Sister Mary C. *The Church and Freemasonry in Brazil, 1872–1875*. Washington, D.C., 1948.

119. Tigner, James Lawrence. "Shindo Remmei: Japanese Nationalism in Brasil." *Hispanic American Historical Review* 41 (1961): 515–32.

120. Tinoco, Brigido. *A vida de Nilo Peçãnha*. Coleção Documentos Brasileiros, no. 114. Rio de Janeiro, 1962.

121. Tôrres, João Camillo de Oliveira. *História de Minas Gerais*. 5 vols. Belo Horizonte, Braz. 1962.

122. Turner, Charles W. *Ruy Barbosa, Brazilian Crusader for the Essential Freedoms.* New York and Nashville, Tenn., 1945.

123. Vianna Filho, Luís. *O negro na Bahia.* Coleção Documentos Brasileiros, no. 55. Rio de Janeiro, 1946.

124. ———. *A vida de Joaquim Nabuco.* São Paulo, 1952.

125. ———. *A vida de Rui Barbosa.* 2d ed. São Paulo, 1952.

126. "Vida e obra do doutor Blumenau." In *Centenário de Blumenau,* pp. 52–113. São Paulo, 1951.

127. Villas-Boas, Naylor Bastos. *A Rui o que é de Rui.* Rio de Janeiro, 1958.

128. Wirth, John P. "Tenentismo in the Brazilian Revolution of 1930." *Hispanic American Historical Review* 44 (1964): 161–79.

# CHILE AND THE ANDEAN REPUBLICS: THE NATIONAL PERIOD

*Frederick M. Nunn*

## INTRODUCTION

The writing of national-period history, whether by professionals or amateurs, obviously depends on the nature of a nation's historical evolution. Race, culture, economic development, social change, foreign affairs, and politics follow distinct patterns throughout Latin America, notwithstanding the seemingly common inheritance from colonial times. The national period, and the scholarly trends in its chronicling, show unique characteristics for each republic and for each historical field. Chile and the Andean countries as a group share much independence and national period history, particularly in the fields of diplomatic and military history. But their histories are quite distinct in other fields—cultural, political, economic, and social, for example. In all of the countries treated in this essay the recent years have seen more scholarly introspection in all fields than ever before, in some instances for similar reasons. Too, there are probably more works being published which approach a synthesis of interpretive and narrative history and are supplemented by documentation, in most instances for dissimilar reasons.

In discussing trends herein, lacunae are indicated but not treated at length. There are several accessible sources which the interested reader should consult to ascertain how trends in Chile and the Andean countries compare and contrast with those in Latin America as a whole or in contiguous areas. The works of Stanley Stein (155), Charles Gibson and Benjamin Keen (74), J. León Helguera (83), Thomas McGann (109), and Howard Cline (38) are especially recommended. In addition there are more specialized bibliographical and historiographical studies utilized in the preparation of this essay which must be consulted by the serious student of Andean and Chilean history. Aside from others mentioned specifically in the text and corresponding notes, the Herculean efforts of Adam Szászdi (159), Charles Arnade (8), and Fredrick Pike (125, 126) are extremely valuable and attractively presented.

Many works and authors have been omitted from this study. Numerous articles, particularly in the field of modern Chilean history, are meritorious and illustrative of scholarly trends, but neither space nor the assignment permits their inclusion in the bibliographic citations. Those works chosen for inclusion are either the most meritorious, the most illustrative, or a combination of the two.

## CHILE

Of the Pacific Coast nations of South America, Chile has the longest scholarly tradition in the field of history (40). The early achievement of political, economic, and social stability; the fact that records and documents have been preserved and cared for since early in the national period; the early development of a national consciousness and sense of history; and an independent history rich in controversy as well as in national achievement all contribute to this tradition.

Contemporary Chilean scholars are not beset with any single, all-consuming national issue which colors their efforts, as is often the case in the Andean countries. Rather, there are a number of issues, some typical of all Latin American countries, others peculiar to Chile, to which historians have turned in interpreting the country's past. A number of biographies of historical figures have been written and rewritten, two nineteenth-century wars and a civil conflict have been and are being chronicled, and sociopolitical movements (particularly since mid-nineteenth century) have consistently merited attention. The continual reediting of scholarly standard works provides an additional link with historical tradition.

To be sure, there are lacunae, but the richness of Chile's history, more than retardation in the development of scholarship, is responsible for them. Further, Chilean history has received more attention than that of the other Pacific nations by United States scholars.[1] In addition to writing book-length studies, United States historians have treated Chilean economic, social, political, military, and cultural history in a growing number of scholarly articles and monographs, too numerous (in comparison with those devoted to Peru, Bolivia, and Ecuador) to discuss here.

---

1. Two recent publications by United States scholars Robert N. Burr (24) and Fredrick B. Pike (126) have been awarded the Herbert Eugene Bolton Prize of the Conference on Latin American History, American Historical Association.

No matter the field, Chilean history since independence has been interpreted by scholars of conservative and moderate views with few exceptions until mid-twentieth century. Studies from the left are a comparatively recent phenomenon.[2] A trend developing since World War II shows more leftist scholarly interpretations, which challenge and incite reactions from the moderates. These fresh works are most valuable to anyone who seeks a balanced view of Chilean history. And as Harold Blakemore (20) has noted, on no issue are historians of the left, right, and center more at odds than on the Civil War of 1891—traditionally a historian's battlefield (55, 84, 132, 133, 171, 172). It is from the left that the most provocative analysis and interpretation—but not always the most profound—emanates.

Traditional Chilean historical writing is heavily documented, and most Chilean historians, until recent times, have limited their scholarly products on the national period to biographies and studies of brief periods or narrow themes. Recently, though, a trend toward syntheses which are both well documented and interpretive has developed. Leading the way in this field are Ricardo Donoso, Guillermo Feliú Cruz, Francisco Antonio Encina, and the late Jaime Eyzaguirre, who was without equal as a conservative interpreter. For example, various works of Donoso, Encina and Eyzaguirre cited in this essay stress a nationalist point of view, thus revising and at times shattering previous notions regarding foreign influences on developments in independence political thought, nineteenth-century liberal and conservative political theory, and constitutional issues.

The most significant work by a Chilean in recent times is the Encina history (for review see 41).[3] Encina's twenty-volume work (the national period begins with volume six) was published between 1941 and 1952; and a three-volume condensation (volumes two and three are on the nineteenth century), superbly supplemented with maps, illustrations, and charts, appeared between 1954 and 1955 under the supervision of art historian Leopoldo Castedo. Encina shocked many traditional Chilean historians with this work. It is not the

---

2. Writing in 1949, Marxist Julio César Jobet (92) lamented that his country's history was eminently erudite but confined for the most part to narrative. Furthermore he proclaimed that scholarship was monopolized by the oligarchy and did not adequately reflect the views of the majority.

3. Another recent multivolume effort of smaller scope is that of Francisco Frías Valenzuela (72). It is a synthesis designed for the general reader, but reflects solid scholarship.

work of a professional historian; it lacks documentation (and until the Castedo edition was remarkably unattractive and sometimes unfathomable) and pays but lip service to bibliography. Its pages consistently tear down idols revered by past historians, destroy myths perpetrated by would-be historians, and refute many new theories of the greats of Chilean historiography, notably Diego Barros Arana. But it is thorough, the product of years of research, and obviously the work of a tough-minded chronicler and interpreter. Encina's interest in administrative, social, and economic history breaks new ground. This sweeping study has outraged footnote aficionados, bibliographers, hero worshipers, historians of Hispanista and Indigenista sentiments, and conservatives and liberals. In size and scope and in style, approach, and content it is the forerunner of modern revisionism and scholarly historical writing in Chile (40, 41, 79).

Since World War II Chilean historical scholars have concentrated heavily on national period sociopolitical and economic themes with great success. This trend is readily noticeable in Encina's volumes as well as in more limited works. Both Donoso (51) and Eyzaguirre (63, 64, 65) have contributed greatly to a better understanding of the evolution of Chilean ideas and sociopolitical issues in the nineteenth century, both stressing indigenous factors and influences; but to date the year 1891, or at best 1900, is a barrier which Chile's leading historians seem loath to pass.

The political scene since World War II has witnessed a breakdown of the traditional party structure to the point where ideology and doctrinaire approach may give way to a nationalistic and developmental approach to national issues by those more versed in economics than in political philosophy. A number of works published since 1945, which reexamine Chile's traditional sociopolitical and economic structure, illustrate this trend (39, 57, 60, 69, 128, 129, 133, 153). Further evidence of the value of the developmental approach is seen in a history of the nitrate industry (18), which is one of the best recent treatments of nineteenth-century Chile. Similarly, northern Chile (the copper and nitrate area) has been examined as an economically influential region. Reflecting this shift in emphasis, economists and historians of all political credos have responded admirably to the need for scholarship that takes into account the changing times since World War II. The classic *Ensayo crítico del desarrollo económico social de Chile* (Santiago de Chile, 1955) by Julio César Jobet, Chile's most distinguished and prolific historian of the left, of Marxism, and of labor, is one of the most widely read treatises on economic and social development in print.

Where social and economic issues do not prevail (or do not seem to prevail) historical scholarship continues along traditional lines: the moderate and conservative viewpoint holds sway. In the field of diplomatic history Chilean scholars continue above all nationalistic (11, 22, 56, 61, 62, 67, 107, 111). National leaders receive praise for defending Chile's interests, Chile's interests are defended, and the defense is always documented or convincingly presented. This remains true for the entire nineteenth century whether the issue is Diego Portales versus the Andean confederation of Peru and Bolivia, the War of the Pacific against the same foes forty years later, the Argentine frontier question, or Chilean–United States relations. Indeed, satisfactory scholarly treatments of diplomatic history since 1920 which do not reflect shrill nationalism, except for several works done by United States historians (23, 24, 125), are yet forthcoming. Chile maintains a purposely aloof stance in the hemispheric system, and her independent way in foreign policy colors all accounts of diplomatic history.

Unlike diplomatic history, which has remained traditional in approach, historical biography has undergone changes in treatment and subject matter since World War II. The content of recent works indicates a lack of satisfaction with routine "life-story" literature and a new concern for the country's social and economic distresses. Furthermore, while focus has shifted from solely independence heroes,[4] the treatment of independence figures has improved markedly (49, 66, 68). Popular and progressive leaders of the nineteenth and twentieth centuries, some of whom could be classified as extremists, have been subjects of recent and numerous scholarly treatments (70, 91, 93, 151). The degree of scholarship diminishes the closer the subject is to the present, but the fact remains that these biographies are extremely valuable. A trend toward providing historians with readily accessible documents which should enable biographers to deal more satisfactorily with their subjects has been established with the extensive publications of the *Archivo Bernardo O'Higgins* (50). Its editors form a *Who's Who* of recent Chilean historiography.

The nature of biography being such that it may include social,

---

4. Diego Portales has not been the subject of a major study since Encina's work of 1934 (58).

political, and economic topics, biography has taken its place among the major works of historical scholarship. The most ambitious study of the early twentieth century is a scholarly but bitterly slanted political biography by Ricardo Donoso of Arturo Alessandri Palma (48), president of Chile, 1920–24, 1925, 1932–38. Although Donoso is most at home when chronicling the nineteenth century, this work, despite some faults, contributes to the revisionist trend. As biography it is a savage attack on Alessandri; as a historical work it is cumbersome but amply, if inconsistently, documented. Few other Chilean historians have proved as ambitious as Donoso.

Alessandri has been the subject of several other recent works, but enough time has not passed for an objective treatment to appear. As if to counter the staggering effects of Donoso's attack there appeared in 1959 a sympathetic treatment by Augusto Iglesias Alessandri (88). The fact that the Alessandri family is still prominent in Chilean politics (Jorge Alessandri Rodríguez served as president from 1958 to 1964 and was a presidential candidate in 1970 may preclude a scholarly, objective approach for some time to come.

Chilean politics has always influenced writers of history—both scholars and nonscholars. Partisans of all political parties have consistently sought to justify and defend their position.[5] Political leaders traditionally publish memoirs and accounts of their years in office or their experiences seeking office. The general quality of these works is high. If not strictly the results of diligent research, they are, more often than not, reflective and of value to the scholar. Chilean politics, so vitally concerned with social and economic issues, is fertile ground for scholarship. Chilean political leaders, highly articulate and sophisticated by Latin American standards, have continued to produce some admirable works based on personal experiences in the last twenty-five years. These works provoke continued interest in the reevaluation of Chilean political history.

For example, Alberto Edwards, author of the widely read *La fronda aristocrática: Historia política de Chile* (54) collaborated with Chile's Christian Democratic leader Eduardo Frei Montalva in a respectable history of Chilean political parties which has become a standard work (53). Though dated, the work has been significant because it is an anatomy of politics and parties which clears up many

---

5. For example, longtime Communist party member Hernán Ramírez Nechochea (134) has written a most subjective history of Chilean Communism.

previously held misconceptions regarding personalities and important issues. Further, the bias of the authors is not an overriding element.

The writing of historical works on the national period by near contemporaries whether or not they are historians appears a constant trend in historical scholarship in the political field. This is as true of the present century as it is of the past. Alessandri's own memoirs of the 1920–25 period, while hardly objective, provide an example of partisan views blended with a sense of historical import. Another example of a historical work by one who helped make history is that of Emilio Bello Codesido (17), who participated in the 1925 civil-military movement leading to Alessandri's reinstatement as president after he had been forced out of office in 1924. The two last mentioned works, the hostile Donoso volumes, and Iglesias' sometimes slavish study of Alessandri comprise the best of the studies on the interwar period career of Chile's great leader, but they do not by any means constitute the whole of that literature. A definitive work still has to be produced.

Recent political history can bring out the worst in professional historians and chroniclers in Chile. This is true of works on the career of Carlos Ibáñez del Campo, president, 1927–31 and 1952–58, the doughty colonel who became Alessandri's chief rival and broke Chile's long tradition of military subservience to civilian leadership. No work published which deals with the interwar period can ignore Ibáñez. Historians and history makers devote page after page to his government, his cult, and his political role out of office. Yet, owing doubtless to historical proximity, there are no outstanding scholarly treatments of this facet of twentieth-century political history. The most widely read works dealing with Ibáñez are either condemnation (170) or hagiography (113). From the point of view of political chronicles there is much activity on this period. From the standpoints of synthesis and scholarship, major works are still to appear.[6] Chilean professionals, with the exception of Donoso, have yet to invade this field, and until they do, scholars must choose with care.

That Chilean historians have begun to assess their country's social and economic development and have produced outstanding biographies bodes well for the future of historical scholarship. For if the

---

6. One of the few scholarly works untinged by partisan subjectivism on the interwar period is Heise González's contribution to the field of constitutional history (82).

use of techniques and methods so ably demonstrated for the early national period is extended for the twentieth century the results should be impressive indeed. A strong sense of nationalism in political, intellectual, and diplomatic history is carrying over into the economic and social field; and it may well be that from these fields the most profound scholarly treatments of recent times will come. Recent times need scholarly treatment in every sense and have received it at the hands of United States scholars in various fields. Chile's archives and libraries abound with source materials. Historical institutes such as the Centro de Investigaciones de Historia de América of the University of Chile, government agencies, and all institutions of higher learning foment historical scholarship on a grand scale by Latin American standards.

## PERU

Recent Peruvian historical scholarship exceeds in quality and quantity that of Peru's Andean neighbors. Trends since 1945 are really continuations of those already existing. Until recent times the chronicling of the national period took the form of examinations of the independence period, biographies of nineteenth-century caudillos, treatments of the War of the Pacific, and studies of politics in the early twentieth century. These themes continue to receive attention, but in a more scholarly·manner than in the past.

Peru has proportionately more professional historians than Bolivia or Ecuador. Once the epicenter of the Viceroyalty of New Castille, Peru possesses a wealth of archival material for the researcher of the colonial period. National period historians likewise have comparatively more to work with than their Bolivian or Ecuadorian counterparts. Institutional history and political history are more fully developed in Peru than in the other Andean countries. Generally what is being produced today is of better quality than pre–World War II efforts, but individual studies still vary widely in scholarly content.

All fields in Peruvian historical scholarship save foreign relations are somehow influenced by a culture conflict which originated as an armed encounter four centuries ago: Indigenismo versus Hispanismo. This conflict has been most recently emphasized as a constant in Peruvian history by Fredrick B. Pike (126). The founding of the Alianza Popular Revolucionaria Americana (APRA) in 1924 by Victor Raúl Haya de la Torre made Indigenismo a political issue of greater significance than ever before. Haya's extremism provoked a political and literary Hispanista reaction, and the "war of the words" has not yet closed. The early Indigenistas, who were often Marxists or extreme leftists, combined ideology with Indigenismo, and in so doing they sacrificed scholarship for the benefit of politically oriented interpretive history. The Indigenista work that most influenced and shaped these early trends is the classic *Siete ensayos de interpretación de la realidad peruana* by José Carlos Mariátegui (105). To counter Mariátegui's socialistically oriented lauding of the Inca past and pleas for vindication of the twentieth-century Indian, Hispanista conservatives of the 1930 wrote from a corporatist slant approximating fascism (46, 139). Thus, just as in Ecuador and Bolivia, the Indian in Peru has been viewed in two divergent ways, ranging from glorification by Indigenista writers to deprecation by Hispanista writers. Following these ideologies, historians, whether scholars or not, were politicized. And the turbulent postdepression decade, in which military men ruled the country for nine years, further polarized historians seeking to interpret—all too often without documentation—Peru's past.

The impact of World War II, the defeat of fascism, and the early stages of the Cold War–Marxist intransigence sobered those involved in the Indian question and tempered Aprismo at the same time. As in Ecuador and the Bolivia the glorification of pre-Andean civilization has proven fallacious. Likewise the staunch defense of all things Spanish, Catholic, or at least European (i.e., Spanish colonial Indian policy) has proved untenable for true scholars. Since 1945 works have appeared which attempt a synthesis between the two extremes and focus on the future rather than the past. As historical scholarship they are significant because they indicate a maturity in treating serious national issues (14, 15).

The new, more objective scholarship, in its effort to resolve the old conflict of ideologies, deals primarily with the colonial and recent periods. The intervening nineteenth century continues to attract Indigenistas and Hispanistas. Whereas nineteenth-century specialists of the pre–World War II period often failed to strike a balance between chronology and narrative on one hand and speculation or interpretation on the other, contemporary scholars strive to make their labors meaningful, to conduct careful research, and to contríbute to knowledge through a diligent effort in interpretive scholarship. However, widespread blending of narrative and interpretive scholarship is still in the future.

This effort to combine narration and interpretation is presently evident in a traditionally fecund field in Peru: biography. The most controversial figure of the nineteenth century, and thus one of the most attractive for biographers, is Ramón Castilla, chief of state, 1845–51 and 1854–62. Because Castilla's politics were those of appeasement of Peru's liberal and conservative factions, one might expect any study of his life and times to reflect moderate viewpoints. However, until the 1950s Castilla fared no better than the Ecuadorian Gabriel García Moreno, who was anything but an appeaser. The obvious need for a juster and more accurate view of Castilla has now in part been answered. The Instituto Libertador Ramón Castilla in Lima has dedicated itself to presenting Castilla as a patriot and nation builder,[7] and to date the publications it has sponsored indicate that while exaltation of Castilla is still the end, scholarly and thoughtful presentation influence the means (5, 9, 165). Regrettably, no other figure of the past century has received the attention Castilla has in recent years. Nicolás de Piérola, the "democratic caudillo" who served as president from 1895 to 1899, is an equally controversial historical figure, but literature on his life does not approach that devoted to Castilla in quantity or quality (36, 52, 162).

Scholarly biography, such as the recent studies of Castilla, has in general been limited to the nineteenth century. Recent biographies of the immediate postindependence period (ca. 1825–45) show the influences of revisionism and reflection on Peru's peculiar independence experience. Agustín Gamarra and José de la Mar have been resurrected by contemporary biographers and metamorphosed from reckless, ambitious predators into heroes of the fatherland (1, 86, 89, 106, 160). This tendency toward more judicious idealization may establish a durable trend in the treatment of lesser caudillos and more recent leaders of national stature. The recent edition of the previously unpublished Mendiburu biographical sketches of leading military figures (45) provides a starting point for biographers so inclined. Contemporary Peruvian biographers have stimulating material to study, and at present they are diligently reexamining their country's independence and postindependence leaders, their ideas, and their deeds in an attempt to balance the effects of the historical roles of Bolívar and San Martín as liberators and national heroes (2, 98, 164).

---

7. Prior to 1945 the most acceptable biographies of Castilla were the sympathetic studies by Paz Soldán (121) and Lavalle (99).

To date, little of a scholarly or objective nature has been done on the lives of Peru's early twentieth-century political leaders. Augusto B. Leguía, Mariátegui, Haya de la Torre, Luis Sánchez Cerro, and Oscar Benavides—the most controversial and best-known figures—with a few notable exceptions (34, 144), are either shrilly attacked by opponents or exalted by friends and followers. After enough time passes, perhaps the techniques which have been successfully applied to nineteenth-century figures will also be used to examine more recent figures.

The writing of Peru's military history has been directly influenced by the political events of that country. Owing to the independence campaigns and international conflicts of the last century, the military was at one time frequently praised as the defender of the fatherland (30, 43, 44). Particularly is this so in literature on Peru's two wars with Chile (always characterized as the aggressor). It is significant that the first critical appraisals of the military did not appear until after World War II, and the best of these were published in the 1960s. Certainly the heavy hand of the military was responsible for the delay. Recently the army has shown itself willing to support social and political changes previously advocated by its severest critics, and publications both favorable and unfavorable to the military have been allowed to appear. Notwithstanding Felipe de la Barra's seminal monograph, *La historia militar y sus fuentes* (10), a recent valuable contribution to the field, there are few scholarly works as such on the military of Peru (166, 167). A useful comparison can be made with historical writings on the church. For like the military, the Peruvian clergy and hierarchy have proven reasonably willing and able to shift with the times. Nevertheless, little scholarship has been produced documenting the changes of the church; and such writings as exist are either confined to the colonial period or largely unconcerned with the role of the church beyond the spiritual realm.

A shift toward moderation and scholarly objectivity can be seen in works on political ideas and philosophies. The disappearance of the traditional nineteenth-century parties—the Civilista and the Democratic—has made studies of their conflicts between 1875 and 1920 purely academic. However, for a brief time prior to World War II writers influenced by Aprismo scored the leaders of both parties and the governments they led. In fact, ever since its founding, APRA itself and its philosophy have been subjects of dispute, viewed with heavy scrutiny by historians. Recently, objectivity and a degree of scholarship have shown through all but the most extreme views of

APRA (37). The fact that APRA itself has modified and moderated its views and programs in recent years (to the point of collaborating officially with the party of former president Manuel A. Odría, one of APRA's worst enemies) has made it impossible for Aprista "historians" like Luis Alberto Sánchez to continue writing didactically. The party has faced reality, and defectors or critics have begun to expose APRA for what it has become. Nevertheless, there is still no fully documented treatment of APRA, but instead only a plethora of works of varying quality (16, 25, 59, 78, 85, 87, 112, 130, 135, 149, 168). The most popular recent treatment of APRA is by Harry Kantor, a North American political scientist (94).

In recent times Peruvian historians have entered the constitutional, diplomatic, economic, and social fields of history with varying distinction. In constitutional history José Pareja Paz Soldán has emerged as Peru's leading scholar, and his work on Peru's constitution (119) is a superior pioneer effort. In Peruvian diplomacy few works which approach a scholarly treatment have been published since the resolution of the Tacna-Arica question in 1929, and only one attempts a full treatment (169). A recent publication by James C. Carey of Kansas State University (27) treats United States relations with Peru in recent times, but it is not a definitive study. In economic history Emilio Romero (142) is Peru's best-known scholar; although his recent works are sound as scholarship, they are not definitive. Social history has attracted almost no following among Peruvians in the last quarter century unless it is concerned with the colonial period or sociopolitical in nature.[8] An exception is Luis Alberto Sánchez's thoughful *Peru: Retrato de un pais adolescente* (150) which deals with national period themes impressionistically at times.

No treatment of Peruvian historiography and scholarly trends can pass without mention of Jorge Basadre. Basadre's career as a historian in itself is a reflection of recent trends in historical scholarship. Basadre was a harsh political and social critic in his youth; but the problems of being a contemporary historian, the passage of some time, and pure expedience have modified his views since World War II. Basadre's widely read *Historia de la república del Perú desde sus orígenes hasta el presente* (13) illustrates the author's development as a historian.

---

8. Defying easy classification, but bordering on nineteenth-century social and economic history are the works of Watt Stewart (156, 157). See also Sánchez's review of Stewart's work (148).

Gradually, through five editions since 1939 Basadre has reduced the number of interpretive conclusions and judgments in his work while concomitantly maintaining a high level of scholarship. Since the fourth edition of the *Historia* in 1949, he has become notably more moderate and optimistic in his criticism. Jorge Basadre is Peru's greatest and most influential historian whether he creates or reflects trends. His name is most often sought to appear at the end of a preface or intro-duction to scholarly monographs. In a field closely related to that of scholarship, the field of publishing, another distinguished contributor must be mentioned. Pareja Paz during the last twenty years has brought out several multivolume histories, compendia, and anthologies which are either sufficiently scholarly or copious to be extremely valu-able (73, 120, 145, 168).

To sum up briefly the most notable trends in historical scholar-ship in Peru, it should be noted that the bulk of the scholarship is devoted to the colonial period, and of that treating other periods, the largest amount is devoted to the nineteenth century. The major field of interest in the twentieth century, political history, continues to be highly interpretive rather than scholarly.[9] Outside the scholarly sphere, of course, most items in print are on contemporary issues.

Growing interest in scholarly interpretation and reinterpretation of Peru's historical past is evident in the activities of historical socie-ties and institutes founded or active since 1945. The Instituto Li-bertador Ramón Castilla has been noted; the Sociedad Histórica del Peru, the Instituto Histórico del Peru, the Instituto Sanmartino, the Centro de Estudios Historico-Militares, and the Centro de Investi-gaciones Históricas at the University of San Marcos have already made contributions to the trends in historical scholarship discussed here. Peruvian historical scholarship remains in the hands of writers of conservative or moderate views. The left has no scholarly champions to goad others along the road to revisionism. Clearly, historians are only beginning to mine the lode of national period sources which exists (for all but economic history) in libraries and archives. The voice of Peruvian conservatism, Hispanismo, and corporatism from the early years of this century until his death in 1944, José de la Riva Agüero y Osma, lamented that Peruvian historical writing was de-

---

9. This is true of post–World War II United States historians writing on Peru as well. Aside from Pike's work there is no full-length scholarly study of Peruvian history. A projected study in the Oxford Press Latin American History Series (James R. Scobie, ed.) includes Bolivia.

void of quality in the postcolonial period in his *Historia en el Peru* (138). Nearly forty years later Watt Stewart writing on Jorge Basadre said much the same (158). Their judgments are still generally valid.

## BOLIVIA

Bolivia has undergone profound change in the period since World War II, and the social upheaval of 1952 has tied trends in historical scholarship in the last twenty-five years to current events. These ties can be said to exist, perhaps, since the Chaco War and the 1936–39 experiments in military socialism, but prior to that time, national period Bolivian historical scholarship was concerned with little outside the pale of the independence era. The link between politics and the writing of history dissuaded would-be historians from essaying contemporary issues before 1945; the link between politics and the writing of history since at least 1952 has influenced the treatment of contemporary issues and those of the past as well. Historical scholarship has been further influenced by the fact that there are are few trained, professional historians in Bolivia. That a historian can be an autodidact is a foregone conclusion, but in Bolivia there are few who really qualify as historians even in this sense.

As is true of many Latin American countries there has been a strong attachment to biographies of controversial historical figures, subjects Bolivia does not lack. A recent biography of Mariano Melgarejo (117) proves superior to any of those done prior to World War II. The search for historical heroes is a result of Bolivia's recent experience in national consciousness and the desire on the part of state and historian alike to dignify the past.

Both the search for national identity and, indeed, the justification of nationhood itself in the midst of an anarchic environment pervade the works of nineteenth-century Bolivian protohistorians. They, and many historians of the early twentieth century, were patricians whose works dealt with independence themes, Bolivia's reasons for existence, archives, libraries, and historical anecdotes. With few exceptions (7), the period following the founding of the republic did not receive much scholarly attention. Nor does it yet in any field, unless it is tied somehow to the one dominant trend in recent times.

The most significant trend in recent Bolivian historical scholarship has been revisionism of the role of the Indian in national life. Such revisionism is the product of two influences. During two and a half centuries of Spanish colonial rule, the Indian was either almost totally ignored by historians or considered merely as an inferior being, a tool of demagogues and tyrants; only for his folkloric contributions or as the object of religious interest was he discussed at all. The political rise of the Movimiento Nacionalista Revolucionario, predicated largely on the integration and vindication of the Indian masses, had a profound impact on history and historians; and under its influence the Indigenista writers began a vigorous reevaluation of the native Indian population. However, Jaime Mendoza (1874–1939) (110), who lived, wrote, and died before the full impact of Indigenismo was felt, must be classified as the first historian to carry historical introspection beyond the realm of justifying national existence and to make it serve the interest of social history.[10]

Prominent among Indigenista historians, Alcides Argüedas is probably Bolivia's most famous man of letters. The mantle of "Protector of the Indians" fell on his shoulders, and his death in 1946 in a way marks the end of traditional Indigenismo and the birth of militant radical Indigenismo, stronger and more pronounced than in Peru or Ecuador. Argüedas was an early radical, and his *Raza de bronce* (6) and *Pueblo enfermo* (Barcelona, 1910) are among the most pessimistic studies (in novel form) ever written of any society. His work—once considered "the word" for militant Indigenistas—has lately come under attack (8), for no longer is pessimism to the degree of a pathological examination of a putrid national corpse in vogue. Argüedas's historical writings, done mainly during the 1920s and covering the national period till around 1922, have been widely criticized and ever more widely read.

Gustavo Adolfo Navarro, writing under the name Tristan Marof, also merits mention as an Indigenista writer and as a historian in a loose sense. Navarro linked the Creole aristocracy, militarism, and the exploited Indian together in his examination of Bolivia's sickness. His pessimism, too, is no longer in vogue. Franz Tamayo, who died

---

10. The *mestizo* (in Bolivia *cholo*) was examined by Alberto Gutiérrez (82). Gutiérrez made of Mariano Melgarejo, the colorful and savage tyrant who ruled over Bolivia from 1864 to 1871, a symbol of the frustrated *cholo* and in so doing explains away Bolivian caudillismo. This, of course, detracts from the book's value, for Gutiérrez's theory intricately tied caudillismo to *mestisaje* and conversely democracy to racial purity. Furthermore Gutiérrez's study, while bridging a gap between early primary source-document bibliophiles and later social and interpretive historians, thrust the socioracial question from the very outset into the interpretive area, a dilemma from which it still has to recover.

less than fifteen years ago, carried the Indigenista banner even further. Augusto Céspedes and Carlos Montenegro were both born in this century, and their works belong chronologically to the transition period encompassing World War II; however, their contributions belong to post-1945 trends, for they have influenced many writers of more recent years. Of the two, Céspedes has probably been the more influential. His condemnation of the aristocracy and the Patiño tin oligarchy (32) brought introspection to an active political level. Céspedes was an early supporter of the MNR as was Montenegro. The works of both authors are written in language suitable for mass consumption, which distinctly sets them apart from the works of their Indigenista predecessors and marks them as exemplary of the new trend. Of the two, Montenegro's works are more sophisticated and objective.

Benevolent, characterized by a social conscience, nationalistic, and more truly popular than any previous government or system, the MNR nevertheless became the status quo in 1952. Despite the overthrow of Victor Paz Estenssoro in 1964, the social, economic, and political programs advocated since the end of the Chaco War and introduced in 1952 remain accomplishments. To Indigenismo, fused with introspection and analysis of Bolivia's problems, has been added critical appraisal of the MNR party program. This complex of ideas affects all fields of national period historical scholarship.[11]

The well-known vindicator of the Indian and advocate of social revolution, Germán Busch, became the subject of one of the first significant publications by Céspedes (31) in the new historiographical era of Bolivia's post–World War II revolutionary period. The book is poorly documented but respectable scholarship. True to Bolivian form it provoked an attack by a fervent critic, Fernando Diez de Medina (116). As Arnade notes (8), the exchanges between author Céspedes and critic Diez de Medina have come to "represent clear statements of militant indianismo and proof that Bolivian history has been absorbed by indianismo."

Bolivia's social revolution actually deterred the development of

---

11. The most scholarly treatments of the revolution of 1952 and its antecedents are by North Americans. The articles of Herbert Klein (95, 96) and Robert J. Alexander's monograph (3) are sound. The most widely known attack of the 1952 overthrow is by Alberto Ostria Gutiérrez (115). It is not a scholarly work nor are most of the revolution-inspired "histories" produced in Bolivia, regardless of the side they take.

researched, documented historical labor just when it was in the embryonic stage and when it might conceivably have been employed to penetrate the fog of the early national period. The Indigenista problem and the Indigenistas themselves will suffer from this for years. Their political, social, economic, and cultural goals and historical scholarship appear for the present to be mutually exclusive. The best-known works of the post-1945 era do not qualify as scholarly ones. As a prime example of the fusion of Indigenismo and social revolutionary ideas in historiography we may cite Fausto Reinaga's *Belzú: Precusor de la revolución nacional* (136). Reinaga presents a Belzú (president, 1848–55) who becomes a popular visionary, precursor to Karl Marx; in truth Isidoro Belzú was little more than a popular demagogue.

But all is not negative. The past quarter century has seen sensitive, if not profound and meaningful, it not professional, historical scholarship on Indigenismo, as well as on other topics. Temperance and sensitivity in Indigenismo can be seen in the pages of the journal *Kollasuyo,* edited for thirteen years by Roberto Prudencio, as well as in the works of Jorge Siles Salinas. Both Prudencio and Siles object to the glorification of the precolonial Indian civilizations and cultures, refuse to place all blame for their country's problems on the European element, and oppose the linking of Indigenismo with dialectical materialism. Both have been free in their criticism of past historians but constructively so.

There is now a maturity in Indigenismo. The Bolivian Indian no longer appears as a noble savage as he did to nineteenth-century romantics and early twentieth-century pamphleteers and propagandists. Tihuanaco was not a terrestrial paradise, or a Babylon, or an Athens. The Black Legend has faded, but the nineteenth century and its politics and social order did not embrace the autochthonous Bolivian. Race conflict in Bolivia is interpreted by Gonzalo Romero (143) in a significant recent publication as a facet of resentment which pervades Bolivian history. Guillermo Francovich (71), who is properly speaking a philosopher, also reflects this attitude toward the Indian, Indigenismo, and their proper place in scholarly fields.

Regardless of the maturation process in Bolivian Indigenista scholarship and writing, research in the field of history is not widely practiced in Bolivia. History has been a part of the curriculum in Bolivian higher education since the first decades of this century, but the demand for professionals has not increased to a point where there are many. Institutional history remains an open field. Bolivia's frontier problems with Paraguay which culminated in the Chaco War produced a few works based on documents and primary source materials (173), but the controversy has long been settled. A reaction to purely interpretive history (whether sound or unsound) and its fusion with politics in recent years has, though, led contemporary Bolivians to realize the value of true historical scholarship.

Barely a quarter century ago Gunnar Mendoza became Director of the National Library and National Archives in Sucre, both of which had long been neglected. Mendoza, not a prolific writer like his father, Jaime Mendoza, is a scholar in the true sense, and his example will doubtless inspire others. Scholarly works have also come from the pens of Guillermo Ovando Sanz and his followers at the Institute of Historical Research of the University of Potosi founded in 1956. The Institute has published scholarly works from other contributors as well, on topics ranging from the colonial period forward. Unfortunately, not enough effort has been devoted by scholars to the modern period. Interpretive history, Indigenismo, and the politicization of historical writing have delayed scholarly treatment of the modern period.[12] Probably the most widely read recent history of Bolivia is the one-volume *Nueva historia de Bolivia* by Enrique Finot published in 1954 in La Paz. It is well written but is based on secondary sources. Clearly the opportunities, the unused source materials, and the subjects are there awaiting scholars to utilize them.

## ECUADOR

Scholarly trends in the writing of national period Ecuadorian history have probed no new fields since 1945 despite a brief focus on the independence period at the time of the 1960 sesquicentennial. For the last quarter century Ecuadorian scholars have merely reflected that which was chronicled earlier with the possible exception of a few works dealing with social problems. In fact, there are few professional historians in Ecuador and altogether too many autodidacts devoid of talent.

The national period history of Ecuador has been shaped in part by the fact that Ecuador passed under the control of several govern-

---

12. The most widely known treatment of the recent period by a Bolivian remains the well-written but thinly researched study by Porfirio Díaz Machicao (47). Díaz's work deals with the 1920–42 period.

ments before its emergence as an independent nation. Originally a part of the Andean conglomerate of the Incas, Ecuador was the Kingdom of Quito in the days of the Spanish viceroys; and, though administered from Quito, it was under the jurisdiction of the Viceroyalty of New Castille (Peru). In 1740 when the Viceroyalty of New Granada was founded for a second time, Ecuador fell under the rule of this new government. Freed from Spanish control in 1822, Ecuador was included in the Bolivarian scheme to create a Gran Colombia—a republican extension of the Viceroyalty of New Granada. Properly speaking, Ecuador emerged as a nation, then, only with the disruption of Gran Colombia in the fourth decade of the past century. Thus, owing to the vicissitudes of the past, Ecuadorian historians have been especially interested in searching for a national identity; and in so doing they have probed their pre-Inca, Inca, and Spanish colonial past with much vigor and some erudition (29, 90). In general their examination of the early national period has been more in the direction of justifying Ecuador's existence as independent from Peru and Colombia than in documenting the early history of a modern nation. The justification of nationhood is a pervasive theme in the pre-1945 era, it subsides only gradually since that time, and it has been combined with treatment of the major fields of Ecuadorian history.

At the outset Ecuadorian history may be divided into two major fields. Writings on the issue of territorial limits—*derecho territorial*—and the long struggle through diplomacy and armed hostilities to maintain Ecuadorian territorial integrity comprise the field which has received the most complete coverage from the standpoint of quality. However, from the standpoint of quantity *derecho territorial* ranks second to that seductive area shared with Ecuador's Andean neighbors, Peru and Bolivia: highly partisan political biography.

The favorite subject of Ecuadorian biographers, and one whose treatment has profoundly influenced Ecuadoran historiography in general, is Gabriel García Moreno (1821–75). García Moreno so dominated national life from 1860 to 1875 and was so significant before 1860 that no other Ecuadorian figure, not even among the independence *próceres,* approaches his position as a historian's subject. A controversial figure from the day he died, August 6, 1875, García Moreno had such a great impact on the politics and history of Ecuador that the nation's national period historiography may never recover from his influence. The controversy surrounding him has made attack and defense appear to be the only Ecuadorian standpoints from which biography is written, no matter the subject and regardless of the chronological period; and post–World War II biographers have still not broken the spell cast over scholarship by the figure of García Moreno. Not only biographers but historians of the national period who seek to document or justify Ecuadorian nationhood, chronicle Ecuadorian liberalism and conservatism, treat economic development, and praise or berate the church inevitably find themselves confronted by the figure of García Moreno. Further, the dominance of this figure is partly responsible for the subjectivism permeating almost all works published since World War II unless they are specifically within the domain of bibliography or do not deal with politico-military themes. It is lamentable that the political odyssey of José María Velasco Ibarra may prove to be equally seductive to future historians and that Velasco may serve to prolong the subjectivity of Ecuadorians treating their national period history.

From the outset there was absolutely no moderation in the treatment of García Moreno's life, and this holds true for the period since 1945 with slight exception. The most impartial recent treatment of García Moreno was published over twenty years ago by Luis Robalino Dávila (140). Yet, as Adam Szászdi (159) notes, this work suffers from defects which stemmed from the extremes of panegyrists on one hand and calumniators on the other. Hearsay, *chismes,* undocumented anecdotes, and the residual effects of nearly a century of anti-Garcían invective find their way into the work. They are also present in the error-ridden 1959 work by the well known Benjamín Carrión (28). Garcían hagiography lives on, too, the result of so many slavish works published from the time of García Moreno's death. García Moreno was a heroic figure to European ultramontanists, Ecuadoran conservatives, and the Catholic faithful everywhere. He is singular in Latin America in having inspired a world-wide literary genre. The Jesuit Severo Gomezjurado's recent works (75, 76) reflect this influence. So do the well-documented works written and edited by Dr. Wilfrido Loor Moreira (100, 101, 102, 103, 104).

The great age of pro-García historiography ended in 1895 when the opposition Liberal Radical party became firmly ensconced, not to be dislodged until 1944. In the interim half century the prosecutors had their heyday and also searched for their own hero. Since 1945 the two sides have been on more even terms as political methods have become more sophisticated. That historical writing in Ecuador is intricately linked to politics is a truism. While there have been others, the hero of the liberals has most often been the autocratic Eloy Alfaro, although he is also highly controversial. Alfaro, president, 1897–1901 and again 1905–11, died by violence as did his historiographical counterpart, García Moreno. Most of the works, and the best ones, dealing with Alfaro were produced between his death and 1944, the end of Ecuador's liberal era (118, 122, 152). In most of the works dealing with Alfaro, the authors, usually consciously, have presented him as the historical counterpoise to García Moreno or as the one Ecuadorian capable of surpassing him in historical significance. This holds true from the earliest (1916) Alfarista panegyrics of Roberto Andrade (4) to the documented but hostile works of the Garciísta Loor (101) published just after the end of World War II. As is the case with Garcian studies the most impartial work—and similarly a recent one—contributes little to our knowledge of Alfaro (80).

Both García Moreno and Alfaro continue to evoke passionate historical literature. The most stimulating works about them continue to be the most subjective. Even with proper and adequate documentation in the truest professional sense, and despite the passage of decades, political history, fused with biography—to which the most attention is devoted—remains an arena rather than a forum. Rarely before or since 1945 have Ecuadorians placed their subjects in a historical context.[13] Political figures of the past are all too often looked upon as omnipotent creators or destroyers, and not as participants and contributors. Finally, it merits note that other leading figures such as the postindependence leaders Vicente Rocafuerte and Juan José Flores have received only cursory treatment, nor does there appear any significant trend to rectify this omission during the last quarter century.

In contrast to biography, historical treatment of the *derecho territorial* question has grown in stature during the period since 1944. Whereas the bulk of literature dealing with boundary disputes was produced prior to the end of World War II, the Peruvian invasion of Ecuador in 1941 fomented the production of a new literature focusing on Ecuador's difficulties with that country. Peru received in 1922 much of the territory lost by Ecuador to Colombia and so became the single target of Ecuadorian *derecho territorial* efforts. These efforts, produced ex post facto and not compiled as legal briefs for

---

13. A highly satisfactory treatment of García Moreno and Garcían historiography is contained in the recent article by Peter H. Smith (154).

the purposes of mediators and arbiters, are history and not simply position papers. A spate of chronicles of the brief 1941 war were produced (35, 114, 131, 141), none of which prove illuminating beyond that incident; but in 1956 appeared a study of the mission of Fray Enrique Varas Galindo to the Spanish archives at the behest of the Alfaro regime (163). Varas's task was to document Ecuador's case in the *derecho territorial* cases with its two powerful neighbors at that time. His work, in Adam Szászdi's words (159) "came to be one of the landmarks in Ecuadorian historiography." The significance of the boundary dispute has led Ecuadorians to write texts on the subject which, though obviously slanted, qualify as sound historical works. *Derecho territorial* became a required subject in primary and secondary education nearly a half century ago, but superior scholarly works appeared only after 1945 (127, 161, 174) and most are designed for use at the university level. The fullest treatment of the subject is Jorge Pérez Concha's *Ensayo crítico de las relaciones diplomáticas del Ecuador con los estados limítrofes* (123).

In sum, Ecuadorian national period historiography, despite able treatment recently of the *derecho territorial* question, has not yet broken the shackles of devotion to partisan biography. There, research, documentation, careful analysis, and the discounting of hearsay still do not prevail.[14] Economic, social, and cultural history, while represented by numerous monographs, is still in the incipient stage only (26, 82). The fusion of regionalism, partisan views arising from it, and political issues continues to influence scholarly trends excessively. As a final note, the dearth of contributions by North American histoirans should be mentioned. Probably the best long-range treatment of Ecuadorian national period political and constitutional development by a United States scholar is that of a political scientist (29); and the most recent scholarly historical work by a North American deals with the seventeenth century (124). Clio has not yet attracted many North American scholars to her Ecuadorian temple.

---

14. The best overall history of Ecuador, that of Cevallos García (33), suffers from these maladies despite the author's recognition of history as a profession and his impressive commentary on his nation's historiography. Another general work which has gone through five editions, that of Oscar Efrén Reyes (137), emphasizes the national period, especially the nineteenth century, but is particularly unsatisfactory in its treatment of the colonial period. See also *Biblioteca ecuatoriana mínima* (19) an anthology project begun in 1960 with four volumes of historical writings by noted historians, church leaders, and politicians.

# BIBLIOGRAPHY

1. Alayza y Paz Soldán, Luis. *El gran mariscal José de la Mar.* Lima, 1941.

2. ———. *Hipólito Unánue, San Martín y Bolívar.* 2d ed. Lima, 1952.

3. Alexander, Robert J. *The Bolivian National Revolution of 1952.* New Brunswick, N.J., 1958.

4. Andrade, Roberto. *Vida˙y muerte de Eloy Alfaro.* New York, 1916.

5. *Archivo Castilla.* 4 vols. Lima, 1956–63.

6. Argüedas, Alcides. *Raza de bronce.* La Paz, 1919.

7. Arnade, Charles W. *The Emergence of the Republic of Bolivia.* Gainesville, Fla., 1957.

8. ———. "The Historiography of Colonial and Modern Bolivia." *Hispanic American Historical Review* 42 (August 1962): 333–84.

9. Barra, Felipe de la. *Castilla: Conductor militar.* Lima, 1962.

10. ———. *La historia militar y sus fuentes.* Lima, 1959.

11. Barros Jarpa, Ernesto. *La "segunda independencia."* Santiago de Chile, 1956.

12. Basadre, Jorge. *Chile, Perú y Bolivia independientes.* Barcelona, 1948.

13. ———. *Historia de la república del Perú desde sus orígenes hasta el presente.* 5th ed. 10 vols. Lima, 1961–64.

14. ———. *Meditaciones sobre el destino histórico del Perú.* Lima, 1947.

15. ———. *La promesa de la vida peruana y otros ensayos.* Lima, 1958.

16. Basombrio, J. L. *Progreso del Perú 1933–1938, durante el gobierno del presidente de la república General Oscar R. Benavides.* Lima, 1945.

17. Bello Codesido, Emilio. *Recuerdos políticos: La junta de gobierno de 1925, su origen y relación con la reforma del régimen constitucional.* Santiago de Chile, 1954.

18. Bermúdez, Oscar. *Historia del salitre desde sus orígenes hasta la guerra del pacífico.* Santiago de Chile, 1963.

19. *Biblioteca ecuatoriana mínima.* 4 vols. Quito, 1960.

20. Blakemore, Harold. "The Chilean Revolution of 1891 and its Historiography." *Hispanic American Historical Review* 45 (August 1965): 393–421.

21. Blanksten, George. *Ecuador: Constitutions and Caudillos.* Berkeley, Calif., 1951.

22. Buines, Gonzalo. *Guerra del Pacífico.* 3 vols. Santiago de Chile, 1911–19.

23. Burr, Robert N. *By Reason or Force: Chile and the Balancing of Power.* Berkeley and Los Angeles, 1966.

24. ———. *The Stillborn Panama Congress: Power Politics and Chilean-Colombian Relations during the War of the Pacific.* Berkeley and Los Angeles, 1962.

25. Bustamante y Rivero, José Luis. *Tres años de la lucha por la democracia en el Perú.* Buenos Aires, 1949.

26. Carbó, Luis Alberto. *Historia monetaria y cambiaria del Ecuador desde la época colonial.* Quito, 1953.

27. Carey, James C. *Peru and the United States, 1900–1960.* Notre Dame, Ind., 1964.

28. Carrión, Benjamín. *García Moreno: el santo del pantíbulo.* Mexico, 1959.

29. ———. *Trece años de cultura nacional: Informe del presidente de la institución, Agosto 1944–Agosto 1957.* Quito, 1957.

30. Casos, Fernando. *La revolución de julio en el Perú.* Valparaiso, Chile, 1872.

31. Céspedes, Augusto. *El dictador suicida: 40 años de historia de Bolivia.* Santiago de Chile, 1956.

32. ———. *Metal del diablo: La vida de un rey de estaño.* La Paz and Buenos Aires, 1946.

33. Cevallos García, Gabriel. *Reflexiones sobre la historia del Ecuador.* 5th ed. 2 vols. Cuenca, Ecua., 1957–60.

34. Chang Rodríguez, Eugenio. *La literatura política de González Prada, Mariátegui y Haya de la Torre.* Mexico, 1957.

35. Chiriboga, Leonardo. *¿Pudo el Ecuador ser agresor en 1941?* Quito, 1952.

36. Chirinos Soto, Enrique. *Nicolás de Piérola.* Lima, 1963.

37. ———. *El Perú frente a junio de 1962.* Lima, 1962.

38. Cline, Howard, ed. *Latin American History: Essays on Its Study and Teaching.* Austin, Tex., 1967.

39. Cohen, Alvin. *Economic Change in Chile, 1929–1959.* Gainesville, Fla., 1960.

40. Cox, Isaac J. Review of vols. 1 and 2 of Francisco Antonio Encina's *Historia general de Chile desde tiempos prehistóricos hasta 1891. Hispanic American Historical Review* 25 (November 1948): 488–90.

41. ———. Review of vols. 6, 7, and 8 of Francisco Antonio Encina's *Historia general de Chile desde tiempos prehistóricos hasta 1891. Hispanic American Historical Review* 26 (May 1949): 261–63.

42. Davis, William Columbus. *The Last Conquistadores: The Spanish Intervention in Peru and Chile, 1863–1869.* Athens, Ga., 1950.

43. Delgado, Luis Humberto. *El militarismo en el Perú, 1821–1930.* Lima, 1930.

44. Dellepiane, Carlos. *Historia militar del Perú*. 2 vols. Lima, 1943.

45. Denegri Luna, Félix, and Manuel Moreyra Paz Soldán, eds. *Biografías de generales republicanos*. Lima, 1963.

46. Deústua, Alejandro O. *La cultura nacional*. Lima, 1937.

47. Díaz Machicao, Porfirio. *Historia de Bolivia*. 5 vols. La Paz, 1954–58.

48. Donoso, Ricardo. *Alessandri, agitador y demoledor: Cincuenta años de historia política de Chile*. 2 vols. Mexico and Buenos Aires, 1952–54.

49. ———. *Antonio José de Irisarri, escritor y diplomático, 1786–1868*. Santiago de Chile, 1966.

50. Donoso, Ricardo, Jaime Eyzaguirre, Guillermo Feliú Cruz, Eugenio Pereira Salas, and Luis Valencia Avaria, eds. *Archivo de Don Bernardo O'Higgins*. Santiago de Chile, 1946–.

51. Donoso, Ricardo. *Las ideas políticas en Chile*. Mexico, 1946.

52. Dulanto Pinillos, Jorge. *Nicolás de Piérola*. 3d ed. Lima, 1953.

53. Edwards, Alberto, and Eduardo Frei Montalva. *Historia de los partidos políticos chilenos*. Santiago de Chile, 1949.

54. ———. *La fronda aristocrática: Historia política de Chile*. Santiago de Chile, 1928.

55. Encina, Francisco Antonio. *Balmaceda*. 2 vols. Santiago de Chile, 1952.

56. ———. *La cuestión de límites entre Chile y Argentina desde la independencia hasta el tratado de 1881*. Santiago de Chile, 1959.

57. ———. *Nuestra inferioridad económica*. Santiago de Chile, 1958.

58. ———. *Portales*. Santiago de Chile, 1934.

59. Enríquez, Luis Eduardo. *Haya de la Torre: la estafa política más grande de América*. Lima, 1951.

60. Escobar Cerda, Luis. *El mercado de valores*. Santiago de Chile, 1959.

61. Espinosa Moraga, Oscar. *El aislamiento de Chile*. Santiago de Chile, 1962.

62. ———. *La postguerra del Pacífico y la puna de Atacama*. Santiago de Chile, 1950.

63. Eyzaguirre, Jaime. *Chile durante el gobierno de Errázuriz Echaurren 1896–1901*. Santiago de Chile, 1957.

64. ———. *Fisonomía histórica de Chile*. Santiago de Chile, 1948.

65. ———. *Ideario y ruta de la emancipación chilena*. Santiago de Chile, 1957.

66. ———. *O'Higgins*. Santiago de Chile, 1954.

67. ———. *La soberanía de Chile en las tierras australes*. Santiago de Chile, 1958.

68. Feliú Cruz, Guillermo, ed. *Memorias militares para servir a la historia de la independencia de Chile del coronel Jorge Beauchef, 1817–1829 y epistolarios, 1815–1840*. Santiago de Chile, 1964.

69. Finer, Herman. *The Chilean Development Corporation.* Montreal, 1947.

70. Fraga, Arturo, and Mario Vergara Gallardo. *Libre pensadores y laicos en Atacama.* Santiago de Chile, 1956.

71. Francovich, Guillermo. *El pensamiento boliviano en el siglo XX.* Mexico and Buenos Aires, 1956.

72. Frías Valenzuela, Francisco. *Historia de Chile.* 4 vols. Santiago de Chile, 1947–49.

73. García Calderón Rey, Francisco. *En torno al Perú y América.* Lima, 1952.

74. Gibson, Charles, and Benjamin Keen. "Trends of United States Studies in Latin American History." *American Historical Review* 62 (July 1957): 855–77.

75. Gomezjurado S.J., Severo. *¿¡Mártir García Moreno!?* Cuenca, Ecua., 1952.

76. ———. *Vida de García Moreno.* 8 vols. Cuenca, Ecua., 1954.

77. González, Julio Heise. *La constitución de 1925 y las nuevas tendencias político-sociales.* Santiago de Chile, 1951.

78. González, Thibaldo. *Haya de la Torre: Trayectoria de una ideología.* Caracas, 1958.

79. Griffin, Charles G. "Francisco Antonio Encina and Revisionism in Chileans History." *Hispanic American Historical Review* 37 (February 1957): 1–28.

80. Guarderas, Francisco. *El viejo de Montecristi.* Quito, 1953.

81. Guevara, Darío C. *Vicente Rocafuerte y la educación pública en el Ecuador.* Quito, 1965.

82. Gutiérrez, Alberto. *El melgarejismo antes y despues de Melgarejo.* La Paz, 1916.

83. Helguera, J. León. "Research Opportunities: The Bolivarian Nations." *The Americas* 18 (April 1962): 365–74.

84. Hell, Jürgen. "Deutschland und Chile." *Wissenschaftliche Zeitschrift der Universität Rostock* 14 (1965): 81–105.

85. Hernández Urbina, Alfredo. *Los partidos y la crisis APRA.* Lima, 1956.

86. Herrera Alarcón, Dante F. *Rebeliones que intentaron desmembrar el sur del Perú.* Lima, 1961.

87. Hidalgo, Alberto. *Porque renuncí al APRA.* Lima, 1954.

88. Iglesias, Augusto. *Alessandri: Una etapa enla democracia en América.* Santiago de Chile, 1959.

89. Jaramillo Alvarado, Pio. *El gran mariscal José de la Mar: Su posición histórica.* Quito, 1950.

90. ———. *La nación quiteña: Perfil biográfico de una cultura.* Quito, 1958.

91. Jobet, Julio César. *Luis Emilio Recabarren: Los orígenes del movimiento obrero y del socialismo chileno.* Santiago de Chile, 1955.

92. ———. "Notas sobre la historiografía chilena." *Atenea* 95 (September–October 1949): 345–77.

93. ———. *Los precursores del pensamiento social de Chile.* 2 vols. Santiago de Chile, 1955–56.

94. Kantor, Harry. *The Ideology and Program of the Peruvian Aprista Movement.* Berkeley and Los Angeles, 1958.

95. Klein, Herbert. "David Toro and the Establishment of 'Military Socialism' in Bolivia." *Hispanic American Historical Review* 45 (February 1965): 25–53.

96. ———. "Germán Busch and the Era of Military Socialism in Bolivia." *Hispanic American Historical Review* 48 (May 1967): 166–84.

97. Lagos Carmona, Guillermo. *Las fronteras de Chile.* Santiago de Chile, 1966.

98. Lastres, Juan B. *Unánue.* Lima, 1955.

99. Lavalle, J. A. "Ramón Castilla, presidente del Perú." *Galería de gobernantes del Perú.* Lima, 1893.

100. Loor Moreira, Wilfrido. *Cartas de García Moreno.* 4 vols. Quito, 1954–55.

101. ———. *Eloy Alfaro.* 3 vols. Quito, 1947.

102. ———. *García Moreno y sus asesinos.* Quito, 1955.

103. ———. *La victoria de Guayaquil.* Quito, 1960.

104. ———. *Los jesuitas en el Ecuador: Su ingreso y expulsión (1850–1852).* Quito, 1959.

105. Mariátegui, José Carlos. *Siete ensayos de interpretación de la realidad peruana.* Lima, 1928.

106. Martínez, Miguel A. *El mariscal de Piquiza: Don Agustín Gamarra.* Lima, 1946.

107. Martinic Beros, Mateo. *Presencia de Chile en la Patagonia austral, 1843–1879.* Santiago de Chile, 1963.

108. Martner, Daniel. *Estudios de política comercial chilena e historia económica.* Santiago de Chile, 1923.

109. McGann, Thomas F. "Research Opportunities: Southern South America." *Americas* 18 (April 1962): 375–79.

110. Mendoza, Jaime. *El factor geográfico en la nacionalidad boliviana.* Sucre, Bol., 1925.

111. Mery Squella, Carlos. *Relaciones entre Chile y los Estados Unidos.* Santiago de Chile, 1965.

112. Miró Quesada Laos, Carlos. *Autopsia de los partidos políticos.* Lima, 1961.

113. Montero Moreno, René. *La verdad sobre Ibáñez*. Santiago de Chile, 1952.

114. Muñoz, Julio H. *La campaña internacional de 1941*. Quito, 1945.

115. Ostria Gutiérrez, Alberto. *The Tragedy of Bolivia: A People Crucified*. New York, 1958.

116. Ovando Sanz, Guillermo, ed. *Una polémica entre Fernando Diez de Medina y Augusto Céspedes en torno a 40 años de historia de Bolivia*. Potosí, Bol., 1957.

117. Paredes, Rigoberto. *El general Melgarejo y su tiempo*. La Paz, 1963.

118. Pareja Diezcanseco, Alfredo. *La hoguera bárbara: Vida de Eloy Alfaro*. Mexico, 1944.

119. Pareja Paz Soldán, José. *Las constituciones del Perú*. Madrid, 1954

120. ———, ed. *Visiones del Perú en el siglo XX*. 2 vols. Lima, 1962.

121. Paz Soldán, Mariano. *Biografía del gran mariscal don Ramón Castilla y Marquesado*. Lima, 1879.

122. Pérez Concha, Jorge. *Eloy Alfaro, su vida, su obra*. Quito, 1942.

123. ———. *Ensayo crítico de las relaciones diplomáticas del Ecuador con los estados limítrofes*. 2 vols. Quito, 1958–59.

124. Phelan, John Leddy. *The Kingdom of Quito in the Seventeenth Century: Bureaucratic Politics in the Spanish Empire*. Madison, Wis., 1967.

125. Pike, Fredrick B. *Chile and the United States, 1880–1962: The Emergence of Chile's Social Crisis and the Challenge to United States Diplomacy*. Notre Dame, Ind., 1962.

126. ———. *The Modern History of Peru*. New York, 1967.

127. Pino Ycaza, Gabriel. *Derecho territorial ecuatoriano, 1493–1830*. 2 vols. Guayaquil, Ecua., 1946–52.

128. Pinto, Francisco Antonio. *Estructura de nuestra economía*. Santiago de Chile, 1959.

129. Pinto Santa Cruz, Aníbal. *Chile: un casco de desarrollo frustrado*. Santiago de Chile, 1959.

130. Portal, Magda. *¡Quienes traicionaron el pueblo!* Lima, 1948.

131. Puente, Rafael A. *La mala fe peruana y las responsables del desastre de Zarumilla*. Quito, 1946.

132. Ramírez Necochea, Hernán. *Balmaceda y la contrarevolución de 1891*. Santiago de Chile, 1958.

133. ———. *La guerra civil de 1891: Antecedentes económicos*. Santiago de Chile, 1951.

134. ———. *Origen y formación del partido comunista en Chile*. Santiago de Chile, 1965.

135. Ravines, Eudocio. *The Yenan Road*. New York, 1951.

136. Reinaga, Fausto. *Belzú: Precursor de la revolución nacional.* La Paz, 1953.

137. Reyes, Oscar Efrén. *Breve historia del Ecuador.* 5th ed. 3 vols. Quito, 1955–56.

138. Riva Agüero y Osma, José de la. *La historia en el Perú.* Lima, 1910.

139. ———. *Por la verdad, la tradición y la patria.* 2 vols. Lima, 1937–38.

140. Robalino Dávila, Luis. *Orígenes del Ecuador de hoy: García Moreno.* Quito, 1948.

141. Rodríguez S., Luis A. *La agresión peruana documentada.* Quito, 1948.

142. Romero, Emilio. *Geografía económica del Perú.* Lima, 1961.

143. Romero, Gonzalo. *Reflexiones para una interpretación de la historia de Bolivia.* Buenos Aires, 1960.

144. Rouillón, Guillermo. *Bio-bibliografía de José Carlos Mariátegui.* Lima, 1963.

145. Sainte Marie, Dario S. *Perú en Cifras.* Lima, 1945.

146. Salinas, Jorge Siles. *La aventura y el orden.* Santiago de Chile, 1956.

147. ———. *Lecciones de una revolución: Bolivia 1952–1959.* La Paz, 1959.

148. Sánchez, Luis Alberto. "Los chineros en la historia peruana." *Cuadernos Americanos* 63 (March–April 1952): 200–212.

149. ———. *Haya de la Torre y el APRA.* Santiago de Chile, 1955.

150. ———. *Perú: Retrato de un país adolescente.* Lima, 1963.

151. Sanhueza, Gabriel. *Santiago Arcos.* Santiago de Chile, 1956.

152. Santovenia, Emeterio S. *Vida de Alfaro.* Havana, 1942.

153. Silvert, Kalman. "The Chilean Development Corporation." Ph.D. thesis, University of Pennsylvania, 1948.

154. Smith, Peter H. "The Image of a Dictator: Gabriel García Moreno." *Hispanic American Historical Review* 45 (February 1965): 1–24.

155. Stein, Stanley J. "Latin American Historiography: Status and Research Opportunities." In *Social Science Research on Latin America,* ed. Charles Wagley. New York, 1964.

156. Stewart, Watt. *Chinese Bondage in Peru: A History of the Chinese Coolie in Peru.* Durham, N.C., 1951.

157. ———. *Henry Meiggs, Yankee Pizarro.* Durham, N.C., 1946.

158. ———. "Jorge Basadre and Peruvian Historiography." *Hispanic American Historical Review* 29 (May 1949): 222–27.

159. Szászdi, Adam. "The Historiography of the Republic of Ecuador." *Hispanic American Historical Review* 44 (November 1964): 503–50.

160. Tauro, Alberto. *Gamarra: Epistolario.* Lima, 1952.

161. Tobar Donoso, Julio, and Alredo Luna Tobar. *Derecho territorial ecuatoriano.* Quito, 1961.

162. Ulloa Sotomayor, Alberto. *Don Nicolás de Piérola: Una época en la historia del Perú.* Lima, 1949.

163. Vargas, Fray José María. *Misiones ecuatorianas en archivos europeos.* Mexico, 1956.

164. Vargas Ugarte, Rubén, S.J. *Historia del Perú: Emancipación 1809–1825.* Buenos Aires, 1958.

165. ———. *Ramón Castilla.* Buenos Aires, 1962.

166. Villanueva Valencia, Victor. *El militarismo en el Perú.* Lima, 1962.

167. ———. *Un año bajo el sable.* Lima, 1963.

168. Villarán, Manuel Vicente. *Páginas escogidas.* Lima, 1962.

169. Wagner de Reyna, Alberto. *Historia diplomática del Perú.* 2 vols. Lima, 1964.

170. Würth Rojas, Ernesto. *Ibáñez: Caudillo enigmático.* Santiago de Chile, 1958.

171. Yrarrázaval Larraín, José Miguel. *El presidente Balmaceda.* 2 vols. Santiago de Chile, 1940.

172. ———. *Tres temas de historia: Portales, "tirano y dictador," la pérdida de la Patagonia, causa y resultados de la revolución de 1891.* Santiago, de Chile. 1951.

173. Zook, David H., Jr. *The Conduct of the Chaco War.* New York, 1960.

174. ———. *Zarumilla-Marañón: The Ecuador-Peru Boundary Dispute.* New York, 1964.

# ARGENTINA:
# THE NATIONAL PERIOD

*Joseph T. Criscenti*

Since the end of World War II, historical writing on Argentina has adhered in the main to the pattern established by the late 1920s. Numerous biographies indicate that the Argentine cult of the heroic has lost none of its earlier vitality. The publication of documental collections, the stress placed on archival research and textual criticism, the critical examination of the independence movement and the early national period—all these are evidence of the persistence of the scientific or positivistic spirit in historical study. The traditional or liberal interpretation of the Argentine past is still dominant, but in addition to its old enemies—the "revisionists," the champions of the caudillo, gaucho, and Juan Manuel de Rosas—it is under increasing attack from scientific and pseudo-Marxists and from ardent nationalists. Most of these critical writers have consulted Argentine and foreign archival collections and other primary sources, though with preconceived notions. Provincial historians continue their efforts to dovetail local with national events. Political history, especially of the pre-1865 period, absorbs the attention of most writers. However, serious investigators are beginning to explore the potentialities of economic and social history. Some show by their dependence on sociology that they are keenly aware of current trends among historians elsewhere in the world.

Several developments suggest that the historical discipline in Argentina will make rapid progress in the foreseeable future. There now are more and better aids to historical research than in 1945. A small but growing number of professional librarians is partly responsible for the appearance of guides and aids of high quality. The Consejo Nacional de Investigaciones Científicas y Técnicas, under the able direction of Ernesto G. Gietz, has published a catalog describing the periodical holdings of 142 Argentine libraries (17). Josefa Emilia Sabor, a professional librarian, is responsible for an important guide to reference works (69). The Fondo Nacional de las Artes, established in 1958, regularly publishes a bibliography of current Argentine publications. Foreign monographs and periodical articles also are noted if they relate to Argentina. Occasionally, the Fondo

Nacional prepares a bibliography on a specific topic or on an important Argentine (32). Professional librarians and historians have likewise compiled special-topic bibliographies on the history of a province, historians, and the Revolución de Mayo (7, 23, 33, 40). In addition there now are indexes to the *Gaceta de Buenos Aires,* the *Revista Nacional,* and the *Nueva Revista de Buenos Aires.*

The postwar years witnessed a continuation of the positivist emphasis on the publication of source materials. These publications have included personal and official correspondence, public records, speeches, diaries, and memoirs. Unfortunately, the private archives of the men who were prominent on the national or provincial scene after 1880 are, with few exceptions, closely held by their descendants and are unavailable to investigators. As a result, would-be editors generally have been forced to focus their attention on the first seventy years of the independence era. Their energies were especially channeled by the celebrations in honor of San Martín and the sesquicentennial anniversary of independence. Numerous documents on the Revolución de Mayo and its antecedents appeared (68, 84). The most ambitious undertaking was that sponsored by the Argentine Senate, the *Biblioteca de Mayo, colección de obras y documentos para la historia argentina,* the first volume of which appeared in 1960. This collection of primary sources is indispensable for scholars who are not interested in first editions or who lack easy access to some of the more important newspapers of the period. It complements two other fundamental works: Emilio Ravignani's six-volume *Asambleas constituyentes argentinas . . .* and the seven volumes edited by the Universidad Nacional de Buenos Aires, Instituto de Historia Argentina "Doctor Emilio Ravignani," entitled *Mayo documental.*

Although editors stressed the independence movement and its antecedents, they have not ignored the period after 1828. Selections from the archives of three provincial leaders—Manuel and Antonio Taboada of Santiago del Estero (76) and Marcos Paz of Tucumán (82)—have already appeared, and those of Juan Facundo Quiroga (79) are in the process of being published. The descendants of two *porteño* leaders—Tomás de Iriarte and Rufino de Elizalde (81)—have released some of their personal papers. There is a special compilation of documents on the Falkland Islands (80). The papers of Bernardino Rivadavia, Juan Manuel de Rosas, and Justo José de Urquiza regrettably have not been assembled in any multivolume set as they justly deserve. For the years after 1880, the scholar must depend essentially on newspapers, speeches, census figures, statistics, and legislative acts. With two notable exceptions, speeches made in Congress or in a provincial legislature are found only in the records of the chamber involved. The Chamber of Deputies of the Province of Buenos Aires is responsible for multivolume works containing the speeches of José Hernández and Leandro N. Alem (9, 10). Some source materials have appeared under the imprint of the Instituto Yrigoyeneano (42), Museo Roca (53), and the Museo y Archivo Dardo Rocha (52), but they are far from satisfactory from the viewpoint of historians.

The availability of materials at hand, national preoccupations, and current scholarly trends have helped shape the writing of Argentine history during the past several decades. A noticeable shift from institutional history to economic and, to a lesser extent, social history has taken place. The example of Juan Alvarez has finally borne fruit, and the field of economic history is being actively cultivated. In this discipline several scholars are particularly outstanding: Enrique M. Barba, Ernesto J. Fitte, Raúl A. Molina, and José M. Mariluz Urquijo. The Department of History at the Universidad Nacional de La Plata, under the aegis of Carlos Heras and Enrique M. Barba, has especially stressed economic topics in its seminars and publications. Among its graduates are such promising young economic historians as Horacio Juan Cuccorese, José Panettieri, and Enrique Wedovoy.

The economic history of the national period is more fully developed than that of the colonial era. Significant efforts have been made to trace and interpret particular aspects of the economy. Some scholars have prepared detailed studies of economic activities rooted in the colonial past. This is true of the original works of Clifton B. Kroeber (44) on the shipping industry, and of Wedovoy (86) on the salt-meat industry. Others have taken a larger time span, and have expanded our knowledge of phases which have acquired special importance in recent times. In this general category also fall the contributions of Sebastián Marotta (46) and Panettieri (57) to labor history, of Cuccorese (22) and Jorge A. Difrieri (25) to financial history, and of H. S. Ferns (29) to the history of Anglo-Argentine economic relations. Ricardo M. Ortiz (55) is the author of a very competent discussion of the Argentine economy from 1850 to 1930. Of the economic historians who have used the Rostow model, Aldo Ferrer (30) probably is the best known in the United States as some of his work has appeared in English.

The economic literature of Argentina is marked by the contemporary concern with Argentine dependence on foreign capital, foreign markets, and foreign manufactures. For economic historians of the early national period (1810–28) and the Rosas era, the issue has become more acute with the growing awareness that manufacturing in Argentina on the eve of the independence movement was fairly diversified. Although they have done so for different reasons, both revisionists and Marxist scholars have attacked the heroes of the traditional or liberal school of historians, and especially Bernardino Rivadavia. For one Marxist (58), the economic policies of Rivadavia were designed to foster the growth of a capitalistic economy, but they were not endorsed by the feudal forces led by Rosas and the caudillos. The revisionists maintain that the liberal administrations that followed Rosas carried out the intent of Rivadavia and surrendered to Great Britain the economic sovereignty of the nation that Rosas had defended (65). In two substantial monographs Sergio Bagú (2) and Ernesto Fitte (31) have come to the defense of Rivadavia. They have stressed the economic realities of the times and the options available to Rivadavia, and have concluded that he followed the best possible choice. Their view has received some support from a revisionist, José María Rosa (67). But the most thoughtful and scholarly study of the Rosas regime, in spite of all the controversy, is still that of Miron Burgin (6).

On another level, serious scholars are seeking to ascertain the reasons for the failure of local industries to develop, the extent and nature of British economic influence, and the role of the landowners. Mariluz Urquijo is preparing what undoubtedly will be the definitive history of the hat industry, and Tulio Halperín Donghi (39) has suggested that local rather than international factors were responsible for the growth of the cattle industry in the Province of Buenos Aires. The economic literature for the remainder of the century is meager (4, 15, 18, 20, 21).

For most of the nineteenth century it is difficult to separate diplomatic history from the political history of Argentina. Historians of the early national period have lost none of their preoccupation with the diplomacy of the Revolución de Mayo, plans for a monarchy, and the efforts to organize a general congress of the provinces. Recent attacks by nationalists have forced a reexamination of the original goal and popularity of the revolution, but without affecting the traditional interpretation of the movement (37, 45, 83). Scholars interested in the Rosas era have made significant contributions to an

understanding of the man himself. Rosas has always been a controversial figure, and the process of reevaluating him began in his own
lifetime. His biographers are numerous, but the most important are
Carlos Ibarguren (41) and Julio Irazusta (43). Noteworthy work has
been done on the French intervention of 1838–40, the English intervention of 1849, and the activities of General José María Paz in the
provinces (11, 16, 51, 63). The first detailed study of the Balcarce
government and the breakup of the Federalist party was prepared by
Gabriel A. Puentes (62). How the office of Encargo de Relaciones
Exteriores helped Buenos Aires to keep alive the concept of an Argentine nation is the subject of a valuable monograph by Victor Tau
Anzoátegui (78).

Students of political and international events from 1852 to 1880
have concentrated on the relations between the Province of Buenos
Aires and the Argentine Confederation and the Paraguayan War,
and have given some passing attention to developments in the interior
provinces. Distinguished scholars who have specialized in the decade
from 1852 to 1862 include Carlos Heras, James R. Scobie, and Beatriz
Bosch. They have consulted both Argentine and foreign archives and
newspapers. Carlos Melo has analyzed political parties in the provinces
from 1860 to 1874 (50). With few exceptions, the prominent men of
the period have their critical and sympathetic biographers. Domingo
F. Sarmiento is a good example. A revisionist accuses him of serving
British economic interests, a distinguished writer tries to destroy his
reputation as an educator and statesman, and a capable French scholar
objectively studies the factors which influenced his intellectual formation between 1839 and 1859 (36, 77, 85). Jorge M. Mayer undertook
with excellent results the most ambitious and comprehensive biography to date of Juan B. Alberdi (47). Revisionists tend to believe
that the Paraguayan War illustrates the dangers of British and
Brazilian imperialism. This is the opinion of José M. Rosa (66), who
has done extensive research in Uruguayan and Brazilian sources. A
different interpretation is advanced in the substantial and thought-
provoking monographs of Efraím Cardozo (13).

The political history of Argentina after 1880 has received little
attention from historians. There is an excellent study of the Unión
Cívica Radical from 1890 to 1916, but it is rather brief (73). Additional
data may be found in an excellent political biography of Leandro
Alem by Roberto Farías Alem (28), and in a history of the party after
1930 by Manuel Augusto A. Gondra (38). For the history of Argentine

socialism, the autobiography of Enrique Dickmann (24) should be consulted. The causes of the Revolution of 1880 are analyzed in two detailed studies (34, 70), and the presidential campaign of 1885–86 is examined in a thoughtful essay (49). The Marxist Luis V. Somni has contributed two studies of the Revolution of 1890 (74, 75). Roberto Etchepareborda probably is the best-informed scholar on the political situation in Argentina at the turn of the century (26, 27). For international relations, the scholarly monograph of Thomas F. McGann (48) on Argentina in inter-American affairs is indispensable.

Other historical topics have not attracted enough scholarly interest to warrant lengthy treatment in this short essay. In the field of diplomatic history, Caillet-Bois (8) has contributed a thorough study of the Falkland Islands question, and Harold F. Peterson (60) has written a pioneer work on United States–Argentine relations. In ecclesiastical history, Cayetano Bruno (5) is preparing a detailed narrative of the Catholic Church in Argentina which is based on archival work in Argentina, Italy, and Spain. The best work on church-state relations is that of Juan Casiello (14), and on the religious reforms of Rivadavia, that of Guillermo Gallardo (35). A promising scholar in the field is Américo A. Tonda. In military history, several surveys of the navy and army have appeared. Jorge Abelardo Ramos (64) has called attention to the role of the army in politics, and Robert A. Potash (61) has made an exceptional study in depth of the military turned politicians from 1928 to 1945.

The history of Argentine letters received a fresh interpretation in a multivolume work edited by Rafael Alberto Arrieta (1). Notable contributions to the history of ideas are those of Leopoldo R. Ornstein (54) on democratic ideas, of Dardo Pérez Guilhou (59) on monarchical ideas, of Bernardo Canal Feijóo (12) on Alberdi, and of Ricardo M. Ortiz (56) on the economic ideas of Echeverría. In demographic studies and immigration history, little progress has been made. The outstanding works in social history are those of James R. Scobie (71, 72). Municipal history is neglected. Joseph T. Criscenti (19) has attempted to reexamine Argentine constitutional history for the first half of the nineteenth century. An important addition to the literature on labor history is the monograph of Samuel L. Baily (3). The areas needing further investigation should become apparent from a reading of Academia Nacional de la Historia, *Historia argentina contemporánea, 1862–1930* (7 vols.; Buenos Aires, 1965–67).

# BIBLIOGRAPHY

1. Alberto Arrieta, Rafael, ed. *Historia de la literatura argentina*. 6 vols. Buenos Aires, 1958–60.

2. Bagú, Sergio. *El plan económico del grupo rivadaviano, 1811–1827: Su sentido y sus contradicciones; sus proyecciones sociales; sus enemigos*. Rosario, Arg., 1966.

3. Baily, Samuel L. *Labor, Nationalism, and Politics in Argentina*. New Brunswick, N.J., 1967.

4. Bollo Cabrios, Palmira S. "Diferencias financieras en la lucha de la Confederación y Buenos Aires, 1857–1862." In *Pavón y la crisis de la Confederación,* ed. by César A. García Belsunce, pp. 167–251. Buenos Aires, 1965.

5. Bruno, Cayetano. *Historia de la Iglesia en la Argentina*. 4 vols. Buenos Aires, 1966–.

6. Burgin, Miron. *The Economic Aspects of Argentine Federalism, 1820– 1852*. Cambridge, Mass., 1946.

7. Caffese, María E., and Carlos F. Lafuente. *Mayo en la bibliografía*. Buenos Aires, 1961.

8. Caillet-Bois, Ricardo R. *Las Islas Malvinas una tierra argentina: Ensayo basado en una nueva y desconocida documentación*. Buenos Aires, 1946.

9. Cámara de Diputados de la Provincia de Buenos Aires. *Obra parlamentaria de Leandro N. Alem*. 6 vols. La Plata, Arg., 1949.

10. ———. *Personalidad parlamentaria de José Hernández*. 3 vols. La Plata, Arg., 1947.

11. Caminos de Artola, Aurora Rosa. *La acción del General Paz en el interior, 1829–1831*. Córdoba, Arg., 1962.

12. Canal Feijóo, Bernardo. *Constitución y revolución: Juan Bautista Alberdi*. Buenos Aires, 1955.

13. Cardozo, Efraím. *Vísperas de la guerra del Paraguay*. Buenos Aires, 1954.

14. Casiello, Juan. *Iglesia y estado en la Argentina, régimen de sus relaciones*. Buenos Aires, 1948.

15. Chiaramonte, José Carlos. "La crisis de 1866 y el proteccionismo argentino de la década del 70." *Anuario del Instituto de Investigaciones Históricas* 6 (1962–63): 213–62.

16. Colli, Néstor S. *Rosas a través de la intervención francesa en el Río de la Plata durante los años 1838 a 1840*. Buenos Aires, 1948.

17. Consejo Nacional de Investigaciones Científicas y Técnicas. *Catálogo colectivo de publicaciones periódicas existentes en bibliotecas científicas y técnicas argentinas*. 2d ed. Buenos Aires, 1962.

18. Cortes Conde, Roberto. "Problemas del crecimiento industrial de la Argentina, 1870–1914." *Desarrollo Económico* 3 (1963): 143–71.

19. Criscenti, Joseph T. "Argentine Constitutional History, 1810–1852: A Re-examination." *Hispanic American Historical Review* 41 (1961): 367–412.

20. Cuccorese, Horacio Juan. "El empréstito inglés para obras públicas: Contribución a la historia financiera de la presidencia de Sarmiento." *Humanidades* 37 (1961): 235–77.

21. ———. *Historia de la conversión del papel moneda en Buenos Aires, 1861–1867.* La Plata, Arg,. 1959.

22. ———. *Historia económica financiera argentina, 1862–1930.* Buenos Aires, 1966.

23. Cutolo, Vicente Osvaldo. *Historiadores argentinos y americanos, 1963–65, con noticias acerca de otros cultores de la temática histórica en todas sus manifestaciones.* Buenos Aires, 1966.

24. Dickmann, Enrique. *Recuerdos de un militante socialista.* Buenos Aires, 1949.

25. Difrieri, Jorge A. *Moneda y bancos en la República Argentina.* Buenos Aires, 1968.

26. Etclhepareborda, Roberto. "La Revolución." In *Hipólito Yrigoyen, pueblo y gobierno,* ed. by Instituto Yrigoyeneano, 3, 105–373. 2d ed. 12 vols. Buenos Aires, 1956.

27. ———. *Tres revoluciones, 1890–1893–1905.* Buenos Aires, 1968.

28. Farías Alem, Roberto.. *Alem y la democracia argentina.* Buenos Aires, 1957.

29. Ferns, H. S. *Britain and Argentina in the Nineteenth Century.* Oxford, Eng., 1960.

30. Ferrer, Aldo. *La economía argentina: Las etapas de su desarrollo y problemas actuales.* 2d ed. Mexico, 1965.

31. Fitte, Ernesto. *Historia de un empréstito: La emisión de Baring Brothers en 1824.* Buenos Aires, 1962.

32. Fondo Nacional de las Artes. *Bibliografía argentina de artes y letras.* Buenos Aires, 1959–.

33. Furlong Cárdiff, Guillermo, and Abel Rodolfo Geoghegan. *Bibliografía de la Revolución de Mayo, 1810–1828.* Buenos Aires, 1960.

34. Galíndez, Bartolomé. *Historia política argentina: La revolución del 80.* Buenos Aires, 1945.

35. Gallardo, Guillermo. *La Política religiosa de Rivadavia.* Buenos Aires, 1962.

36. Gálvez, Manuel. *Vida de Sarmiento, el hombre de autoridad.* Buenos Aires, 1945.

37. Gandía, Enrique de. *Historia del 25 de mayo: Nacimiento de la libertad y de la independencia argentina.* Buenos Aires, 1960.

38. Gondra, Manuel Augusto A. *Declinación del radicalismo y política del futuro.* Buenos Aires, 1957.

39. Halperín Donghi, Tulio. "La expansión ganadera en la campaña de Buenos Aires, 1810–1852." *Desarrollo Económico,* 3 (1963): 57–100.

40. Haulde de Pérez Guilhou, Margarita. *Contribución a una bibliografía histórica de Mendoza.* Mendoza, Arg., 1962.

41. Ibarguren, Carlos. *Juan Manuel de Rosas: Su vida, su drama, su tiempo.* Buenos Aires, 1948.

42. Instituto Yrigoyeneano. *Hipólito Yrigoyen, pueblo y gobierno.* 2d ed. 12 vols. Buenos Aires, 1956.

43. Irazusta, Julio. *Vida política de Juan Manuel de Rosas, a través de su correspondencia.* 5 vols. Buenos Aires, 1941–.

44. Kroeber, Clifton B. *The Growth of the Shipping Industry in the Rio de la Plata Region, 1794–1860.* Madison, Wis., 1957.

45. Marfany, Roberto. "Vísperas de mayo." *Historia* 5 (1960): 87–158.

46. Marotta, Sebastián. *El movimiento sindical argentino: Su génesis y desarrollo.* Buenos Aires, 1960–.

47. Mayer, Jorge M. *Alberdi y su tiempo.* Buenos Aires, 1963.

48. McGann, Thomas F. *Argentina, the United States, and the Inter-American System, 1880–1914.* Cambridge, Mass., 1957.

49. Melo, Carlos R. *La campaña presidencial de 1885–1886.* Córdoba, Arg., 1946.

50. ———. "Las provincias durante la presidencia de Sarmiento, 1868–1874." *Humanidades* 37 (1961): 149–96.

51. Muñoz Azpiri, José Luis. *Rosas frente al imperio inglés: Historia íntima de un triunfo argentino.* Buenos Aires, 1960.

52. Museo y Archivo Dardo Rocha. *Fundación de la Ciudad de La Plata: documentos para su estudio.* La Plata, Arg., 1956.

53. Museo Roca. *Publicaciones.* Documentos, no. 1–. Buenos Aires, 1964–.

54. Ornstein, Leopoldo R. *Historia de la democracia argentina.* Buenos Aires, 1946.

55. Ortiz, Ricardo M. *Historia económica de la Argentina, 1850–1930.* 2 vols. Buenos Aires, 1955.

56. ———. *El pensamiento económico de Echevarría: Trayectoria y actualidad.* Buenos Aires, 1953.

57. Panettieri, José. *Los trabajadores.* Buenos Aires, 1968.

58. Paso, Leonardo. *Rivadavia y la línea de mayo*. Buenos Aires, 1960.

59. Pérez Guilhou, Dardo. *Las ideas monárquicas en el Congreso de Tucumán*. Buenos Aires, 1966.

60. Peterson, Harold F. *Argentina and the United States, 1810–1960*. New York, 1964.

61. Potash, Robert A. *The Army and Politics in Argentina, 1928–1945: Yrigoyen to Perón*. Stanford, Calif., 1969.

62. Puentes, Gabriel A. *El gobierno de Balcarce: División del partido Federal, 1832–1833*. Buenos Aires, 1946.

63. ———. *La intervención francesa en el Río de la Plata: Federales, unitarios, y románticos*. Buenos Aires, 1958.

64. Ramos, Jorge Abelardo. *Ejército y semi-colonia*. Buenos Aires, 1968.

65. Rosa, José Maria. *Defensa y pérdida de nuestra independencia económica*. 3d ed. Buenos Aires, 1962.

66. ———. *La guerra del Paraguay y las monternas argentinas*. Buenos Aires, 1965.

67. ———. *Rivadavia y el imperialismo financiero*. Buenos Aires, 1964.

68. Rui-Guiñazú, Enrique. *Epifanía de la libertad: Documentos secretos de la Revolución de Mayo*. Buenos Aires, 1952.

69. Sabor, Josefa Emilia. *Manual de fuentes de información; obras de referencia: Enciclopedias, diccionarios, bibliografías, biografías, etc.* Buenos Aires, 1957.

70. Sanucci, Lia E. M. *La renovación presidencial de 1880*. La Plata, Arg., 1959.

71. Scobie, James R. *Argentina: A City and a Nation*. New York, 1964.

72. ———. *Revolution on the Pampas: a Social History of Argentine Wheat, 1860-1910*. Austin, Tex., 1964.

73. Sigal, Silvia, and Ezequiel Gallo. "La formación de los partidos políticos contemporáneos: La Unión Cívica Radical, 1890–1916." *Desarrollo Económico* 3 (1963): 173–230.

74. Sommi, Luis V. *La crisis del liberalismo argentino*. Buenos Aires, 1957.

75. ———. *La revolución del 90*. Buenos Aires, 1948.

76. Taboada, Gaspar, ed. *Recuerdos históricos: "Los Taboada", luchas de la organización nacional, documentos seleccionados y coordinados.* 5 vols. Buenos Aires, 1929–50.

77. Tamagno, Roberto. *Sarmiento, los liberales y el imperialismo inglés*. Buenos Aires, 1963.

78. Tau Anzoátegui, Victor. *Formación del Estado Federal Argentino (1820–1852): Intervención del gobierno de Buenos Aires en los asuntos nacionales*. Buenos Aires, 1965.

79. Universidad Nacional de Buenos Aires, Instituto de Historia Argentina "Doctor Emilio Ravignani." *Archivo del brigadier general Juan Facundo Quiroga.* 2 vols. Buenos Aires, 1957–.

80. Universidad Nacional de Buenos Aires, Instituto de Historia Argentina "Doctor Emilio Ravignani." *Colección de documentos relativos a la historia de las islas Malvinas.* 3 vols. Buenos Aires, 1957–.

81. Universidad Nacional de Buenos Aires, Instituto de Historia Argentina "Doctor Emilio Ravignani." *Correspondencia Mitre-Elizalde.* Buenos Aires, 1960.

82. Universidad Nacional de La Plata, Instituto de Historia Argentina. *Archivo del coronel doctor Marcos Paz.* 7 vols. La Plata, Arg., 1959–66.

83. Urquijo, José M. Mariluz. *Los proyectos españoles para reconquistar el Río de la Plata, 1820–1833.* Buenos Aires, 1958.

84. Vargas Peña, Benjamín. *Paraguay-Argentina: Correspondencia diplomática, 1810–1840.* Buenos Aires, 1945.

85. Verdevoye, Paul. *Domingo Faustino Sarmiento, éducateur et publiciste entre 1839 et 1852.* Paris, 1963.

86. Wedovoy, Enrique. "Burguesía comercial y desarrollo económico nacional: Examen del problema a la luz de la historia ganaderil." *Humanidades* 35 (1960): 55–109.

# MEXICO:
# THE NATIONAL PERIOD

*Charles A. Hale and Michael C. Meyer*

It is indeed ironic that Mexico, a country with a historical tradition dating from the moment of the initial European contact, and a tradition nurtured through and enriched by four and a half centuries of concerted scholarship, dedication, and considerable talent, should not yet have come to grips with its own historiographical reality. Mexico has not produced historiographical studies at all comparable to those of Guillermo Feliú Cruz (49, 50, 51, 52) in Chile, Rómulo D. Carbía (22, 23) in Argentina, José Manuel Pérez Cabrera (106) in Cuba, or José Honório Rodrígues in Brazil (119, 120, 121, 122). Until recently Mexican efforts in this field have been sparse and the large majority of those works purporting to be historiographical in essence constituted little more than annotated bibliographies of an extended nature on the one hand or philosophies of history on the other. Those studies which properly can be considered historiographical were all limited by scope of coverage, structural framework, and intent of author. Most often they treated the scholarly output of a single individual and failed even to place him within the intellectual currents of his own day.

The historiographical enterprise has improved markedly in the last decade, and while Mexicanists cannot yet turn to a single cohesive volume, a number of recent perceptive essays are quite helpful to the student seeking a conceptualization of Mexican historical output. These recent endeavors also provide a useful starting point for those who take it upon themselves to mold their own historiographical perspective (2, 35, 46, 56, 109, 125, 126, 157).

## I. INDEPENDENCE TO 1910

The last twenty-five years have seen a dramatic increase in scholarly publication pertaining to nineteenth-century Mexican history. In 1964–65 the *Handbook of Latin American Studies* listed five times more entries on the subject than it did for 1945. The ranks of serious students of Mexican history emerging from Mexican, North American, and European universities have swollen by a similar proportion. This quantitative increase in scholarship is marked by two trends, complementary in part, but also in part divergent. On the one hand, historiography stimulated by ideology and patriotism reached a peak by the late 1960s. On the other hand, these same years have seen a remarkable expansion of professionalism, both within Mexico and abroad. Historical writing on the nineteenth century might be said to have come of age. The first tendency owes much to coincidence, to the celebration during recent years of the centennial and sesquicentennial of the two heroic ages of Mexican liberalism, the Reforma–French Intervention (1854–67) and the Revolution for Independence (1808–15). The critical temper of the new professionalism has made inroads into centennial historiography, but nationalism and political ideology still appear to be durable quantities in Mexico.

The historiography of nineteenth-century Mexico has been affected by a unique crystallization of events. Sharply delineated political periods and classic conflicts between federalism and centralism, republicanism and monarchy, dictatorship and anarchy make the national history of Mexico more tractable for the historian than is that of Argentina, Brazil, or Chile. For the latter countries, "there is less agreement with respect to a meaningful focus of attention" (65). However, this tractability may have inhibited, at least until quite recently, the search by historians for new patterns of organization based upon economic and social change.[1] Thus the nature of nineteenth-century events themselves, as well as the strength of Revolutionary ideology and nationalism, has resulted in the fact that most publications are still devoted to political topics.

Centennial historiography is at best a mixed bag. It includes books and articles by the best of Mexico's historians as well as a flood of polemical, eulogistic, and semischolarly occasional essays. The uneven quality of this production has drawn barbed comments from editor after editor of the Mexican section of the *Handbook of Latin American Studies*.[2] Certainly the outpouring of Mexican centennial literature is due in part to a characteristic of all Hispanic countries, namely,

---

1. Perhaps symptomatic of this fact is Charles Cumberland's reliance upon standard political periodization in his recent economic and social history (41). His work could be contrasted in this respect to two other works in the same series by James R. Scobie on Argentina and Rollie Poppino on Brazil.

2. For example one can consult comments in the *Handbook of Latin American Studies* by Frank Knapp in volume 22 (1960) and by Luis González y González in volume 28 (1966) as well as the historiographical essay by Potash (109).

that the publication cost for a large portion of historical writings is borne directly by the government (165). In the case of Mexico, as Luis González indicated in volume 28 of the *Handbook of Latin American Studies,* the centennials of the 1950s and 1960s have been particularly productive because "our present government . . . recognizes as relatives only figures and episodes of Independence and the Reforma."

Centennial historiography, however, has been far more than mere government-subsidized patriotic rhetoric. The recent intense interest in the nineteenth century is in part a search for historic guideposts by a nation that has experienced revolutionary upheaval since 1910 and an apparent rupture with its past. Historians have increasingly sought meaning and justification for the objectives of Mexican policy since 1940—national integration, development, social justice—in the political ideas and policies of the nineteenth century (161). Perhaps the leading exponent of this use of nineteenth-century antecedents to guide a "revolutionary" Mexico is Jesús Reyes Heroles, elected on August 7, 1968, to the select Academia Mexicana de la Historia. In his inaugural lecture, Reyes Heroles said he was attracted to the study of the past century because of a desire to combat the popular idea that the Revolution of 1910 developed spontaneously. He set out, instead, to demonstrate the continuity of modern Mexican history, and the result was his three-volume *El liberalismo mexicano* (1957–61). The historian, he argues, must reject "historicism"—the belief in the existence of unique events in the past and the nonexistence of laws of historical development. Like the nineteenth-century revolutionaries who saw revolution as the culmination of the historical process, so the historian as revolutionary must now use history as the means and the justification for transforming reality. Citing E. H. Carr, Reyes Heroles argues that the historian should not shun "subjectivity," but should instead recognize, and indeed exploit, the intimate connection that exists between history and action (116).[3] The question to be asked is at what point such present-mindedness ceases to be a natural search for relevance and becomes instead what Daniel Cosío Villegas calls "historiographical sleight-of-hand," a gross distortion of historical reality. Unfortunately, this question can be asked of much of the recent literature on the Independence movement and the Reforma.

The heroes of independence have continued to draw the attention

3. In response Arturo Arnáiz y Freg predicted that the works of Reyes Heroles would emerge as one of the best defenses of the "historical significance of the Mexican Revolution," like those of Emilio Rabasa for the Porfiriato (105, 117).

of serious scholars. Whereas nineteenth-century historians looked askance at Hidalgo and Morelos as agents of social upheaval, since 1910 each has been seen as the "prophetic precursor of the revolutionary program" (101). The standard Mexican treatments in this genre by Alfonso Teja Zabre (170) and Luis Castillo Ledón (25) have been supplemented by more critical studies of Hidalgo on the bicentenary of his birth.[4] More recently Hugh M. Hamill, Jr. (74, 75) has cut through the Hidalgo myth by demonstrating, as did Mora and Alamán, the contradictions of his revolt. It is significant that the "conservative" leader, Agustín de Iturbide, has been little studied in Mexico, though there did appear in the United States a scholarly biography by W. S. Robertson (118).

The sesquicentennial of the Constitution of Apatzingán (1814) occasioned significant interest in that "insurgent" constitution (145, 147), but the landmark in constitutional studies of the independence era is the work of Nettie Lee Benson (11, 12), who has spent an entire career probing the impact of the Spanish Constitution of 1812 on incipient Mexican legal institutions.[5] While outside the scope of this paper, it should be noted that numerous questions are being raised about periodization, suggesting 1760 as a more significant turning point than 1810 or 1821. This inquiry is bound to have its effect on future studies of the Independence era, as historians increasingly seek the political and intellectual continuities of the century following the advent of the Bourbon monarch Charles III (48, 76, 89).

Amid the prolific literature on the heroic mid-century civil war, there have appeared a number of significant contributions. We now have new editions of Francisco Zarco's *Historia* and *Crónica* of the Constituent Congress of 1856–57 (171, 172, 173), though we lack a thorough study of its actions. Benito Juárez still awaits definitive biographical treatment, though numerous Juárez materials have been published (142, 156).[6] Ernesto de la Torre Villar has edited a selection

---

4. See the articles by Juan Hernández Luna, Catalina Sierra Casasus, Manuel Carrera Stampa, Ernesto de la Torre Villar, and Moisés González Navarro in volume 3 of *Historia Mexicana* and the impartial and scholarly study by W. H. Timmons (144).

5. See also the recent article by Charles Macune (87).

6. The republication of the works of leading liberal figures have not been limited to the Reforma. For example, the second edition of José María Luis Mora's *México y sus revoluciones* appeared in 1950 and his *Obras sueltas* in 1963 (97, 98). The *Obras completas* of Justo Sierra were also republished in the early post–World War II period (133).

of documents on the Three Years War, and, along with Lilia Díaz, has brought to light the vast materials available in French archives for the history of the mid-century era (44, 88, 146, 148, 149). While the major liberal leaders, ideas, and policies have been studied repeatedly (though seldom in depth), minor figures have received less attention; and as Martín Quirarte has remarked, "There are few [scholars] who have wanted to commit themselves to the study of the French Intervention and the Second Empire" (112).[7] The twenty-eight volumes of varying quality that appeared as a result of the Congreso Nacional de Historia para el Estudio de la Guerra de Intervención (1962) present a uniformly liberal and republican viewpoint.[8]

As the heroic liberal cycle (viewed in centennial terms) draws to a close, and as the era of Porfirio Díaz approaches, one wonders what turn commemorative writing will take. Will there emerge a more benign view of the Díaz regime, emphasizing its liberal antecedents and its affinity with present-day policies?[9] Or will the law of centennials give way to growing professionalism, resulting in a wider and more sophisticated choice of political topics for study?

The professionalization of Mexican historiography can be said to have begun with the founding of El Colegio de México in 1940. As Jorge Manrique noted, it marks the "change from the isolated student to the researcher working within the confines of favorable institutions" (157). The establishment of the Colegio's Centro de Estudios Históricos was followed soon after by the initiation of training programs at the Escuela Nacional de Antropologia e Historia and at the Instituto de Historia of the National University and by the appearance of *Historia Mexicana* in 1951. The role of Spanish refugee scholars in these events cannot be overestimated. Out of these institutional developments came the creation of the Seminar in the Modern History of Mexico by Daniel Cosío Villegas and the subsequent publication of the multivolume *Historia moderna de México* (34). This is

---

7. Among the few good treatments of mid-century liberalism are those of Reyes Heroles, O'Gorman (102), Scholes (131), Fuentes Mares (60, 61, 62, 63), and Valadés (154). The forthcoming dissertation by Richard N. Sinkin (136) may strike a new note.

8. See the annotated list in Torre Villar (150). Less partisan is the unusual collection of essays by Frenchmen and Mexicans edited by Arnáiz y Freg (5).

9. For example, Jorge Fernando Iturribarría's study of Díaz (79). There are also indications of a revisionist view of Sebastián Lerdo de Tejada, president from 1872 to 1876, by Daniel Cosío Villegas (37). Cosío emphasizes the heretofore unjust treatment of Lerdo except in Frank A. Knapp's outstanding work (82).

easily the most important historiographical effort on the nineteenth century to appear in the last twenty-five years. The achievement of Cosío and his followers has been to defy the centennial impulse and to demonstrate critically and dispassionately that the years 1867–1910 constituted the formative period of modern Mexico. The *Historia moderna* not only is a massive and balanced synthesis, but it has also been a stimulus for younger investigators to venture out on untrod paths of diplomatic and especially economic and social history. Reviews and commentary on the work have been overwhelmingly favorable (127), though one suspects that more than one scholar has been discouraged by the prospect of reading through eight such stout volumes. The Cosío Villegas achivement indicates, among other things, the need to study other neglected political periods of the nineteenth century, for example, the Bustamante administration of 1830–32 and the seemingly dismal decade of 1834–46.

The history of Mexican foreign relations is one of the fields that shows the influence of the new professionalism. For example, Carlos Bosch García (18) has brought new scholarship and new objectivity to a traditionally emotional subject, Mexican–United States relations prior to the War of 1846–48.[10] Advancing beyond the recent spate of patriotic essays on the McLane-Ocampo Treaty of 1859, José Fuentes Mares (60, 61, 62, 63) has brought new insight, if not new dispassion, to the diplomacy of the civil war era. Mexico's relations with France and Spain over a broad time span have also been the subject of significant publications (43, 44, 146, 148, 159, 164). Finally, Cosío Villegas himself has done much to revive interest in the study of diplomatic history. Not only has he served as director since 1960 of the long-standing Archivo Histórico Diplomático Mexicano, but he has devoted volumes 5 and 6 of the *Historia moderna* and several other studies to Mexico's foreign relations after 1867 (33, 36, 152). On a more specific note, the long career of the diplomat and financier Matías Romero is attracting special attention from scholars (13, 38, 95).

Certainly one of the striking developments in Mexican historiography since the early forties is the burgeoning of the genre known as the "history of ideas." The origins of this movement date back to 1925, when German historicist and existentialist philosophy made its entry into Mexico through the ideas of José Ortega y Gasset (123).

---

10. The war with the United States is the focus of at least three forthcoming studies by United States scholars Robert E. Quirk, David M. Pletcher, and Ralph E. Weber, and one recently completed study by George W. Smith (137).

More recently, the impetus came from the Seminar in the History of Ideas initiated at El Colegio de México by José Gaos, a Spanish refugee philosopher. In their search for the roots and distinctive features of Mexican national culture, such scholars as Leopoldo Zea (174, 175, 176), Edmundo O'Gorman (100), Luis Villoro (162), and Francisco López Cámara (86) have focused attention on the nineteenth century. It should be noted that these historian-philosophers in quest of *lo mexicano* work from premises quite different from those of Cosío Villegas and his colleagues and from those of most practitioners of "intellectual history" in the United States and Europe. They categorically reject the effort of the historian to be "objective" and "scientific." If the past is in any way detached from the present, it becomes dead and meaningless. These assumptions appear similar to those of the more politically oriented Reyes Heroles, discussed above. Yet the latter's dismissal of "historicism" shows that there may be basic points of intellectual divergence within the "history of ideas," considered as a broad category (161). Since the history of ideas in Mexico has been appropriated in large part by philosophers, the more empirical study of ideas in their socioeconomic and institutional context has been left with a few exceptions (6, 71, 94) to foreign scholars (32, 73, 114, 139).[11] For example, the intellectual life of the post-1867 period does not receive special treatment in the *Historia moderna*. It might also be noted that the history of education and of science are subjects badly in need of emphasis.

Perhaps the most noteworthy result of the new professionalism is the awakening interest in social and economic history. Symptomatic of this new interest is the fact that observers are now increasingly citing the need for research based on sociological, economic, and quantitative methods which will examine the "juxtaposition of traditional and ultramodern institutions" and the intricacies of social structure and social change (8, 88, 141).

The study of nineteenth-century land tenure and its relation to social and political conflict is beginning to attract researchers. With a few exceptions (17, 78) the hacienda as an institution has been generally neglected, but several investigators are working from heretofore unused materials to clarify the complicated but immensely important ties between the church and the landed property of the nation (8, 15,

11. There are at least ten recently completed or in progress dissertations in intellectual history at United States institutions. The Díaz period is particularly popular.

39, 84). Such studies will help us to understand the social basis of political conflict and the socioeconomic aftermath of the Reforma— exactly what happened to church property transferred as a result of anticlerical measures. François Chevalier has advanced suggestions concerning the liberal-conservative conflict and several other researchers are examining the role of Spaniards in Mexican politics and economic life (27, 54, 55, 67, 135). An annotated and expanded edition of Mme Calderón de la Barca's *Life in Mexico* (53) portrays several of the great families of mid-nineteenth-century Mexico City, which await some enterprising student.[12] At the other extreme of society, revolutionary concerns have aroused much interest in the nineteenth-century plight of the indigenous population (34, 59, 70, 110, 134). More recently there has also emerged an increased awareness of the role of peasant populations in the modernization process, a world phenomenon for which Mexico provides an interesting case study (29, 31, 90, 115).

There are even indications that the long-neglected field of economic history is being cultivated. Thanks to Miguel A. Quintana (111), Howard F. Cline (29), Robert A. Potash (108), and Luis Chávez Orozco (26) we are now aware of a tradition of government-financed modern textile manufacturing, established in 1830 upon late colonial precedents.[13] Catalina Sierra has opened up the economic history of the independence era (132). An ambitious effort to survey the Mexican economy from 1867 to 1910 appears in three volumes of the *Historia moderna* (34). It is perhaps an indication of the rapid advances being made, however, that these volumes are already being criticized by younger Mexican scholars (9, 57). Michael P. Costeloe's study (39) of ecclesiastical banking dramatizes the need to investigate the origins of the modern banking system which replaced the church in the 1860s. Perhaps if we get a more precise idea of the dimensions of economic development during the Díaz regime, we can better explain the agrarian upheaval of 1910 and in turn its relation to the more recent industrial revolution (14, 28, 107, 141, 160).

---

12. There is a dissertation in progress by Doris Ladd Spech of Stanford on the Mexican aristocracy in 1821 and one by Miguel Marín of Columbia on the society of neocolonial Puebla from 1780 to 1830.

13. Dawn Keremitsis (81) is completing a dissertation at the University of California on the nineteenth-century cotton industry.

## II. 1910 TO THE PRESENT

During the past fifty years, within the general field of Mexican history, an inordinate proportion of the historical writing has centered on the Revolution. For some, even after years of study and research, the Mexican Revolution continues to hold a certain attraction—a unique flavor which helps carry one through the drudgery that archival research can sometimes be. Certainly Pancho Villa, Pascual Orozco, and Emiliano Zapata must rank high on anyone's list of most unforgettable characters. To the most pragmatic, the Revolution was, after all, the first serious social upheaval in twentieth-century Latin American history, and one of the great social revolutions in world history. But what of the historiographical results of this protracted interest in a dynamic and significant historical subject? Unfortunately, until the last fifteen or twenty years the overwhelming majority of Mexicanists, both in the United States and in Mexico, have not given the subject the type of attention which it merits.

In purely quantitative terms, the historical literature produced during the first three decades of the Revolution is rich. To state it another way, it is almost frightening in terms of sheer bulk. In the last analysis, however, it is the quality rather than the quantity that is of primary concern. As one begins to examine the nature of the literature produced during the first thirty or thirty-five years of the Revolution, it quickly becomes obvious that most of it simply is not well grounded in historical fact. An alarming percentage is distorted by blatant partisanship. Most of the practitioners were amateurs, even dilettantes, not professionals schooled in the proper use of evidence.

The positivist tradition which permeated historical scholarship during the *porfiriato* was discredited along with the social philosophy embodied in Mexican *cientificismo*. But unfortunately, as the positivists retired from the field no serious group rose up to take their place. Antipositivism in itself, even with its vigorous attacks on materialist explanations, was insufficient to rally any school of historical thought. While the negative label could bind a group together in terms of what it was against, it offered nothing with respect to what it was for. The Mexican philosopher was quickly able to accept or reject something new—the pragmatism and subsequently the Christian dualism of Antonio Caso. The artist could embrace or reject the new *indigenista* muralist movement. But the historian had only something old to discard. Grasping at straws, he finally opted for the very antithesis of any system of rational thought—exaggerated *personalismo*—that type of blind commitment not to ideology, not to program, but simply to the image which the individual caudillo is able to project. The various *"ismos"* continue even today to be very important to that generation of Mexicans who lived through and participated in the early Revolution. The historical literature produced by that generation is strongly colored by Villismo, or Zapatismo, or Carrancismo, or Obregonismo.

In addition, as the 1910 uprising gradually began to mushroom into a social upheaval, and as it began to yield its first positive fruit, the Revolution—that rather nebulous phenomenon—began to be viewed as the very essence of the Mexican state. Nationalism and *mexicanidad* became inexorably intertwined with the revolutionary ideal. To be Mexican, in the full meaning of the word, was tantamount to being a revolutionary. As a logical corollary, a counterrevolutionary, or someone judged to be a counterrevolutionary, was not viewed simply as a political opponent but rather as something less than a true Mexican.

History became one of the many vehicles for the apotheosis of the Revolution. It was conceived as a pragmatic device for keeping the Revolution alive and exalting its successes. Biographers of those men who had in some way opposed the quickly accepted apostles of the Revolution invariably made use of shamelessly long lists of pejoratives to depict their various apostates. The heroes, on the other hand, had to be defended, their indiscretions notwithstanding. Historical narratives artfully concealed documentation or testimony which seemed to refute favorite hypotheses and preconceived prejudices. Time-honored methods of authentication were either overlooked or purposely ignored. The crimes of the Revolution were dismissed or excused on grounds of political necessity while those of the opposition were painted as barbarities of the worst kind.

Must one then concede a vast totalitarian conspiracy undermining the girders of historical scholarship? Formal censorship was not a significant factor. The Mexican Revolutionary historian, when confronted with a seemingly irreconcilable dichotomy, decided that he would rather be loved than candid. Once accepting that the Revolution embodied all virtue, it was necessary to deprecate the enemies of the movement in the most scathing terms. The bulk of the historical literature was designed simply to serve the interests of the movement rather than those of historical scholarship itself. The result of this very pervasive frame of reference was finally the development of a school—a prorevolutionary school.

The *personalista* tradition and the prorevolutionary bias were not at all incompatible. To the contrary, they complemented one another perfectly. The prorevolutionary umbrella, as the official party itself, was made large enough to shelter some differences. Some historians became adherents of Pancho Villa and others of Emiliano Zapata. Some opted for a Carrancista interpretation while still others preferred an Obregonista interpretation. The differences, although real, were severely circumscribed by a fundamental commitment to the Revolution. The practitioners merely differed on which of the protagonists most closely approximated the ultimate ideal, revolutionary orthodoxy.

It would be foolhardy indeed to expect that the Mexican historian of the period 1910–45 could have divorced himself entirely from the partiality wrought by his social and political environment. But even granting that historians are likely to reflect the prejudices of their age, one cannot help being outraged by the extent to which subjectivism pervaded the historical output.

Shortly after the foundation of El Colegio de México and the Instituto de Historia of the National University the professionalization of historiography, noted for the nineteenth century, began to manifest itself in Revolutionary studies as well. The Mexican government, too, contributed to upgrading professional standards as it provided funds to bring together and purchase major documentary collections and make them available to investigators. In the past ten years at least three major revolutionary collections have been acquired: The Espinosa de los Monteros Archive, which focuses on the Reyista movement, is now housed in the historical annex to Chapultepec Castle; the Secretaría de Hacienda y Crédito Público acquired the 66,000-item Archivo Madero; and the National University managed to purchase the Zapata papers. Private industry has played an important role as well. CONDUMEX, S.A., has established a cultural center and a historical archive which contains the papers of Venustiano Carranza and Francisco León de la Barra. But perhaps the most important single acquisition is that of the University of the Americas, which recently obtained the Archivo Díaz, comprising almost one million folio pages.

The results of the professionalization in the postwar period have not yet all come in, and there are those in Mexico who fail to acknowledge that the changes which have occurred are for the better. Old-line revolutionaries such as Alfonso Taracena, for example, have flailed out at the work being done at El Colegio de México. Leaning heavily on his Yankeephobic crutch, Taracena insists that the best interests of Clio cannot be served by any institution which deigns to accept financial assistance from the Rockefeller Foundation (143). In spite of invectives such as his, much of the postwar production is encouraging.

In general, evaluations of the Revolution have become more guarded. Studies have begun to depart from the oversimplified prorevolutionary patterns and have begun to show the shortcomings as well as the successes of the movement. They reflect a new consciousness which is not totally permeated by the type of Mexican nationalism which prostituted so much of the earlier work. More specifically, they reflect a new consciousness which is not overpowered by the concept of the Revolution. At least one substantial work frankly antagonistic to the Revolution was produced in the 1950s (158).

In the field of biography Mexicanists for the first time began to take an active interest in the methodological considerations prerequisite to serious scholarship: the proper relationship of the individual to the historical process, personal leadership versus environmental considerations, and the nature of the decision-making process within a revolutionary setting. The emergent works demonstrated clearly that the paladins of the first twenty years of the conflict fell conspicuously short of perfect and the heretics were not always malicious and depraved.

The 1950s were the important years of transition. As an example one can point to three biographies of Francisco I. Madero—two written in the United States by Stanley R. Ross (128, 129) and Charles C. Cumberland (40), and one written in Mexico by José C. Valadés (155). Unlike the hundreds of books, pamphlets, and articles which had been written about Madero previously, all three of these studies were based upon serious archival research. While none of the three departed drastically from the prorevolutionary frame of reference, it is accurate to label them sympathetic biographies, certainly not eulogistic or panegyric. Because of the nature of the research and the development of the argumentation, the burden of proof rests heavily with any who would dissent from the conclusions presented.

Another important trend initiated in the 1950s was the beginning of the interdisciplinary approach. Many Mexican historians began to recognize the desirability, indeed the necessity, of enlarging their own frame of reference in order to incorporate the findings and, when applicable, even the methodology of sister disciplines in the humanities and the social or behavorial sciences. The interdisciplinary approach is best represented by the efforts of Howard F. Cline (30), Frank Brandenburg (19), and most recently in the pioneering study of James Wilkie (167). Wilkie utilizes quantitative methodology but avoids the jargon so often associated with works of the behavioralist genre.

Within Mexico the new professionally oriented school is engaging in some very meaningful work. Exhaustive bibliographical work is currently being produced, especially by a group of Mexican and United States scholars at El Colegio. Three bibliographical volumes have appeared thus far on books and pamphlets devoted to the Revolution (69), two on periodical literature which make possible for the first time the efficient use of Mexico City's Hemeroteca Nacional (130), one on the holdings of the Archivo de Relaciones Exteriores de México (153), and one is being prepared currently by Luis Muro on the holdings of the Archivo Histórico de la Defensa Nacional.

One of the most heartening trends in the last two decades is the cultivation of regional histories. Because the fight against the exaggerated centralism of the Porfirist state ushered in a period of extreme regionalism and sectionalism, the Revolution, to be fathomed, must be viewed against a background of disparate regional interests pursuing different ends and utilizing different means. State histories (1, 42, 58, 64, 124, 177) and studies of state and regional leaders (10, 16, 20, 92) are still in their infancy. Hopefully, those works which have appeared mark only the beginning. The regional histories are complemented nicely by a growing emphasis on Revolutionary institutions and by topical studies moving across the Revolutionary period. Thus the mining industry (14), the Revolutionary army (85), the social security system (4), the church (103), and the role of organized labor (3) have been researched with considerable care.[14] The development of Mexican nationalism, an important subject long avoided, has only recently been given the broad interpretive type of attention which it warrants (68, 93, 151).

United States–Mexican relations during the Revolution have provided a subject of nationalistic diatribe for years. Only in the last decade have the bitter invectives lost ground as a younger generation of diplomatic historians have begun to consult the foreign relations

---

14. At least three recent doctoral dissertations have been devoted to the church-state conflict: those of Dooley (45), Hanley (77), and Williams (168).

archives of both countries in an attempt to strike some balance. Robert Quirk's excellent study of the invasion of Veracruz (113) set the moderate tone. The most significant Mexican contribution is Lorenzo Meyer's scholarly analysis (91) of the oil conflict—a work based upon the diplomatic records of both participants. German and English scholars have provided new dimensions in the field of diplomatic history (21, 80), and a group of young United States historians, having gained access to Mexico City's Archivo de Relaciones Exteriores de México, are beginning to make known the results of their endeavors (66, 72, 166).

Finally, in the last five or six years, new documentary publications have been rapidly made available. The most notable group engaged in this field, but by no means the only one, is the Comisión de Investigaciones Históricas de la Revolución Mexicana, which was founded by Isidro Fabela and directed by him until his death several years ago. The Comisión has already published fifteen volumes of documents on the early revolutionary period (six on the Carranza era, five on the Madero period, one on the Flores Magón brothers, one on other precursors, and two on the Pershing punitive expedition) and is projecting a total of twenty-three (47). When completed, this project might well be the most important of its kind ever undertaken in Mexico.[15]

The record of Revolutionary historiography of the past twenty-five years is scarcely of uniformly high quality. Stanley Ross's characterization of the last two years in volume 30 of the *Handbook of Latin American Studies*—"the resulting compilation is not one to cause the scholarly community to celebrate"—is not inappropriate for the postwar period in general. Professionalization has not yet penetrated very deep. The amount of work coming off the presses is still tremendous and library shelves continue to be filled with works of very poor quality. The major difference, however, is that the percentage of serious work has increased markedly in the past several decades.

The changes in the historical literature for the nineteenth and twentieth centuries are but one segment of a very profound mutation in Mexico's entire scholarly, literary, and artistic output. Modern

---

15. The only comparable undertaking in modern Mexican history has been the publication of the Díaz papers (24). The published Díaz archive is not nearly as impressive as the thirty volumes might seem to indicate. No discernible system of selecting important documents was used, and as a result hundreds of documents of only marginal interest are included.

Mexican art, for example, has closed the door on the great muralist movement of a generation ago. The Mexican literary community has turned its back on the novel of the Revolution. Musical productions are departing drastically from the stereotyped Ballet Folklórico. The Ballet Folklórico today is primarily for foreign consumption, for Expo 67, Hemisfair 68, or the cultural Olympics, not for the Mexicans.

All of these changes in Mexico's scholarly, literary, and artistic endeavors have at least one important ingredient in common. They indicate the demise of traditional Mexican Revolutionary nationalism in the search for the more universal. Perhaps the most important lesson to be gleaned from the new approach is that Mexico obviously has begun to mature. It has begun to outgrow what Samuel Ramos referred to in his brilliant essay, *El perfil del hombre y la cultura en México,* as the national inferiority complex. Mexico is beginning to show that it can continue to progress without using the Revolution as a crutch for every step. In short, the historians have made the beginning of a contribution. They have come a long way since World War II, but much work remains to be done.

# BIBLIOGRAPHY

1. Almada, Francisco R. *La revolución en el estado de Chihuahua.* 2 vols. Mexico, 1964–65.

2. Al'perovich, M. S. "Instoriia Otnoshenii Mezhdu Meksikoi i SSha v Poslevoennoi Meksikanskoi Istoriografi." *Voprosy Istorii* 3 (1958): 171–83.

3. Araiza, Luis. *Historia del movimiento obrero mexicano.* 4 vols. Mexico, 1964–65.

4. Araujo, Lucila Leal. *Aspectos económicos del Instituto Mexicano del Seguro Social.* Mexico, 1966.

5. Arnáiz y Freg, Arturo, ed. *La intervención francesa y el imperio de Maximiliano, cien años después, 1862–1962.* Mexico, 1965.

6. ———. "Prologo." In *José María Luis Mora: Ensayos, ideas y retratos.* Mexico, 1941.

7. Ashby, Joe C. *Organized Labor and the Mexican Revolution under Lázaro Cárdenas.* Chapel Hill, N.C., 1967.

8. Bazant, Jan. "La desamortización de los bienes corporativos de 1856." *Historia Mexicana* 16 (1966): 193–212.

9. ———. *Historia de la deuda exterior de México, 1823–1949.* Mexico, 1968.

10. Beezley, William. "Revolutionary Governor: Abraham González and the Mexican Revolution in Chihuahua, 1910–1913." Ph.D. dissertation, University of Nebraska, 1968.

11. Benson, Nettie Lee. *La diputación provincial y el federalismo mexicano.* Mexico, 1955.

12. ———, ed. *Mexico and the Spanish Cortes, 1810–1822.* Austin, Tex., 1966.

13. Bernstein, Harry. "Mocedades de Matías Romero." *Historia Mexicana* 10 (1961): 588–612.

14. Bernstein, Marvin D. *The Mexican Mining Industry, 1890–1950.* Albany, N.Y., 1965.

15. Berry, Charles R. "The Reform in the Central District of Oaxaca, 1856–1857: A Case Study." Ph.D. dissertation, University of Texas, 1967.

16. Blaisdell, Lowell L. *The Desert Revolution: Baja California, 1911.* Madison, Wis., 1962.

17. Boorstein Couturier, Edith. "Modernización y tradición en una hacienda (San Juan Hueyapan: 1902–1911)." *Historia Mexicana* 18 (1968): 35–55.

18. Bosch García, Carlos. *Historia de las relaciones entre México y los Estados Unidos, 1819–1848.* Mexico, 1961.

19. Brandenburg, Frank. *The Making of Modern Mexico.* Englewood Cliffs, N.J., 1964.

20. Bryan, Anthony T. "General Bernardo Reyes and Mexican Politics, 1900–1913." Ph.D. dissertation, University of Nebraska, 1969.

21. Calvert, Peter. *The Mexican Revolution, 1910–1914: The Diplomacy of the Anglo-American Conflict.* New York, 1968.

22. Carbía, Rómulo D. *Historia crítica de la historiografía argentina desde sus orígenes en el siglo XVI.* Buenos Aires, 1940.

23. ———. *Historia de la historiografía argentina.* La Plata, Arg., 1925.

24. Careño, Alberto María, ed. *Archivo del General Porfirio Díaz.* 30 vols. Mexico, 1947–60.

25. Castillo Ledon, Luis. *Hidalgo: Vida del heroe.* 2 vols. Mexico, 1948–49.

26. Chávez Orozo, Luis. *Historia de Mexico, 1808–1836.* Mexico, 1947.

27. Chevaliér, François. "Conservateurs et libéraux au Mexique: Essai de sociologie et géographie politique de l'independance a l'intervention française." *Cahiers d'Histoire Mondiale* 8 (1964): 457–74.

28. ———. "Un facteur décisif de la révolution agraire au Mexique: Le soulèvement de Zapata." *Annales Economies, Sociétés, Civilisations* 16 (1961): 66–82.

29. Cline, Howard F. "The 'Aurora Yucateca' and the Spirit of Enterprise of Yucatán." *Hispanic American Historical Review* 27 (1947): 30–60.

30. ———. *Mexico: Revolution to Evolution, 1940–1960.* New York, 1963.

31. ———. "The Sugar Episode in Yucatán, 1825–1850." *Inter-American Economic Affairs* 1 (1948): 79–100.

32. Cockcroft, James G. *Intellectual Precursors of the Mexican Revolution, 1900–1913.* Austin, Tex., 1968.

33. Cosío Villegas, Daniel. *Estados Unidos contra Porfirio Díaz.* Mexico, 1956.

34. ———, ed. *Historia moderna de México.* 8 vols. Mexico, 1955–65.

35. ———. *Nueva historiografía política del México moderno.* Mexico, 1965.

36. ———. *The United States versus Porfirio Díaz,* Lincoln, Nebr., 1963.

37. ———. "Sebastián Lerdo de Tejada, mártir de la república restaurada." *Historia Mexicana* 17 (1967): 167–99.

38. Cosío Villegas, Emma, ed. *Diario personal de Matías Romero, 1855–65.* Mexico, 1960.

39. Costeloe, Michael P. *Church Wealth in Mexico: A Study of the "Juzgado de Capellanías" in the Archbishopric of Mexico, 1800–1856.* Cambridge, Eng., 1967.

40. Cumberland, Charles. *Mexican Revolution: Genesis under Madero.* Austin, Tex., 1952.

41. ———. *Mexico: The Struggle for Modernity*. New York, 1968.

42. Dabdoub, Claudio. *Historia del Valle del Yaqui*. Mexico, 1964.

43. Delgado, Jaime. *España y México en el siglo xix*. 3 vols. Madrid, 1950.

44. Díaz, Lilia. *Versión francesa de México: Informes diplomáticos, 1853–1858, 1858–1862*. 2 vols. Mexico, 1963–64.

45. Dooley, Francis P. "Mexico's Cristeros: Rebels for Religion." Ph.D. Dissertation, University of Maryland, in progress.

46. Esquenazi-Mayo, Roberto. "Historiografía de la guerra entre México y los EE. UU." *Duquesne Hispanic Review* 2 (1962): 34–77.

47. Fabela, Isidro, ed. *Documentos históricos de la Revolución Mexicana*. 15 vols. Mexico, 1960–69.

48. Fariss, N. M. *Crown and Clergy in Colonial Mexico, 1759–1821*. London, 1968.

49. Feliú Cruz, Guillermo. *Barros Arana, historiador*. 2 vols. Santiago de Chile, 1958.

50. ———. *Historiografía colonial de Chile*. Santiago de Chile, 1958.

51. ———. *Medina y la historiografía americana: Un ensayo sobre la aplicación del método*. Santiago de Chile, 1933.

52. ———. *Las obras de Vicuña Mackenna*. Santiago de Chile, 1932.

53. Fisher, Howard T., and Marion H. Fisher, eds. *Life in Mexico: The Letters of Fanny Calderón de la Barca*. Garden City, N.Y., 1966.

54. Flores Caballero, Romeo. "La consolidación de vales reales en la economía, la sociedad y la política novohispanas." *Historia Mexicana* 18 (1969): 334–78.

55. ———. *La contrarevolución el la independencia: Los españoles en la vida política, económica y social de México*. Mexico, 1969.

56. Florescano, Enrique. "Las investigaciones históricas en México." *Cahiers des Amériques Latines* 1 (1968): 200–207.

57. ———, and Alejandra Moreno Toscano. "Historia económica y social." *Historia Mexicana* 15 (1965–66): 314–15, 351.

58. Fowler, Heather. "The Agrarian Revolution in the State of Veracruz, Mexico." Ph.D. dissertation, American University, in progress.

59. Fraser, Donald J. "The Disposition of Communal Lands in Mexico, 1856–1911." Ph.D. dissertation, University of Florida, in progress.

60. Fuentes Mares, José. *Juárez y los Estados Unidos*. Mexico, 1960.

61. ———. *Juárez y el imperio*. Mexico, 1963.

62. ———. *Juárez y la intervención*. Mexico, 1962.

63. ———. *Juárez y la república*. Mexico, 1965.

64. Gámiz Olivas, Everado. *La revolución en el estado de Durango.* Mexico, 1963.

65. Gibson, Charles. "Spanish American Historiography: A Review of Two Decades." *Handbook of Latin American Studies* 28 (1966): 60–66.

66. Gilderhus, Mark T. "The United States and the Mexican Revolution, 1915–1920: A Study of Policy and Interest." Ph.D. dissertation, University of Nebraska, 1968.

67. Gleizes, Catherine. "Le Role des 'Ilustrados' et des liberaux creoles et espagnols dans le mouvement d'indépendance au Mexique." Ph.D. dissertation, University of Paris, in progress.

68. Gómez Quiñones, Juan H. "Mexican Nationalism: The Formative Years, 1890–1912." Ph.D. dissertation, UCLA, in progress.

69. González, Luis, ed. *Fuentes de la historia contemporánea de México: Libros y folletos.* 3 vols. Mexico, 1961–62.

70. González Navarro, Moisés. "Instituciones indígenas en México independiente." In *Métodos y resultados de la política indigenista en México*, ed. Instituto Nacional Indigenista, pp. 113–169. Mexico, 1954.

71. ———. *El pensamiento político de Lucas Alamán.* Mexico, 1952.

72. Grieb, Kenneth J. *The United States and Huerta.* Lincoln, Nebr., 1969.

73. Hale, Charles A. *Mexican Liberalism in the Age of Mora, 1821–1853.* New Haven, Conn., 1968.

74. Hamill, Hugh M. "Early Psychological Warfare in the Hidalgo Revolt." *Hispanic American Historical Review* 41 (1961): 206–35.

75. ———. *The Hidalgo Revolt: Prelude to Mexican Independence.* Gainesville, Fla., 1966.

76. Hamnett, B. R. "The Intendant System and the Landed Interest in Mexico: The Origins of Independence, 1768–1808." Ph.D. dissertation, Cambridge University, 1968.

77. Hanley, Timothy C. "The Role of the National League for the Defense of Religious Liberty in the Church-State Conflict in Mexico, 1910–1929." Ph.D. dissertation, Columbia University, in progress.

78. Harris, Charles H. III. *The Sánchez Navarros: A Socio-economic Study of a Coahuilan Latifundio, 1846–1853.* Chicago, 1964.

79. Iturribarría, Jorge Fernando. *Porfirio Díaz ante la historia.* Mexico, 1967.

80. Katz, Friedrich. *Deutschland, Díaz and die mexikanische Revolution.* Berlin, 1964.

81. Keremitsis, Dawn K. "The Development of the Cotton Industry in Nineteenth Century Mexico." Ph.D. dissertation, University of California, Berkeley, in progress.

82. Knapp, Frank A. *The Life of Sebastian Lerdo de Tejada: A Study of Influence and Obscurity.* Austin, Tex., 1951.

83. Knauth, Josefina Zoraída de. "Historia de la educación." *Historia Mexicana* 15 (1965–66): 293.

84. Knowlton, Robert J. "Chaplaincies and the Mexican Reform." *Hispanic American Historical Review* 48 (1968): 421–37.

85. Lieuwen, Edwin. *Mexican Militarism: The Political Rise and Fall of the Mexican Army.* Albuquerque, N. Mex., 1968.

86. López Cámara, Francisco. *La Génesis del liberalismo mexicano.* Mexico, 1954.

87. Macune, Charles W., Jr. "A Test of Federalism: Relations between the Province and State of Mexico and the Mexican Nation, 1823–1824." *Paisano* 4 (1965): 39–57.

88. Mauro, Frédéric. "Comment développer les recherches françaises sur l'histoire de l'Amérique Latine?" *Revue d'Histoire Moderne et Contemporaine* 14 (1967): 426–28.

89. McAlister, Lyle N. *The "Fuero Militar" in New Spain, 1764–1800.* Gainesville, Fla., 1957.

90. Meyer, Jean. "Décolonisation et sous-développement: Vues sur le Mexique au xixᵉ siècle." *Revue d'Histoire Modern et Contemporaine* 14 (1967): 406–23.

91. Meyer, Lorenzo. *México y Estados Unidos en el conflicto petrolero (1917–1942).* Mexico, 1968.

92. Meyer, Michael C. *Mexican Rebel: Pascual Orozco and the Mexican Revolution, 1910–1915.* Lincoln, Nebr., 1967.

93. Michaels, Albert L. "Nationalism in Mexico, 1920-1940." Ph.D. dissertation, University of Pennsylvania, 1967.

94. Miranda, José. *Humboldt y México.* Mexico, 1962.

95. Monroy, Guadalupe. *Archivo histórico de Matías Romero.* Mexico, 1965.

96. Moore, Barrington, Jr. *Social Origins of Dictatorship and Democracy: Lord and Peasant in the Making of the Modern World.* Boston, 1966.

97. Mora, José María Luis. *México y sus revoluciones.* 3 vols. Mexico, 1950.

98. ———. *Obras sueltas.* Mexico, 1963.

99. Munch, Francis J. "Anglo-American Petroleum in the Mexican Revolution, 1910–1915." Ph.D. dissertation, University of Nebraska, in progress.

100. O'Gorman, Edmundo. *Fray Servando Teresa de Mier.* Mexico, 1945.

101. ———. "Hidalgo en la historia." *Memorias de la Academia Mexicana de la Historia* 23 (1964): 239.

102. ———. "Precedentes y sentido de la revolución de Ayutla." In *Plan de Ayutla.* ed. Mexico, Universidad Nacional, pp. 113–69. Mexico: 1954.

103. Olivera Sedano, Alicia. *Aspectos del conflicto religioso de 1926 a 1929.* Mexico, 1966.

104. Oswald, J. Gregory. "La revolutión Mexicana en la historiografía soviética." *Historia Mexicana* 10 (1960): 340–57.

105. Otero, Mariano. *Obras.* 2 vols. Mexico, 1967.

106. Pérez Cabrera, José Manuel. *Fundamentos de una historia de la historiografía cubana.* Havana, 1959.

107. Pletcher, David M. *Rails, Mines, and Progress: Seven American Promoters in Mexico, 1867–1911.* Ithaca, N.Y., 1958.

108. Potash, Robert A. *El Banco de Avío de México: El fomento de la industria, 1821–1846.* Mexico, 1959.

109. ———. "The Historiography of Mexico since 1921." *Hispanic American Historical Review* 40 (1960): 383–424.

110. Powell, Thomas G. "The Indian Question in Central Mexico, 1867–1876." Ph.D. dissertation, Indiana University, in progress.

111. Quintana, Miguel. *Estevan de Antuñano, fundador de la industria textil en Puebla.* 2 vols. Mexico, 1957.

112. Quirarte, Martín. "Historia política: Siglo xix." *Historia Mexicana* 15 (1965–66): 411.

113. Quirk, Robert. *An Affair of Honor: Woodrow Wilson and the Occupation of Veracruz.* Lexington, Ky., 1962.

114. Raat, William D. "Leopoldo Zea and Mexican Positivism: A Reappraisal." *Hispanic American Historical Review* 48 (1968): 1–18.

115. Reed, Nelson. *The Caste War of Yucatán.* Stanford, Calif., 1964.

116. Reyes Heroles, Jesús. "La historia y la acción." *Cuadernos Americanos* 161 (1968): 65–85.

117. ———. "El liberalism mexicano y su significación social." *Cuadernos Americanos* 161 (1968): 91–92.

118. Robertson, William S. *Iturbide of Mexico.* Durham, N.C., 1952.

119. Rodrígues, José Honório. *História e historiadores do Brasil.* São Paulo, 1965.

120. ———. *Historiografía del Brasil.* 2 vols. Mexico, 1957–63.

121. ———. *Historiografía e bibliografía do domínio holandês no Brasil.* Rio de Janeiro, 1949.

122. ———. *Vida e historia.* Rio de Janeiro, 1966.

123. Romanell, Patrick. *Making of the Mexican Mind.* Lincoln, Nebr., 1952.

124. Romero Flores, Jesús. *Historia de la Revolución en Michoacán.* Mexico, 1964.

125. Ross, Stanley R. "Aportación norteamericana a la historiografía de la Revolución Mexicana." *Historia Mexicana* 10 (1960): 282–308.

126. ———. "Bibliography of Sources for Contemporary Mexican History." *Hispanic American Historical Review* 39 (1959): 234–38.

127. ———. "Cosío Villegas' *Historia moderna de México*." *Hispanic American Historical Review* 46 (1966): 276–79.

128. ———. *Francisco I. Madero: Apostle of Mexican Democracy.* New York, 1955.

129. ———. *Francisco I. Madero: Apóstol de la democracia mexicana.* Mexico, 1959.

130. ———, ed. *Fuentes de la historia contemporánea de México: Periódicos y revistas.* 2 vols. Mexico, 1965–66.

131. Scholes, Walter. *Mexican Politics during the Juárez Regime, 1855–1872.* Columbia, S.C., 1957.

132. Sierra, Catalina. *El nacimiento de México.* Mexico, 1960.

133. Sierra, Justo. *Obras completas.* 14 vols. Mexico, 1948–49.

134. Silva Herzog, Jesús. *El agrarismo mexicano y la reforma agraria.* Mexico, 1959.

135. Sims, H. D. "The Expulsion of the Spaniards from Mexico, 1821–1828." Ph.D. dissertation, University of Florida, 1968.

136. Sinkin, Richard N. "Development of Nationalism in Mexico, 1855–76." Ph.D. dissertation, University of Michigan, in progress.

137. Smith, George W. *Chronicles of the Gringos: The U.S. Army in the Mexican War, 1846–1848.* Albuquerque, N. Mex., 1968.

138. Somolinos d'Ardois, Germán. "Historia de la ciencia." *Historia Mexicana* 15 (1965–66): 269–90.

139. Stabb, Martin S. "Indigenism and Racism in Mexican Thought: 1857–1911." *Journal of Inter-American Studies* 1 (1959): 405–23.

140. Stein, Stanley J. "The Historiography of Brazil, 1808–1889." *Hispanic American Historical Review* 40 (1960): 278.

141. ———. "Tasks Ahead for Latin American Historians." *Hispanic American Historical Review* 41 (1961): 424–25.

142. Tamayo, Jorge L., ed. *Benito Juárez: Documentos diversos y correspondencia.* 2 vols. Mexico, 1965.

143. Taracena, Alfonso. *La labor social.* Satillo, Mex., 1958(?).

144. Timmons, W. H. *Morelos: Priest, Soldier, and Statesman of Mexico.* El Paso, Tex., 1963.

145. Torre Villar, Ernesto de la, ed. *La constitución de Apatzingán y los creadores del estado mexicano.* Mexico, 1964.

146. ———, ed. *Correspondencia diplomática franco-mexicana, 1808–1839.* Mexico, 1957.

147. ———, ed. *Estudios sobre el decreto constitucional de Apatzingán.* Mexico, 1964.

148. ———, ed. *Las fuentes francesas para la historia de México y la guerra de intervención.* Mexico, 1962.

149. ———, ed. *El triunfo de la república liberal, 1857–1860.* Mexico, 1960.

150. ———, and Arturo Gómez Camacho. "La intervención francesa." *Historia Mexicana* 15 (1965–66): 584–85.

151. Turner, Frederick C. *The Dynamics of Mexican Nationalism.* Chapel Hill, N.C., 1968.

152. Ulloa Ortiz, Berta. "Historia diplomática." *Historia Mexicana* 15 (1966): 495–530.

153. ———. *La revolución mexicana a través del Archivo de la Secretaría de Relaciones Exteriores.* Mexico, 1963.

145. Valadés, José C. *Don Melchor Ocampo, reformador de México.* Mexico, 1954.

155. ———. *Imaginación y realidad de Francisco I. Madero.* 2 vols. Mexico, 1960.

156. ———. *El pensamiento político de Benito Juárez.* Mexico, n.d.

157. *Veinticinco años de investigación histórica en México.* Mexico, 1966.

158. Vera Estañol, Jorge. *La revolución mexicana: Orígenes y resultados.* Mexico, 1957.

159. Verges, Josep María Miguel i. *La diplomacia española en México, 1822–23.* Mexico, 1956.

160. Vernon, Raymond. *The Dilemma of Mexico's Development.* Cambridge, Mass., 1963.

161. Villoro, Luis. "Historia de las ideas." *Historia Mexicana* 15 (1965–66): 161–195.

162. ———. *La revolución de independencia: Ensayo de interpretación histórica.* Mexico, 1953.

163. Wagley, Charles, ed. "Latin American Historiography." In *Social Science Research on Latin America,* pp. 94–105. New York, 1964.

164. Weckmann, Luis. *Las relaciones franco-mexicanas, 1823–67.* 2 vols. Mexico, 1961–62.

165. Whitaker, Arthur P. "Recent Developments of the Past Decade in the Writing of Latin American History." *Revista de Historia de América* 29 (1950): 129–30.

166. White, David Anthony. "Mexico in World Affairs, 1928–1968." Ph.D. dissertation, UCLA, 1968.

167. Wilkie, James. *The Mexican Revolution: Federal Expenditure and Social Change since 1910.* Berkeley, Calif., 1967.

168. Williams, Peter W. "The Mexican Cristero Rebellion, 1926–1929." Ph.D. dissertation, Yale University, in progress.

169. Womack, John, Jr. *Zapata and the Mexican Revolution.* New York, 1969.

170. Zabre, Alfonso Teja. *Vida de Morelos.* Mexico, 1934.

171. Zarco, Francisco. *Actas oficiales y minutario de decretos del congreso constituyente de 1856–1857.* Mexico, 1957.

172. ———. *Crónica del congreso extraordinario constituyente, 1856–1857.* Mexico, 1957.

173. ———. *Historia del congreso extraordinario constituyente, 1856–1857.* Mexico, 1956.

174. Zea, Leopoldo. *Apogeo y decadencia del positivismo en México.* Mexico, 1944.

175. ———. *Dos etapas del pensamiento en Hispanoamérica.* Mexico, 1949.

176. ———. *El positivismo en México.* Mexico, 1943.

177. Zuno, José G. *Historia de la Revolución en el estado de Jalisco.* Mexico, 1964.

# THE CARIBBEAN:
# THE NATIONAL PERIOD

*Thomas G. Mathews*

No other region in the New World has experienced such history-making political and economic changes in the last twenty-five years as the Caribbean area. Four new fully independent nations, Jamaica, Trinidad and Tobago, Barbados, and Guyana, with an aggregate population of over four million, have been formed. Ten other polities, formerly Dutch, English, and American colonies, have attained an autonomous status with full internal self-government. While the Dominican Republic freed itself from one of the most depraved dictators of any Spanish-speakng country, Haiti came under the control of a high priest of the voodoo cult who retains the loyalty of the superstitious masses through fear. The economic and political revolution in Cuba has monopolized the attention of three continents and at one point almost precipitated an atomic holocaust. Finally, the peaceful economic transformation of the once poverty-plagued island of Puerto Rico has impressed all but the hypercritical social scientist.

As one could rightly expect, then, there has emerged an impressive collection of historical writings from those communities experiencing the euphoric drive of nationalism. Such motivation does not always produce the best works of history. In fact, the revisionists, whether they be the nationalists of Trinidad or the Marxists of Cuba, have produced histories with clearly discernible political motives. The best studies have been those which have transcended national boundaries either by considering the area as a geographic whole or by analyzing a particular regional institution.

One of the most impressive works dealing with the history of the Caribbean appeared in 1956 under the modest title *A Short History of the West Indies* (52). The two authors, J. H. Parry, a student of the colonial empires of the New World, and Philip M. Sherlock, a dedicated teacher concerned with the local heritage of his islands, accomplished the extraordinary achievement of bridging the divisions of the artificial political systems which separated the colonial history of Jamaica from that of Cuba and that of Haiti from its neighbor, the Dominican Republic. No other work has ever attempted to integrate into one concise history the story of the competitive building of Caribbean colonial empires and the embryonic growth of a Caribbean community. Authoritatively and engagingly written, this brief volume has become the cornerstone of Caribbean historical works.

A second major work which transcends the limitations of a national history by dealing with an institution which left its diabolical impression on every island community appeared one year before the period under study, but because of its importance, reference must be made to it. *Capitalism and Slavery* (67), by the brilliant Trinidadian historian Dr. Eric Williams, whose professional interests have been more recently sacrificed to politics, stands as a monumental classic in Caribbean studies. A few who would detract from its value point to its Marxist orientation, but none have refuted its thesis that slavery only began to decline when it was no longer profitable to the commercial interests which had created such a monstrous abomination.

There are studies, written mostly by non-Caribbeanists, which are either marginal to the field of history or not concerned exclusively with the Caribbean. Some deal with the history of the Negro people, the predominant racial group in the Caribbean: for example, the late Frank Tannenbaum's study *Slave and Citizen: The Negro in the Americas* (64), and the sociologist H. Hoetink's recent work entitled *The Two Variants in Caribbean Race Relations* (31). Other works, such as Noël Deerr's *History of Sugar* (17) and Leland Jenks's *The Sugar Industry of the Caribbean* (33), deal with the once all-important agricultural product grown on almost every island of the Caribbean. Strangely enough, no historian has produced a study of the plantation in the Caribbean, although individual monographs on the several varieties of this social institution have been published, such as Sidney Mintz's *Worker in the Cane* (45), Richard Pares's *A West Indian Fortune* (51), Roland Ely's *Cuando Reinaba su Majestad el Azúcar* (20), and Guy Laserre's "Une plantation de canne aux Antilles" (34). Each of these, as well as others, deals with specific islands rather than presenting a comparative and comprehensive study of the institution in the Caribbean. No attempt has been made to focus on the historical development of the Caribbean as a commercial center, as Fernand Braudel did with the Mediterranean, although English, Spanish, and American historians certainly have written about a particular nation's exploitation of the people of the Caribbean. Dexter Perkins's *The United States and the Caribbean* (54), and the Chaunus' *Seville et l' Atlantique* (10) can be cited as examples.

In Central America the same scarcity of works dealing with the region as a whole is noted. Most of the historical works which transcend national interests, such as that by Pedro Joaquín Chamorro (8), deal with the short-lived Central American Federation. Although not of book length, Robert Chamberlain's excellent study, *Francisco Morazán* (7), is worthy of mention. Although great strides have been recently made toward economic integration in the Caribbean and particularly in Central America, the historical writings in the area have not reflected this movement; instead, divisive nationalist sentiments abound in both regions. In the case of the Caribbean countries this may be easier to understand, since these are comparatively new nations, concerned with defining their national culture and clarifying for themselves their nation's heritage.

Since 1954 the Dutch areas of the Caribbean, the Netherlands Antilles and Surinam, have participated as self-governing members with Holland in the Kingdom of the Netherlands. The creation of these two nearly independent states with full local autonomy has stimulated the people to consider themselves as communities with their own unique development, related to but separate from that of Holland. No strong nationalist or independence movement has developed as yet in either Caribbean country, but there are signs in both Surinam and the Netherlands Antilles that a concern for national pride is growing.

In the Netherlands Antilles, Johan Hartog, a long-time Dutch resident of the island of Aruba, where he serves as director of the public library, has turned out a series of historical works on the islands belonging to Holland entitled *The History of the Netherlands Antilles* (28). Based on only an amateur's training in history, Hartog's works, lacking the historian's usual accouterments of cited sources, either through footnotes or bibliography, should be used with care. As would be expected, the works, some of which are translated into English, reflect a natural Dutch bias, but at least they provide a base for later more specialized professional studies.

On the basis of a very promising first essay, one would venture to predict that Alejandro Paula, currently serving as curator of the Netherlands Antilles archives, will be preparing important historical monographs on the history of his islands. This study, entitled *From Objective to Subjective Barriers* (53), makes excellent use of historical material to point out the need for exploration of the past to capture the full personality of the native Antillian.

In contrast to the Netherlands Antilles, Surinam has a much more heterogeneous population, with Javanese, East Indians, Bush Negroes, and American Indians all trying to live together and forge a new nation. The feeling of identity with Holland is not as strong as in the islands; thus interest is expressed in the historical development of Surinam as a nation. As yet no dedicated local historian free from his racial ties and committed only to the as yet undefined nationality of Surinam has come forth. Several rather pedantic studies written from a specialized professional viewpoint have been published. Jan Adhin's *Development Planning in Surinam in Historical Perspective* (2) and F. E. M. Mitrasing's *Tien Jaar Suriname* (46) are examples.

In the French-speaking areas of the Caribbean, the clear orientation offered by Jean Price-Mars in Haiti and Aimée Césaire in Martinique have carried over into the postwar period. The French islands of Guadeloupe and Martinique continue as integrated departments of France, but recently there have been signs of growing interest in local autonomy if it can be secured without weakening the cultural and economic support received from Paris. Césaire's influence, as shown by its Marxist and black orientation, is evident in an outstanding historical study, *La Guadeloupe* (5), of the island of Guadeloupe by the skilled surgeon and current mayor of Pointe-à-Pitre, Dr. Henri Bangou. Monographs are being prepared by a group of young historians led by M. Adelaide, who has specialized in the study of slavery and its abolition on the islands. Aimée Césaire's contribution in bringing out a new edition (1948) of Victor Schoelcher's famous study *Esclavage et colonisation* (61) should not be overlooked. For the colonial period of the French West Indies, the works of Gabriel Debien have provided indispensable material. The most important studies are *Les engagés pour les Antilles* (15) and "La nourriture des esclaves sur les plantations des Antilles francaises au XVIII siècles" (16).

In impoverished Haiti, as Edmund Wilson has observed, more publications per person see the light of day than in any other Latin American country. The recently deceased Jean Price-Mars continued to set the pace and orientation (first expressed in his *Ainsi parla l'oncle,* 1928) for the Haitian historians with his study *Jean Pierre Boyer Bazelais et le drame de Miragoane* (56). The awakening which occurred in Haiti from 1946 on was well expressed in Etienne Charlier's work *Aperçu sur la formation historique de la nation haitienne* (9). The confusion within the avant-garde of the black revolution caused by the enigmatic François Duvalier can be best appreciated by referring to Leslie Manigat's study *Haiti in the Sixties* (41). Momentarily thwarted by the actions of one of its recognized leaders, black nationalism will continue to search for the authentic national spirit of Haiti and will not return to the discarded philosophy of Dantes Bellegarde and his followers.

The wide-spread English-speaking islands offer what appears to be two separate and distinct schools of historians. The one group has specialized in highly skilled monographs dealing with the conditions of slavery, indentured servants, and abolition and its effects on the economy. The distinguished Professor Elsa Goveia, who holds the chair in West Indian history at the University of the West Indies, has established herself as one of the recognized leaders of this school with her *Slave Society in the Leeward Islands in the Seventeenth Century* (22). Another important figure in this group is Professor Douglas Hall, chairman of the history department at UWI who has produced an economic history of nineteenth-century Jamaica entitled *Free Jamaica* (27). Others in the group include Keith Laurence (Trinidad), Woodville Marshall (43), who has worked on the Windward Islands, and Robert Moore of Guyana.

The second school is more concerned with the political problems of the creation of a national or even a regional character. Their works are addressed to a wider audience, rely less on methodical ,archival research, and are more directly concerned than the previous group with correcting the errors of European or American historians. The undisputed leader of the group is the one-time historian and current prime minister of Trinidad-Tobago, Dr. Eric Williams, who presented to his nation on the day of independence a formidable tour de force, *The History of the People of Trinidad and Tobago* (68), written and published within a twelve-month period. Another versatile member of this school is the erudite Professor Gordon Lewis, whose impressive *Growth of the Modern West Indies* (38) is a provocative mixture of scholarship and opinion. Other works belonging to this group include Sir John Mordacai's *The West Indies: The Federal Negotiations* (49), Sir Philip Sherlock's *The West Indies* (62), and Francis Mark's *The History of the Barbados Workers' Union* (42).

On occasion the two schools clash, as evidenced by Elsa Goveia's caustic demolition of Dr. Williams's unfortunate excess in his *British Historians and the West Indies* (66). But for the most part the two schools complement one another, and in the long run each is essential to the other. The historians of the area eagerly await the long-announced three-volume historical study of the entire Caribbean currently being prepared under the guidance of the historians at the University of the West Indies. Hopefully, this work will bridge the cultural cleavages in the Caribbean which as yet have only been successfully hurdled in the works of Gordon Lewis.

Only recently have the small Virgin Islands produced any local works of history. Two authors acknowledge their indebtedness to José Antonio Jarvis, the outstanding local historian of the previous generation. Modest in scope and depth, both Valdemar Hill's *A Golden Jubilee* (29) and Darwin Creque's *The U.S. Virgins and the Eastern Caribbean* (12) are characteristic of the type of historical writing being done by a proud people exploring the past so as to better fulfill their responsibilities as an independent nation in the future.

Two distinct groups of historical writings can be discerned in Puerto Rico. One is concerned with the colonial period and most of its publications are based on research carried out almost exclusively in the Archivo de Indias in Seville. Perhaps the most typical writer of this school is the Spanish priest, Vicente Murga (50), whose four formidable volumes on the colonization of the island constitute a veritable gold mine of new information concerning Juan Ponce de León and other early colonizers. Others in this category include Bibiano Torres (65), who treats the problem of the heirs of Columbus and the career of Alejandro Ramírez, and Arturo Dávila (14), whose speciality is ecclesiastical art history. Some of the work of this group has been sponsored by the Institute of Puerto Rican Culture.

The other group, although also concentrating their efforts on the colonial period, is much less restricted to Spanish archival sources. The works, while equally based on solid scholarship, are more concerned with the creation of a national heritage. Many of these historians, such as Professor Lidio Cruz Monclova (who, because of his prolificacy, is not typical of this group), were trained by the outstanding Puerto Rican historian of the previous generation, Antonio S. Pedreira. Cruz Monclova's best work, in contrast to the weighty tomes on the nineteenth century, is perhaps his concise study of the tragic year of 1887 (13). Other writers belonging to this group include Luis Díaz Soler, with his *Historia de la esclavitud negra en Puerto Rico* (18) and the political biography *Rosendo Matienzo Cintrón* (19); Arturo Morales Carrión, who wrote *Puerto Rico and the Non-Hispanic Caribbean* (48); and Isabel Gutiérrez Arroyo (25), whose studies in historiography are well known and widely respected.

There is a reluctance on the part of the Puerto Rican professional historian to treat the history of the present century. In Puerto Rico, as in most Latin American countries, politics premeates all groups, and even the most objective native historian is likely to avoid any accusation of partisanship simply by ignoring recent history. Thus works on recent Puerto Rican history have been produced by long-time non-native residents of the island such as Robert Anderson, with his *Party Politics in Puerto Rico* (3); Gordon Lewis with *Puerto Rico: Freedom and Power in the Caribbean* (39); and Thomas Mathews, with *Puerto Rican Politics and the New Deal* (44).

In contrast to the generous number of historical studies of Puerto Rico, the study of history in the Dominican Republic has suffered from the stultifying restrictions of Trujillo and the uncertainty of the chaotic aftermath of his dictatorship. One historian, Emilio Rodríguez Demorizi, has continued to produce impressive works during both periods, although at times he has identified himself too closely with the interests of the Trujillo family. Solidly based on archival research, the work of Rodríguez Demorizi includes *Documentos para la historia de la República Dominicana, 1844–1865* (58), and *El Cancionero de Lilís*.

The earlier anti-Haitian bias of much of the historical work being done in the Dominican Republic, such as Joaquín Balaguer's *Dominican Reality* (4), seems to be disappearing. No work at all is being done on the colonial period. Recently Dr. Harmannus Hoetink, a sociologist with a strong inclination toward history, has published a series of well-researched articles in *Caribbean Studies* on the late nineteenth century when, from all appearances, the basic economic and social structure of the contemporary republic was established. One of the very few benefits of the overthrow of Juan Bosch was the guarantee that historians would soon have the advantage of his extremely perceptive and penetrating analysis of the social history of the Dominican Republic. This work will be available shortly.

Just as in the Dominican Republic, so in Cuba the historical writings can be divided into "before" and "after" categories. Prior to the Castro revolution the most important historical work was the publication of the ten-volume *Historia de la nación cubana* (24), to which some thirty distinguished Cuban historians contributed. The editors of the series included Ramiro Guerra y Sánchez, José M. Pérez Cabrera, Juan J. Ramos, and Emeterio Santovenia. Evaluations of this monu-

mental collection have been consistently favorable. One of the younger and more promising contributors to the study, Julio Le Riverend
Brusone (36, 37), has continued to publish impressive monographs on
the early colonial development of Cuba. Others, such as the recently
deceased Emilio Leuschenring, while no less Marxist in their interpretations, have been somewhat less than objective in their contributions
to the postrevolutionary reevaluation of Cuban history.

With one or two exceptions, the quality of historical works in the
pre-Castro period was superior to that in the postrevolutionary period.
Herminio Portell Vilá's excellent study of Narciso López (55) and the
events of the mid-nineteenth century and Ramiro Guerra y Sánchez's
history of the Ten Years' War (1868–78) (23) are two outstanding examples of the careful interpretive works which were published in the
earlier period. Although not works of history, the fertile studies of
African influence on Cuban music by the sociologist Fernando Ortiz
are of such monumental importance to an understanding of the Cuban
people that recognition must be offered.

The death of a number of prolific Cuban writers, such as Fernando
Ortiz, Ramiro Guerra y Sánchez, and Emilio Roig de Leuschenring,
and the exile of others, such as Pérez Cabrera and Herminio Portell
Vilá, have naturally reduced the number and quality of historical
works in the new Cuba. Significant work continues to be turned out
in *Bohemia* by Julio Le Riverend Brusone, but except for an occasional study, most of the work published in Cuba now is of a revisionist nature. This new work relies heavily on reinterpretation and is
rarely based on a reexamination of archival material. Of all the outpouring from Cubans in exile, only one work is worthy of mention.
This is Andrés Suárez's recent study, *Cuba: Castroism or Communism*
(63).

The growing nationalism of the Caribbean area, as reflected in
the historical writings of the region, should have yielded a number of
impressive biographies of leading Caribbeanists. Unfortunately, this is
not the case. More personalities untouched by the adulations of a
biographer can be noted, such as José Martí, Luis Muñoz Rivera,
Antenor Fermin, and Gregorio Luperón than those who have been
more fortunate, like Rafael Leonidas Trujillo, Henri Christophe, and
Eugenio María de Hostos. More works have been written about Toussaint L'Overture and Fidel Castro, but the questionable quality of
most of them precludes reference to them. Three exceptions might be
mentioned: Jesús de Galíndez's *La Era de Trujillo* (21), which cost

the author his life, the admirable work of Robert Crassweller on the Dominican dictator (11), and the recent balanced work by Herbert Matthews on Fidel Castro.

Even scarcer are good autobiographies. In an area where politicians are caught up in the full-time task of political survival, not to mention mere physical survival, few have found time to take up the pen in their own defense. Dr. Cheddi Jagan, who has been kept out of his rightful office by scheming colonial bureaucrats and interfering CIA agents, has penned a highly ex parte polemic entitled *The West on Trial* (32). The indefatigable Dr. Eric Williams has just published his premature biography, *Inward Hunger* (69), while still enjoying a very successful tenure as prime minister of his nation. Others now in forced retirement, such as Luis Muñoz Marín and Norman Manley, could better engage themselves in writing than in futile attempts to help their fallen parties regain power. Finally, if one might project into the future, the memoirs of Eugenio María de Hostos, now guarded under lock and key in the Library of Congress, will be made available to the public in 1975.

With the struggle against old-style colonialism in the Caribbean obviously over, and new nations and their founding fathers being challenged by the younger generation, the next twenty-five years to the close of this century should provide a mellowing of outlook and a more measured evaluation by historians more skillfully prepared than most of those whose works have been under review in this paper.

# BIBLIOGRAPHY

1. Adelaide, Jacques. "La colonisation française aux Antilles à la fin du XVIIᵉ siècle, d'après les 'Voyages aux Isles d'Amerique' du Père Labat." *Bulletin de la Societé d'Histoire de la Guadeloupe* 8 (1967).
2. Adhin, Jan. *Development Planning in Surinam in Historical Perspective.* Groningen, Neth., 1961.
3. Anderson, Robert. *Party Politics in Puerto Rico.* Stanford, Calif., 1965.
4. Balaguer, Joaquín. *Dominican Reality.* Mexico, 1949.
5. Bangou, Henri. *La Guadeloupe.* 2 vols. Paris, 1962–63.
6. Césaire, Aimée, ed. *Esclavage et colonisation.* Paris, 1948.
7. Chamberlain, Robert. *Francisco Morazán: Champion of Central America Federation.* Coral Gables, Fla., 1950.
8. Chamorro, Pedro Joaquín. *Historia de la Federación de la América Central 1823–1840.* Madrid, 1951.
9. Charlier, Etienne. *Aperçu sur la formation historique de la nation haitienne.* Port-au-Prince, 1954.
10. Chaunu, Pierre et Huguette Chaunu. *Seville et l'Atlantique.* Paris, 1955.
11. Crassweller, Robert. *Trujillo: The Life and Times of a Caribbean Dictator.* New York, 1966.
12. Creque, Darwin. *The U.S. Virgins and the Eastern Caribbean.* Philadelphia, 1968.
13. Cruz Monclova, Lidio. *Historia del año de 1887.* Río Piedras, P.R., 1958.
14. Dávila, Arturo. *Las encíclicas sobre la Revolución Hispanoamericana y su divulgación en Puerto Rico.* San Juan, 1965.
15. Debien, Gabriel. *Les engagés pour les Antilles.* Paris, 1952.
16. ———. "La nourriture des esclaves sur les plantations des Antilles francaises au XVIII siècle," *Caribbean Studies* 4 (1964): 3–27.
17. Deerr, Noël. *History of Sugar.* London, 1949–50.
18. Díaz Soler, Luis. *Historia de la esclavitud negra en Puerto Rico.* Río Piedras, P.R., 1953.
19. ———. *Rosendo Matienzo Cintrón.* Río Piedras, P.R., 1960.
20. Ely, Roland. *Cuando Reinaba su Majestad el Azúcar.* Buenos Aires, 1963.
21. Galíndez, Jesús de. *La era de Trujillo.* Santiago de Chile, 1956.
22. Goveia, Elsa. *Slave Society in the Leeward Islands in the Seventeenth Century.* New Haven, Conn., 1965.

23. Guerra y Sánchez, Ramiro. *Guerra de los Diez Años 1868–78*. Vols. 1 and 2. Havana, 1952.

24. ———, et al. *Historia de la nación cubana*. 10 vols. Havana, 1952.

25. Gutiérrez Arroyo, Isabel. *Historiografía puertorriqueña desde la memoria de Melgarejo*. San Juan, 1957.

26. ———. *El reformismo ilustrado en Puerto Rico*. Mexico, 1953.

27. Hall, Douglas. *Free Jamaica*. New Haven, Conn., 1959.

28. Hartog, Johan. *The History of the Netherlands Antilles*. 3 vols. Oranjestad- Aruba, Neth. W.I. 1961.

29. Hill, Valdemar. *A Golden Jubilee*. New York, 1967.

30. Hoetink, Harmannus. "Materiales para el estudio de la República Dominicana en la segunda mitad del siglo XIX." *Caribbean Studies* 5 (1966): 3–21; 7 (1968): 3–34; 8 (1969): 3–37; 9 (1970): 5–26.

31. ———. *The Two Variants in Caribbean Race Relations*. London, 1967.

32. Jagan, Cheddi. *The West on Trial*. London, 1966.

33. Jenks, Leland. *The Sugar Industry of the Caribbean*. N.P., 1944.

34. Laserre, Guy. "Une plantation de canne aux Antilles," *Les Cahiers, d'Outre Mer* 5 (1952): 297–329.

35. Laurence, Keith. "Evolution of Long-Term Labour Contracts in Trinidad and British Guiana." In *The Caribbean in Transition,* ed. by Fuat Andic and Thomas Mathews. Madrid, 1965.

36. Le Riverend Brusone, Julio, ed. "Documentos para la historia económica y social de Cuba." *Boletín del Archivo Nacional* (Havana) 55 (1957): 9–37.

37. ———. "Relaciones entre Nueva España y Cuba 1518–1820." *Revista de Historia de América*. 37–38 (1954): 45–108.

38. Lewis, Gordon. *Growth of the Modern West Indies*. London, 1968.

39. ———. *Puerto Rico: Freedom and Power in the Caribbean*. New York, 1963.

40. Lugo Lovatón, Ramón. [Francisco] *Sánchez*. Vols. 1 and 2. Ciudad Trujillo, 1947–48.

41. Manigat, Leslie. *Haiti in the Sixties*. Washington, D.C., 1964.

42. Mark, Francis. *The History of the Barbados Workers' Union*. Bridgetown, Barbados, n.d.

43. Marshall, Woodville. "Social and Economic Problems in the Windward Islands, 1838–65." In *Caribbean in Transition,* ed. by Fuat Andic and Thomas Mathews. Madrid, 1965.

44. Mathews, Thomas. *Puerto Rican Politics and the New Deal*. Gainesville, Fla., 1960.

45. Mintz, Sidney. *Worker in the Cane*. New Haven, Conn., 1960.

46. Mitrasing, F.E.M. *Tien Jaar Suriname.* Leiden, Neth., 1969.

47. Monclus, Miguel Angel. *El caudillismo en la República Domincana, 1801–1916.* Ciudad Trujillo, n.d.

48. Morales Carrion, Arturo. *Puerto Rico and the Non-Hispanic Caribbean.* Río Piedras, P.R., 1952.

49. Mordacai, John. *The West Indies: The Federal Negotiations.* London, 1968.

50. Murga, Vicente. *Historia documental de Puerto Rico.* 4 vols. Rio Piedras, P.R., 1956.

51. Pares, Richard. *A West Indian Fortune.* London, 1950.

52. Parry, John H. and Philip Sherlock. *A Short History of the West Indies.* New York, 1956.

53. Paula, Alejandro. *From Objective to Subjective Barriers.* Curaçao, Neth. Antilles, 1967.

54. Perkins, Dexter. *The United States and the Caribbean.* New York, 1947.

55. Portell Vilá, Herminio. *Narciso López y su época 1848–1850.* Havana, 1952.

56. Price-Mars, Jean. *Jean Pierre Boyer Bazelais et le drama de Miragoane.* Port-au-Prince, 1948.

57. Rodrigo, Facio. *Trayectoria y crisis de la Federación Centroamericana.* San José, C.R., 1949.

58. Rodríguez Demorizi, Emilio. *Documentos para la historia de la República Dominicana, 1844–1865.* Santiago, D.R., 1944–47.

59. Roig de Leuchsenring, Emilio. *La guerra libertadora cubana de los treinta años 1868–1898.* Havana, 1952.

60. Ruben, Vera, ed. *Plantations Systems of the New World.* Washington, D.C., 1969.

61. Schoelcher, Victor. *Esclavage et colonisation.* Paris, 1948.

62. Sherlock, Philip. *The West Indies.* London, 1966.

63. Suárez, Andrés. *Cuba: Castroism or Communism.* Boston, 1967.

64. Tannenbaum, Frank. *Slave and Citizen: The Negro in the Americas.* New York, 1947.

65. Torres, Bibiano. *Historia de Puerto Rico en la segunda mitad del siglo XVIII.* San Juan, 1968.

66. Williams, Eric. *British Historians and the West Indies.* London, 1966.

67. ———. *Capitalism and Slavery.* Chapel Hill, N.C., 1944.

68. ———. *The History of the People of Trinidad and Tobago.* New York, 1964.

69. ———. *Inward Hunger.* London, 1969.

# Part Two

# RESEARCH IN
# POLITICAL SCIENCE

# 2. RESEARCH IN
# POLITICAL SCIENCE

Scholarship in Latin American political science in the last twenty-five years has concentrated heavily on institutional developments and inter-American relations. The institutional studies have focused on the Roman Catholic Church, the organized labor movement, and the military establishment. In each case one can discern a definite trend away from the general study covering the entire Latin American area to more specific works treating the development of the institution in individual countries or carefully defined geocultural subregions. The pioneer efforts of J. Lloyd Mecham on the church, Edwin Lieuwen on the military, and Moisés Poblete Troncoso on organized labor continue to serve as starting points for the research scholar, but some of the initial findings are being questioned, refined, expanded, and in some cases reversed. Indeed, the pioneers are often in the vanguard of the revisionist movement and are not hesitant to suggest that some of their tentative hypotheses may no longer be applicable and should be subjected to the test of the individual country.

The study of inter-American relations continues to occupy the political scientist, the diplomatic historian, the journalist, and the retired diplomat much as it has since the Western Hemisphere severed political ties with Europe in the late eighteenth and early nineteenth centuries. While the demise of polemicism is scarcely upon us, the last twenty-five years has witnessed an increase in serious studies by professional scholars quite willing to put in their time, if permitted, in the pertinent foreign relations archives.

Without question the greatest change in the nature of political science scholarship on Latin America in the post–World War II period is the rapid growth and increasing acceptance of empirical studies. Frederick Turner, writing on the church, and Stephen Rozman on the military, find quantitative methodology much more pervasive than do Robert Alexander, analyzing studies on labor, and Roger Trask, who considers inter-American relations. But if trends in the 1960s augur anything for the future, one could reasonably expect that models and typologies will soon be used extensively in analyses of the labor movement and the diplomatic relations of the United States and Latin America.

All four of the contributors, while acknowledging improvement, recognize that much remains to be done. They call for both United States and Latin scholars to respond to the challenges posed by the new methodology and the need for more systematic archival research.

# ORGANIZED LABOR

*Robert J. Alexander*

Latin American trade unionism and labor relations is an area which has received relatively little study, either by Latin Americans or North Americans. Since World War II some books and pamphlets have been written on organized labor in the area as a whole and some studies have been made of the labor movements of particular countries. There is a growing number of articles on one aspect or another of labor problems in the region; in the last decade a few doctoral theses and other unpublished studies have been completed, and some are currently in progress.

Of course, the labor organizations of the various countries of the region have turned out a large amount of material, which is one kind of prime source for the study of labor in Latin America. This includes reports of congresses, periodicals, and studies of particular unions or of problems they have faced. Such material is too extensive and too diffuse to occupy us in this paper, which will be confined to the more general type of treatment of the subject. We shall also not deal with the question of labor and social legislation, which has been a major preoccupation of Latin American researchers in the field. We shall take note only of studies which have centered on organized labor and contain considerable material on the actual functioning of the organized workers' groups. Finally, a number of periodicals since World War II have dealt more or less extensively with organized labor in Latin America. At the end of this piece, we shall note the most important of these.

## GENERAL STUDIES IN ENGLISH AND SPANISH

Several volumes have been published since the end of World War II which have dealt in general terms with the Latin American labor movement. One of the earliest of these was Moisés Poblete Troncoso's *El movimiento obrero latinoamericano* (65). Two other pioneer studies were the pamphlet of Stephen Naft, *Labor in Latin America* (58), published as Confidential Report No. 22 by News Background in 1947, and Robert J. Alexander's *Labour Movements of Latin America* (10). Alexander also wrote a study which was published in Spanish by the Pan American Union in 1950. This work, *Reseña del movimiento*

155

*obrero en la América Latina* (13), was withdrawn from publication a few months after its release because of protests from the Venezuelan dictatorship of that time against references to organized labor in that country.

Víctor Alba has been a prolific writer about the Latin American labor movement. His first work in this field was *Le mouvement ouvrier en Amerique Latine* (5), published in 1953. He later published three additional studies in various languages: *Esquema histórico del movimiento obrero en América Latina* (2), *Historia del movimiento obrero en América Latina,* and *Politics and the Labor Movement in Latin America* (6), a sketch of ideological tendencies within Latin American labor during the twentieth century. Another general study of Latin American labor in English is the work of the Chilean Moisés Poblete Troncoso, one of the earliest students of Latin American labor, and Ben G. Burnett, a United States scholar, entitled *The Rise of the Latin American Labor Movement* (66). In 1962 the New York State School of Industrial and Labor Relations published Myles Gavin's pamphlet *Unionism in Latin America* (35). Finally, in the category of general studies in English, Robert J. Alexander's *Organized Labor in Latin America* (11) should be mentioned.

Several studies have been made of international labor organizations in the Latin American area. One of the most important of these is Sinclair Snow's *The Pan American Federation of Labor* (85). Another volume in this category is a publication of the Research Center in Economic Development and Cultural Change of the University of Chicago entitled *U.S.–Latin American Relations: United States Business and Labor in Latin America* (71), a study prepared at the request of the Subcommittee on the American Republics Affairs of the Committee on Foreign Relations of the United States Senate. Also of interest are two theses, one of which is H. W. Berger's doctoral dissertation, "Union Diplomacy: American Labor's Foreign Policy in Latin America" (19), prepared at the University of Wisconsin in 1966 under the supervision of Professor William Appleman Williams; the other is a master's essay submitted to Rutgers University in 1958 by Marcos Perera Raphael, entitled "United States Labor and the Inter-American Labor Movement" (62).

Another book in this general category which is worthy of particular note is Serafino Romualdi's posthumous autobiographical work, *Presidents and Peons* (76). For fifteen years Romualdi was the Latin American representative of the American Federation of Labor and the

AFL-CIO; the organizer of the American Institute for Free Labor Development, he knew the Latin American labor movement at first hand probably better than any other North American citizen. A French study in this same general area should also be mentioned. This is Pedro Reiser's *L'Organisation regionale interamericaine des travailleurs (ORIT) de la confederation internationale des syndicats libres (CISL) de 1951 a 1961* (69).

Most of the works cited above are either descriptive or historical. There have been relatively few attempts to theorize about the Latin American labor movements. However, one such effort is worthy of note: *Sindicato y comunidad, dos tipos de estructura sindical Latino Americana* (88), written by Torcuato di Tella, Lucien Brams, Jean Daniel Reynaud, and Alain Touraine. This work is an attempt to develop a model for Latin American trade unionism, based largely on the unions in Chile.

## CHAPTERS IN BOOKS

In addition to the books which are generally concerned with a discussion and analysis of Latin American organized labor, a number of works have been published since World War II containing chapters dealing with the labor movement. Some of these volumes are general studies of Latin American politics and government. Chapters on labor include Alexander Edelmann's chapter entitled "Labor: A Fair Share or Else" in his *Latin American Government and Politics* (31); Harry Stark's chapter "Labor and Social Security Programs" in *Social and Economic Frontiers in Latin America* (86); and the chapter "Labor and Social Legislation" in *Governments of Latin America* (63) by William Pierson and Federico Gil. In the same category is Robert J. Alexander's chapter "Organized Labor and Politics" in the volume edited by Harold Eugene Davis, *Government and Politics in Latin America* (28).

Several chapters have also appeared in books by Latin Americans which have dealt with the organized labor movement. These include the chapter entitled "Inadequadas condições de trabalho" in the volume *Situação social da América Latina* (23), published by the Centro Latino Americano de Pesquisas em Ciencias Sociais (Rio de Janeiro), as well as the chapter entitled "Nascimento do movimento operario" in *América Latina a luz do marxismo,* published in São Paulo in 1965.

Finally, in this category there are several chapters on organized labor in books published in the United States which are not textbooks on Latin American politics and government but deal more generally with the Latin American area. Two such chapters are Robert J. Alexander's "Latin America's Secular Labor Movement as an Instrument of Social Change," and Emilio Máspero's "Latin America's Labor Movement of Christian Democratic Orientation as an Instrument of Social Change," both of which are to be found in the volume edited by William V. D'Antonio and Frederic Pike entitled *Religion, Revolution, and Reform: New Forces for Change in Latin America* (27). In this same category is Henry Landsberger's chapter "The Labor Elite: Is It Revolutionary?" in *Elites in Latin America,* edited by Seymour Martin Lipset and Aldo Solari (50). This last is, to a considerable degree, a polemic against the position maintained by Alexander in the chapter of the book by D'Antonio and Pike mentioned above. Finally, Robert J. Alexander's study *Communism in Latin America* (8) has a chapter entitled "Communists in the Latin American Labor Movement."

### Studies in English of National Labor Movements

A number of volumes have been written, and several published, in English since World War II treating the labor movements in one or more of the Latin American countries. One of the most important of these is Robert J. Alexander's *Labor Relations in Argentina, Brazil, and Chile* (9), published in 1962. Several studies have dealt with the labor movement of Argentina, one of the oldest and largest trade union groups in Latin America. These include Samuel Baily's *Labor, Nationalism, and Politics in Argentina* (17) and John Deiner's "ATLAS— A Labor Instrument of Argentine Expansionism Under Perón" (29), an unpublished Ph.D. thesis presented at Rutgers University in 1969.

One very good study has been made of the rural labor movement of Brazil. This is Cynthia Naegele Hewitt's "An Introduction to the Rural Labor Movement of Pernambuco" (36), published in mimeographed form by the Institute of Latin American Studies of Columbia University in September, 1965. The Chilean labor movement has been the subject of several studies. These include Henry Landsberger's "Ideology and Practical Politics: Two Years of Christian Democratic Labor Policy" (48) and the same author's *Do Ideological Differences Have Personal Correlates? A Study of Chilean Labor Leaders at the*

*Local Level* (47). There is also James O. Morris's *Elites, Intellectuals, and Consensus: A study of the Social Question and the Industrial Relations System* (57), dealing with early labor organization in Chile and the forces responsible for passage of that country's early labor legislation. The labor movement of Colombia is the subject of one excellent study, a doctoral thesis by M. Urrutia, "The Development of the Colombian Labor Movement" (96), presented at the University of California in 1967.

Trade unionism and labor relations in Cuba, particularly since the advent of the Castro regime, have been tested by several authors. These studies include *Labor Conditions in Communist Cuba* (26), published by the Cuban Economic Research Project of the University of Miami; Maurice Zeitlin's *Revolutionary Politics and the Cuban Working Class* (98), a study of workers' attitudes, based on a survey made by the author in Cuba in 1962; and Camilo Mesa Lago's *The Labor Sector and Socialist Distribution in Cuba* (54), which deals particularly with the controversy over "material" versus "moral" incentives in the labor relations of Castro's Cuba. One volume has appeared which has dealt with the problem of labor in Ecuador. This is B. R. Salz's *Human Element in Industrialization* (80), published by the American Anthropological Association in 1955. A pioneer study in English of Latin American trade unionism was made in the early 1950s with regard to Guatemala. This is Archer Bush's *Organized Labor in Guatemala* (21), a thesis presented to Colgate University, and subsequently published by Colgate in mimeographed form in 1950.

The Mexican labor movement has probably received more attention than any other in Latin America from scholars in the United States. Within the last few years, dissertations have been prepared by M. E. Thompson (90), H. A. Levenstein (49), and R. C. Miller (55). Recently published volumes treating Mexican labor include Joe C. Ashby's *Organized Labor and the Mexican Revolution Under Cárdenas* (16) and Robert Paul Millon's biographical study *Mexican Marxist: Vicente Lombardo Toledano* (56), dealing with one of the country's major trade union leaders. One of the most important labor studies concerning a particular Latin American country has been James L. Payne's *Labor and Politics in Peru* (60). It presents a novel view of the strategy and tactics used by the organized workers of that country. One study of labor relations in Puerto Rico has been of some importance. This is L. F. Silva's Ph.D. thesis, "Public Wage Fixing and Its Effect on Collective Bargaining and the Labor Movement in

Puerto Rico" (83), presented at the University of Wisconsin in 1962. Organized labor in the West Indies has also received some attention from those writing in English. Two volumes are worthy of special mention. The first was the International Labor Organization's *Labor Policies in the West Indies* (41), published in 1952. Interesting, too, is the biography of the Barbadian labor leader Sir Grantley Adams by F. A. Hoyos, entitled *The Rise of West Indian Democracy: The Life and Times of Sir Grantley Adams* (37). Also of major importance in this area is William H. Knowles' *Trade Union Development and Industrial Relations in the Bristish West Indies* (46), written by a long-time professor of economics and labor relations at the Inter-American University of Puerto Rico.

Finally, two volumes have been published by the International Labor Organization concerning trade unionism and labor conditions in Venezuela during the dictatorship of General Marcos Pérez Jiménez in the 1950s. These are *Freedom of Association and Conditions of Work in Venezuela* (39), a report of an ILO mission sent to the country as a result of complaints by Venezuelan unionists; and *Freedom of Association and Conditions of Work in Venezuela: Observations of the Government of Venezuela on the Report of the ILO Mission* (40), released in 1951 as an answer to the earlier report.

## CHAPTERS ON LABOR IN SPECIFIC COUNTRIES

Several volumes in English which have treated one or another of the Latin American countries in general include chapters on organized labor. Thus, Robert J. Alexander has several chapters on organized labor in his books *The Peron Era* (12), *The Bolivian National Revolution* (7), and *The Venezuelan Democratic Revolution* (14). Ronald Schneider likewise devotes chapters 6 and 7 to organized labor in his *Communism in Guatemala, 1944–1954* (82), and Daniel James similarly assigns chapter 6, "The Key—Labor," to the same subject in his *Red Design for the Americas: Guatemalan Prelude* (42). Karl Schmitt also deals with labor in chapter 4, "Organized Labor and the Communists," in his *Communism in Mexico* (81).

Other more general books, not dealing in their entirety with Latin America, also contain chapters about Latin American labor. These include Robert J. Alexander's chapter, "Brazil, Argentina, and Chile," in Walter Galenson's *Labor in Developing Economies* (33), and Alexander's chapter, "Organized Labor in the Bolivian Revolution," which appeared in Everett M. Kassalow's *National Labor Movements in the Post War World* (45). Similarly, the book by William Z. Foster, long-time leader of the Communist Party of the United States, entitled *Outline Political History of the Americas* (32), devotes considerable attention to the labor movement in the area.

## Spanish- and Portugese-Language Studies of Labor in Particular Countries

Various books have been published during the last two and a half decades in the various Latin American countries dealing with the labor movements in those nations. Such studies have been particularly important in a few countries of the region. Argentine organized labor particularly has been treated extensively by national writers. One of the most notable books on Argentine organized labor is Sebastián Marotta's two-volume *El movimiento sindical argentino* (52). Marotta is an old-time syndicalist and for many years was a leader of the country's printing trades workers unions. A third volume by Marotta is said to be in preparation, although it has not yet been published. Another significant volume is Roberto Carri's *Sindicatos y poder en la Argentina* (22), an apologia for Augusto Vandor, the leader of the Metal Workers Union and a Peronista with independent ideas; probably the most important post-Perón trade union leader, Vandor was murdered in Buenos Aires in June, 1969.

Juan C. Juárez's *Los trabajadores en función social* (44) has both a sketch of Argentine labor history and an analysis of then existing unions, from a Peronista point of view. Luis Ramicone's *Apuntes para la historia: La organización gremial obrera en la actualidad* (68) also treats the history of Argentine labor. Jerónimo Remorino's *La nueva legislación social argentina* (70) is a study of Argentine labor legislation, particularly that passed under Perón, by one of the principal figures in the Perón regime, written against the background of the country's labor history. Several writers since the fall of Perón have sought to interpret the impact of his administration on the labor movement. One of these was the Socialist leader David Tieffenberg, who dealt with these matters in his study *Exigencias proletarias a la revolución y la legislación obrera en el régimen peronista* (91). Another point of view is presented in *El movimiento obrero en los orígenes del peronismo* (67) by Juan Carlos Portantiero and Miguel Marmis, which analyzes the subject from a Marxist perspective.

Two other books on Argentine labor are worthy of notice. One is José Panettieri's *Los trabajadores en tiempo de la inmigración masiva en Argentina, 1870–1910* (59), which studies the early years of Argentine organized labor. The other is Eustaquio Tolosa's *El problema portuario argentino resuelto* (92), concerned particularly with the port workers' organizations.

In recent years several volumes have been published in Portuguese dealing more or less directly with organized labor in Brazil. These include Leoncio Rodrigues's *Conflito industrial e sindicalismo no Brasil* (74), Luiz Pereira's *Trabalho e desenvolvimento no Brasil* (61), Asis Simão's *Sindicato e estado* (84), a study of the relations between the unions and the government, and Evardo Dias's *História das lutas sociais no Brasil* (30), which chronicles the labor movement and its struggles as well as other social conflicts in the republic. Finally, the origins of the Brazilian labor movement are treated extensively in *O ano vermelho: A revolução russa e seus reflexos no Brasil* (18), a study of the impact of the Russian Revolution on Brazil, by Moniz Bandeira, Clovis Melo, and A. T. Andrade.

Several studies of Chilean organized labor have also appeared since World War II. Two of these, Francisco Walker Linares's *Panorama del derecho social chileno* (97) and Moisés Poblete Troncoso's *El derecho del trabajo y la seguridad social en Chile* (64), are basically studies of labor and social legislation, but also contain considerable information on labor history. The third, Julio César Jobet's *Recabarren: Los orígenes del movimiento obrero y del socialismo chilenos* (43), is a study of one of the principal early leaders of the Chilean labor movement. *Trayectoria y administración del movimiento sindical chileno, 1946–1962* (95), published by the Instituto de Organización y Administración of the Faculty of Economic Sciences of the University of Chile in 1963, is a study of the post–World War II Chilean labor movement.

As yet, no real study in any language has been made of the labor movement of Bolivia. For a somewhat distorted report on the post-1952 Central Obrera Boliviana, one can consult chapters 6 and 7 of *El marxismo en Bolivia, informe en mayoría de la Comisión Designada por el II Congreso de la Confederación Interamericana de Defensa del Continente, sobre la situación interna de Bolivia* (53).

So far, we have not encountered any extensive treatment of the post-Castro labor movement in Cuba. However, for a survey of the pre-Castro unions, with particular reference to their legal position, one might consult Fausto Clavijo Aguilera's *Los sindicatos en Cuba* (25). No thorough study has been made, either, of the unions of the Dominican Republic. However, Jesús de Galíndez has a chapter on labor in his famous *La era de Trujillo* (34).

The Mexican labor movement has probably been more extensively studied than any other by Spanish-speaking writers. Undoubtedly the most prolific author has been Rosendo Salazar, who had published several things on the subject before World War II, and since that conflict has produced *La carta del trabajo de la Revolución Mexicana* (77), a study of the influences which were responsible for the labor clauses of the Constitution of 1917. Salazar's *Historia de la CTM* (78) is a study of what is still the largest central labor body in Mexico and a volume which has been described by Howard Cline as "patchy but important." Salazar's *Líderes y sindicatos* (79) is a study of the leaders of the Mexican trade union movement. Luis Araiza has also written two large works on Mexican labor. One, *Historia de la casa del obrero mundial* (15), is a survey of the first trade union group formed after the beginning of the Mexican Revolution. Another, *Historia del movimiento obrero mexicano,* was to be a four-volume history of the Mexican labor movement, which was scheduled for publication in 1964, although we do not know whether it has yet appeared.

Ricardo Treviño, one of the oldest Mexican labor leaders, and a founder of the CROM in 1918, published a volume *El movimiento obrero en México, su evolución ideológica* (93). Other studies of Mexican labor include Alfonso López Aparicio's *El movimiento obrero en México: Antecedentes, desarrollo y tendencias* (51), Dolores Beatriz Chapoy Bonifaz's *El movimiento obrero y el sindicato en México* (24), and José Revueltas's *Ensayo sobre un proletariado sin cabeza* (72), a severe criticism of the labor leadership of the early 1960s from a left-wing Marxist point of view. Victor Alba also published a study of Mexican labor leadership entitled *El líder: Ensayo sobre el dirigente sindical* (1) in 1957.

Mention should be made of three other volumes which, although not dealing directly with the Mexican organized labor movement, contain extensive information about it. These are Guadalupe Rivera Marín's *El mercado del trabajo: Relaciones obrero-patronales* (73), R. Rojas Carria's *Tratado de cooperativismo mexicano* (75), and Chapter XIII, "El problema obrero," in Victor Alba's *Las ideas sociales contemporáneas en México* (4) which treats the ideologies which have dominated Mexican organized labor. Finally, mention should be made of an unpublished study by Ben Stephansky, long-time United States labor attaché in Mexico and subsequently U.S. ambassador in Bolivia, entitled "The Mexican Labor Movement: An Interpretation of a Political Labor Movement" (87). Dr. Stephansky is currently associated with a private research organization in Washington, D.C.

Two small volumes about Peruvian trade unionism have been published since World War II. These are Alberto Bolognesi's *Teoría y táctica del sindicalismo moderno* (20) and Ricardo Temoche's *El sindicato moderno* (89), published by the Escuela Sindical Autónoma de Lima, a trade union training school of the Confederación de Trabajadores del Perú.

## LATIN AMERICAN LABOR IN REFERENCE WORKS

Latin American organized labor has been dealt with in a few reference books. For instance, the 1962 edition of the *Handbook of Latin American Studies* has a section treating labor which was written by Edwin W. Bishop. Somewhat earlier, Robert J. Alexander had an article, "Unions in Latin America and the Caribbean Area," in the *International Labor Directory and Handbook, 1955* (38). Also, the United States Department of Labor published a *Directory of Labor Organizations in the Western Hemisphere* in May, 1964 (94).

## ARTICLES AND PERIODICALS

During the quarter of a century since World War II a large number of articles have been published on organized labor in Latin America. These are too numerous to mention in detail. However, some brief mention of them should be made in any general survey of the bibliography of this subject. Particularly significant are the long series of articles by the late Serafino Romualdi which appeared during the late 1940s and the 1950s in the *American Federationist,* the monthly periodical of the American Federation of Labor. These are an invaluable source of information on the Latin American labor movement during this period, when Romualdi was probably in closer contact with the Latin American unions than was any other North American. The present writer also wrote numerous articles on the subject during the fifteen years or more following World War II. These include "Perón's Labor Missionaries," in *The Reporter,* February 28, 1950; "Union Movements in Latin America," in *Labor and Nation,* September, 1951; "Labor and Inter American Relations," in the *Annals of the American Academy of Political and Social Science,* March, 1961; and "International Labor Groups in the Americas," in the *Labor Law Journal,* July, 1962.

Many other people have published one or more individual articles in a variety of English-language periodicals since World War II. However, rather than listing a large sampling of these, it is more useful, perhaps, to note the various publications devoting particular attention to the subject of Latin American organized labor in the period being considered. The AFL's publication, *American Federationist,* which we have already noted, has contained many articles over the years in addition to those written by Serafino Romualdi. Another AFL publication dealing extensively with the subject was the *International Free Trade Union News,* which after the merger of the AFL and CIO in 1955 became the *AFL-CIO Free Trade Union News.* The Spanish-language monthly publication of the AFL, and AFL-CIO, *Noticiario Obrero Norteamericano,* also contains frequent and valuable contributions. During most of the 1950s the United States Department of Labor put out a mimeographed monthly publication which is a very useful source of information on Latin American labor during the post–World War II period; the periodical was entitled *Foreign Labor Information. The Monthly Labor Review,* the more general periodical of the Department of Labor, has carried articles about Latin American unionism but less regularly.

Several inter-American and international labor periodicals have also specialized in articles on the Latin American labor movement. These have included *Inter-American Labor Notes,* published by the Inter-American Confederation of Workers (CIT) between 1948 and 1951, and the *Inter-American Labor Bulletin,* published by the CIT's successor, the Organización Inter-Americana de Trabajadores (ORIT) for fifteen years after its establishment in 1951. *Free Labor World,* organ of the International Confederation of Free Trade Unions, with which the ORIT is affiliated, regularly carries Latin American articles. A Spanish-language version of this periodical, *Mundo del Trabajo Libre,* has been published for several years at the ORIT headquarters in Mexico.

The Communist-controlled Latin American group, the Confederación de Trabajadores de América Latina (CTAL), published for almost two decades *Noticiero de la CTAL,* which carried an English translation of most of the articles it contained. However, this publication came to an end with the liquidation of the CTAL in 1963. The

*World Trade Union Movement,* monthly organ of the Communist World Federation of Trade Unions usually carries at least one article on Latin America in each issue.

The Latin American affiliate of the International Federation of Christian Trade Unions, the Confederación Latino Americana de Sindicalistas Cristianas, has recently begun issuing *CLASC News,* a mimeographed monthly periodical, published in New York. Its parent group, which changed its name in 1969 to World Labor Confederation, has for many years published *Labor,* a periodical carrying occasional articles on the trade union situation in Latin America.

Finally, mention should be made of three publications which do not deal principally with labor problems but have dealt amply for long periods with labor problems and the trade union movement. These are *Industria,* a publication of McGraw-Hill, which for much of the 1950s carried a monthly column on labor-management relations in Latin America; *Hemispherica,* organ of the Inter-American Association for Democracy and Freedom, which had a similar column during most of the 1950s, and subsequently has continued to make frequent reference to the Latin American labor movement; and *Hispanic American Report,* issued until 1964 by the Hispanic American and Luso-Brazilian Institute of Stanford University, which in its month-by-month account of events in Latin America paid frequent attention to labor matters.

## Conclusion

Organized labor in Latin America is still a relatively undeveloped field, insofar as research is concerned, particularly by North American scholars. Histories remain to be written of the national labor movements of most of the countries of the area; analyses of labor-management relations are largely conspicuous by their absence. This is a field which will provide ample material for innumerable studies yet to be made.

# BIBLIOGRAPHY

1. Alba, Víctor. *El líder: Ensayo sobre el dirigente sindical.* Mexico, 1957.
2. ———. *Esquema histórico del movimiento obrero en América Latina.* Mexico, 1957.
3. ———. *História del movimiento obrero en América Latina.* Mexico, 1964.
4. ———. *Las ideas sociales contemporáneas en México.* Mexico, 1960.
5. ———. *Le mouvement ouvrier en Amerique Latine.* Paris, 1953.
6. ———. *Politics and the Labor Movement in Latin America.* Stanford, Calif., 1968.
7. Alexander, Robert J. *The Bolivian National Revolution.* New Brunswick, N.J., 1964.
8. ———. *Communism in Latin America.* New Brunswick, N.J., 1957.
9. ———. *Labor Relations in Argentina, Brazil, and Chile.* New York, 1962.
10. ———. *Labour Movements of Latin America.* London, 1947.
11. ———. *Organized Labor in Latin America.* New York, 1965.
12. ———. *The Peron Era.* New York, 1951.
13. ———. *Reseña del movimiento obrero en la América Latina.* Washington, D.C., 1950.
14. ———. *The Venezuelan Democratic Revolution.* New Brunswick, N.J., 1964.
15. Araiza, Luis. *Historia de la casa del obrero mundial.* Mexico, 1963.
16. Ashby, Joe C. *Organized Labor and the Mexican Revolution under Cárdenas.* Chapel Hill, N.C., 1967.
17. Baily, Samuel. *Labor, Nationalism, and Politics in Argentina.* New Brunswick, N.J., 1968.
18. Bandeira, Moniz, Clovis Melo, and A. T. Andrade. *O ano vermelho: A revolução russa e seus reflexos no Brasil.* Rio de Janeiro, 1967.
19. Berger, H. W. "Union Diplomacy: American Labor's Foreign Policy in Latin America." Ph.D. dissertation, University of Wisconsin, 1966.
20. Bolognesi, Alberto. *Teoría y táctica del sindicalismo moderno.* Lima, 1955.
21. Bush, Archer. *Organized Labor in Guatemala, 1944–1949.* Mimeographed. Hamilton, N.Y., 1950.
22. Carri, Roberto. *Sindicatos y poder en la Argentina.* Buenos Aires, 1967.
23. Centro Latino Americano de Pesquisas em Ciencias Sociais. *Situação social da América Latina.* Rio de Janeiro, 1965.
24. Chapoy Bonifaz, Dolores Beatriz. *El movimiento obrero y el sindicato en México.* Mexico, 1961.

167

25. Clavijo Aguilera, Fausto. *Los sindicatos en Cuba.* Havana, 1954.

26. Cuban Economic Research Project, University of Miami. *Labor Conditions in Communist Cuba.* Coral Gables, Fla., 1963.

27. D'Antonio, William V., and Frederick Pike. *Religion, Revolution, and Reform: New Forces for Change in Latin America.* New York, 1964.

28. Davis, Harold Eugene, ed. *Government and Politics in Latin America.* New York, 1958.

29. Deiner, John. "ATLAS—A Labor Instrument of Argentine Expansionism Under Perón." Ph.D. dissertation, Rutgers University, 1969.

30. Dias, Evardo. *História das lutas sociais no Brasil.* São Paulo, 1962.

31. Edelmann, Alexander. *Latin American Government and Politics.* Homewood, Ill., 1965.

32. Foster, William Z. *Outline Political History of the Americas.* New York, 1951.

33. Galenson, Walter. *Labor in Developing Countries.* Berkeley, Calif., 1963.

34. Galíndez, Jesús de. *La era de Trujillo.* Santiago de Chile, 1956.

35. Gavin, Myles. *Unionism in Latin America.* New York, 1962.

36. Hewitt, Cynthia Naegele. "An Introduction to the Rural Labor Movement of Pernambuco." Mimeographed. Institute of Latin American Studies, Columbia University, 1965.

37. Hoyos, F. A. *The Rise of West Indian Democracy: The Life and Times of Sir Grantley Adams.* Bridgetown, Barbados, 1963.

38. *International Labor Directory and Handbook, 1955.* New York, 1955.

39. International Labor Organization. *Freedom of Association and Conditions of Work in Venezuela.* Geneva, 1950.

40. ———. *Freedom of Association and Conditions of Work in Venezuela: Observations of the Government of Venezuela on the Report of the ILO Mission.* Geneva, 1951.

41. ———. *Labor Policies in the West Indies.* Geneva, 1952.

42. James, Daniel. *Red Design for the Americas: Guatemalan Prelude.* New York, 1954.

43. Jobet, Julio César. *Recabarren: Los orígenes del movimiento obrero y del socialismo chilenos.* Santiago de Chile, 1955.

44. Juárez, Juan C. *Los trabajadores en función social.* Buenos Aires, 1947.

45. Kassalow, Everett M. *National Labor Movements in the Post War World.* Evanston, Ill., 1963.

46. Knowles, William H. *Trade Union Development and Industrial Relations in the British West Indies.* Berkeley, Calif., 1960.

47. Landsberger, Henry. "Do Ideological Differences Have Personal Correlates? A Study of Chilean Labor Leaders at the Local Level." Mimeographed. 1967.

48. ———. "Ideology and Practical Politics: Two Years of Christian Democratic Labor Policy." Paper read at Colloquium on Overall Development in Chile, March, 1967, at the University of Notre Dame. Mimeographed.

49. Levenstein, H. A. "The United States Labor Movement and Mexico." Ph.D. dissertation, University of Wisconsin, 1966.

50. Lipset, Seymour Martin, and Aldo Solari, eds. *Elites in Latin America*. New York, 1967.

51. López Aparicio, Alfonso. *El movimiento obrero en México: Antecedentes, desarrollo y tendencias*. Mexico, 1952.

52. Marotta, Sebastián. *El movimiento sindical argentino*. 2 vols. Buenos Aires, 1960–1961.

53. *El marxismo en Bolivia, informe en mayoría de la Comisión Designada por el II Congreso de la Confederación Interamericana de Defensa del Continente, sobre la situación interna de Bolivia*. Santiago de Chile, 1957.

54. Mesa Lago, Camilo. *The Labor Sector and Socialist Distribution in Cuba*. New York, 1968.

55. Miller, R. C. "The Role of Labor Organization in a Developing Country: The Case of Mexico." Ph.D. dissertation, Cornell University, 1966.

56. Millon, Paul. *Mexican Marxist: Vicente Lombardo Toledano*. Chapel Hill, N.C., 1966.

57. Morris, James A. *Elites, Intellectuals, and Consensus: A Study of the Social Question and the Industrial Relations System*. Ithaca, N.Y., 1968.

58. Naft, Stephen. *Labor in Latin America*. Confidential Report No. 22 of News Background, 1947.

59. Panettieri, José. *Los trabajadores en tiempos de la inmigración masiva en Argentina, 1870–1910*. La Plata, Arg., 1966.

60. Payne, James L. *Labor and Politics in Peru*. New Haven, Conn., 1965.

61. Pereira, Luiz. *Trabalho e desenvolvimento no Brasil*. São Paulo, 1965.

62. Perera Raphael, Marcos. "United States Labor and the Inter-American Labor Movement." Master's thesis, Rutgers University, 1958.

63. Pierson, William, and Federico Gil. *Governments of Latin America*. New York, 1957.

64. Poblete Troncoso, Moisés. *El derecho del trabajo y la seguridad social en Chile*. Santiago, de Chile, 1949.

65. ———. *El movimiento obrero latinoamericano.* Mexico, 1946.

66. Poblete Troncoso, Moisés and Ben G. Burnett. *The Rise of the Latin American Labor Movement.* New Haven, Conn., 1960.

67. Portantiero, Juan Carlos and Miguel Marmis. *El movimiento obrero en los orígenes del peronismo.* Buenos Aires, 1969.

68. Ramicone, Luis. *Apuntes para la historia: La organización gremial obrera en la actualidad.* Buenos Aires, 1963.

69. Reiser, Pedro. *L'Organisation regionale interamericaine des travailleurs (ORIT) de la confederation internationale des syndicats libres (CISL) de 1951 a 1961.* Geneva, 1962.

70. Remorino, Jerónimo. *La nueva legislación social argentina.* Buenos Aires, 1953.

71. Research Center in Economic Development and Cultural Change of the University of Chicago. *U.S.–Latin American Relations: United States Business and Labor in Latin America.* Washington, D.C., 1960.

72. Revueltas, José. *Ensayo sobre un proletariado sin cabeza.* Mexico, 1962.

73. Rivera Marín, Guadalupe. *El mercado del trabajo: Relaciones obrero-patronales.* Mexico, 1955.

74. Rodrigues, Leoncio. *Conflito industrial e sindicalismo no Brasil.* São Paulo, 1966.

75. Rojas Carria, R. *Tratado de cooperatismo mexicano.* Mexico, 1952.

76. Romualdi, Serafino. *Presidents and Peons: Recollections of a Labor Ambassador in Latin America.* New York, 1967.

77. Salazar, Rosendo. *La carta del trabajo de la Revolución Mexicana.* Mexico, 1959.

78. ———. *Historia de la CTM.* Mexico, 1956.

79. ———. *Líderes y sindicatos.* Mexico, 1953.

80. Salz, B. R. *Human Element in Industrialization.* n.p., 1955.

81. Schmitt, Karl. *Communism in Mexico.* Austin, Tex., 1965.

82. Schneider, Ronald. *Communism in Guatemala, 1944–1954.* New York, 1959.

83. Silva, L. F. "Public Wage Fixing and its Effect on Collective Bargaining and the Labor Movement in Puerto Rico." Ph.D. dissertation, University of Wisconsin, 1962.

84. Simão, Asis. *Sindicato e estado.* São Paulo, 1966.

85. Snow, Sinclair. *The Pan American Federation of Labor.* Durham, N.C., 1964.

86. Stark, Harry. *Social and Economic Frontiers in Latin America.* Dubuque, Iowa, 1961.

87. Stephansky, Ben. "The Mexican Labor Movement: An Interpretation of a Political Labor Movement." Unpublished manuscript.

88. Tella, Torcuato di; Lucien Brams; Jean Daniel Reynaud; and Alain Touraine. *Sindicato y comunidad, dos tipos de estructura sindical Latino Americana*. Buenos Aires, 1967.

89. Temoche, Ricardo. *El sindicato moderno*. Lima, 1962.

90. Thompson, M. E. "The Development of Unionism Among Mexican Electrical Workers." Ph.D. dissertation, Cornell University, 1966.

91. Tieffenberg, David. *Exigencias proletarias a la revolución y la legislación obrera en el régimen peronista*. Buenos Aires, 1956.

92. Tolosa, Eustaquio. *El problema portuario argentino resuelto*. Buenos Aires, 1969.

93. Treviño, Ricardo. *El movimiento obrero en México, su evolución ideológica*. Mexico, 1948.

94. United States, Department of Labor. *Directory of Labor Organizations in the Western Hemisphere*. Washington D.C., 1964.

95. Universidad de Chile. Instituto de Organización y Administración, Facultad de Ciencias Económicas. *Trayectoria y administración del movimiento sindical chileno, 1946–1962*. Santiago de Chile, 1963.

96. Urrutia, M. "The Development of the Colombian Labor Movement." Ph.D. dissertation, University of California, 1967.

97. Walker Linares, Francisco. *Panorama del derecho social chileno*. Santiago de Chile, 1946.

98. Zeitlin, Maurice. *Revolutionary Politics and the Cuban Working Class*. Princeton, N.J., 1967.

# THE ROMAN
# CATHOLIC CHURCH

*Frederick C. Turner*

In the quarter century since the end of World War II, both the nature of Latin American Catholicism and the writings about it have changed considerably in attitude and in scope. The diversity of Catholic positions on social issues has grown sharply with the rise of progressivism and Christian Democracy, and conservative reactions against them. Polemicists and religious activists have defended their doctrinal stances in numerous books and pamphlets, while lay historians, sociologists, and political scientists have analyzed Catholicism from the standpoint of divergent disciplines rather than from opposing doctrinal perspectives. With the broader range of controversy and activity within the church, the new appraisals by clerics and lay scholars reflect the evolution of the church as an institution and as a body of doctrine.

In this twenty-five-year period, three foci of intellectual interest have become especially evident: historical description, sociological analysis, and attempts at religious and social persuasion. The three orientations are not entirely separate and distinct, and a variety of viewpoints gains expression under each of these three rubrics. Some of the same priests have produced emotive tracts and sociological surveys, for example, while other persuaders in the church have promoted such divergent goals as collaboration with leftist revolutionaries or a return to the highly stratified, clerically oriented organization of the Middle Ages. No single essay can fully cover the broad sweep of recent writings on Catholicism. At best, it can establish the trends in the literature, illustrate and compare their approaches, and evaluate some of the contrasting images of Latin American Catholicism which they present.

## I

Among the studies written by spokesmen for opposing Catholic positions, the most extreme confrontation is between archconservatism and the advocacy of leftist revolution. Whereas conservatives condemn agrarian reform as a sin against God (33) or advocate a return to corporatist politics and clerical direction of society (21), the late Father Camilo Torres called for sweeping change and for Christians

173

to join Marxist revolutionaries to bring about that change (16, 17, 39). In contrast to these more extreme viewpoints, however, the major weight of Catholic writings now supports social change and religious revitalization in a nonrevolutionary context. One of the best sources of statements on this new middle position is the volumes of papers presented at yearly meetings of the Catholic Inter-American Cooperation Program (CICOP) (8, 9, 10, 36, 37).

The new position emphasizes the need to overcome social problems without massive violence. In doing so, its advocates rely upon the overhanging threat of violence to spur others to join their activity. As Rafael Caldera wrote in a CICOP paper (10) four years before his 1968 election to the presidency of Venezuela, "Either we carry out a peaceful, constructive and Christian revolution, or our peoples will be dragged to their own misfortune, into a violent, materialistic and destructive one." The nonviolent approach to development basically tries to align the church with reform and popular aspirations. Many churchmen do not agree with Father James A. Clark (6), who after studying the role of the church in the Dominican Republic crisis of 1965, concluded that the church not only ought to assist "the people" but also "ought to abandon the rich, who can always provide for their religious needs." Rather than abandoning the rich, others want to bring them to realizations of the need for societal reconstruction. To the extent that such writings actually bring the church over to champion the egalitarian revolution which is gradually sweeping Latin America, as well as other parts of the world in the twentieth century, they will be among the most influential documents on the contemporary church.

Critics want to apply both ethics and pragmatism to the issues of development. Mario Zañartu, an economist and Chilean Jesuit, argues in favor of establishing a Christian mystique of economic development (9). A Catholic educator in Venezuela, Arístides Calvani, points out that, when medical advances of the industrialized countries come to Latin America, they exacerbate the dual problems of sharp population increase and massive unemployment (36). Since such spokesmen recognize that the experience and situation of the developing countries differ categorically from those of industrialized societies, there seems to be a particular need for moral and religious imperatives to humanize as well as stimulate the development process.

Development is a major theme in the writing of Dom Hélder Câmara (5), the influential Bishop of Recife and Olinda in the Northeast of Brazil. Dom Hélder champions concern for the poor; he wants the presently industrialied societies to contribute far more heavily to the developing countries without trying to control them. He raises the fundamental question of whether Latin Americans can work toward a more egalitarian society in the context of a democratic political system. Pointing out that many young Brazilians have lost faith in democracy as the best means of effecting change, he suggests that democrats need to join together to transform basic laws and then to implement them. Whether this transformation takes place under a centralized or decentralized system of power is of less significance to Dom Hélder than is the necessity for the transformation itself.

The essential humanism of such statements has given them wide appeal and self-assurance. They concentrate on human achivement rather than divine ordination, and they maintain an attractive if potentially self-deceptive and beguiling faith in man's capacities. As Eduardo Frei wrote just before leading his Christian Democratic Party to victory in the Chilean elections of 1964, Christian Democracy is "inspired by its trust in man," by its "belief that we are witnesses to the crisis of a world exhausted, to the death of paternalism, and to the birth of a civilization of work and solidarity *with man as its center*" (12). Frei has maintained this orientation, despite the powerful obstacles which his regime encountered and despite the defection of the crucial left wing of his party in 1969.

When viewed uncritically, the new Catholic justification for nonviolent development seems to have immense power and support. Men who are committed to furthering both religion and development quite naturally link appeals for them, and such advocates gradually come to assume the eventual triumph of the cause for which they work. Typifying the censorious but optimistic interpretation is *The Church and the Latin American Revolution,* a widely read study by two European priests, François Houtart and Emile Pin (20), who each studied sociology at the University of Chicago. Somewhat paradoxically, the work lengthily documents the failures of Latin American Catholicism but ends by assuming that the Church will overcome these failures.

Fathers Houtart and Pin may well overestimate both the inherent power of Catholicism and the weight of what they call "progressivism" within it. In a chapter on religious practice, they demonstrate the essential superficiality of the national census figures which list Latin American populations as being more than 90 percent Catholic. A more realistic figure reveals that weekly attendance at mass in Latin

American cities, where priests are far more available than in the countryside, does not run higher than 17 or 18 percent. From an involved rather than analytic position, however, Houtart and Pin ultimately conclude that Latin American Catholicism, "since it embraces more than 90 percent of the inhabitants, carries a very heavy responsibility." Similarly, another chapter shows that religious motivations are ritualistic and often have nothing to do with the broader issues of social development. Yet Houtart and Pin conclude that Catholicism is providing new motivation for development and that "the progressive forces are winning out in Latin American Catholicism (and the Vatican Council has shown this), even if a few centers of resistance are still powerful." Both inside and outside Latin America, what they call the "centers of resistance" may even now be more powerful than they originally assumed in the euphoric atmosphere of the Vatican Council.

## II

In addition to analyzing the roles of the church in processes of Latin American development and modernization, recent studies have presented comprehensive interpretations of church politics and institutions. Missing have been quasi-journalistic accounts of contemporary confrontations within the church, as no one has written the sort of in-depth study of conflict which Xavier Rynne provides for the Vatican Council (34). Instead, researchers have supplied information on the historical and institutional framework for Catholic politics. While the analyses of this framework enrich the context in which future studies will be written, they also raise a number of specific issues which need to be studied through a combination of traditional and behavioral approaches.

The writing of Fredrick Pike both describes church experience and challenges stereotypes concerning it. Besides succinctly interpreting the broad sweep of church activities in Latin America (27), Pike cogently questions standard interpretations of Catholic politics in specific countries. After years of research in Chile and Peru and after writing separate books on each country, Pike implicitly criticizes the common assumption of the uniquely advanced position of the Chilean clergy. He details ways in which the Chilean clergy has come to promote individual initiative and political pluralism (28), but demonstrates parallel development in church policies and attitudes for Peru as well (26, 29). His work underlines the need for the sort of comparisons which J. Lloyd Mecham makes among the different Latin American countries.

In a 1966 revision of his *Church and State in Latin America,* for many years the best historical treatment of church-state conflict, Mecham chronicles the substantial losses of property, support, and separate legal status which the church has undergone in the nineteenth and twentieth centuries (25). By concentrating on constitutional restrictions and on the political conflicts between the two major institutions of secular and ecclesiastical authority, Mecham demonstrates the curtailment of clerical power. His chapters on the individual Latin American countries show the gradual, uneven, but irreversible nature of the limitations which successive governments have placed upon the direct political powers which churchmen enjoyed in the colonial period.

An important point which Mecham raises but does not stress is the fact that, once the church has come to accept these limitations, its leaders can work informally to influence progressive politicians in the new Christian Democratic parties with less fear of traditional opposition to clerical intervention. As more and more priests combine concern for social welfare with acceptance of the institutional framework of Latin American liberalism, their political orientation as well as the restraints on their direct political activities makes them more acceptable to contemporary politicians. Consequently, as Mecham points out at the end of his study, since about 1950 such countries as Ecuador and Venezuela have relaxed former restrictions on the church. Since the revision of Mecham's study, this relaxation has continued to lessen anticlerical tendencies, thereby encouraging the victory of such Christian Democratic candidates as Rafael Caldera in Venezuela.

The Mecham volume combines sound historical scholarship with some major implications for future research. Based largely upon a detailed study of secondary sources, it provides a wealth of background information and a useful bibliography. In its country-by-country context, it also challenges researchers to pick up and extend ideas and issues which it raises. In discussing Haiti, for example, Mecham points to the basic confrontation which led to the nationalist expulsion of the white French clergy. As Rémy Bastien has also pointed out, French priests appear to be cultural imperialists to nationalist leaders who want to stress a black heritage and the native voodoo religion (11). More generally, the sheer political importance of both Catholicism and nationalism in Latin America requires further study of their inter-relationships (22, 40).

As Edward Williams suggests in the first major study of Christian Democratic parties in Latin America (43), this force of nationalism works to blunt and modify the international thrust of the Christian Democratic movement. Williams may underestimate the degree to which Christian Democratic leaders can adust their political appeals to the requisites of nationalism; he probably overestimates the disadvantage which the European origins of the movement pose for its growth in Latin America. By tracing aims and programs of the movement, however, he provides useful interpretation of the diverse forces which promote and retard its development. Williams' approach, like that of Pike or Mecham, contrasts with the approach of a series of sociologically oriented studies.

### III

Unlike historical and institutional descriptions, recent sociological analyses focus upon the values and attitudes of Latin American Catholics. While sometimes drawing upon historical data and usually having clear implications for the church as an institution, they approach the subject by concentrating on the beliefs and values of religious activists and elites. They establish models and typologies, describe contrasting orientations in different national contexts, and develop hypotheses through questionnaire surveys. With strongly comparative and empirical tendencies, they point the direction for newer lines of research.

Ivan Vallier (41), in one of the best known studies of Latin American Catholicism, asks to what extent the changing orientations of Catholic elites can affect solidarity among groups, legitimate reforms in secular institutions, and help to bring presently marginal groups into more active social participation. He separates the clerical elite into four segments: politicians, papists, pluralists, and pastors. Whereas the politicians uphold conservative norms, hierarchical organization, and direct ties to secular politics, the papists prefer the progressive goals of papal encyclicals, reject direct political roles for churchmen, and encourage laymen to effect new social policies. The pluralists stress cooperation with non-Catholic groups to achieve the specific goals of development, while the pastors strengthen the religious norms of parishioners and so give the norms renewed power to legitimate the process of change.

When seen in terms of the model of development which Vallier establishes, his differentiation of Catholic elites is impressive. The categories remain ideal types, as Vallier recognizes. Although the work of individual churchmen may relate to more than one category, therefore, it has in fact proved important for "papists" to cut the ties of traditional involvement before new norms could gain wider support. Somewhat wishfully, Vallier's assumption of the "bankruptcy" of the "politicians" may underestimate their continuing power, and the implication that the "pastors" can now be successful in winning broad adherence to religious norms may prove to be far more optimistic than Vallier suggests. In refining and extending his approach, what is needed at this point is empirical analysis which actually tests his propositions among the clergy of different countries.

In looking at religious orientations in one country, such sociologists as Nathan Whetten frequently concentrate on popular rather than priestly attitudes (42). Unlike other writers on the Guatemalan church, Whetten considers the religious values of the mass of citizens. There is certainly a place for contrasting country studies of the historical conflict of church and state or the pattern of church administration; studies of these topics in Guatemala by Mary Holleran (19) and Bruce Calder (4) provide significant additions to the literature. But Whetten's study goes one step further. By carefully appraising the differences in religious norms and activities among different Guatemalan groups and regions, he shows the popular effects and limited innovational possibilities of Catholicism in this context. Working from demographic data, anthropological sources, and an intimate personal knowledge of religious variations in the country, Whetten's work points the way to future studies which could similarly approach popular religious values among a variety of other groups.

Emile Pin's study of popular orientations throughout Latin America (31) presents some of the hypotheses which such country studies could test. Pin describes general patterns of religious beliefs, motivations, and behavior. He repeatedly indicates ways in which customary practices contravene Catholic norms, although he sympathetically understands how personal hardships and what he calls "a false idea of God's patience" lead to the indulgence of vices. At some points, he raises issues whose scope extends far beyond the treatment which he can give to them in a general discussion. What, for instance, are ·the causes and social ramifications of the fear which he characterizes as the basic attitude of many Indians toward God? What changes are now occurring in attitudes of religious resignation and abnegation? While providing a useful set of questions, Pin himself does not enter into the survey research which he says is necessary to obtain more complete answers.

At the time that Father Pin was calling for more survey research, Joseph Fichter (15), a Jesuit sociologist who now teaches at the Harvard Divinity School, was undertaking such research in Chile. With the help of numerous Chileans, Fichter sent questionnaires to 782 priests and 1,500 Catholic activists in the diocese of Santiago. Despite disappointingly low response rates, the ways in which the questionnaire was constructed allowed the survey to provide excellent data on attitudes toward social change, politics, religion, and the role of the church. Significant differences in attitude appeared among different classes, age groups, and educational levels, just as they did between men and women, bachelors and married persons, clergymen and laymen, and the Chilean and foreign clergy. In retrospect, some of the implications of the study have proved to be mistaken, as when 62.2 percent of the respondents predicted that Chile would have a revolution within five years. Even in such cases, however, it is of great value to have information on the perceptions of different groups at the time, and it is revealing to see that predictions of revolution were widespread in 1961 just as they continue to be today.

Complementary survey research by Renato Poblete (32), the Jesuit sociologist who has directed a number of studies at the Centro Bellarmino in Santiago, addresses the fundamental causes for the scarcity of religious vocations in Chile. After outlining the elements in the Chilean environment which affect the scarcity of vocations, Poblete presents the results of surveys taken in Catholic seminaries and schools. His research uncovered important information, such as the fact that friendship with a priest ranked highest among the motivations which seminarians gave for their desire to enter the priesthood. With personal friendship and admiration thus ranking well above family, school, or religious group influences, the surveys still revealed that the practice of Catholicism among the parents of seminarians was considerably higher than that among the parents of the students in regular Catholic schools. The research provided such indirect benefits as measurements for the common assumption of higher levels of religious practice among women than among men, and dealt with the key issues of class background and age structure in ways which later surveys can extend even further.

The work of Poblete and Fichter also exemplifies an even more significant research trend. One of the points which stands out clearly in the overall structure of writings on the church during the past twenty-five years is that researchers are gradually applying more rigorous, empirical approaches which try to compare situations and test hypotheses. The vineyard of ecclesiastical studies in Latin America remains ample and largely unworked; there is a continuing need for historical as well as sociological studies. But, given the range of hypotheses now generated on Latin American Catholicism, the most pressing priority has become the testing rather than the restatement of these hypotheses. Through comparison and a more precise formulation of the theoretical variables in question, historical or contemporary country studies can provide valuable data and evaluations. Through depth interviews, questionnaires, and participant observer techniques, social scientists can test hypotheses on the pervasiveness, consistency, and effects of the religious attitudes and activities of differing lay and clerical groups. If such studies do test the conclusions of past tracts, descriptions, and surveys, then the research of the next quarter century will build upon and significantly extend that of the recent past.

# BIBLIOGRAPHY

1. Alonso, Isidoro, and Gines Garrido. *La iglesia en América Central y el Caribe: Estructuras eclesiásticas.* Bogotá, 1962.
2. Badanelli, Pedro. *Perón, la iglesia, y un cura.* 4th ed. Buenos Aires, 1960.
3. Bialek, Robert W. *Catholic Politics: A History Based on Ecuador.* New York, 1963.
4. Calder, Bruce J. "Growth and Change in the Guatemalan Catholic Church, 1944–1966." Master's thesis, University of Texas, 1968.
5. Câmara, Hélder. *Revolução dentro da paz.* Rio de Janeiro, 1968.
6. Clark, James A. *The Church and the Crisis in the Dominican Republic.* Westminster, Md., 1967.
7. Coleman, William J. *Latin American Catholicism: A Self-Evaluation.* Maryknoll, N.Y., 1958.
8. Considine, John J., ed. *The Church in the New Latin America.* Notre Dame, Ind., 1964.
9. ————, ed. *The Religious Dimension in the New Latin America.* Notre Dame, Ind., 1966.
10. ————, ed. *Social Revolution in the New Latin America: A Catholic Appraisal.* Notre Dame, Ind., 1965.
11. Courlander, Harold, and Rémy Bastien. *Religion and Politics in Haiti.* Washington, D.C., 1966.
12. D'Antonio, William V., and Fredrick B. Pike, eds. *Religion, Revolution, and Reform: New Forces for Change in Latin America.* New York, 1964.
13. "De Camilo Torres a Hélder Câmara: La iglesia en América Latina." *Cuadernos de Marcha,* no. 9 (January 1968).
14. Dewart, Leslie. *Christianity and Revolution: The Lesson of Cuba.* New York, 1963.
15. Fichter, Joseph H. *Cambio social en Chile: Un estudio de actitudes.* Santiago de Chile, 1962.
16. Guzmán, Germán. *Camilo Torres.* Trans. by John D. Ring. New York, 1969.
17. Habegger, Norberto. *Camilo Torres, el cura guerrillero.* Buenos Aires, 1967.
18. Haddox, Benjamín Edward. *Sociedad y religion en Colombia (estudio de las instituciones religiosas colombianas).* Trans. by Jorge Zalamea. Bogotá, 1965.
19. Holleran, Mary P. *Church and State in Guatemala.* New York, 1949.

20. Houtart, François, and Emile Pin. *The Church and the Latin American Revolution.* Trans. by Gilbert Barth. New York, 1965.

21. Hübner Gallo, Jorge Iván. *Los católicos en la política.* Santiago de Chile, 1959.

22. "La iglesia en el mundo de hoy." *Mensaje* (anniversary number, 1951–66) 15, no. 153 (October 1966).

23. Kennedy, John J. *Catholicism, Nationalism, and Democracy in Argentina.* Notre Dame, Ind., 1958.

24. "La libertad religiosa." *Criterio* 37, no. 1465–66 (December 24, 1964).

25. Mecham, J. Lloyd. *Church and State in Latin America: A History of Politico-Ecclesiastical Relations.* Chapel Hill, N.C., 1966.

26. Pike, Fredrick B. "The Catholic Church and Modernization in Peru and Chile." *Journal of International Affairs* 20, no. 2 (1966): 272–88.

27. ———. "Catholicism in Latin America Since 1848." Unpublished manuscript, 1968.

28. ———. "Church and State and Political Development in Chile." *A Journal of Church and State* 10, no. 1 (Winter 1968): 99–113.

29. ———. "Church and State in Peru and Chile Since 1840: A Study in Contrasts." *American Historical Review* 73, no. 1 (October 1967): 30–50.

30. ———, ed. *The Conflict between Church and State in Latin America.* New York, 1964.

31. Pin, Emile. *Elementos para una sociología del catolicismo latinoamericano.* Bogotá: 1963.

32. Poblete Barth, Renato. *Crisis sacerdotal.* Santiago de Chile, 1965.

33. Proença Sigaud, Geraldo de; Antonio de Castro Mayer; Plinio Corrêa de Oliveira; and Luis Mendonça de Freitas. *Reforma agrária, questão de consciência.* 4th ed. São Paulo, 1962.

34. Rynne, Xavier. *Letters from Vatican City. Vatican Council II (First Session): Background and Debates.* Garden City, N.Y., 1964.

35. Sanders, Thomas G. "Catholicism and Development: The Catholic Left in Brazil." In *Churches and States: The Religious Institution and Modernization,* ed. by Kalman H. Silvert. New York, 1967.

36. Shapiro, Samuel, ed. *Cultural Factors in Inter-American Relations.* Notre Dame, Ind., 1968.

37. ———, ed. *Integration of Man and Society in Latin America.* Notre Dame, Ind., 1967.

38. Tiseyra, Oscar. *Cuba marxista vista por un católico.* Buenos Aires, 1964.

39. Torres Restrepo, Camilo. *Obras escoguidas.* Montevideo, 1968.

40. Turner, Frederick C. "The Compatibility of Church and State in Mexico." *Journal of Inter-American Studies* 9, no. 4 (October 1967): 591–602.

41. Vallier, Ivan. "Religious Elites: Differentiations and Developments in Roman Catholicism." In *Elites in Latin America,* ed, by Seymour Martin Lipset and Aldo Solari. New York, 1967.

42. Whetten, Nathan L. "Religion and the Church." Chapter 14 in *Guatemala: The Land and the People*. New Haven, Conn., 1961.

43. Williams, Edward J. *Latin American Christian Democratic Parties.* Knoxville, Tenn., 1967.

# THE MILITARY

*Stephen L. Rozman*

Perhaps the most relevant generalities regarding the literature on the Latin American military are the lack of empirical data and the largely historical and unsystematic approach taken by the authors. In part this may be attributed to the difficulties encountered in employing modern methodology because of the prevailing secrecy and inapproachability of the military leadership. Supposedly, the armed forces are apolitical. Therefore research which assumes a political role is not likely to meet with a warm reception, cooperation, and candor on the part of military officers.

Unfortunately, the barriers in obtaining empirical data seem to have offered an excuse to allow many writers to draw conclusions which are difficult to substantiate and often appear to be normatively derived, reflecting the author's values, aspirations, and goals more than current Latin American realities. Lamentably, ethnocentrism appears quite evident in much of the literature related to the implicit belief that Latin American political systems would be much more similar to that of the United States if the military was not an obstacle to such a development. Following this line of reasoning, the armed forces must be disbanded (as in Costa Rica) or be socialized to adopt democratic values. Furthermore, more interest is sometimes expressed in the potential contribution of the individual Latin American military establishments to United States security goals than in their relevance to purely internal or domestic considerations.

Strong criticism of methodological shortcomings has come from Lyle N. McAlister, himself a specialist on the Latin American military. He decries the fact that many studies "are based on inadequate data and are generally expressed in continental-wide generalizations which often do not apply to specific situations." Consequently, "careful studies of individual countries are needed as bases for a truly comparative evaluation of the role of the military in Latin America" (23). (One should note that this is not the only area where the development of macro-theory has far outpaced the micro-studies to substantiate it.) However, McAlister does not dispute the practice of treating Latin America as a region, observing that "it is quite possible that historically, Latin America or at least the Hispanic world provides a functional as well as a convenient unit for the study of civil-military relations" (24). Of particular concern to McAlister is the tendency to explain militarism as an aberration in an otherwise healthy process, an outlook which ignores interaction between the military and civilian interest groups, and relates to the inclination to stereotype the military rigidly as a conservative force which has been holding back progress (25).

McAlister distinguishes between the "traditional" and "revisionist" writers on the Latin American military and links himself to the second category. The traditionalists find nothing beneficial in the roles of the military and simply view the armed forces as deterring progress through political intervention and enormous budgetary demands. The need, then, is to abolish or greatly reduce them and place them under civilian control. Revisionists, on the other hand, while also basically antimilitarist, look at militarism as "an expression of, rather than a basic cause of, political instability in Latin America." They also feel that is is impracticable to abolish the military or place it under civilian control; they hold that the military does perform useful tasks, notably in civic action, and that these roles should be encouraged. McAlister stresses that both traditionalists and revisionists fail to offer ample empirical evidence and are inclined to stereotype (23).

The methodological deficiencies are perhaps related to the dearth of background material on the Latin American military, combined with the fact that the overwhelming bulk of the literature has been published within the past decade. Víctor Alba, who wrote one of the earliest works on the Latin American armed forces (1960), lamented the glaring paucity of material on this interest group and expressed the hope that his contribution would stimulate further and more profound studies (which it did) (1). Aside from Alba's stimulus, the expansion of the literature during the past decade seems to have resulted from at least two factors. First, the approach to the study of Latin American politics until recently was highly institutional, relating the powers of the executive, legislative, and judicial branches to the respective constitutional framework. Interest group approaches have only recently come into vogue. Thus, military takeovers were related to *caudillismo,* which in turn was associated with the strong, personalistic executive, whether he be military or civilian. The recent advent of the institutional coup as opposed to the earlier predominance of the personalistic coup (related to the *cuartelazo*) helped develop the study of the military as an interest group. Second, the Cuban revolution and the resulting communist threat have led observers to search for weaknesses in the Latin American fabric, and the political role of the military has normally been treated as such a fault. Indeed, Alba, in his original and highly normative work, bemoaned the irony of the neglect of the military in literature at a time when militarism was presenting a serious danger for democratic stability in Latin America (1). Latin America had a global image of militarism and frequent *golpes de estado* long before serious studies of these phenomena were undertaken.

Charles Wolf, Jr., and Martin C. Needler provide examples of a very limited use of empirical data and illustrate the difficulties impeding a more extensive application. Wolf warns against unsubstantiated cause-and-effect relationships and proceeds to provide data which destroy hypotheses that the extent of foreign military aid, the size of a country's defense budget, or military expenditures per capita are related to the degree of militarism found in a Latin American nation. He stresses the need for multivariate analysis, since a complexity of variables is probably related to the political role of the military. Furthermore, it is difficult to determine when a political effect is produced, since "the kinds of political change that we can observe directly tend to be confined to sharp, discrete changes: a coup or a revolution" (36).

Needler, unlike Wolf, uses empirical data for a positive goal, relating four factors to frequency of coups and types of insurrection. His categories include coups which were reformist; those which were low in violence; coups that overthrew constitutional governments; and those that occurred around election time. Working with a sample of fifty-six coups, divided into three periods between 1935 and 1964 (1935–44, 1945–54, and 1955–64), he concludes from his data that reformist coups have declined in percentage from one period to the next; that coups low in violence have similarly declined; that the percentage of coups overthrowing constitutional governments has increased from one period to the next; and that coups around election time have similarly increased (30). In this case, statistical tests were not utilized nor were cause-and-effect relationships established. Yet the quantitative orientation itself has made Needler's study a contribution beyond earlier efforts.

Perhaps the best example to date of the utilization of empirical data is provided by Robert D. Putnam in his statistical testing of hypothetical causes of military intervention in politics. He establishes a military intervention index, rating countries over a ten-year period (1956–1965) on a scale from zero to three, based on the extent of military intervention in a particular year. He then relates this intervention ranking to rankings on aspects of socioeconomic development, aspects of political development, characteristics of the military establishment itself, and foreign influences. His findings are as follows. There is a fairly strong negative correlation (–.56) between social mobilization and military intervention; a small, but still rather surprising, correlation (+.26) exists between economic development and military intervention; but a lack of any meaningful correlation is found regarding factors of political development (widespread participation in elections, strong parties and pressure groups, and freedom from political violence) and regarding the role of foreign training missions. Especially in showing the lack of relationship between political development and military intervention, Putnam's use of statistical testing explodes some rather prevalent notions of traditionalists (33).

Some nonquantitative conceptual development has emerged from the typologies of the military in Latin America established by several writers. However, the methodology employed has frequently left much to be desired. The most common approach has been to fit the military into three categories: those countries where the military dominates the political system; those countries in transition—moving away from militarism—or where militarism is occasional; and those countries where the military is nonpolitical. The second category lends itself to the greatest controversy and appears to manifest the greatest methodological weakness, especially in the case of writers like Edwin Lieuwen who prefer the "transitional" label to that of "occasional." Writing in 1960, Lieuwen held that Cuba, Guatemala, Venezuela, Peru, Ecuador, Argentina, and Brazil had military establishments which were in transition from political to nonpolitical institutions (17). Lieuwen was assuming a tendency toward declining militarism in Latin America, a continuous shift from political to nonpolitical roles. No classification of transitions in the opposite direction, from nonpolitical to political or from occasional militarism to dominance, was provided. Since the publication of his study, Brazil seems to offer an example of the latter variety of shift. And certainly the political role of the Argentine and Peruvian military has recently become more pronounced. The word "transitional" seems to relate to a culture-bound ethnocentrism, which will be dealt with shortly.

Alba presents a similarly optimistic trichotomy, with the trend working against militarism and in favor of democracy; but his typology seems somewhat more sophisticated than Lieuwen's. Whereas the latter's framework is based on a country's recent experience with militarism (equating militarism with overt political activity, especially coups d' etat themselves), Alba's framework is based on the technical and intellectual training of the officer corps. The distinction is made between barracks, school, and laboratory officers. Barracks officers are the traditionalists, often lacking professional training and intervening in politics on behalf of status quo interests or personal goals. School officers are more middle class in origin, have received professional training, have a technological orientation, and are often attracted to democratic values. However, they are sometimes attracted to other ideologies, including communism, so their position is still questionable. Laboratory officers represent the youngest group, that with the best technical and intellectual training. This is the wave of the future, and they do represent antimilitarism, according to Alba (1).

Those writers who substitute "occasional" for "transitional" manifest a less normative approach and, accordingly, less optimism that progress is steadily being made toward the goal of democracy. Theodore Wyckoff and John Duncan Powell both refer to occasional military intervention in depicting the stage between constant intervention and the total absence of a political role (32, 37). Nonetheless, even this substitution fails to reconcile the typology with empirical evidence. Wyckoff, for example, classifies El Salvador as an "occasional" country even though it has not had a single civilian government since 1931. Peru and Argentina, similarly categorized, have experienced more than occasional militarism by any standard. The problem seems to lie in the absence of meaningful definitions to distinguish the three categories of the trichotomy. The terms are descriptive rather than analytical and are difficult to make operational.

A conceptual confusion is manifested by the fact that Wyckoff places six countries in the "military-dominant" category, twelve in the "occasional" category, and only two in the "never" category, whereas Powell distributes them in corresponding groups of seven, nine, and three (leaving Cuba out). Lieuwen deviates considerably from this pattern, with a seven, seven, and six distribution (17). Immediately, the reader wonders why Wyckoff considers only Costa Rica and Uruguay to be totally free of militarism, while Powell adds Mexico to this group, and Lieuwen throws in Chile, Colombia, and Bolivia.[1] Evi-

---

1. Other conflicts among these writers are found in the classification of Panama (Lieuwen places it in the "dominant" category); Guatemala (Lieuwen places it in the "transitional" category); and El Salvador (in Wycoff's "occasional" category).

dently, the problem lies in the definition of what constitutes a military role in politics. Lieuwen appears most prone to limiting such a role to actual coups d' etat or other blatant interventionism, while Wyckoff would appear to include an exaggerated interest group role as an example of militarism. If the latter evaluation is sound, Wyckoff's approach would seem more meaningful, provided that data were offered to substantiate a claim of exaggerated political involvement, together with the criteria for distinguishing between normal and exaggerated activity. Indeed, the political scientist must reject the notion of nonpolitical armed forces, since an interest group such as the military must inevitably enter the political system in the advancement of its institutional goals.

Some of the literature attempts to provide an explanation for the presence or absence of militarism in connection with the typologies. Wyckoff, in particular, sees the "military-dominant" countries as small, isolated, stratified, and lacking a middle class to cushion the gap between great wealth and abject poverty; the "occasional" countries as large in area and population, socially and economically diverse, with such complexities that the government is "effectively beyond the reach of anything more than nominal military-political control"; and the "never" countries as ethnically homogeneous, with a sizable middle class, some social mobility, and a tradition of reformist government and democratic processes (37).

Other typologies are offered by Needler and McAlister, without the rigid categorizing of countries into one of three classes. Needler distinguishes between the military as an interest group, as the guardian of the constitution, as the holder of a veto power, as wielding open military rule, and as supporting a personal military dictator. The guardian role often provides an excuse for a coup, while the veto power works to bar the presidency to contenders found objectionable by the military. The personal dictator represents the extreme end of the continuum because he neither relies on the military as his exclusive base of power nor has to share his decision making with other higher officers (28). McAlister, on the other hand, distinguishes between the praetorian, gendarmist, garrison, and civilist states, reflecting, respectively, frequent military coups for nonmilitary purposes, typical of nonprofessional militaries; personalistic takeovers and rule based on the military as a prop; the overall militarization of both state and society (atypical of Latin America); and civilian supremacy over the military (24).

Again, Putnam provides the best relationship between theory and empirical data. Similar to Needler and McAlister, he avoids the rigid trichotomy; but beyond this, he refuses to classify many countries dogmatically into any set category because of the vicissitudes in the political role of their armed forces in recent years. On the basis of his military intervention index, he establishes four categories of countries: those where the military role has been limited to that of a "minor pressure group on strictly military matters"; those where civilian institutions and power groups have prevailed, but with the military "still a significant political force in nonmilitary matters"; those where civilians and military each have powerful influence, regardless of which is in power; and those where the military rules, and civilian influence is very limited (33). By adding a category to the usual trichotomy, Putnam is able to distinguish between the minor pressure-group role of the military in Uruguay and Costa Rica (referring to the latter's police force), and the somewhat more extensive role in Mexico, Chile, and Colombia, without having to lump these latter three countries with Argentina, Peru, El Salvador, Ecuador, and Brazil, such as Wyckoff was compelled to do with his awkward trichotomy. Moreover, Putnam's framework enables him to avoid the serious pitfalls of the "occasional" category used in trichotomies as Wycoff's.

Treatment of militarism as an aberration, combined with the implication in some of the typologies that all progress leads toward democracy, reflects the ethnocentrism found in much of the literature (most of which has been written by United States authors). Russell H. Fitzgibbon manifests a blatant ethnocentrism in his assertion that "dictatorship . . . is becoming anachronistic in Latin America and it is to a significant degree being forced into conjunction with another anachronism: the military man in the presidency" (8). Such commentary is highly normative, strongly implying that modernization inevitably means democratic government anywhere in Latin America. Alba likewise exemplifies the normative approach, contending that the term militarism should refer only to those interventions where the military undermines a civilian-democratic regime, not to military action against a dictatorship (2). Another normative approach is to assume that the desired democratic development will occur inevitably as the middle class grows and develops. Some writers appear to be culture-bound, analyzing the middle class in Latin American countries in terms of the same values one would attribute to the U.S. middle class. Robert J. Alexander, among others, views the Latin American middle class as a democratic, antimilitaristic, and stabilizing force (3). (Empirical data have come to reveal middle-class sectors as the instigators of some coups, a matter which will be treated subsequently.)

A further type of ethnocentrism not only relates to the application of U.S. values to the Latin American culture, but treats Latin America as subordinate to U.S. national security priorities. Lieuwen exemplifies this tendency, with comments such as the following: "It is only at the expense of its long-range world-wide image and security interests that the United States can accept military dictatorship or Nasserism as short cuts and forfeit the democratic means of attaining social and economic reform in Latin America" (18). Such an approach quite obviously undermines the scientific detachment of the author. It implies the right of the U.S. to impose its own standards and assumes that it can, by carrot and stick, control political processes in Latin American countries. Needler takes a similar approach, calling upon the U.S. to thwart a budding coup by warning key military leaders that reprisals will be forthcoming if the military action takes place (30).

On the other hand, there are also antiethnocentric currents in the literature. Kurt Conrad Arnade, writing as early as 1950, warned that "external diplomatic or economic pressures can in no way alter the internal structure of these countries [because] Latin American political factors are derivative of other internal factors, including problems of economy, communication, education, population groups, and terrain" (5). More recently, McAlister has taken up this banner, decrying the democratic orientation and value system employed in the treatment of the Latin American military: "The traditional view is basically teleological. It interprets Latin-American history in terms of the 'Struggle for Democracy' or 'Progress toward Democracy'" (23). In harmony with Arnade, he observes that "Anglo-Saxon constitutional norms are not automatically transferable to nations with differing cultural heritages" (23). Moreover, he takes sharp issue with positions like those of Lieuwen and Needler, remarking that he deplores "the general propensity for North Americans to pronounce on how Latin-Americans should run their affairs" (23).

Even the few writers who are somewhat favorably inclined toward the Latin American military manifest a democratic orientation and value system. A good example is offered by Wyckoff (37), who observes that

> under certain conditions the military—far from being a threat to democratic institutions—may serve as a force to uphold and safeguard

them. Constitutional provisions might even be rewritten so as to formalize this arrangement, making of the top uniformed officers a sort of judiciary, with power to interpret the rightness or wrongness of acts of the executive and the legislative branches of government. If this hypothesis should prove to be correct, democracy in such countries would have nothing to fear from the political role of the military. [P. 762]

The surfeit of normative studies and ethnocentric approaches has influenced analyses of military socialization processes, in the absence of empirical data. What are the forces that contribute to military socialization? Are military officers being inculcated with democratic values? Does military socialization overcome earlier socialization? These are some of the questions which relate to conflicting viewpoints in the literature.

In essence, those writers who see a trend toward greater democratic government and a corresponding decline in militarism point to steadily increasing recruitment of military officers from the middle class and characterize this class as prodemocratic and imbued with antimilitaristic values. Accordingly, these middle-class values are influencing the orientation of the military toward politics in a manner favorable to the eventual demise of militarism. Alba's school and laboratory illustrate this position. He stresses their adherence to the values of "that middle class which in Iberoamerica is the ferment of progress, which gives orientation to the nationalistic revolutionary movement that forms the barrier to dictatorial ambitions and communist maneuvers, and which has given to the countries of our hemisphere the few and brief epochs of democracy which they have enjoyed" (1). (The barracks officers, reflecting traditional autocratic values, are steadily becoming an anachronism. Unable to inculcate these younger middle-class officers with their archaic values, their demise and that of militarism is inevitable, especially when the laboratory officers come to dominate.)

The writings of Alexander, Fitzgibbon, Alexander T. Edelmann, Magnus Mörner, Gino Germani and Kalman Silvert, and, initially, John J. Johnson reflect very similar positions, especially with regard to the antimilitaristic nature of the middle class and its growing influence upon the military. Mörner comments that "the evident desires in the middle class environment to attain more democratic political forms, have also been accepted by a steadily growing number of military officers" (27). Germani and Silvert suggest that as the middle class grows larger, militarism declines because of middle-class dedication to civilian government and democratic procedures (9). Alexander adds that the growth of political parties has further worked to undermine militarism (3); and both Alexander and Edelmann refer to organized labor as another contributor to the undermining of the military's political role (3, 7). Fitzgibbon optimistically sees currently growing economic opportunity as the key to promoting stable democracy (8). Johnson, with more restraint than most of the others, adds his voice to the chorus, remarking that channels for the orderly transfer of government are "beginning to work," thus undermining militarism bit by bit (16).

Many of these writers are implying that military coups are increasingly coming to take place in a vacuum, based on the sheer power of the military vis-à-vis relatively helpless civilian sectors. However, such implications normally do not go quite to the extreme of depicting the coup as something totally in a vacuum. Jesús Silva Herzog is an exception to this rule, at least to the point of characterizing military governments as being totally isolated, "without any more support than the weapons of the soldiery" (34). His position is quite ironic, since it was written twenty years ago (1949), whereas most other writings of this inclination are much more recent and refer to the coup in a vacuum as a new phenomenon which has not yet reached the extreme of total isolation from civilian support. Nor do they treat military rule in such an extreme fashion.

Again, Putnam's empirical study appears to destroy an unfounded hypothesis, in this case the belief that political development decreases military intervention. Correlating several political development variables with his military intervention index, he arrives at the following conclusions: constitutional limits on military activity do not curtail militarism; popular political participation does not inhibit military intervention; "strong and articulate parties and pressure groups do not necessarily inhibit military intervention, nor do weak parties and pressure groups necessarily encourage intervention" (33). If Putnam's conclusions are accurate, it would appear that either Silva Herzog is right (that militarism is simply a product of the application of superior force against a helpless civilian population, thus rendering irrelevant the degree of development of civilian political institutions in a particular country), or that the development of civilian institutions does not necessarily signify a growing public attitude that the military should abandon its political role.

This latter position has been advanced by a large and growing number of writers. Increasingly, the literature has been dealing with military coups as phenomena which cannot be treated exclusively as the product of military whims independent of civilian encouragement or at least passivity. Writers with this approach decry the tendency of "traditionalists" to treat the military as an anomaly. McAlister, for example, contends that "implicit in traditional thinking is the assumption that the military is not really a component of the social order which created it. It is, rather, an alien and demoniac force which does not interact with other social groups but simply acts against them" (23). He also rejects the proposition that the emergence of labor, industrialists, middle sectors, intellectuals, and other such groups has served to undermine the political importance of the military. McAlister asserts that more pluralistic societies do not work against militarism. "Although they may inhibit unilateral action, they do not preclude alliances between military elements and aggressive, disgruntled, or frustrated civilian groups (25).

In like manner, Wyckoff observes that "the political role of the military is not a 'political disease'; rather it is but a symptom of a condition of political immaturity." Therefore, the military "is not by itself primarily responsible for the absence or presence of democracy or democratic institutions" (37). Silvert (35) confirms that

> it would be erroneous to presume that politicized military groups in Latin America move in an entirely simplistic and uninhibited fashion. In carrying out their internal political policing functions, the military interact with their peer groups or with those to which they aspire. There is no divorce, then, between the armed forces and the social elements comprising the most effective civilian political groups; on the contrary, often the identification is all too close. [P. 761]

Needler goes so far as to proclaim that "very frequently the conspirators are in touch with civilian politicians and respond to their advice. . . . This relationship sometimes takes the form of a coup only reluctantly staged by the military at the insistence of civilian politicians" (30). Arnade, on the other hand, claims that military coups and their acceptance by the public are mainly due to the fact that Latin American countries, except for Chile and Uruguay, are not basically democracies, that the democracy is a facade, "essentially a democracy of the upper classes," a clique which "controls the press and radio, molds public opinion, and dictates political policy" (5).

Such linking of militarism with upper class domination of the political system has become increasingly rare in more recent literature. A growing number of writers attribute this role to the middle class (though not necessarily in conflict with the upper class), and refer to the military as the instrument of the middle class in most Latin American countries. Accordingly, militarism is explained as the product of undemocratic leanings on the part of the middle class. Irving Louis Horowitz and José Nun are perhaps the clearest proponents of this hypothesis. Horowitz observes that middle-class sectors, including the large bureaucracy

> support the military out of a fear that any civilian regime which would run its natural course, naturally and inevitably, yields its power to the numerically superior popular classes. An informal bargain is thus reached which exchanges political democratization for a fundamental integration of society along middle-class lines. [Pp. 152–53]

He adds that even the urban working class and socialists stimulate militarism, hoping to convert the military into "a positive force for national redemption. They seem to await a military messiah who can perform for the Latin American area what President Nasser achieved in Egypt or what Premier Sukarno sought to achieve in Indonesia— a socialist construction imposed from above" (13). Obviously, this position is diametrically opposed to that of writers who see the military as becoming steadily more isolated.

Nun, for his part, sees the middle class as weak, divided, unorganized, lacking a coherent ideology, and, in essence, "at the mercy of circumstances." Thus, in crisis situations, its relative helplessness in organizing and uniting to defend its interests often leads to military intervention to bail it out (31). Johnson and Lieuwen take a milder view along these lines; but the former's position is becoming increasingly indistinguishable from that of Horowitz and Nun, in contrast to his former praise of the middle class as the champion of democracy (14).

Somewhat related to the position that military coups are basically in conflict with civilian aspirations and not products of civil-military interaction, is the belief that the military's political role is at least as much the product of interaction with foreign powers and foreign military counterparts as with civilian sectors within their own countries. Horowitz suggests that the military elite's position in the national power structure is "dependent upon foreign support and foreign supplies" (13). Alexander links militarism to the training that many Latin American armies received from German military missions in the late

nineteenth and early twentieth centuries: "This Prussian junker training reinforced already existing beliefs of the military men in their
peculiar destiny and their right to be the final arbiters of national
affairs" (3).

Lieuwen, Alba, Johnson, and William Gutteridge credit the United
States military with the ability to influence its Latin American counterparts to divest themselves of their political roles and work to promote
and safeguard democratic processes. Lieuwen observes that "the attitudes of United States officers toward their profession and their role
in society . . . did not fail to influence somewhat the outlook and the
attitudes of their Latin-American colleagues" (19), although he seems
to feel that the U.S. could be shaping these attitudes to a far greater
extent (reflecting Lieuwen's position that it could and should be
ardently promoting democracy). Alba asserts that the training of Latin
American officers in the United States has oriented them towards the
viewpoints of U.S. officers regarding the military role, moving them
away from political involvement (1): whereas Gutteridge simply refers
to U.S. military aid to Latin America as "an important force tending
at last to produce a detached professionalism" (12). Johnson expressed
similar sentiments in his earlier writings (15), but has since come to
relate military values much more to internal (local) factors.

On the other hand, several writers have viewed U.S.–Latin American military interaction as stimulating rather than deterring militarism. Lieuwen, partially inclined toward both views, observes that
there are serious doubts as to "whether the military emphasis in United
States policy toward Latin America is not seriously out of line with
our political and economic objective and long-term interests" (17).
Fitzgibbon takes a more unequivocal stand, criticizing the United
States' "unfortunate policy" of military assistance to Latin American
countries, which better enables them to suppress their own people (8).
Powell echoes this feeling, commenting that "it is difficult to escape the
conclusion that it is a contributory cause of militarism in Latin
America" (32).

McAlister and Putnam challenge the position that socialization
from foreign sources is the overriding factor. The former contends
that the attitudes of Latin American military officers are shaped much
more by their national environment than by external, international
factors (25); whereas the latter again applies statistical method to
manifest that foreign military missions have not had much influence
over the Latin American military, either in promoting militarism or

discouraging it (33). Wolf's data, referred to earlier, support this conclusion (36).

Two further themes have been the subject of controversy in the literature: the effects of militarism and military rule, and whether or not the military has a meaningful role to play. Regarding the first theme, differences of opinion center around the question of whether military intervention in politics or military rule can ever be beneficial. Alba's position is extreme on the negative side: "There is not . . . any achievement, nothing constructive, that can be attributed to military men in power" (1). In contrast, McAlister sums up the positive position by referring to "a tendency among reformist writers to believe that, in certain situations, civilian governments lack the power or the will to undertake essential economic and social reforms and that only an enlightened military can provide the necessary impetus" (23). Lieuwen also calls to mind some beneficial effects from military rule, observing that the masses "unquestionably benefited, materially and psychologically, from the social and economic reforms introduced by the new-type military leaders," including the impetus to industrialization, the development of communications and public works projects, their restoration of political stability which has improved the economic situation, and the fact that reformist military leaders have "tended to bring about greater equality in income and social position" (19).

Most writers, nonetheless, are inclined to believe that current problems are too complex for military rulers, that they normally work to preserve the status quo, and that their political role may actually foster the growth of communism, especially if they reinforce the status quo and destroy faith in the likelihood of change through democratic processes. Horowitz comments that "nearly every Latin American republic would stand politically to the Left of where it now is," were it not for the military (13).

Regarding the second theme, Alba again exemplifies the negative extreme in asserting that the armed forces have no meaningful role to play, that they "do not carry out any socially useful function; nor do they contribute to the development of the country nor assure its defense" (1). However, he wrote his book shortly before military civic action programs in the form of highway building, colonization, building construction, educational and medical programs, reforestation, etc., came into vogue. These programs notwithstanding, Horowitz discounts the benefits of civic action, claiming that the military simply uses it for political ends, so that the disadvantages of such projects outweigh the advantages (13). Those who fail to encounter a meaningful military role are most vociferous in their claims that the military is a parasite, sucking the lifeblood of the nation in the form of its huge budgetary allotment. (Actually, there are few writers who do not attack the size of these allotments.)

Those writers who believe that the military does play a positive role refer principally to civic action projects, and some urge the stimulation of such activities as a convenient vehicle to depoliticize the armed forces (on the theory that their political activity is mainly due to boredom and the lack of a mission). McAlister, Johnson, and Edward Glick especially stress the need to encourage military civic action programs (10, 16, 25). Moreover, a few writers refer to a positive military role in nation building. Luis Mercier Vega refers to the army as the only organization that encompasses the entire national territory and can work out of the capital to any distant area, thus coping with problems "not dealt with on a national scale by civilian governments" (26). McAlister adds that the military has been "a significant influence in overcoming regionalism and localism," through its nation-wide recruitment; and in "teaching patriotism and exalting national values" (24).

# BIBLIOGRAPHY

1. Alba, Víctor. *El militarismo*. Mexico City, 1960.

2. ———. "The Stages of Militarism in Latin America." In *The Role of the Military in Underdeveloped Countries,* ed. by John J. Johnson, pp. 165–83. Princeton, N.J., 1962.

3. Alexander, Robert J. "The Army in Politics." In *Government and Politics in Latin America,* ed. by Harold E. Davis, pp. 147–65. New York, 1958.

4. ———. *Today's Latin America*. 2nd ed. New York, 1968.

5. Arnade, Kurt Conrad. "The Technique of the Coup d'Etat in Latin America." In *The Evolution of Latin American Government,* ed. by Asher N. Christensen, pp. 309–17. New York, 1951.

6. Calvert, Peter. "The 'Typical Latin American Revolution.'" *International Affairs* 43 (January 1967): 85–95.

7. Edelmann, Alexander T. *Latin American Government and Politics*. Homewood, Ill., 1965.

8. Fitzgibbon, Russell H. "What Price Latin American Armies?" *Virginia Quarterly Review* 36 (Autumn 1960): 517–32.

9. Germani, Gino, and Kalman Silvert. "Politics, Social Structure and Military Intervention in Latin America." *Archives Européennes de Sociologie* 2 (Spring 1961): 62–81.

10. Glick, Edward Bernard. "The Feasibility of Arms Control and Disarmament in Latin America." *Orbis* 9 (Fall 1965): 743–59.

11. ———. "The Nonmilitary Use of the Latin American Military." In *Latin America: Politics, Economics, and Hemispheric Security,* ed. by Norman A. Bailey, pp. 179–91. New York: 1966.

12. Gutteridge, William. *Military Institutions and Power in the New States*. New York: 1965.

13. Horowitz, Irving Louis. "The Military Elites." In *Elites in Latin America,* ed. by Seymour Martin Lipset and Aldo Solari, pp. 146–89. New York, 1967.

14. ———. "The Military of Latin America." *Economic Development and Cultural Change* 13 (January 1965): 238–42.

15. Johnson, John J. "The Latin-American Military As a Politically Competing Group in Transitional Society." In *The Role of the Military in Underdeveloped Countries,* ed. by John J. Johnson, pp. 91–129. Princeton, N.J., 1962.

16. ———. *The Military and Society in Latin America*. Stanford, Calif., 1964.

17. Lieuwen, Edwin. *Arms and Politics in Latin America*. New York, 1961.

18. ———. *Generals vs. Presidents.* New York, 1964.
19. ———. "Militarism and Politics in Latin America." In *The Role of the Military in Underdeveloped Countries,* ed. by John J. Johnson, pp. 131–63. Princeton, N.J., 1962.
20. ———. "Militarism in Latin America: A Threat to the Alliance for Progress." *World Today* 19 (May 1963): 193–99.
21. ———. "The Military: A Force for Continuity or Change." In *Explosive Forces in Latin America,* ed. by John J. TePaske and Sidney Nettleton Fisher, p. 59–79. Columbus, Ohio, 1964.
22. ———. *The United States and the Challenge to Security in Latin America.* Columbus, Ohio, 1966.
23. McAlister, Lyle N. "Changing Concepts of the Role of the Military in Latin America." *Annals of the American Academy of Political and Social Science* 360 (July 1965): 85–98.
24. ———. "Civil-Military Relations in Latin America." *Journal of Inter-American Studies* 3 (July 1961): 341–50.
25. ———. "The Military." In *Continuity and Change in Latin America,* ed. by John J. Johnson, pp. 136–60. Stanford, Calif., 1964.
26. Mercier Vega, Luis. *Mecanismos del poder en América Latina.* Buenos Aires, 1967.
27. Mörner, Magnus. "Cuadillos y militares en la evolución hispanoamericana." *Journal of Inter-American Studies* 2 (1960): 295–310.
28. Needler, Martin C. *Latin American Politics in Perspective.* Princeton, N.J., 1962.
29. ———. "Political Development and Military Intervention in Latin America." *American Political Science Review* 60 (September 1966): 616–26.
30. ———. *Political Development in Latin America.* New York, 1968.
31. Nun, José. "A Latin American Phenomenon: The Middle-Class Military Coup." In *Latin America: Reform or Revolution,* ed. by James Petras and Maurice Zeitlin, pp. 145–85. New York, 1968.
32. Powell, John Duncan. "Military Assistance and Militarism in Latin America." *Western Political Quarterly* 18 (June 1965): 382–92.
33. Putnam, Robert D. "Toward Explaining Military Intervention in Latin American Politics." *World Politics* 20 (October 1967): 83–110.
34. Silva Herzog, Jesús. "Las juntas militares de gobierno." *Cuadernos Americanos* 8 (May–August 1949): 7–13.
35. Silvert, K. H. "Political Change in Latin America." In *The United States and Latin America,* ed. by Herbert L. Matthews, pp. 61–85, 2d. ed. Englewood Cliffs, N.J., 1963.

36. Wolf, Charles, Jr. "The Political Effects of Military Programs: Some Indications from Latin America." *Orbis* 8 (Winter 1965): 871–93.

37. Wyckoff, Theodore. "The Role of the Military in Latin American Politics." *Western Political Quarterly* 13 (September 1960): 745–63.

# INTER - AMERICAN RELATIONS

*Roger R. Trask*

Latin Americanists have produced a substantial amount of literature in the field of inter-American relations since the end of World War II. As a result, knowledge and understanding of the inter-American system and United States relations with the Latin American region and its individual nations have been enhanced. These works, however, vary greatly in quality, and neglect some important aspects of inter-American relations. Thus much remains to be accomplished.

With the possible exception of the Good Neighbor era, the role of the United States in Latin America since the late nineteenth century has been controversial. The intervention policy of the "colossus of the north" in the early twentieth century, and the tendency of the United States since 1945 to slight Latin America in favor of areas considered more critical, have contributed to the controversy. Latin American writers, with few exceptions, are very critical of the hemisphere policy of the United States. Their hostility explains the polemical emphasis, even in otherwise scholarly works, when Latin Americans write about U.S. policy and actions. While many U.S. scholars are similarly critical of their nation's policy, they usually avoid polemics. Latin American writers too often fail to use United States sources, contributing to the one-sided views frequently presented. U.S. students of inter-American relations, perhaps because of the availability of financial aid, usually do a better job of using Latin American sources, but often, sometimes because of inaccessible archives, their works are narrowly based too. There have been few scholarly, comprehensive, and non-polemical studies based extensively on the primary resources of both Latin America and the United States.

These generalizations can provide a basis for an examination of works on inter-American relations. The works cited are significant for various reasons and are representative of what students of and participants in inter-American affairs have concerned themselves with in the years since the end of World War II.

The author wishes to acknowledge the assistance in the preparation of this essay of M. Gary Forbes, a senior history student at Macalester College 1968–69.

203

## BIBLIOGRAPHIES

Students of inter-American relations will find useful *A Bibliography of United States–Latin American Relations Since 1810: A Selected List of Eleven Thousand Published References* (1968), edited by David F. Trask, Michael C. Meyer, and Roger R. Trask (132). Less comprehensive and somewhat out of date but still useful is R. A. Humphreys's *Latin American History: A Guide to the Literature in English* (68), published in 1958. The annual volumes of the *Handbook of Latin American Studies* (1936–   ) are indispensable for Latin Americanists (64). *A Guide to Latin American Studies,* edited by Martin H. Sable (115), is also helpful.

## THE INTER-AMERICAN SYSTEM

Several books on the historical development of the inter-American system have appeared in recent years. In a provocative series of essays, *The Western Hemisphere Idea: Its Rise and Decline* (135), Arthur P. Whitaker traces the development of the idea of hemispheric common interests. Wilfrid H. Callcott's *The Western Hemisphere: Its Influence on United States Policies to the End of World War II* (17) discusses factors which historically encouraged the idea of hemispheric unity in the United States. A Mexican writer, Antonio Gómez Robledo, in *Idea y experiencia de América* (59), surveys with a juridical-political emphasis the history of the "idea of America" from the sixteenth century. Harry Bernstein, in *Origins of Inter-American Interest, 1700–1812* (9) and *Making an Inter-American Mind* (8), discusses the bases for the development of interest by U.S. citizens in Latin America through the nineteenth century.

There has been considerable interest, especially in Latin America, in the historical development of the Pan-American movement. A Chilean, Alejandro Magnet (88), surveys the growth of Pan-Americanism to 1889, and José Sanson-Terán (120) carries the history through the 1948 Bogotá conference and presents a useful collection of documents. In preparation for the 1954 conference at Caracas, the Venezuelan government sponsored a contest for works on Simón Bolívar's influence on the development of the inter-American system. Jesús M. Yepes won the first prize and Francisco Cuevas Cancino the second. Each produced a useful two-volume work entitled *Del Congreso de Panamá a la Conferencia de Caracas, 1826–1954: El genio de Bolívar a través de la historia de las relaciones interamericanas* (33, 140). Enrique V. Corominas, onetime Argentine representative in the OAS, presents his personal observations and criticism of the United States in *Historia de las conferencias interamericanas: Desde el Congreso de Panamá hasta la Conferencia Interamericana de Caracas en 1954* (24). Two Brazilians, Olímpio de Souza Andrade (3) and Luis Gomes (58), discuss the role of the great Brazilian stateman Joaquim Nabuco in the development of Pan-Americanism.

Two well-known Latin Americanists in the United States recently have published accounts of the inter-American system. John Lloyd Mecham (94) emphasizes the concepts of security, regionalism, and universalism, and the special role of the United States. Mecham concludes that there is a vital need for regional organization in the Western Hemisphere. Less useful and somewhat superficial is Samuel G. Inman's *Inter-American Conferences, 1826–1954: History and Problems* (71). *The Inter-American System,* by Gordon Connell-Smith (23), an English scholar, should not be overlooked, but it must be used cautiously because of Connell-Smith's hostile and sometimes distorted interpretation of U.S. policy. Other more specilized works are C. Neale Ronning's *Law and Politics in Inter-American Diplomacy* (114), Donald R. Shea's *The Calvo Clause* (121), Mary A. Gardner's *The Inter-American Press Association: Its Fight for Freedom of the Press, 1926–1960* (56), and Sinclair Snow's *The Pan American Federation of Labor* (125).

The Organization of American States has been the subject of many books in the last two decades. *The Organization of American States* (130), by Ann Van Wynen Thomas and A. J. Thomas, Jr., is a valuable legalistic study of OAS institutions, but fails to provide a living picture of OAS operations. Jerome Slater's *The OAS and United States Foreign Policy* (122) fills this void well but lacks scholarly respectability. John C. Dreier, U.S. ambassador to the OAS for a decade, optimistically analyzes the OAS as an institution in his *The Organization of American States and the Hemisphere Crisis* (42). Dreier argues that nonintervention, a doctrine Latin Americans hold sacred, is also a serious obstacle to a more effective OAS. Latin Americans fear that strengthening the OAS might increase the possibility of political domination of the hemisphere by the United States. O. Carlos Stoetzer (128) and Charles G. Fenwick (51) provide historical and institutional surveys. An interesting and insightful personal account by the man who was the U.S. ambassador to the OAS from 1961 to 1963 is Delesseps S. Morrison's *Latin American Mission: An Adventure in Hemisphere Diplomacy* (97).

UNITED STATES RELATIONS WITH LATIN AMERICA: GENERAL AND
PERIOD STUDIES

Since World War II there have been few attempts to synthesize the history of United States–Latin American relations. Nothing has appeared to replace or extend Samuel F. Bemis's *The Latin American Policy of the United States* which, although published in 1943, is still useful. J. Lloyd Mecham's *A Survey of United States–Latin American Relations* (93), a textbook, provides country and chronological surveys. *U.S. Policy in Latin America: A Short History* (77), by Edwin Lieuwen, is brief and of limited usefulness. Dexter Perkins, in *The United States and Latin America* (103), presents three useful essays which emphasize the history of the Monroe Doctrine and U.S.–Latin American political and economic relationships. In a valuable study, *No Transfer: An American Security Principle* (81), John A. Logan, Jr., argues that the "no transfer" principle helped lead logically to the Monroe Doctrine.

Instead of writing broad syntheses, U.S. scholars have concentrated on period studies, mainly of twentieth century relations. For the early twentieth century, a good book, based mainly on U.S. sources, is Dana G. Munro's *Intervention and Dollar Diplomacy in the Caribbean, 1900–1921* (98). Munro argues that strategic considerations rather than business interests were the primary influences on U.S. policy. The Good Neighbor period has attracted several leading U.S. scholars. Alexander DeConde, in an admirable book using both U.S. and Latin American sources, *Herbert Hoover's Latin American Policy* (37), argues that the Good Neighbor policy had its origins during the Hoover administration. Helpful but not highly interpretive is Edward O. Guerrant's *Roosevelt's Good Neighbor Policy* (63). *The Making of the Good Neighbor Policy* (137), by Bryce Wood, is perceptive and provocative, and is the most detailed survey of the Roosevelt and Hoover periods. Wood has also written *The United States and Latin American Wars, 1932–1942* (138), which discusses the limited U.S. role in the Chaco, Leticia, and Marañon controversies. David H. Zook, in *Zarumilla-Marañon: The Ecuador-Peru Dispute* (142), analyzes one of these wars, with reference to related inter-American diplomacy, in great detail. Donald M. Dozer's book *Are We Good Neighbors? Three Decades of Inter-American Relations, 1930–1960* (38) covers the Good Neighbor policy and the post–World War II deterioration in U.S.–Latin American relations. Using Latin American newspapers, although not systematically, Dozer sheds considerable light on Latin American attitudes toward the United States. *The Americas: The Search for Hemisphere Security* (43), by Laurence Duggan, a Latin American specialist in the State Department from 1930 to 1944, covers realistically and not uncritically the Good Neighbor policy and the immediate postwar period. A Mexican historian, Francisco M. Cuevas Cancino, wrote *Roosevelt y la Buena Vecindad* (34), based in part on interviews with U.S. leaders, including Cordell Hull, Nelson Rockefeller, Sumner Welles, and others.

The establishment of the Alliance for Progress in the early 1960s signaled an apparent shift in emphasis in the policy of the United States, although in practice it has seemed something less. One of the earliest books on the Alliance was edited by John C. Dreier (41) and contains essays by Milton Eisenhower, Raúl Prebisch, José Figueres, Teodoro Moscoso, and Dean Rusk. The study by Nino Maritano and Antonio H. Obaid (87) is encouraging about the future of the Alliance while examining some of its problems. Lincoln Gordon, a State Department official and ambassador to Brazil who helped develop the Alliance, presents another optimistic view (60), but Víctor Alba, a Spanish journalist and political scientist living in Mexico, argues that Latin American oligarchies and the failure of the U.S. to identify with Latin American masses have crippled the Alliance (2). William D. Rogers, once deputy coordinator of the Alliance, feels that the United States did respond to the need for social revolution in Latin America when establishing the Alliance. He presents a strong defense in *The Twilight Struggle: The Alliance for Progress and the Politics of Development in Latin America* (113). A hostile interpretation emerges in Simon G. Hanson's study (65), which argues that the Alliance has intensified Latin American political instability and widened the gap between the rich and the poor.

Many U.S. writers have presented general appraisals of the post-1945 Latin American policy of their nation. Included are J. Fred Rippy (112), who emphasizes economic relations, and Herbert L. Matthews, who edited a study for the American Assembly (90). Adolf A. Berle, a onetime State Department official, wrote *Latin America: Diplomacy and Reality* (7), a useful book, although it generally ignores Latin American sources. John Gerassi, in *The Great Fear: The Reconquest of Latin America by Latin Americans* (57), aims devastating criticism at both U.S. policy and Latin American oligarchs and asserts that Latin American change through violent revolution is inevitable.

Milton S. Eisenhower, in *The Wine Is Bitter: The United States and Latin America* (45), agrees that revolution will come but expects it to be nonviolent in most Latin American countries. In part an account of his missions to Latin America for his brother, Eisenhower's book is not completely uncritical of U.S. policy. Robert N. Burr (14), in *Our Troubled Hemisphere: Perspectives on United States–Latin American Relations* (1967), advocates strengthening the OAS and the Alliance for Progress as means of improving relations. Edwin Lieuwen, in two books, considers the long-existing problem of Latin American militarism. In *Arms and Politics in Latin America* (75), after a comparative historical survey of Latin American armed forces, Lieuwen criticizes the nature of U.S. relations with the military. In a sequel, *Generals vs. Presidents: Neomilitarism in Latin America* (76), Lieuwen analyzes seven military coups between 1962 and 1964. While the Kennedy administration was cautious and slow to recognize the new governments, according to Lieuwen, the Johnson administration returned to the more pragmatic approach of relatively quick recognition. The old dilemma—how to reconcile assumed security needs with military governments which usually were undemocratic—remained.

Since World War II there has been a flood of critiques of U.S. policy from the pens of Latin American writers. Many have a historical framework, although few break new ground in historical scholarship. Usually highly critical and polemical in tone, they are valuable mainly as indicators of Latin American opinion of the U.S. and its policy. Perhaps the classic is Juan Arévalo's *The Shark and the Sardines* (5) (published in Buenos Aires in 1956 as *Fábula del tiburón y las sardinas: América Latina estrangulada*). For Arévalo, president of Guatemala between 1944 and 1951, the U.S. is the "shark," and the "sardines" are the Latin American republics, dominated by U.S. dollar diplomacy. Arévalo's *Anti-Kommunism in Latin America* (4) argues similar themes. Comparable in argument but more moderate and well balanced is *Andanzas de América* (83), by the Venezuelan Rodolfo Luzardo. In a useful but not brilliant book, *Latin America between the Eagle and the Bear* (85), Salvador de Madariaga analyzes Latin America's position between the U.S. "eagle" and the Soviet "bear." A Mexican writer, Vicente Sáenz, attacks U.S. and European economic imperialism in two books (117, 118), and the Chilean Carlos Dávila argues the same theme, but more moderately and responsibly, in *We of the Americas* (36).

Ramón Oliveres, who edited *La Prensa* in Buenos Aires during the Perón era, bitterly denounces U.S. imperialism (99), as does Genaro Carnero Checa (19). Two works which see Pan-Americanism as an instrument of U.S. domination are Ricardo A. Martínez's *De Bolívar a Dulles: El Panamericanismo, doctrina y práctica imperialista* (89), and Alonso Aguilar Monteverde's *El Panamericanismo: De la Doctrina Monroe a la Doctrina Johnson* (1). The latter work discusses the Dominican intervention of 1965 as an example of the "Johnson Doctrine." In *Los Estados Unidos y América Latina, 1930–1965* (109), Hernán Ramírez Necochea, a Chilean historian with Communist connections, argues that the U.S. through the Alliance for Progress and otherwise, has officially promoted a reformist policy while discouraging any real change in Latin America. Isidro Fabela, Mexican diplomat, historian, and journalist, has written three books which criticize U.S. policy: *Las Doctrinas Monroe y Drago* (49), *Buena y mala vecindad* (46), and *Intervención* (48).

## UNITED STATES RELATIONS WITH LATIN AMERICA: COUNTRY STUDIES

Some of the most solid books in the field of inter-American affairs published since World War II consider bilateral relations between the U.S. and individual Latin American nations. Most of these country studies have been written by U.S. scholars, although there are a few useful ones by Latin Americans. Four U.S. historians recently have produced surveys of relations with Argentina. Arthur P. Whitaker's *The United States and Argentina* (134) is brief but scholarly and informative. Much more extensive is *Argentina, the United States, and the Inter-American System, 1880–1914* (92), by Thomas F. McGann. Based on both Argentine and United States sources, McGann's book examines Argentina's European orientation beginning in the 1880s and its competition with the United States for hemispheric leadership. Harold F. Peterson's valuable *Argentina and the United States, 1810–1960* (105), a very detailed account, balances with McGann's book by paying some attention to aspects of U.S.-Argentine cooperation. Oscar E. Smith, in *Yankee Diplomacy: U.S. Intervention in Argentina* (123), covers relations since 1930 but especially criticizes U.S. intervention during the Perón era, which helped break down the Good Neighbor policy.

Only one major study of United States–Brazilian relations has appeared in recent years. E. Bradford Burns's *The Unwritten Alliance: Rio Branco and Brazilian-American Relations* (13) is an excellent monograph which stresses the shift of Brazil away from England and its rapprochement with the United States from 1902 to 1912. Further studies of other periods in U.S.-Brazilian relations are badly needed. For Chile, there is Frederick B. Pike's *Chile and the United States, 1880–1962: The Emergence of Chile's Social Crisis and the Challenge to United States Diplomacy* (106). Using Chilean sources, Pike emphasizes social problems in Chile and U.S. relations, which, he contends, included support for the upper classes. Carlos Mery Squella studies an earlier period in a book of limited usefulness, *Relaciones diplomáticas entre Chile y los Estados Unidos de América, 1829–1841* (126). Among other things Squella discusses Chilean–U.S. disputes during Chile's war with the Peru-Bolivian Confederation (1835–1839). Colorful but naive is *Chile through Embassy Windows, 1939–1953* (12), by Claude G. Bowers, U.S. ambassador to Chile during the years indicated.

James C. Carey's *Peru and the United States, 1900–1962* (18) is a perceptive study emphasizing economic relations, but it is not of the same high quality as the McGann and Peterson studies on Argentina and the Pike study on Chile. Peru's neighbor, Colombia, is the subject of *Eduardo Santos and the Good Neighbor, 1938–1942* (16), by David Bushnell. In a thorough study, Bushnell considers domestic developments in Colombia and their effects on relationships with the U.S. at the peak of the Good Neighbor era.

Dexter Perkins, in *The United States and the Caribbean* (104), surveys the political, economic, and social problems of the area and their effffects on U.S. policy. Perkins seems opposed to U.S. intervention more because it is useless than because it is wrong. A recent example of intervention, in which he was involved, is analyzed by Ambassador John Barlow Martin in *Overtaken by Events: The Dominican Crisis from the Fall of Trujillo to the Civil War* (88). Martin believes there was a genuine Communist threat in the Dominican Republic in 1965 and upholds President Lyndon Johnson's decision to dispatch the Marines. Not an apology for U.S. policy, this book is well worth reading.

There have been only a few books on U.S. relations with Central American nations. Lawrence O. Ealy (44) documents Panama's role as an independent country in international politics, and argues that Panama has not been a puppet of the United States. More recently Sheldon B. Liss published *The Canal: Aspects of United States–Panamanian Relations* (80), which sheds some new light on the controversy over the isthmian canal. Watt Stewart studies the activities of one of the founders of the United Fruit Company in *Keith and Costa Rica: A Biographical Study of Minor Cooper Keith* (127). Although essentially a narrative, the book is interesting and useful. U.S.-Nicaraguan relations in the late 1920s and early 1930s are in part the subject of Neil Macaulay's *The Sandino Affair* (84). The main argument in Vicente Sáenz's *Rompiendo cadenas: Las del imperialismo en Centro América y en otros repúblicas del continente* (119) is that Central America must cast off the bonds of U.S. political and economic control.

Cuban–United States relations have naturally interested many scholars. The role that the U.S. played in securing Cuban independence and the more recent problems with Fidel Castro have insured this interest. A useful study of early U.S. policy is Basil Rauch's *American Interest in Cuba, 1848–1855* (110). Philip S. Foner thus far has produced two volumes of a projected series entitled *A History of Cuba and Its Relations with the United States* (53), which brings the story up to 1895. David F. Healy's *The United States in Cuba, 1898–1902: Generals, Politicians, and the Search for Policy* (66) has great merit. Healy stresses the importance of the War Department in establishing Cuban policy and sees the Platt Amendment as a realistic approach to the Cuban situation. Allan R. Millett details the initial U.S. intervention in Cuba, based on the Platt Amendment, in *The Politics of Intervention: The Military Occupation of Cuba, 1906–1909* (96). Robert F. Smith's well-documented survey, *The United States and Cuba: Business and Diplomacy, 1917–1960* (124), criticizes U.S. policy which, he contends, was dominated by business interests from 1898 to the advent of Fidel Castro. Even more critical is William Appleman Williams in *The United States, Cuba, and Castro: An Essay on the Dynamics of Revolution and the Dissolution of Empire* (136). According to Williams, the U.S. must bear the blame for the leftist orientation of Castro's revolution. Although an interesting indictment, Williams's book must be read cautiously. One of the most perceptive observers of Castroism, Theodore Draper, has written two very helpful and balanced books which deal in part with Cuban–U.S. relations (39, 40). Enrique V. Corominas has written *México, Cuba y la OEA* (25), an important analysis of Mexico's attitude toward Cuba and its refusal to honor the OAS call for its members to sever diplomatic relations with Cuba.

The location of Mexico, its importance in Latin America,· the significance of its revolution, and accompanying problems with the

United States help to explain the wide interest in Mexican-American relations. Almost a classic is Howard F. Cline's *The United States and Mexico* (22). Somewhat mistitled, this perceptive book details Mexican history, especially since 1910, more than U.S.–Mexican relations. It is essential reading for students of Mexico and its relations with the U.S. Another recent survey, journalistic and somewhat superficial, is Daniel James's *Mexico and the Americans* (73). A Mexican author, Alberto M. Carreño, has written *La diplomacia extraordinaria entre México y Estados Unidos, 1789–1947* (20). The two volumes of this useful work divide at the Mexican War. An objective, unemotional, and well-documented study of the initial period in Mexican-American relations is Carlos Bosch Garcia's *Historia de las relaciones entre México y los Estados Unidos, 1819–1848* (11). Two good books which consider long-standing controversies are Sheldon B. Liss's *A Century of Disagreement: The Chamizal Conflict, 1864–1964* (79), and *Dividing the Waters: A Century of Controversy Between the United States and Mexico,* by Norris Hundley, Jr. (69).

The eminent Mexican historian, Daniel Cosío Villegas, has devoted two volumes in his comprehensive history of the Díaz period to foreign relations: *Historia moderna de México: El Porfiriato, la vida política exterior* (30). Using Mexican and some U.S. sources, Cosío Villegas has produced an extremely valuable work. A briefer study by Cosío, *Estados Unidos contra Porfirio Díaz* (29), emphasizes the initial years of Díaz's rule between 1876 and 1880. Cosío's account compliments Díaz and gives him credit for successfully countering U.S. pressures. David M. Pletcher's valuable monograph, *Rails, Mines, and Progress: Seven American Promoters in Mexico, 1876–1911* (107), recounts the business activities of some U.S. citizens in Mexico. No recent U.S. historian has produced a general study of Mexican-American relations in the Díaz period, although the author of this essay has one under way.

Several studies of Mexican-American relations during the first decade of the Mexican Revolution have appeared in recent years. Robert E. Quirk argues in his well-written *An Affair of Honor: Woodrow Wilson and the Occupation of Veracruz* (108) that poor communications and rumors contributed to Wilson's decision to occupy Veracruz in 1914. Isidro Fabela, Venustiano Carranza's foreign minister, has written two volumes on this same period. The first, *Revolución y régimen constitucionalista, Vol. III: Carranza, Wilson y el ABC* (50), concludes that Carranza won a diplomatic victory during the 1914 controversy. In *Historia diplomática de la Revolución Mexicana, II (1912–1917)* (47), Fabela begins with the Niagara Falls Conference (1914) and carries his narrative to 1918.

A solid and useful study of another phase of Wilson's Mexican policy is *The United States and Pancho Villa: A Study in Unconventional Diplomacy,* by Clarence C. Clendenen (21). Louis M. Teitelbaum's *Woodrow Wilson and the Mexican Revolution (1913–1916): A History of United States-Mexican Relations from the Murder of Madero until Villa's Provocation across the Border* (129) provides some useful information, but because of its poor organization, has limited value and little scholarly status. The activities of Ricardo Flores Magón in Baja California during the Revolution and U.S.–Mexican relations in the area are discussed by Lowell L. Blaisdell in *The Desert Revolution* (10). *The Cabinet Diaries of Josephus Daniels, 1913–1921* (32), edited by E. David Cronon, shed additional light on Mexican-American relations.

Aarón Sáenz, who for a time was Alvaro Obregón's secretary for foreign affairs, discusses the 1920–24 period in *La política internacional de la Revolución: Estudios y documentos* (116). With polemics Sáenz defends Obregón from charges that he gave in to U.S. pressures. Alberto J. Pani's book dealing with the same period, *Las Conferencias de Bucareli* (102), has more value. Lorenzo Meyer's *México y Estados Unidos en el conflicto petrolero (1917–1942)* (95) is documented from Mexican and U.S. sources and has merit because of its coverage and general objectivity. E. David Cronon's masterful biography, *Josephus Daniels in Mexico* (31), chronicles Daniels's work as U.S. ambassador between 1933 and 1942 and his important contributions to the development and implementation of the Good Neighbor policy. Also useful are Daniels's memoirs of his Mexican service (35).

## CONCLUSIONS

This survey of the literature of inter-American relations since 1945 suggests the need for more scholarly work on the subject in both the United States and Latin America. While much of value has been produced, especially in the United States, much remains to be done. Both U.S. and Latin American scholars should consider the possibility of writing syntheses of the history of United States–Latin American relations. These same scholars need to produce more country studies—especially for the smaller, less obvious nations. Such studies would facilitate the eventual writing of the syntheses called for above.

Students of Latin America need to make more use of each other's primary resources—diplomatic archives and other official and unofficial sources. This depends in part, of course, on the willingness of Latin American governments to open their archives for full research. Finally, more objectivity is needed, especially although not exclusively by Latin American writers. Their hostility toward the United States has legitimate historical and contemporary foundations; but one can hope that they will be able to overcome their fears and prejudices as they produce scholarly works which could contribute substantially to the improvement of relationships among the nations of the Western Hemisphere.

# BIBLIOGRAPHY

1. Aguilar Monteverde, Alonso. *El Panamericanismo: de la Doctrina Monroe a la Doctrina Johnson.* Mexico, 1965.

2. Alba, Víctor. *Alliance without Allies: The Mythology of Progress in Latin America.* New York, 1965.

3. Andrade, Olímpio de Souza. *Joaquim Nabuco e o Pan-Americanismo.* São Paulo, 1950.

4. Arévalo, Juan J. *Anti-Kommunism in Latin America.* New York, 1964.

5. ———. *The Shark and the Sardines.* New York, 1961.

6. Bailey, Norman A. *Latin America in World Politics.* New York, 1967.

7. Berle, Adolf A. *Latin America: Diplomacy and Reality.* New York, 1962.

8. Bernstein, Harry. *Making an Inter-American Mind,* Gainesville, Fla., 1961.

9. ———. *Origins of Inter-American Interest, 1700–1812.* Philadelphia, 1945.

10. Blaisdell, Lowell L. *The Desert Revolution.* Madison, Wis., 1962.

11. Bosch García, Carlos. *Historia de las relaciones entre México y los Estados Unidos, 1819–1848.* Mexico, 1961.

12. Bowers, Claude G. *Chile through Embassy Windows, 1939–1953.* New York, 1958.

13. Burns, E. Bradford. *The Unwritten Alliance: Rio Branco and Brazilian-American Relations.* New York, 1966.

14. Burr, Robert N. *Our Troubled Hemisphere: Perspectives on United States–Latin American Relations.* Washington, D.C., 1967.

15. Burr, Robert N., and Roland D. Hussey. *Documents on Inter-American Cooperation.* 2 vols. Philadelphia, 1955.

16. Bushnell, David. *Eduardo Santos and the Good Neighbor, 1938–1942.* Gainesville, Fla., 1967.

17. Callcott, Wilfrid H. *The Western Hemisphere: Its Influence on United States Policies to the End of World War II.* Austin, Tex., 1968.

18. Carey, James C. *Peru and the United States, 1900–1962.* Notre Dame, Ind., 1964.

19. Carnero Checa, Genaro. *El aguila rampante: El imperialismo yanqui sobre América Latina.* Mexico, 1956.

20. Carreño, Alberto M. *La diplomacia extraordinaria entre México y Estados Unidos, 1789–1947.* 2 vols. Mexico, 1951.

21. Clendenen, Clarence C. *The United States and Pancho Villa: A Study in Unconventional Diplomacy.* Ithaca, N.Y., 1961.

22. Cline, Howard F. *The United States and Mexico.* 3d. ed. Cambridge, Mass., 1963.

215

23. Connel-Smith, Gordon. *The Inter-American System.* London, 1966.

24. Corominas, Enrique V. *Historia de las conferencias interamericanas: Desde el Congreso de Panamá hasta la Conferencia Interamericana de Caracas en 1954.* Buenos Aires, 1959.

25. ———. *México, Cuba y la OEA.* Buenos Aires, 1965.

26. Cosío Villegas, Daniel. *American Extremes.* Austin, Tex., 1964.

27. ———. *Change in Latin America: The Mexican and Cuban Revolutions.* Lincoln, Nebr., 1961.

28. ———. *Cuestiones internacionales de México, una bibliografía.* Mexico, 1966.

29. ———. *Estados Unidos contra Porfirio Díaz.* Mexico, 1956. Eng. ed., Lincoln, Nebr., 1964.

30. ———. *Historia moderna de México: El Porfiriato, la vida política exterior.* 2 vols. Mexico, 1960–1963.

31. Cronon, E. David. *Josephus Daniels in Mexico.* Madison, Wis., 1960.

32. ———, ed. *The Cabinet Diaries of Josephus Daniels, 1913–1921.* Lincoln, Nebr., 1963.

33. Cuevas Cancino, Francisco M. *Del Congreso de Panamá a la Conferencia de Caracas, 1826–1954: El genio de Bolívar a través de la historia de las relaciones interamericanas.* 2 vols. Caracas, 1955.

34. ———. *Roosevelt y la Buena Vecindad.* Mexico, 1954.

35. Daniels, Josephus. *Shirt-Sleeve Diplomat.* Chapel Hill, N.C., 1947.

36. Dávila, Carlos. *We of the Americas.* Chicago, 1949.

37. DeConde, Alexander. *Herbert Hoover's Latin American Policy.* Stanford, Calif., 1951.

38. Dozer, Donald M. *Are We Good Neighbors? Three Decades of Inter-American Relations, 1930–1960.* Gainesville, Fla., 1959.

39. Draper, Theodore. *Castroism: Theory and Practice.* New York, 1965.

40. ———. *Castro's Revolution: Myths and Realities.* New York, 1962.

41. Dreier, John C., ed. *The Alliance for Progress: Problems and Perspectives.* Baltimore, 1962.

42. ———, ed. *The Organization of American States and the Hemisphere Crisis.* New York, 1962.

43. Duggan, Laurence. *The Americas: The Search for Hemisphere Security.* New York, 1949.

44. Ealy, Lawrence O. *The Republic of Panama in World Affairs, 1903–1950.* Philadelphia, 1951.

45. Eisenhower, Milton S. *The Wine Is Bitter: The United States and Latin America.* Garden City, N.Y., 1963.

46. Fabela, Isidro. *Buena y Mala Vecindad*. Mexico, 1958.

47. ———. *Historia diplomática de la Revolución Mexicana, II (1912–1917)*. Mexico, 1959.

48. ———. *Intervención*. Mexico, 1959.

49. ———. *Las Doctrinas Monroe y Drago*. Mexico, 1957.

50. ———, ed. *Revolución y régimen constitucionalista, Vol. III: Carranza, Wilson y el ABC*. Mexico, 1962.

51. Fenwick, Charles G. *The Organization of American States: The Inter-American Regional System*. Washington, D.C., 1963.

52. Fitte, Ernesto J. *La agresión norteamericano a las Islas Malvinas*. Buenos Aires, 1966.

53. Foner, Philip S. *A History of Cuba and Its Relations with the United States*. 2 vols. New York, 1962.

54. Fuchs, Jaime. *La penetración de los trusts yanquis en la Argentina*. 2nd ed. Buenos Aires, 1959.

55. Gantenbein, James W., ed. *The Evolution of Our Latin American Policy: A Documentary Record*. New York, 1950.

56. Gardner, Mary A. *The Inter-American Press Association: Its Fight for Freedom of the Press, 1926–1960*. Austin, Tex., 1967.

57. Gerassi, John. *The Great Fear: The Reconquest of Latin America by Latin Americans*. New York, 1963.

58. Gomes, Luis S. *Joaquim Nabuco e o Pan-Americanismo*. Rio de Janeiro, 1950.

59. Gómez Robledo, Antonio. *Idea y experiencia de América*. Mexico, 1958.

60. Gordon, Lincoln. *A New Deal for Latin America: The Alliance for Progress*. Cambridge, Mass., 1963.

61. Graber, Doris A. *Crisis Diplomacy: A History of U.S. Intervention Policies and Practices*. Washington, D.C., 1959.

62. Gregg, Robert W., ed. *International Organization in the Western Hemisphere*. Syracuse, N.Y., 1968.

63. Guerrant, Edward O. *Roosevelt's Good Neighbor Policy*. Albuquerque, N.Mex., 1950.

64. *Handbook of Latin American Studies*. 20 vols. Cambridge, Mass., 1936–51 (vols. 1–13); Gainesville, Fla., 1951–68 (vols. 14–30).

65. Hanson, Simon G. *Five Years of the Alliance for Progress: An Appraisal*. Washington, D.C., 1967.

66. Healy, David F. *The United States in Cuba, 1898–1902: Generals, Politicians, and the Search for Policy*. Madison, Wis., 1963.

67. Houston, John A. *Latin America in the United Nations*. New York, 1956.

68. Humphreys, R. A. *Latin American History: A Guide to the Literature in English.* London, 1958.

69. Hundley, Norris, Jr. *Dividing the Waters: A Century of Controversy between the United States and Mexico.* Berkeley, Calif., 1966.

70. Ibarguren, Carlos. *De Monroe a la Buena Vecindad.* Buenos Aires, 1946.

71. Inman, Samuel G. *Inter-American Conferences, 1826–1954: History and Problems.* Washington, D.C., 1965.

72. Inter-American Institute of International Legal Studies. *The Inter-American System: Its Development and Strengthening.* Dobbs Ferry, N.Y., 1966.

73. James, Daniel. *Mexico and the Americans.* New York, 1963.

74. Krehm, William. *Democracia y tiranías en el Caribe.* Mexico, 1949.

75. Lieuwen, Edwin. *Arms and Politics in Latin America.* New York, 1960.

76. ———. *Generals vs. Presidents: Neomilitarism in Latin America.* New York, 1964.

77. ———. *U.S. Policy in Latin America: A Short History.* New York, 1965.

78. Link, Arthur S. *La política de Estados Unidos en América Latina, 1913–1916.* Mexico, 1960.

79. Liss, Sheldon B. *A Century of Disagreement: The Chamizal Conflict, 1864–1964.* Washington, D.C., 1965.

80. ———. *The Canal: Aspects of United States–Panamanian Relations.* Notre Dame, Ind., 1967.

81. Logan, John A., Jr. *No Transfer: An American Security Principle.* New Haven, Conn., 1961.

82. López Jiménez, Ramón. *El principio de no intervención en América y la nota uruguaya.* Buenos Aires, 1947.

83. Luzardo, Rodolfo. *Andanzas de América.* Caracas, 1962.

84. Macaulay, Neil. *The Sandino Affair.* Chicago, 1967.

85. Madariaga, Salvador de. *Latin America between the Eagle and the Bear.* New York, 1962.

86. Magnet, Alejandro. *Orígenes y Antecedentes del Panamericanismo.* Santiago de Chile, 1945.

87. Maritano, Nino, and Antonio H. Obaid. *An Alliance for Progress: The Challenge and the Problem.* Minneapolis, Minn., 1963.

88. Martin, John Barlow. *Overtaken by Events: The Dominican Crisis from the Fall of Trujillo to the Civil War.* Garden City, N.Y., 1966.

89. Martínez, Ricardo A. *De Bolívar a Dulles: El Panamericanismo, doctrina y práctica imperialista.* 2d ed. Mexico, 1959.

90. Matthews, Herbert L., ed. *The United States and Latin America.* 2d ed. Englewood Cliffs, N.J., 1963.

91. McClellan, Grant S., ed. *United States Policy in Latin America*. New York, 1963.

92. McGann, Thomas F. *Argentina, the United States, and the Inter-American System, 1880–1914*. Cambridge, Mass., 1957.

93. Mecham, John Lloyd. *A Survey of the United States–Latin American Relations*. Boston, 1965.

94. ———. *The United States and Inter-American Security, 1889–1960*. Austin, Tex., 1961.

95. Meyer, Lorenzo. *México y Estados Unidos en el conflicto petrolero (1917–1942)*. Mexico, 1968.

96. Millett, Alan R. *The Politics of Intervention: The Military Occupation of Cuba, 1906–1909*. Columbus, Ohio, 1968.

97. Morrison, Delesseps S. *Latin American Mission: An Adventure in Hemisphere Diplomacy*. New York, 1965.

98. Munro, Dana G. *Intervention and Dollar Diplomacy in the Caribbean, 1900–1921*. Princeton, N.J., 1964.

99. Oliveres, Ramón. *El imperialismo yanqui en América: La dominación política y económica del continente*. Buenos Aires, 1952.

100. Palacios, Alfredo L. *Nuestra América y el imperialismo*. Buenos Aires, 1961.

101. Pan American Union. *Inter-American Treaty of Reciprocal Assistance Applications*. 2 vols. Washington, D.C., 1964.

102. Pani, Alberto J. *Las conferencias de Bucareli*. Mexico, 1953.

103. Perkins, Dexter. *The United States and Latin America*. Baton Rouge, La., 1961

104. ———. *The United States and the Caribbean*. Rev. ed. Cambridge, Mass., 1966.

105. Peterson, Harold F. *Argentina and the United States, 1810–1960*. New York, 1964.

106. Pike, Frederick B. *Chile and the United States, 1880–1962: The Emergence of Chile's Social Crisis and the Challenge to United States Diplomacy*. Notre Dame, Ind., 1963.

107. Pletcher, David M. *Rails, Mines, and Progress: Seven American Promoters in Mexico, 1867–1911*. Ithaca, N.Y., 1958.

108. Quirk, Robert E. *An Affair of Honor: Woodrow Wilson and the Occupation of Veracruz*. Lexington, Ky., 1962.

109. Ramírez Necochea, Hermán. *Los Estados Unidos y Amèrica Latina, 1930–1965*. Santiago de Chile, 1965.

110. Rauch, Basil. *American Interest in Cuba, 1848–1855*. New York, 1949.

111. Reidy, Joseph W. *Strategy for the Americas*. New York, 1966.

112. Rippy, J. Fred. *Globe and Hemisphere: Latin America's Place in the Postwar Foreign Relations of the United States.* Chicago, 1958.

113. Rogers, William D. *The Twilight Struggle: The Alliance for Progress and the Politics of Development in Latin America.* New York, 1967.

114. Ronning, C. Neale. *Law and Politics in Inter-American Diplomacy.* New York, 1963.

115. Sable, Martin H., ed. *A Guide to Latin American Studies.* 2 vols. Los Angeles, 1967.

116. Sáenz, Aaron. *La política internacional de la Revolución: Estudios y documentos.* Mexico, 1961.

117. Sáenz, Vicente. *Hispano América contra el coloniaje.* Mexico, 1949.

118. ———. *Nuestra América en la cruz.* Mexico, 1960.

119. ———. *Rompiendo cadenas: Las del imperialismo en Centro América y en otras repúblicas del continente.* 2d ed. Mexico, 1951.

120. Sanson-Terán, José. *El interamericanismo en marcha: De Bolívar y Monroe al Rooseveltianismo.* Washington, D.C., 1949.

121. Shea, Donald R. *The Calvo Clause: A Problem of Inter-American and International Law and Diplomacy.* Minneapolis, Minn., 1955.

122. Slater, Jerome. *The OAS and United States Foreign Policy.* Columbus, Ohio, 1967.

123. Smith, Oscar E. *Yankee Diplomacy: U.S. Intervention in Argentina.* Dallas, 1953.

124. Smith, Robert F. *The United States and Cuba: Business and Diplomacy, 1917–1960.* New York, 1960.

125. Snow, Sinclair. *The Pan American Federation of Labor.* Durham, N.C., 1964.

126. Equella, Carlos Mery. *Relaciones diplomáticas entre Chile y los Estados Unidos de América, 1829–1841.* Santiago de Chile, 1965.

127. Stewart, Watt. *Keith and Costa Rica: A Biographical Study of Minor Cooper Keith.* Albuquerque, N.Mex., 1964.

128. Stoetzer, O. Carlos. *The Organization of American States: An Introduction.* New York, 1965.

129. Teitelbaum, Louis M. *Woodrow Wilson and the Mexican Revolution (1913–1916): A History of United States–Mexican Relations from the Murder of Madero until Villa's Provocation across the Border.* New York, 1967.

130. Thomas, Ann Van Wynen, and A. J. Thomas, Jr. *The Organization of American States.* Dallas, 1963.

131. Tischendorf, Alfred, and E. Taylor Parks, eds. *The Diary and Journal of Richard Clough Anderson, Jr., 1814–1826.* Durham, N.C., 1964.

132. Trask, David F.; Michael C. Meyer; and Roger R. Trask; comps. and eds. *A Bibliography of United States–Latin American Relations since 1810: A Selected List of Eleven Thousand Published References.* Lincoln, Nebr., 1968.

133. Uribe Vargas, Diego. *Panamericanismo democrático: Bases para una transformación del sistema continental.* Bogotá, 1958.

134. Whitaker, Arthur P. *The United States and Argentina.* Cambridge, Mass., 1954.

135. ———. *The Western Hemisphere Idea: Its Rise and Decline.* New York, 1954.

136. Williams, William Appleman. *The United States, Cuba and Castro: An Essay on the Dynamics of Revolution and the Dissolution of Empire.* New York, 1962.

137. Wood, Bryce. *The Making of the Good Neighbor Policy.* New York, 1961.

138. ———. *The United States and Latin American Wars, 1932–1942.* New York, 1966.

139. Wythe, George A. *The United States and Inter-American Relations: A Contemporary Appraisal.* Gainesville, Fla., 1964.

140. Yepes, Jesús M. *Del Congreso de Panamá a la Conferencia de Caracas, 1826–1954: El genio de Bolívar a través de la historia de las relaciones interamericanas.* 2 vols. Caracas, 1955.

141. Yrarrázaval Concha, Eduardo. *América Latina en la guerra fría.* Santiago de Chile, 1959.

142. Zook, David H. *Zarumilla-Marañon: The Ecuador-Peru Dispute.* New York, 1964.

# Part Three

# LITERARY CURRENTS SINCE WORLD WAR II

# 3. LITERARY CURRENTS SINCE WORLD WAR II

Since World War II the Latin American literary world has seen great activity and experimentation as writers have sought new avenues of expression after modernism, which for so long inspired the major literary output of that part of the world. The merit of the best of this new writing is reflected in the world recognition it has received, including Nobel literature prizes to Gabriela Mistral (Lucila Godoy y Alcayaga) of Chile and Miguel Angel Asturias of Guatemala and a Stalin award to Pablo Neruda (Neftalí Ricardo Reyes) of Chile.

Since litererary movements do not happen spontaneously but are part of a continuing evolution, the essays in this section give us a helpful perspective by presenting the prewar contexts in which the postwar developments have occurred. Luis Leal and Fábio Lucas, taking a similar approach in studying the two main literary worlds in Latin America, the Spanish and the Portuguese, follow chronologically the rich output that began in the late thirties and still shows signs of strength and innovation.

Jorge Luis Borges, María Luisa Bombal, and Agustín Yáñez opened a new era in Spanish American fiction, which continues to provide effective experimentation in the works of Carlos Fuentes and Gabriel García Márquez. One can detect in them a kind of sophistication that overrides the exclusively social preoccupation of Ciro Alegría and Jorge Icaza. There is a new and sincere approach to structure, style, and psychological impact. In his chronological description, Luis Leal underlines the poetic significance of the new novels, as if to redeem the authors from the exclusively social and political commitments. More than a study of the criticism of the novel, Professor Leal's essay points out the outstanding examples of creativity and experimentation. This, in our judgment, is a refreshing approach, since the critic must react to the impact of the new narrators such as García Márquez.

Fábio Lucas employs a similar approach in examining the Brazilian novel and short story, but underlines the fact that in Brazil two distinct tendencies of realism-naturalism survived into the postwar period: "fiction reinforced by documentary evidence, and exaggerated character portrayal." The awareness of new methods used by foreign writers is clear in Brazilian fiction, but those methods are adapted to local moods and circumstances. Actually, the literary revolution in Brazil,

225

according to Professor Lucas, is aimed not only at bringing about a new society, but at establishing a "relation between its own created reality and the means of literary expression." The achievements of Brazilian fiction writers have been stimulated by experimentation, Guimarães Rosa being one of the outstanding examples.

Bernard Gicovate and Wilson Martins underline the year 1945 as a major turning point in both Spanish American and Brazilian poetry. In the former, that year marks the beginning of "historical investigation and stylistic analysis," although marred by "excessive professionalism." In the case of the latter, the end of World War II marks the beginning of a most powerful effort to remove "that gigantic corpse of modernism." However, in both there is a clearly discernible tendency toward innovation and experimentation, both in creativity and in criticism.

# THE SPANISH AMERICAN NOVEL AND SHORT STORY

*Luis Leal*

In his short but interesting essay *Notes on the Novel* (1925) (66) the Spanish philosopher José Ortega y Gasset expressed the opinion that the novel was a decadent art form and that therefore it would probably die out in the near future. He believed that the novelist had exhausted the supply of themes; that it was not easy to write a good novel then, since it is difficult to please a reader who has read the great novels of the past and who knows more psychology than is known by the average novelist. Therefore, concluded Ortega, the writing of a good novel at that time required the aptitudes and intelligence of a genius. Keeping these observations in mind while thinking about the many excellent novels that have been written in Spanish America since 1925, we come to the conclusion that either Ortega was wrong or that Spanish American writers have conspired to prove him wrong.

Jorge Luis Borges (b. Argentina, 1899), for instance, was a member of the vanguard school, and his early literary activities were confined to the writing of poetry. In 1935 he published his first works of fiction. By that year the two trends in the development of the novel, the psychological and the socially oriented, were well established. The next decade (1935–45) saw the birth of a new type of fiction, the fantastic story. The social novel declined in popularity and there was a new interest in the writing of experimental novels.

By 1935 the taste of the reader of novels had changed in Latin America, just as it had elsewhere. The Spanish American novel written after that year, with some exceptions, is more like that written in Europe and the United States, more like those of André Gide *(Faux-monayeurs,* 1926), Virginia Woolf *(Orlando,* 1928), Aldous Huxley *(Point Counter Point,* 1928), William Faulkner *(The Sound and the Fury,* 1929), and Ernest Hemingway *(A Farewell to Arms,* 1929). In 1935 Borges published his *Historia universal de la infamia* (24), a fundamental work in the development of Spanish American narrative prose. His style is at the opposite pole of that regarded as typical of Spanish American novelists, of that of José Eustasio Rivera, Ricardo Güiraldes, Rómulo Gallegos, and Jorge Icaza, which is overburdened with ornamentation.

Borges's style is terse, straightforward, limited in vocabulary, and yet sophisticated, rich in contextual references, and intellectually exciting. In this first book we already find the characteristics that will later make Borges famous as a short-story writer, the characteristics that will predominate in the stories collected in *Ficciones* (1944) (23), *El aleph* (1949) (22), and *La muerte y la brújula* (1951) (25). *Historia universal de la infamia* is a collection of stories based on the lives of men famous for their infamous deeds. The settings are international (China, Japan, Persia, Chile, the United States), as are the characters. As Borges himself says, these stories are comments upon other books, which in turn are as heterogeneous as the settings and the characters, with those in English predominating. The themes treated demonstrate Borges's interest in the fantastic, in science fiction, and in the detective story. Imaginative literature is his main interest and therefore his own stories are attempts to create a nonrealistic, nonsocial fiction, a fiction which although it may not be considered characteristic of Latin America, is nevertheless just as important as the more typical. In a great measure the new trend toward fantastic literature is due to Borges. To his school belong such important novelists and short-story writers as Adolfo Bioy-Casares (b. Argentina, 1914), Enrique Anderson-Imbert (b. Argentina, 1910), Virgilio Piñera (b. Cuba, 1914), Juan José Arreola (b. Mexico, 1918), and Julio Cortázar (b. Argentina, 1914).

The psychological novel is represented during this period by the Chilean María Luisa Bombal (b. 1910), best known by her short story "El árbol," in which she combines theme and structure to bring out the agonizing nature of the life of a young girl married to an old man. In her two novels, *La última niebla* (1935) (21) and *La amortajada* (1938) (20), she presents psychological problems related to the sexual life of women. In the first the protagonist, lacking the love of her husband (still in love with his first wife, now dead), compensates by creating an imaginary lover. In the second work Bombal goes a step further in the development of her narrative technique by re-creating the love life of the protagonist just before her funeral. In both works the nebulous settings, the poetic style, and the introspective nature of the characters give the narratives a dreamlike tone, a quality very well suited to the themes treated.

By 1940 the foundations for the contemporary novel in Spanish America had been laid. The years 1940 and 1941 mark, more than any others, a turning point in the development of narrative fiction, since during those two years several significant novels were published. In 1940 Adolfo Bioy-Casares published *La invención de Morel* (18), a science fiction novel dealing with the nature of reality. The same year Eduardo Mallea (Argentina, b. 1903) published *La bahía de silencio* (56), his second novel (*Fiesta en noviembre* (57) had appeared in 1938), in which he dissects life in a metropolitan center, in this case Buenos Aires, thus beginning a trend toward the urban-centered novel. If *La bahía de silencio* lacks unity of place (the protagonist makes a trip to Italy, taking the reader along with him), and is overburdened with long essays on the nature of *argentinidad*, it is nevertheless important, for it analyzes life in the city as a whole and succeeds in presenting a vivid picture of social relations and their motivations. Mallea's following novel, *Todo verdor perecerá* (1941) (58), is better structured; the characters, especially Agata, the protagonist, come to life in their struggle against a hostile environment. The theme of sterility is very well embodied in the main character, Agata, and reflected in her environment through well-integrated imagery.

In Mexico the new novel, that is, the novel produced since 1940, reflects the tendencies of the European and North American novel. At the same time, it does not lose its Mexican identity, since it does not break entirely with tradition, as in other countries. The influence of the novelists of the Revolution—Mariano Azuela, Martín Luis Guzmán, José Rubén Romero—is evident in the selection of themes, in the creation of backgrounds, and in the techniques of characterization. But the influence of the European and North American novel is evident in the treatment of the national themes, in the form, and in the introduction of new points of view. Of the North American novelists, William Faulkner, John Dos Passos, and Ernest Hemingway have had the strongest influence; of the English, James Joyce, Virginia Woolf, and Aldous Huxley; of the French, Alain Robbe-Grillet and Nathalie Sarraute. The application of new techniques to the development of Mexican subject matter has produced an original novel that, without losing its national identity, has become universal.

In 1943 José Revueltas (b. 1914) published *El luto humano* (70) (translated into English under the title *The Stone Knife*, 1947), the first novel written by a Mexican author in which an attempt was made to apply modern novelistic techniques. Although in some respects it shows the influence of Azuela, Guzmán, and Gregoria López y Fuentes, in others that of William Faulkner predominates. This novel represents a contribution to the development of Spanish American fiction because Revueltas tried to solve the problems of narrative technique without abandoning native subject matter. If he failed, his lesson was not lost, and soon after there appeared novelists who produced works of high quality.

In the following year, 1944, Rubén Salazar Mallén (b. Mexico, 1905) published a short novel, *Soledad* (*Loneliness*) (81), in which he carried the psychological process farther than Revueltas had done. If in *El luto humano* we still find social preaching, in *Soledad* nothing remains but the interest in the psychological presentation of the central character, Aquiles Alcázar, a government worker in Mexico City haunted by a persecution complex. Alcázar, very much like Juan Carlos Onetti's Eladio Linacero, is a symbol of the man whose life is a vacuum; he is a symbol of modern man, isolated from his fellow men by his own fear, incapable of carrying out any constructive action, without any will power to conquer, always thinking about the negative significance of the most inconsequential actions and words of his fellow workers. In order to present the psychological aspect of Alcázar's life, the author makes use of the stream-of-consciousness technique, thus giving the reader a direct insight into the character's mind.

Some critics may object that Salazar Mallén's novel is too short, that it lacks, like Onetti's *El pozo*, depth and complexity. This could not be said of the novel of Agustín Yáñez (b. Mexico, 1904), *Al filo del agua* (*At the Edge of the Storm*) (94), which appeared in 1947 and represents perhaps the most ambitious undertaking in the field of the novel by a Mexican writer. It brings together several trends that had been present in Mexican fiction; it is a work of art that is, at the same time, national and universal, artistic and social. If some critics consider it a novel of the Revolution, it is because we find in it the best literary explanation of why the Revolution took place. The novelist selected a dramatic moment not only in the life of his characters, but also in the history of Mexico. The Mexican people, so well represented in this novel, were at the brink of an explosion in 1909; the unfolding of the novel is parallel to the unfolding of Mexican history. The causes to which the author attributes the Revolution are not stated explicitly in the novel, but the reader can easily reach the conclusions from the actions of the characters. Yáñez has created a community that is completely isolated from the main cultural currents, not by its own will, but by a severe censorship imposed by civil and religious authorities. It is a community where free thinking is unknown, where repressed sexual desires drive both men and women to insanity, where reading a daily newspaper is considered a major sin. No wonder, then, that there is an explosion of gigantic proportions. Yáñez obtains depth by using a dense, almost baroque style, very appropriate for telling about the nature of these tormented souls, of their spiritual conflicts, of their motivations (sex, greed, ambition). No less important is the structure of the novel, divided, like a symphony, into four parts, and each in turn into four chapters. To obtain density the novelist presents simultaneous scenes. The first four chapters, which take place during the same night at four different places, reveal to us what is going on in the minds of four of the town's important persons at the same time. The *tempo lento* of the narrative adds to the effectiveness of the novel, which ends appropriately with an explosion in the char-acters' souls, synchronized with the national explosion of 1910. Better than anyone else, Yáñez has brought to life that world of the last years of Díaz's regime, at the precise moment when stagnant society was ready for a change.

One year before the publication of *Al filo del agua*, Miguel Angel Asturias, who was awarded the Nobel Prize in literature for 1967, finally published, also in Mexico City, his novel *El señor Presidente* (14), a work he had written in Paris between 1925 and 1932, and based on an earlier short story, "Los mendigos políticos" (1922). In the novel Asturias dissects the method employed by a dictator to rule (or rather, misrule) a country. The suffering his family had undergone at the hands of the dictator Manuel Estrada Cabrera in his native Guatemala had left an indelible impression on Asturias's mind. He later used all these experiences to write the novel, adding motifs taken from Maya mythology, as found in *Popol Vuh* (69), the book he had translated into Spanish from the French version of George Raynaud. By associating the dictator Estrada Cabrera to the Mayan god Tohil, the god of fire, he has presented a character that is more a myth than a flesh-and-blood person. His dictator is unlike that of Don Ramón del Valle Inclán, whose novel *Tirano Banderas* (1926) (90) presents a grotesque tyrant, a true *esperpento*. Nor is his dictator like that created by the Guate-malan Rafael Arévalo Martínez (b. 1884), the first to make Estrada Cabrera a character in a work of fiction. In Arévalo's short story, *Las fieras del trópico* (8), completed in January, 1915, but for obvious rea-sons not published until 1922 (two years after Estrada Cabrera's fall), the dictator José de Vargas is a ferocious tiger more than a human being. The social impact of Arévalos's story is further diluted by mak-ing Don José governor of an imaginary country, Orolandia. This, of course, was necessary for political reasons, but it destroys the emo-tional appeal which is so effective in *El señor Presidente*.

To strengthen the myth, Asturias associates the figure of the dictator with the Maya-Quiché divinity. In his translation of *Popol Vuh* we
read (pp. 84–86) that Tohil had given fire to his people. But the first
sacred fire went out as a result of a great rain, and once more Tohil
had to provide it, this time by rubbing his sandals together. As pay-
ment he demanded human sacrifices. In Asturias's novel there is a
chapter entitled "Tohil's Dance" in which Mr. President, at a reception
in his palace, asks Cara de Angel, the protagonist, to go to Washington
as his personal representative. Cara de Angel accepts (he has to accept;
no one would dare contradict the president), but before he leaves the
dance he has a vision:

> Near and far the plaintive voices of the tribesmen abandoned in the
> forest were heard . . . requesting from Tohil, *The Fire Giver,* that
> he return to them the burning firewood. . . . Tohil demanded human
> sacrifices. The tribesmen brought to him loaded slingshots. "and these
> men, what will they hunt? Will they hunt men?" . . . "Anything you
> request," answered the tribesmen, "provided you return the fire to
> us, you, *The Fire Giver,* so that our flesh may not grow cold."

This prophetic vision symbolizes Cara de Angel's sacrifice. Before
he arrives at the port to take the ship to Washington, he is arrested,
returned to the capital, and placed in a dungeon. Thus, the Indian
mythology motifs are very well integrated into the novel by means
of dreams and visions; they are, at the same time, suborinated to an
overall archetypal sturcture, that of the fall of Lucifer from Paradise.
Cara de Angel, "beautiful and evil like Satan," revolts against the
president and is therefore punished. Asturias's purpose, very skillfully
attained, is to paint the degrading conditions which people living in
Latin American countries ruled by dictators have to endure.

Although *El señor Presidente* is a novel of social protest, Asturias
is able to give its message an artistic form. The book is read not only
as the best example of life under a dictatorship but also for its aesthetic value. In a recent article about the novel as a literary genre,
Francisco Ayala (15) had this to say about Asturias' book:

> That a novel with a strong, aggressive thrust, as is in its own right
> Miguel Angel Asturias' *El señor Presidente,* should besides being a
> passionate allegation against dictatorships and their degrading effects,
> be a work having a high poetic quality whose intensity gives it perma-
> nent value, seems to us to be an exceptional case. We find ourselves
> in the presence of an artist who is able to triumph over the most
> adverse conditions.

What permanent values was Ayala thinking about? Doubtless he had in mind the novel's structure, its style, its psychological impact. The work has an original structure; it is divided into three parts, the first of which takes place in three days, the second in four days, and the last in weeks, months, years, or an eternity. The epilogue is a scene which suggests that the whole frightful story is to be repeated again and again. The theme of treason (the treason of Cara de Angel) is very well expressed through images that give a sensation of coldness. Dante placed Satan in the last circle of Hell, frozen in ice. Asturias makes use of that imagery of European origin but blends it with that found in the New World. In *Popol Vuh,* Tohil made the tribesmen consent to offer him human sacrifices by allowing the fire to go out and letting the tribe freeze to death; in his novel Asturias recreates this mythical scene by the use of images of coldness to express Cara de Angel's punishment. Fear, the second important theme, is given expression through the use of onomatopoeic language. By this technique Asturias brings to life characters that, through their fear of the dictator, act as if they were walking in sleep. The constant repetition of onomatopoeic phrases, words, and syllables reflects a world in which people move and behave mechanically. But this artistic aspect of *El señor Presidente* should not be overemphasized at the cost of diminishing the value of its message. The author himself has not done so. "For me," he wrote in 1950, "the value of this novel, if it has any, is to be found in the lesson it contains for the countries of Latin America, by portraying what happens to the people that place on a pedestal a man who controls all social forces." Thus in this novel Miguel Angel Asturias, as was to be done by Yáñez the following year in *Al filo del agua,* unifies the two main currents present in Spanish American fiction, that of the social novel and that of the artistic novel. These two works are unique in Spanish American narrative prose.

Toward the end of the forties the psychological novel and the novel of life in a metropolitan center were well represented with the works of the Argentines Ernesto Sábato (b. 1911) and Leopoldo Marechal (b. 1898). Sábato's *El túnel* (1948) (80) represents the existentialist novel, a novel similar to those being written in Europe during the same years, best represented by the works of Albert Camus. In *El túnel* Sábato places the reader in the mind of Castel the narrator-protagonist, from the very first sentence, *"Yo la maté,"* and keeps him there until the end. Although the external structure is archetypal (the prisoner who writes a confession), it is given originality by making the main image, the tunnel, the unifying element. That same image expresses the theme of the novel, man's inability to abandon the mind's prison, which is like a tunnel without exits. The abnormal condition of the unreliable narrator adds to the significance of the work by provoking in the reader a desire to speculate about the true nature of Castel's world.

Sábato's second novel, *Sobre héroes y tumbas* (79), did not appear until 1962. In a prefatory note he says:

> There is a type of fiction by means of which the author tries to liberate himself from an obsession which is not clear even to himself. Good or bad, this is the only type I can write. . . . In 1948 I decided to publish one of them, *El túnel*. In the thirteen years that passed after that, I continued exploring that dark labyrinth that leads to the central secret of our lives. Again and again I tried to express the result of my search, but discouraged by the poor results, I destroyed the manuscripts. Now, some friends that have read [this one] have encouraged me to publish it.

Much more ambitious than *El túnel*, this second novel is a complex presentation of the same theme, man's inability to overcome mental blocks. Loosely structured, it consists of four parts, dealing with the love of Martín for a demoniacal woman, Alejandra. She ends up by killing Fernando, her father, setting their home on fire, and burning to death along with him. The third part, "Informe sobre ciegos," presented in first person by Alejandra's father, serves to give the novel a new perspective. It is not, as some critics have said, totally unrelated to the central narrative plot. "To have deleted this part of the novel to obtain a greater logical coherence," the author wrote, "would have been like deleting man's dreams in an integral vision of his life." Sábato's novels, it could be said, represent in Spanish American fiction the psychological trend carried to its limits.

*Adán Buenosayres* (1948) (59), by Leopoldo Marechal, on the other hand, represents the novel concerned with the problems of the people in a modern metropolis. The book, which took eighteen years to write, is a work not unlike Joyce's *Ulysses,* but marred by innumerable hermetic, private anecdotes, as well as references to friends and acquaintances of the author. Unlike Sábato, Marechal has a sense of humor that gives the novel a light if sometimes sarcastic touch. He mocks pseudo scientists, intellectuals, pompous ladies, and all that world that is to be found in any large center of population. The novel is important because it points the way for such future works as Carlos

Fuentes's *La región más transparente* (46), Cortázar's *Rayuela* (38), and José Lezama Lima's *Paradiso* (54).

By 1950 the Spanish American novel, as I believe I have demonstrated, had produced some exceptional works. And yet, during the next two decades the genre was to be enriched by some really outstanding contributions from the pens of, among others, Alejo Carpentier, Manuel Rojas *(Hijo de ladrón,* 1951) (74), Arreola, Juan Rulfo, Fuentes, Augusto Roa Bastos, Cortázar, Fernando Alegría *(El cataclismo,* 1960) (3), Enrique Anderson-Imbert *(Fuga,* 1953) (6), Carlos Martínez Moreno *(El paredón,* 1962) (60), Vicente Leñero, Salvador Elizondo, Fernando del Paso, Gabriel García Márquez, and Lezama Lima.

The Cuban Alejo Carpentier (b. 1904), who had joined the ranks of the fiction writers in 1933 with *Ecue-Yamba-O* (29), published in 1944 the short story "Viaje a la semilla" and the novel *El reino de este mundo* (31). The short story is significant because of the handling of time, which flows backward, from the present to the past. This preoccupation with time, not as a theme (as in Borges) but as a technique, as a discovery, is what characterizes Carpentier's fiction, and especially *Los pasos perdidos* (1953) (30), *El acoso* (1956) (28), and *El siglo de las luces* (1962) (32). In the first he skillfully contrasts two ways of life, the sophisticated but meaningless existence in the large city and the primitive but significant life in the jungles. The hero, a man of Spanish American descent living in New York (or a city like New York), is sent to the jungle, by a museum, in search of a primitive musical instrument. There he finds not only love, but also the inspiration to write the musical composition he had not been able to compose in the city, where he had placed his talent at the service of commercial enterprises. Although the plot unfolds on two continents and the settings are diametrically opposed to each other, the novel is unified by means of musical motifs, skillfully integrated into the overall archetypal structure, a journey through time and space. But it is in *El acoso* that Carpentier's preoccupation with time really comes to the fore. Here he has combined time and space to give us one of the best-structured short novels in Spanish American fiction. The life of the hunted man *(el acosado),* the life of the music lover and sex driven *taquillero,* and the life of the prostitute Estrella (the only fixed point of reference in the novel) form the sides of a triangle held together in time by the music of Beethoven's *Eroica.* Within this framework the dramatic life of the antihero, *el acosado,* unfolds inexorably, as in a Greek tragedy.

It was during the fifties also that Juan Rulfo (b. Mexico, 1918) published his two books, the collection of short stories *El llano en llamas* (1953) (76) and the novel *Pedro Páramo* (1955) (77). Both works deal, dramatically, with the problems of humble people in the countryside. The novel is a unique work in many respects. Through a poetic style, Rulfo is able to give life to a dead town, a town that has been choked to death by the local *cacique*, Pedro Páramo. The novel has a poetic structure, that is, the transitions from scene to scene are not carried out by introducing formal linking elements; they are, like the stanzas in a poem, juxtaposed, united only by the central theme. The reader passes from one place to another (since most of the characters are dead) as in a poem, by means of the introduction of lyrical motifs, which Rulfo can use with great effectiveness. But *Pedro Páramo* is also a novel of unforgettable characters. There we find people tormented by overpowering passions: Susana by a great love, Páramo by a desire to dominate his fellow men, Father Rentería by remorse, Miguel Páramo by sexual desire. Although they are dead, this fact does not make them less real. Rulfo has been able to make his characters seem alive by using the first-person narrative and letting each tell his own story from his own point of view, much like Dante in his *Inferno*.

A contemporary of Rulfo, Juan José Arreola (b. Mexico, 1918), represents in his country's fiction the trend toward universal, often fantastic, always satirical literature. His two books of short stories, *Varia invención* (1949) (12) and *Confabulario* (1952) (9), published together in 1962 under the title *Confabulario total* (10), represent a high point in the development of Spanish American short fiction. In the first Arreola reveals himself as a great stylist and storyteller, although not all the selections included may be catalogued as short stories. Some of these prose works, poetic in style, are an excellent introduction to the magic world of Arreola, a world he flagellates in ironical, often sardonic terms, as to him our world is one in which the foolish acts of foolish men set the tone of life. The same characteristics are found in his second book, written in an effective style that is, at the same time, ironic and poetic. There we find such well-known stories as "El guardagujas," En verdad os digo," and "Pueblerina." The essence of the short stories of Arreola, as seen in the second of these three, is not so much the creation of fantastic settings and characters, but the subtlety with which he can make fun of the social institutions and the most respected ideas of modern man. The biblical camel and needle serve him to mock scientists. With a great sense of humor he relates the anecdote of the scientist who has discovered a way to make the camel go through the needle's eye. If successful, the invention will make it possible for the rich to enter heaven. If he fails, they will also be saved, as they will be poor after spending their money to finance the experiment. Not less important than his short stories is his only novel, *La feria* (1963) (11), a satire of life in a provincial town, in this case his native town, Ciudad Guzmán in the state of Jalisco. By making use of a mosaiclike structure, he is able to incorporate small vignettes, confessions, sketches, diaries, and historical information into a harmonious whole, framed by the religious celebration offered annually to the patron saint of the town, Señor San José. The result is a hilarious and yet significant portrayal of life in a small town.

Of a different nature are the works of Mexico's most prestigious novelist, Carlos Fuentes (b. 1928), the author of *La región más transparente* (1958) (46), *Las buenas conciencias* (1959) (43), *Aura* (1962) (42), *La muerte de Artemio Cruz* (1962) (45), *Zona sagrada* (1967) (47), and *Cambio de piel* (1967) (44). The first is an experimental novel in which the author gives expression to the spirit of Mexico City, the region where the air is clear, a metaphor used ironically. The structure of the novel, much like that of Dos Passos's *Manhattan Transfer,* is built up through the accumulation of scenes in Mexico City. But instead of passing, as in Yáñez' *Al filo del agua* or Rulfo's *Pedro Páramo,* from the mind of one character to that of another, the reader is transported from one social group to another. We may find ourselves in the street with a prostitute; in the home of an old Revolutionary leader now turned capitalist and owner of a bank and large real estate holdings; in the primitive hut of Teódula, a symbol of the Indian past; or with Zamacona, representative of the new intellectuals. In order to integrate these diverse elements, Fuentes makes use of a mythical character, Ixca Cienfuegos, who moves from group to group with great ease. But it is the city, of which he is a symbol, that really comes to life, leaving the reader the sense of its being the real protagonist. In *La muerte de Artemio Cruz* Fuentes integrates the elements of his novel much better by creating a central character, Artemio Cruz, who on his deathbed, at the age of seventy one, reviews his entire life. The novel covers a long period of Mexican history, from the age of Santa Anna to the present. Each chapter is dedicated to an important historical event, but also to an incident which has changed the protagonist's life. Cruz is a man whose only preoccupation is survival and material well-being. To secure this he tramples upon his fellow men, even his friends and his own family. All the scenes in the novel have one purpose: to show how this self-made man has survived, how he has become selfish, arrogant, and hard even to the point of despising his own family, his best friends, and his own country. In his last two novels Fuentes is less successful in the creation of unforgettable characters like Artemio Cruz.

Much like Fuentes, the Colombian Eduardo Caballero Calderón (b. 1910) in *El Cristo de espaldas* (1952) (26), the Paraguayan Augusto Roa Bastos (b. 1918) in *Hijo de hombre* (1960) (71), and the Peruvian Mario Vargas Llosa (b. 1936) in *La ciudad y los perros* (1963) (92) and *La casa verde* (1966) (91) are excellent representatives of the neorealistic trend in Spanish American fiction. *El Cristo de espaldas* is the novel that best represents the violent nature of the social conflicts which beset Latin America. *Hijo de hombre,* on the other hand, makes good use of an international conflict, the Chaco War between Paraguay and Bolivia, to give expression to the terrible consequences that can result from a senseless fight over a wasteland. At the same time, Roa Bastos's novel transcends the war theme by depicting events dealing with man's suffering; by representing man as the inheritor, not of Christ's redemption, but of Christ's suffering on earth.

In 1963 Vargas Llosa became famous as a novelist with *La ciudad y los perros* (literally, "The City and the Dogs," translated into English under the title *The Time of the Hero,* 1966), a bitter denunciation of military education in Peru and, by implication, in Latin America. Beyond the military college setting, which looks more like a reform school, there is a denunciation also of society in general as other institutions come under fire. The work is significant not only for its theme but also for the nature of the language. The author reproduces the raw dialogue of the cadets (the "dogs" of the title), whose behavior is not too far removed from that of the animals in the jungle. Force is the rule in the school, and no spiritual spark, however insignificant, could prevail. The material nature of the world of the novel is overpowering. Equally violent, but much more artistic, is Vargas Llosa's second novel, *La casa verde (The Green House,* 1968), in which he creates several tragic characters whose lives, told separately, integrate through their relations with less important persons. Although the heroes and heroines move in different worlds (but all Peruvian), often in different times, and their stories are told by different narrative voices, the total effect is harmonious and well unified. The green house, the house of prostitution which we see built and destroyed, serves as a point of reference around which the story of the several characters unfolds, both in space and in time. The social forces that have molded Peruvian society are excellently depicted in their struggle for power.

Unlike the neorealists, the Argentine Julio Cortázar (b. 1918) has developed under the influence of Borges and the narrators of fantastic stories. His fiction reflects the latest trends in the art of the novel, in both Europe and the United States. At the same time, he follows closely the writings of the Spanish American novelists of his generation. He began publishing with *Bestiario* (1951) (34), a collection of short stories in which he already demonstrates an interest in the mysterious nature of life. His first novel, *Los premios* (1960) (37), is a continuation of this trend, but in an extended form. The action takes place aboard a ship at sea. In this microcosm, which resembles those of Kafka, Cortázar reveals a situation bordering on the absurd: the inability of most of the passengers to reach a certain area of the ship. As in life, the important thing is not so much to reach the goal as the desire to attempt it. The existence of an unattainable goal (for most human beings), as we shall see, reappears in Cortázar's second novel, *Rayuela* (1963) (38).

In 1959 Cortázar published a collection of five short stories, *Las armas secretas* (33), in which he included "Las babas del diablo," utilized by Antonioni for his movie *Blowup*, and "El perseguidor," the life of a black musican in Paris. The latter story marks a turning point in the development of Cortázar's fiction, for here for the first time he abandons the creation of fantastic worlds to concentrate on a lifelike situation and on the development of the central character in depth. This story foreshadows the Parisian world we find in the first part of *Rayuela*.

After an interlude, with the publication of the unrealistic short fiction of *Historias de Cronopios y de Famas* (1962) (35), Cortázar returns to the world he had created in "El perseguidor" with a full-length novel, *Rayuela*, excellently translated by Gregory Rabassa under the title *Hopscotch* (1966). Divided into three parts, this work depicts life in Paris and in Buenos Aires. The two worlds, which also appear in one of Cortázar's short stories, "El otro cielo" (in the collection *Todos los fuegos el fuego*, 1966) (36) are loosely integrated through the presence of the principal narrator and hero of the novel, who goes from Paris to Buenos Aires in search of La Maga, the woman with whom he had lived in Paris and who had abandoned him after the death of their infant son, which is tragically described. He is, of course, unable to find her, just as those who play hopscotch are often unable to reach the last square of the diagram, symbolic of heaven. Structurally, *Rayuela* is a complex work. It can be read in two ways, either from the beginning to the end, or following the suggestions provided by the author, skipping certain chapters, just as one jumps while playing hopscotch. The third part of the novel (the first is set in Paris and the second in Buenos Aires) is a collection of the novelist's notes and papers while writing the novel, dealing with a theory of fiction (according to Morelli, a ficticious character who represents the author himself), which help the reader to integrate the first and second parts of the work. The author's intention in including this part is to force the reader to participate in the creative process, to make him believe that he is writing the novel. How well this purpose is attained depends upon whether or not the reader follows the author's instructions. Nevertheless, it is an attempt to get away from the traditional novelistic structure. Although the unique structure has perhaps attracted more attention than any other element in the novel, it must not be forgotten that Cortázar's intention here is also to destroy the trite, traditional narrative style characteristic of the Hispanic novelist. This effort is worthy of study, for it is precisely the preoccupation with language, with style, that has given the new Spanish American novelist the prestige that they now enjoy. *Hopscotch* is a landmark in the development of the novel in a new key, as it embodies an original structure, a new style, a new approach to reality, and in general a new concept of the novel.

This new novel is represented by a group of writers among whom we find the Mexicans Vicente Leñero (b. 1933), Fernando del Paso (b. 1935), and Salvador Elizondo (b. 1932); the Colombians Manuel Mejía Vallejo (b. 1923) and Gabriel García Márquez (b. 1927); the Cubans Guillermo Cabrera Infante (b. 1929) and José Lezama Lima (b. 1912); the Uruguayan Mario Benedetti (b. 1920); and the Chileans José Donoso (b. 1924) and Carlos Droguett (b. 1915). The novel *Farabeuf* (1965) (39) by Elizondo is the first attempt in Mexican fiction to write an antinovel like those of Sarraute and Robbe-Grillet. The subtitle, "Chronicle of an Instant," reveals the structure, which is based on the minute reconstruction, in the minds of the characters, of a significant moment in their lives. More than the narrative element, the minute descriptions of the scenery create interest. The theme is the torment given to a Chinese prisoner, a torment that is associated with sex drives and desires. The book is illustrated with a picture of a Chinese man being dismembered, an image that is central to the novel and which leaves the reader with a sense of horror. Elizondo's last novel, *El hipogeo secreto* (1968) (40) is a novel about a novel. The reader is reading as the novelist is writing. The reader thus becomes also the writer of the novel. The Hipogeo Secreto is a society whose purpose is to guess what will come next in the novel. By this technique Elizondo is able to obliterate completely the limits between reality and the novel. The characters in the narrative, the author, and the reader become part of the same world. The basic reality is language. It is fitting that we should end this survey of the Spanish American novel with a work that turns its back on European techniques to renew a lost narrative art, the art of telling a story for its own merits without capitalizing on a complicated structure or stylistic pyrotechnics. For García Márquez's novel, *Cien años de soledad* (1967) (48), is written with gusto, with the same attitude toward reality and in the same style as some of the earliest Spanish American chronicles. It is, at the same time, the history of a family (the Buendías), of a town (Macondo), of a nation (Colombia?), and of a continent. Here we find the same spirit of adventure that characterized the early explorers, the same faith in life as that found in the earliest settlers, the same attitude toward a wondrous nature that is found in the writings of the early *cronistas*. The author forgoes all interest in intellectualizing life, and the result is a charming tale that we read for the pleasure of reading. Spanish American narrative art has come a full cycle with *Cien años de soledad*.

# BIBLIOGRAPHY

1. Alcalá, Hugo Rodríguez. *El arte de Juan Rulfo.* Mexico, 1965.
2. Aldrich, Earl, Jr., "The Quechua World of José María Arguedas." *Hispania* 45 (1962): 62–67.
3. Alegría, Fernando. *El cataclismo.* Santiago de Chile, 1960.
4. ———. *Historia de la novela hispanomericana.* 2d ed. Mexico, 1965.
5. Anderson-Imbert, Enrique. *Los cuentos fantásticos de Rubén Darío.* Cambridge, Mass., 1967.
6. ———. *Fuga.* Tucumán, Arg., 1953.
7. Archer, William H., and Gerald E. Wade. "The *indianista* Novel since 1889." *Hispania* 33 (1950): 211–20.
8. Arévalo Martínez, Rafael. *Las fieras del trópico.* Guatemala City, 1922.
9. Arreola, Juan José. *Confabulario.* Mexico, 1952.
10. ———. *Confabulario total.* Mexico, 1962.
11. ———. *La feria.* Mexico, 1963.
12. ———. *Varia invención.* Mexico, 1949.
13. Asturias, Miguel Angel. "Leyendas de Guatemala." In *Obras escogidas,* p. 29. Madrid, 1959.
14. ———. *El señor Presidente.* Mexico, 1946.
15. Ayala, Francisco. "Nueva divagación sobre la novela." *Revista de Occidente* 5 (September 1967): 303.
16. Azuela, Mariano. "Marcel Proust." *Obras Completas* 3 (1960): 934–70.
17. Benedetti, Mario. *Literatura uruguaya del siglo XX.* Montevideo, 1965.
18. Bioy-Casares, Adolfo. *La invención de Morel.* Buenos Aires, 1940.
19. Bollo, Sarah. *Literatura uruguaya, 1808–1965.* Montevideo, 1965.
20. Bombal, María Luisa. *La amortajada.* Buenos Aires, 1938.
21. ———. *La última niebla.* Santiago de Chile, 1935.
22. Borges, Jorge Luis. *El aleph.* Buenos Aires, 1949.
23. ———. *Ficciones.* Buenos Aires, 1944.
24. ———. *Historia universal de la infamia.* Buenos Aires, 1935.
25. ———. *La muerte y la brújula.* Buenos Aires, 1951.
26. Caballero Calderón, Eduardo. *El Cristo de espaldas.* Buenos Aires, 1952.
27. Cañas, Salvador. "Homenaje a Miguel Angel Asturias." *Repertorio Americano* 30 (March 1950): 83.
28. Carpentier, Alejo. *El acoso.* Buenos Aires, 1956.
29. ———. *Ecue-Yamba-O.* Madrid, 1933.
30. ———. *Los pasos perdidos.* Mexico, 1953.

31. ———. *El reino de este mundo.* Caracas, 1958.
32. ———. *El siglo de las luces.* Mexico, 1962.
33. Cortázar, Julio. *Las armas secretas.* Buenos Aires, 1959.
34. ———. *Bestiario.* Buenos Aires, 1951.
35. ———. *Historias de Cronopios y de Famas.* Buenos Aires, 1962.
36. ———. "El otro cielo." In *Todos los fuegos el fuego.* Buenos Aires, 1966.
37. ———. *Los premios.* Buenos Aires, 1960.
38. ———. *Rayuela.* Buenos Aires, 1963.
39. Elizondo, Salvador. *Farabeuf.* Mexico, 1965.
40. ———. *El hipogeo secreto.* Mexico, 1968.
41. Englekirk, John E. "The Discovery of *Los de abajo* by Mariano Azuela." *Hispania* 18 (1935): 53–62.
42. Fuentes, Carlos. *Aura.* Mexico, 1962.
43. ———. *Las buenas conciencias.* Mexico, 1959.
44. ———. *Cambio de piel.* Mexico, 1967.
45. ———. *La muerte de Artemio Cruz.* Mexico, 1962.
46. ———. *La región más transparente.* Mexico, 1958.
47. ———. *Zona sagrada.* Mexico, 1967.
48. García Márquez, Gabriel. *Cien años de soledad.* Buenos Aires, 1967.
49. Harss, Luis. *Los nuestros.* Buenos Aires, 1966. [Translation of *In the Main Stream.*]
50. Irvy, James E. *La influencia de William Faulkner en cuatro narradores hispanoamericanos.* Mexico, 1956.
51. Keyserling, Count Hermann. *South American Meditations.* New York, 1932.
52. Leal, Luis. *Historia del cuento hispanoamericano.* Mexico, 1966.
53. ———. "El realismo mágico en la literatura hispanoamericana." *Cuadernos Americanos* 26 (1967): 230–35.
54. Lezama Lima, José. *Paradiso.* Havana, 1966.
55. Lichblau, Myron I. *El arte estilístico de Eduardo Mallea.* Buenos Aires, 1967.
56. Mallea, Eduardo. *La bahía de silencio.* Buenos Aires, 1940.
57. ———. *Fiesta en noviembre.* Buenos Aires, 1938.
58.———. *Todo verdor perecerá.* Buenos Aires, 1941.
59. Marechal, Leopoldo. *Adán Buenosayres.* Buenos Aires, 1948.
60. Martínez Moreno, Carlos. *El paredón.* Barcelona, 1962.
61. Mejía Sánchez, Ernesto, ed. *Cuentos completos de Rubén Darío.* Mexico, 1951.

62. Meléndez, Concha. *La novela indianista en Hispanoamérica (1832–1889).* 2d ed. Río Piedras, P.R., 1961.

63. Monegal, Emir Rodríguez. "The New Novelties [Novelists]." *Encounter* 25 (September 1965): 97–109.

64. Monguió, Luis. "Reflexiones sobre un aspecto de la novela hispanoamericana actual." In *La novela iberoamericana,* ed. by Arturo Torres-Ríoseco, pp. 89–104. Albuquerque, N.Mex., 1952.

65. Onetti, Juan Carlos. "Tiempo de abrazar." *Marcha* 3 (June 18, 1943) and 4 (December 31, 1943).

66. Ortega y Gasset, José. *Notas.* Madrid, 1925.

67. Paz, Octavio. "Salvador Elizondo: El placer como crítica de la realidad y el lenguaje." *Siempre!* 819 (March 5, 1969).

68. Rama, Angel. "Orígen de un novelista y de una generación literaria." In *El pozo* by Juan Carlos Onetti, pp. 57–111. 2d ed. Montevideo, 1965.

69. Raynaud, George, ed. *Popol Vuh.* Trans. with notes by Miguel Angel Asturias. Mexico, 1939.

70. Revueltas, José. *El luto humano.* Mexico, 1943.

71. Roa Bastos, Augusto. *Hijo de hombre.* Buenos Aires, 1960.

72. Rodríguez Monegal, Emir. *Literatura uruguaya del medio siglo.* Montevideo, 1966.

73. Roggiano, Alfredo A. "El modernismo y la novela en la América Hispana." In *La novela iberoamericana,* ed. by Arturo Torres-Ríoseco, pp. 25–45. Albuquerque, N.Mexico., 1952.

74. Rojas, Manuel. *Hijo de ladrón.* Santiago de Chile, 1951.

75. Romero, José Rubén. "La vida inútil de Pito Pérez." In *Obras completas.* 2d. ed. Mexico, 1963.

76. Rulfo, Juan. *El llano en llamas.* Mexico, 1953.

77. ———. *Pedro Páramo.* Mexico, 1955.

78. Sábato, Ernesto. *El escritor y sus fantasmas.* 2d ed. Buenos Aires, 1964.

79. ———. *Sobre héroes y tumbas.* Buenos Aires, 1962.

80. ———. *El túnel.* Buenos Aires, 1948.

81. Salazar Mallén, Rubén. *Soledad.* Mexico, 1944.

82. Scari, Robert M. "Ciencia y ficción en los cuentos de Leopoldo Lugones." *Revista Iberoamericana* 30 (1964): 163–87.

83. Shaw, Donald L. "Eduardo Mallea y la novela hispanoamericana." *Razón y Fábula* 7 (March 1968): 19–24.

84. Sommers, Joseph. *After the Storm.* Albuquerque, N.Mex., 1968.

85. ———. "Changing View of the Indian in Mexican Literature." *Hispania* 47 (1964): 47–55.

86. ———. "El ciclo de Chiapas: Nueva corriente literaria." *Cuadernos Americanos* 23 (1964): 246–61.

87. ———. "The Indian-Oriented Novel of Latin America: New Spirit, New Forms, New Scope." *Journal of Inter-American Studies* 6 (April 1964): 249–65.

88. Spell, J. R. "The Historical and Social Background of *El Periquillo Sarniento*." *Hispanic American Historical Review* 36 (1956): 447–70.

89. ———. "The Intellectual Background of Fernández de Lizardi as Reflected in *El Periquillo Sarniento*." *PMLA* 71 (1956): 414–32.

90. Valle Inclán, Ramón del. *Tirano Banderas*. Madrid, 1926.

91. Vargas Llosa, Mario. *Las casa verde*. Barcelona, 1966.

92. ———. *La ciudad y los perros*. Barcelona, 1963.

93. Weber, Frances W. "*El acoso:* Alejo Carpentier's War on Time." *PMLA* 68 (1963): 440–48.

94. Yáñez, Agustín. *Al filo del agua*. Mexico, 1947.

# SPANISH AMERICAN POETRY

*Bernard Gicovate*

## I

The criticism of poetry may proceed to the evaluation of specific poems through analysis of form or to the study of the poetry of the past through historical investigation. Although stylistic studies are fashionable in Spanish America today, historical studies have abounded since the moment Spanish Americans found they had a body of literature to deal with. One noticeable trait of historical studies there as elsewhere is the progressive approximation to the present. No study of books can be truly contemporary, not even the book review, since it assumes at least the publication and dating of the work being examined. And yet, we can notice the progressive elimination of what formerly was considered the necessary perspective of time. Perhaps this phenomenon is part of the americanization of the world. America has been in the painful position of needing a past in a hurry and has often tried to invent it rapidly. Juan María Gutiérrez in his *América poética* (37) of 1846 was one of the first to utilize the methods of historical scholarship on the creative output of the recent past. Since his day the anthology has been one of the most serviceable tools of historical investigation and criticism. Before studying works of general and special criticism of poetry, a consideration of the critical function of anthologies may be useful in a survey of the trends in this field.

The ideal anthology must offer critical introductions of the most generous impartiality. It has to devise groupings into sections to fit the readers' tastes and interests without distorting a complex history. It should include every important original manifestation of thought, but never the work of derivative rhymesters. For each poet it must offer an accurate definition and evaluation of his work, followed by a selection of poems which show the evolution of his thought from apprenticeship to maturity. The importance of each poet should determine the number of pages devoted to his works, and complete bibliographies should invite further reading.

The work of the nineteenth and early twentieth centuries set the tone for the postwar anthologies and culminated in 1934 with the publication of the *Antología de la poesía española e hispanoamericana (1882–1932)* (49) by Federico de Onís. Except for minor details of

247

critical unawareness or disagreement of taste, this anthology measures
up to the ideal set forth above. It is guided by that ideal and it is
this book that the anthologies of the postwar period must seek to
emulate. Onís comes as close to including the most recent production
of young poets as is possible for a book of this size and scope. Some
of the poems selected had been published in books dated 1931. The
next anthology, that of Xavier Villarrutia, Emilio Prados, Juan Gil
Albert, and Octavio Paz, *Laurel: Antología de la poesía moderna en
lengua española* (67), was much less a critical statement than a gather-
ing of poetry at its best. In both inclusion and exclusion it was whimsi-
cal but yet successful.

The challenge was perhaps too overwhelming. And furthermore,
as the poetry of Spanish America continued to be published, the
field became less and less manageable in its richness and diversity.
In the fifties Ginés de Albareda and Francisco Garfias attempted the
compilation of a comprehensive anthology of all Spanish American
poetry, divided by countries. This ten-volume *Antología de la poesía
americana* (1), published by Biblioteca Nueva of Madrid, lacks selec-
tivity and is handicapped by some unliterary biases. It is of great
value as a work of reference, but it has little interest as a critical tool.
For different reasons the *Antología de la poesía hispanoamericana* (12)
by Julio Caillet Boïs, has failed to bring up to date the critical effort
of Federico de Onís. More than five hundred poets are assembled
here, but many important names are left out, while some of the in-
clusions are obviously expendable. Introductory and bibliographical
materials are not satisfactory. We must conclude that these two large
attempts provide samplings rather than anthological aids to evaluation. Perhaps the historical scope—from the pre-Colombian poets to
this day—is too vast for the work of one person. Obviously, the geographical vastness is already burden enough, although these books
have excluded Spain to make the effort more feasible.

Yet this limitation of scope is not only one of convenience. The
opposition of Spain and Spanish America is becoming clearer in the
minds of historians and literary critics. It may not derive from any
reality outside their narrow field of vision (Mexico and Chile are as
different from each other as Spain is from Argentina, for instance),
but the cleavage has been established, and Spanish American poetry
is anthologized and studied apart from Spanish poetry. Even so, the
field has to be narrowed further in order to achieve some kind of
completeness and excellence.

Limiting the field historically has proved fruitful, especially with recent studies of the *modernista* movement. As examples one can cite the compilations of Carlos García Prada, *Poetas modernistas hispanomericanos* (33); Raúl Silva Castro, *Antología crítica del modernismo hispanoamericano* (62); and Homero Castillo, *Poetas modernistas hispanoamericanos* (14). The work of the period immediately following the *modernista* movement has been anthologized by Eugenio Florit and José Olivio Jiménez in *La poesía hispanoamericana desde el modernismo* (27). A confusion of historical and cultural concepts in the latter book produced the strange arrangement of historical sections (I. Modernismo, II. Post modernismo, III. Vanguardismo, IV. Post vanguardismo) in which one section is conceived ahistorically, forcing the anthologists to give selections of the same poet in two different sections. All four of the foregoing anthologies are essentially didactic, aimed at preparing students for examinations rather than at encompassing an age. Of the four, Raúl Silva Castro's is perhaps least interested in following a syllabus format, but his anthology is disfigured by a narrow nonhistorical understanding of *modernismo*.

A much more fruitful narrowing of scope has been the limitation of anthologies to the poetry of a single country. Numerous anthologies of the poetry of each country have been published in this century —and even before—and some of them are still of critical interest. Among the most valuable are Carlos García Prada's *Antología de líricos colombianos* (32), Juan Ramón Jiméz, José María Chacón y Calvo, and Camila Henríquez Ureña's *La poesía cubana en 1936* (40), and Jorge Luis Borges, Silvina Ocampo, and Adolfo Bioy-Casares, *Antología poética argentina* (11). Sometimes anthologists are even more restricted, as is Jorge Cuesta's famous *Antología de la poesía mexicana moderna* (20). The anthologies of *poesía negra* are of great interest, although, unfortunately, studies of this phenomenon are not exhaustive. Emilio Ballagas has published the best-known collections: *Antología de la poesía negra hispanoamericana* (8) and *Mapa de la poesía negra americana* (9).

Since it is impossible to list the many anthologies of the postwar period, those of Mexico may serve as a case study. The partial works of Luis Castro Leal (15) and Max Aub (6), together with many other efforts, seemed to have prepared the way for the recent publication of José Emilio Pacheco's *La poesía mexicana del siglo XIX, antología* (51) and Carlos Monsiváis's *La poesía mexicana del siglo XX, antología* (48). These two volumes together constitute the most comprehensive and best-presented anthology of the poetry of any country in Spanish America. The authors present a study of the historical development of their country's poetry, and each poet, selected with critical impartiality, is allotted the necessary space. The inclusion of lists of significant events and publications in other countries and languages, while not entirely new, is testimony to a conception of literature that makes it a living part of history and of Mexico's maturity in the world. A different type of anthology, which includes a personal statement of values rather than a comprehensive view of a closely limited period is *Poesía en movimiento: México, 1915– 1966* (53) by Octavio Paz, Alí Chumacero, José Emilio Pacheco, and Homero Aridjis.

Among the efforts in other countries, many of them of great value in their fields, the *Antología de la poesía peruana* (24) by Alberto Escobar should be singled out. The critical introduction of this work presents a panoramic view of Peruvian poetry, poets are well represented, and the critical comments are sensitve and intelligent.

Together with the task of anthologizing, scholars must present the bibliographical tools that will serve students in the future. And the above-mentioned anthologies supply the desirable listings. In addition, many general bibliographies of literature complement these endeavors with lists of recent studies on each author. Worthy of special note is the annotated bibliography of poetry and studies on poetry in the *Handbook of Latin American Studies* published by the Library of Congress since 1936. Current anthologies, books of verse, and critical studies are reviewed succinctly as a guide to students in the field.

## II

Paralleling the effort at compiling anthologies, whether organized by period or by country, numerous general studies of Spanish American poetry have appeared since Marcelino Menéndez y Pelayo's encyclopedic history and anthology of Spanish American poetry published in Madrid in 1895. Attempts of this magnitude are no longer possible or indeed desirable. It is futile to try, since no greater depth can be achieved and failure is likely, as proved by a few attempts that have been unanimously ignored or lambasted by reviewers. On the other hand, general studies can contribute a great deal to the understanding of Spanish American poetry when they are limited to the treatment of a theme, a form, an idea, or a period.

Of the studies devoted to a specific period, the most numerous deal with *modernismo*. Among them, the *Breve historia del modernismo* (38), by Max Henríquez Ureña, is of extraordinary significance. This book integrates a great body of scholarship on the subject. In spite of its many defects, it is still the most reliable history of a movement. Before its publication, the *modernista* movement was the center of controversy and polemics, and it has remained so. Charges and countercharges might be dismissed as so much nonsense, if it were not that beneath the surface there are many problems of historical accuracy and aesthetic evaluation that are seldom faced clearly. On the one hand, one encounters the contention of Pedro Salinas in *Literatura española, siglo XX* (59) that the Spanish writers are not part of hispanic history. The argument is carried to the extreme in Guillermo Diaz Plaja's *Modernismo frente al noventa y ocho* (23), which suggests that the Generation of '98 rejected *modernismo*. Yet poets such as Blas de Otero disprove the thesis by demonstrating a close Spanish dependence on Rubén Darío. Ricardo Gillón in *Direcciones del modernismo* (36), his "Prólogo" to Juan Ramón Jiménez's *El modernismo: Notas de un curso* (39), and other writings defends the theory of one historical period on both sides of the Atlantic. The many aspects of the controversies about *modernismo* are studied in Ned J. Davison's *The Concept of Modernism in Hispanic Criticism* (22), a survey of opinion on this subject. *Estudios críticos sobre el modernismo* (13), edited by Homero Castillo, is an anthology of the most important essays on all sides of the question. In my *Conceptos fundamentales de literatura comparada: Iniciación de la poesía modernista* (34), I have tried to clarify the complex issues of theory and literary history underlying this controversy.

In addition to general studies of periods, geographical limitations have made the work of the scholar more manageable. *La poesía chilena* (3), by Fernando Alegría, presents a survey of the history of poetry in one country with sober accuracy and insight. A further limitation, of country and period, has permitted Luis Monguió in his *La poesía post-modernista peruana* (46) to produce a work of greater detail in exegesis and criticism within the framework of a historical account. It would be tedious to list the numerous studies of this type in all the countries of Spanish America, since they are listed in the appropriate bibliographies. Cintio Vitier's *Lo cubano en la poesía* (68), Frank Dauster's *Ensayos sobre poesía mexicana: Asedio a los "contemporáneos"* (21), and Merlin H. Forster's *Los contemporáneos, 1920–32:*

*Perfil de un experimento vanguardista mexicano* (29) are examples
of attempts at defining what is essentially national in the poetry of
a country, of a generation, or of a group.

This type of general study limited by the interest in defining the
common undertakings of a group is similar to the efforts of critics
to define concepts of the criticism of poetry, for instance, as in Luis
Monguió's "El concepto de la poesía en algunos poetas hispanoamericanos representativos" (44) and "De la problemática del modernismo:
La crítica y el cosmopolitismo" (45). The pursuit of the elusive notion
of what is American in the poetry of the greatest writers of the continent is found in Octavio Paz's *Las peras del olmo* (52), in Ramón
Xirau's *Poesía hispanoamericana y española* (69), and, in a strange
way, in the theories of Antonio de Undurraga on the primitivism of
America in "La poesía lírica y la mente mestiza en América" (66).

Another possible limitation of the scope of critical undertakings
is achieved by restricting the study to one form. Unfortunately, this
procedure seems doomed to failure, essentially since the preliminary
study of historical development preempts the field of investigation.
Nevertheless, exceptions to this rule are found. The haiku as a novelty
has a definite place in history and can be studied as a form produced
by specific desires and influencing both style and modes of thought
in a clearly established period of time. Gloria Ceide Echevarría's
*El haikai en la lírica mexicana* (16) is an example of what can be
done in this immense field when the subject is approached with
devotion and sensitivity. The few studies of the sonnet as a form
and the anthologies of sonnets have not been quite as successful.
A little different perhaps is the effort to study the function and
meaning of the anthology in the criticism of poetry. Héctor H. Orjuela,
in his *Las antologías poéticas de Colombia: Estudio y bibliografía* (50)
has prepared the way with an exhaustive study of the problem in
Colombia.

The study of themes in poetry is often fruitless, but a few attempts
deserve mention because they seem to define something very special
in a country. For instance, Angel Mazzei's "El tema del día domingo"
(43) is illuminating in what it says, and in what it does not say, when
seen against the background of the poetry of *tono menor* in Argentina.
Akin to these studies are the general studies of foreign influences in
the poetry of Spanish America. Fernando Alegría, for example, has
brought together all the information about his subject in *Walt Whitman en Hispanoamérica* (4). Other books of similar scope have not

been quite as successful. But in the histories of periods and in introductory chapters of monographic studies, a great deal of the influence
of French literature has been studied. Marie Josèphe Faurie's *Le
modernisme hispano-américain et ses sources françaises* (25), Max
Henríquez Ureña's *Breve historia del modernismo* (38), monographs
on *modernista* poets, and many partial articles have already cleared
the way for the study of the influence of major French poets from
Baudelaire to St.-John Perse in Spanish America.

Several attempts to encompass the exuberance of recent developments in Spanish American poetry are noteworthy. "Dos mares y cinco
patrias" (19), by Pablo Antonio Cuadra, tries to synthesize the achievements of Spanish American poetry through the study of five figures:
César Vallejo, Pablo Neruda, Ricardo Molinari, Octavio Paz, and
Joaquín Pasos. Roberto Fernández Retamar's "Situación actual de la
poesía hispanoamericana" (26) is an attempt at surveying the evolution of poetry in the last decades.

One historical event of great social significance—the emancipation
of women—has been accompanied by an interest in their poetry as
feminine poetry. Such an attitude has no validity in literary criticism,
and there is no reason to assign women to a special section in an
anthology or study, as does even Federico de Onís in his *Antología
de la poesía española e hispanoamericana* (49), yet the custom prevails.
Sidonia C. Rosenbaum's *Modern Women Poets of Spanish America*
(58) was one of the first studies of this type. Of all the studies limited
by this external distinction, *La poesía femenina argentina* (54), by
Helena Percas, is the most comprehensive and careful.

### III

By far the most numerous studies on Spanish American poetry
are the books, monographs, and articles treating individual poets.
The two main directions of criticism—historical and stylistic—are
well represented in many valuable essays. Many studies combine these
two approaches, and there are varieties within the main currents
and in many combinations. It may well be that each poet and each
critic, when they converge in a study, create a new method, and consequently, every critical view must be unique to be valuable. Nevertheless, general trends can be discerned.

Among historical studies, the biographical presentation of a writer
is the narrowest. But when dealing with an important personality,

biographies are indispensable introductions to more complex or profound thoughts. Rubén Darío has fared better than any other poet in this respect. Among the many conscientious and at the same time imaginative biographies of him published in the last decades are Arturo Torres Ríoseco's *Vida y poesía de Rubén Darío* (65) and A. Oliver Belmás's *Este otro Rubén Darío* (10). A few recent studies of a period in his life are also helpful, such as G. Alemán Bolaños's *La juventud de Rubén Darío (1890–1893)* (5) and Raúl Silva Castro's *Rubén Darío a los veinte años* (64). In this respect the publications of the *Revista hispánica moderna* devoted to one author are outstanding, since they include biographical, bibliographical, and anthological selections.

Biographical criticism can be made more valuable if the critic tries to illuminate individual psychological problems of importance in the development of culture. In this respect, studies on Sor Juana Inés de la Cruz and her poetry have been the most interesting of those dealing with the colonial period. Sor Juana's *Primero sueño* especially has been the subject of a great deal of recent research. Outstanding examples include Gerald Cox Flynn's "The Alleged Mysticism of Sor Juana Inés de la Cruz" (28), José Gaos's "El sueño de un sueño" (30), and Ludwig Pfändl's *Sor Juana Inés de la Cruz, la décima musa de México: Su vida, su poesía, su psique* (55), a translation of the German original of 1946. A great deal more has been done in the study of colonial poetry, from Mexico to Argentina, to the point that what half a century ago was considered a cultural wasteland has emerged as a very rich period indeed.

A more profound use of biographical material in the interpretation of poetry can be found in many books of recent critics, the best of which is *El viajero inmóvil: Introducción a Pablo Neruda* (57), by Emir Rodríguez Monegal. The critic here takes as his premise the belief that the interpretation of Neruda's poetry has to be based on the intimate knowledge of his life. Another poet who has recently been the subject of many critical biographies is Gabriela Mistral, studied by, among others, Raúl Silva Castro in *Producción de Gabriela Mistral de 1912 a 1918* (63) and Fernando Alegría in *Genio y figura de Gabriela Mistral* (2).

The analysis of the themes of poetry can be made a basis for studies of form and is based on the knowledge of the concerns of each poet in his life. Consequently, studies of themes are somewhat biographical and to some extent concerned with stylistics. Rubén Darío has been a favorite in this type of study, since Arturo Marasso in 1934 published his masterly *Rubén Darío y su creación poética* (42), which has been expanded in later editions. Pedro Salinas's *La poesía de Rubén Darío* (60) examines the major themes of his poetry, but forgets at times Darío's religious concerns and imaginative depth. Among books that try to combine thematic studies with biographical-historical background and some analysis of technique, we find the examples of André Coyné's *César Vallejo y su obra poética* (18) and Angel I. Augier's two-volume *Nicolás Guillén: Notas para un estudio bio-gráfico-crítico* (7).

Studies of the relation of other arts to poetry have been scarce, in spite of the valuable insights they provide in the understanding of personality and cultural changes. Discussion of the influence of painting on poets is often found in passing references in biographical or stylistic monographs. Two attempts to relate music and poetry deserve notice: Manuel Corripio Rivero's "Sor Juana y la musica: Commentarios musicales" (17), which appeared as a series of articles in *Abside,* and Erika Lorenz's *Rubén Darío "bajo el divino imperio de la música": Estudio sobre la significación de un principio estético* (41).

The study of influences as a springboard to the understanding of style is also part of research in the history of culture. Criticism of this type has to be both historical and general in its view of the period, biographical in its analysis of the poet's reactions to foreign innovations, and stylistic in its discussion of technique. One of the best books of this kind published recently is J. M. Monner Sanz's *Julián del Casal y el modernismo hispanoamericano* (47). My own *Julio Herrera y Reissig and the Symbolists* (35) is an attempt to study the milieu of *modernismo* and the poetic technique of Julio Herrera y Reissig through an analysis of French influences.

Especially successful articles have been written explaining the abstruse poetry of Neruda or Vallejo and analyzing their technical skill. Among them are Luis García-Abrines's "La forma en la última poesía de Neruda" (31) and John H. R. Polt's "Elementos gongorinos en 'El gran océano' de Pablo Neruda" (56), both published in the *Revista Hispánica Moderna,* and Noël Salomon's "Sur quelques aspects de 'Lo humano' dans *Poemas humanos* . . . de César Vallejo" (60), published in *Caravelle.*

The poets most often discussed in recent criticism are Rubén Darío, Gabriela Mistral, and César Vallejo. A phenomenon that should not go unnoticed is the publication of many issues as *homenajes* to one poet; in the case of the centenary of Darío in 1967, many journals published issues in his honor. There is a journal devoted exclusively to studies on César Vallejo, *Aula Vallejo,* published in Córdoba, Argentina. The study of Luis Palés Matos is beginning to produce excellent articles, such as those in the issues devoted to his poetry by *Asomante* in 1959 and *La Torre* in 1960, but we have not yet seen a critical book of the scope and exactness his poetry deserves.

Before 1945 the main weakness of criticism in Spanish America was dilettantism. Journals were filled with impressionistic articles, which were later put together in disorderly books. Since then, critics have become well aware of the need for discipline, and the many studies mentioned here prove that the methods of historical investigation and stylistic analysis have been mastered. Yet the outpouring of emotional pages on favorite poets and poems continues. Unfortunately and inexplicably, the advent of professional criticism has not driven out the journalistic essay. There is a clear disparity in the material in this field: the academic publications are usually competent in method and reliable in scholarship; literati, on the other hand, still fancy the careless and garrulous essay. As a consequence, the two temptations that beckon the beginner at this moment are the old one of easy and chatty emotionalism and a new one of excessive professionalism. Perhaps the latter one is more dangerous today, since the former one has been thoroughly discredited. A warning seems necessary at this point when we begin to notice a lack of sensitivity and imagination in some of the most concientious critical writing. Perhaps critics are submerging their intuition beneath the mechanics of a well-learned method.

# BIBLIOGRAPHY

1. Albareda, Ginés de, and Francisco Garfias. *Antología de la poesía americana.* 10 vols. Madrid, 1961.
2. Alegría, Fernando. *Genio y figura de Gabriela Mistral.* Buenos Aires, 1966.
3. ———. *La poesía chilena.* Mexico, 1954.
4. ———. *Walt Whitman en Hispanoamérica.* Mexico, 1964.
5. Alemán Bolaños, G. *La juventud de Rubén Darío (1890–1893).* Guatemala, 1958.
6. Aub, Max. *Poesía mexicana, 1950–1960.* Mexico, 1960.
7. Augier, Angel I. *Nicolás Guillén: Notas para un estudio biográfico-crítico.* 2 vols. Santa Clara, Cuba, 1962.
8. Ballagas, Emilio. *Antología de la poesía negra hispanoamericana.* Madrid, 1935.
9. ———. *Mapa de la poesía negra americana.* Buenos Aires, 1946.
10. Belmás, A. Oliver. *Este otro Rubén Darío.* Barcelona, 1960.
11. Borges, Jorge Luis, Silvina Ocampo, and Adolfo Bioy-Casares. *Antología poética argentina.* Buenos Aires, 1941.
12. Caillet Bois, Julio. *Antología de la poesía hispanoamericana.* Madrid, 1958.
13. Castillo, Homero, ed. *Estudios críticos sobre el modernismo.* Madrid, 1968.
14. ———. *Poetas modernistas hispanoamericanos.* Waltham, Mass., 1966.
15. Castro Leal, Luis. *La poesía mexicana moderna.* Mexico, 1953.
16. Ceide Echevarría, Gloria. *El haikai en la lírica mexicana.* Mexico, 1967.
17. Corripio Rivero, Manuel. "Sor Juana y la música: Comentarios musicales." *Abside* (Mexico) 26 (1962): 436–84, 27 (1963): 174–95, 28 (1964): 479–96.
18. Coyné, André. *César Vallejo y su obra poética.* Lima, 1959.
19. Cuadra, Pablo Antonio. "Dos mares y cinco patrias." In *Torres de Dios: Ensayos sobre poetas.* Managua, 1958.
20. Cuesta, Jorge. *Antología de la poesía mexicana moderna.* Mexico, 1928.
21. Dauster, Frank. *Ensayos sobre poesía mexicana: Asedio a los "contemporáneos."* Mexico, 1963.
22. Davison, Ned J. *The Concept of Modernismo in Hispanic Criticism.* Boulder, Colo., 1966.
23. Díaz Plaja, Guillermo. *Modernismo frente al noventa y ocho.* Madrid, 1951.

257

24. Escobar, Alberto. *Antología de la poesía peruana.* Lima, 1965.

25. Faurie, Marie Joséphe. *Le modernisme hispano-américain et ses sources françaises.* Paris, 1966.

26. Fernández Retamar, Roberto. "Situación actual de la poesía hispanoamericana." *Revista Hispánica Moderna* 24 (1958): 321–30.

27. Florit, Eugenio, and José Olivio Jiménez. *La poesía hispanoamericana desde el modernismo.* New York, 1968.

28. Flynn, Gerald Cox. "The Alleged Mysticism of Sor Juana Inés de la Cruz," *Hispanic Review* 28 (1960): 233–44.

29. Forester, Merlin H. *Los contemporáneos, 1920–32: Perfil le un experimento vanguardista mexicana.* Mexico, 1964.

30. Gaos, José. "El sueño de un sueño." *Historia Mexicana* 10 (1960): 54–71.

31. García-Abrines, Luis. "La forma en la última poesía de Neruda." *Revista Hispánica Moderna* 25 (1951): 303–11.

32. García Prada, Carlos. *Antología de líricos colombianos.* 2 vols. Bogotá, 1936–37.

33. ———. *Poetas modernistas hispanoamericanos.* Madrid, 1956.

34. Gicovate, Bernard. *Conceptos fundamentales de literatura comparada: Iniciación de la poesía modernista.* Puerto Rico, 1962.

35. ———. *Julio Herrera y Reissig and the Symbolists.* Berkeley, Calif., 1957.

36. Gillón, Ricardo. *Direcciones del modernismo.* Madrid, 1964.

37. Gutiérrez, Juan María. *América poética.* Buenos Aires, 1846.

38. Henríquez Ureña, Max. *Breve historia del modernismo.* Mexico and Buenos Aires, 1954.

39. Jiménez, Juan Ramón. *El modernismo: Notas de un curso.* Mexico, 1962.

40. ———, José María Chacón y Calvo, and Camila Henríquez Ureña. *La poesía cubana en 1936.* Havana, 1937.

41. Lorenz, Erika. *Rubén Darío "bajo el divino imperio de la música": Estudio sobre la significación de un principio estético.* Trans. by Fidel Coloma González. Managua, 1960.

42. Marasso, Arturo. *Rubén Darío y su creación poética.* La Plata, Arg., 1934.

43. Mazzei, Angel. "El tema del día domingo." In *Estudios de poesía.* Buenos Aires, 1964.

44. Monguió, Luis. "El concepto de la poesía en algunos poetas hispanoamericanos representativos." In *Estudios sobre literatura hispanoamericana y española.* Mexico, 1958.

45. ———. "De la problemática del modernismo: La crítica y el cosmopolitismo." *Revista iberoamericana* 28 (1962): 75–86.

46. ———. *La poesía post-modernista peruana.* Berkeley, Calif., 1955.

47. Monner Sanz, J. M. *Julián del Casal y el modernismo hispanoamericano.* Mexico, 1952.

48. Monsiváis, Carlos. *La poesía mexicana del siglo XX, antología.* Mexico, 1966.

49. Onís, Federico de. *Antología de la poesía española e hispanoamericana (1882–1932).* Madrid, 1934.

50. Orjuela, Héctor H. *Las antologías poéticas de Colombia: Estudio y bibliografía.* Bogotá, 1966.

51. Pacheco, José Emilio. *La poesía mexicana del siglo XIX, antología.* Mexico, 1966.

52. Paz, Octavio. *Las peras del olmo.* Mexico, 1957.

53. ———, Alí Chumacero, José Emilio Pacheco, and Homero Aridjis. *Poesía en movimiento: Mexico, 1915–1966.* Mexico, 1966.

54. Percas, Helena. *La poesía femenina argentina.* Madrid, 1958.

55. Pfändl, Ludwig. *Sor Juana Inés de la Cruz, la décima musa de México: Su vida, su poesía, su psique.* Mexico, 1963.

56. Polt, John H. R. "Elementos gongorinos en 'El gran océano' de Pablo Neruda." *Revista Hispánica Moderna* 27 (1961): 21–31.

57. Rodríguez Monegal, Emir. *El viajero inmóvil: Introducción a Pablo Neruda.* Buenos Aires, 1966.

58. Rosenbaum, Sidonia C. *Modern Women Poets of Spanish America.* New York, 1945.

59. Salinas, Pedro. *Literatura española, siglo XX.* Mexico, 1941.

60. ———. *La poesía de Rubén Darío.* Buenos Aires, 1948.

61. Salomon, Noël. "Sur quelques aspects de 'Lo humano' dans *Poemas humanos* . . . de César Vallejo." *Caravelle* (Toulouse) 2 (1967): 97–133.

62. Silva Castro, Raúl. *Antología crítica del modernismo hispanoamericano.* New York, 1963.

63. ———. *Producción de Gabriela Mistral de 1912 a 1918.* Santiago de Chile, 1957.

64. ———. *Rubén Darío a los veinte años.* Madrid, 1956.

65. Torres Ríoseco, Arturo. *Vida y poesía de Rubén Darío.* Buenos Aires, 1944.

66. Undurraga, Antonio de. "La poesía lírica y la mente mestiza en América." *Política* (Caracas) 5 (1966): 37–51.

67. Villarrutia, Xavier, Emilio Prados, Juan Gil Albert, and Octavio Paz. *Laurel: Antología de la poesía moderna en lengua española.* Mexico, 1941.

68. Vitier, Cintio. *Lo cubano en la poesía.* Havana, 1958.

69. Xirau, Ramón. *Poesía hispanoamericana y española.* Mexico, 1961.

# THE BRAZILIAN NOVEL
# AND SHORT STORY

*Fábio Lucas*

### LITERARY TRENDS

While understanding the difficulty of pinpointing historical events and of dating any period of cultural development, we will take the period after World War II as a point of departure for this study of contemporary Brazilian fiction. Brazilian modernism, as a movement representing a break with the past in literature, the arts, and culture, had been fermenting in the 1920s and strengthened its position in the 1930s. The battle was waged against the old-fashioned writers, the domination of the Parnassians in poetry, the frivolous literature of prose fiction, and the type of theater that was then prevalent.

Genuine modernism arrived in the postwar period, but with some qualities of the old-fashioned style. Notwithstanding the efforts to destroy old traditions and implant a new national point of view in literature and the arts, it still made concessions to symbolism in its poetry and to realism-naturalism in its prose. Brazilian fiction after the war in a way shows the exhaustion of the revolutionary impulse. The best-known writers of the 1930s failed to demonstrate a renovating spirit. They repeat old formulas, petrify the real revolutionary impetus, and fall into a regular literary routine. They appear to be content with living in past memories. The writers who were associated with the novel of the Northeast of Brazil as well as the followers of Machado de Assis and the adherents of the psychological novel felt they had already delivered their message, and they retired into the pages of literary history. Thus ended a period of great literary activity and fermentation in the country.

Within the bounds of modernism, there survived in Brazil two distinct tendencies of realism-naturalism: fiction reinforced by documentary evidence, and exaggerated character portrayal. The documentary approach became dominant in the social novel, while character exaggeration was employed principally in the psychological novel. Utilizing these methods, the writers from the northeastern part of Brazil have given ample coverage to the patriarchal rural society in that area. The evidence produced by each writer came from personal observations of the problems existing in his part of the

261

country. They attempted to represent reality as accurately as possible within the patterns of normal linguistic usage. Modernism gave the writers freedom of syntax and vocabulary quite distinct from the usages which persisted in Portugal. These modernists are credited with "brazilianizing" the literary language and giving it a colloquial and spontaneous quality.

The originality of the fiction writers, those concerned with society in the rural areas as well as those who criticized the bourgeois customs of the city, lies in the fact that they attack the evils of social organization as the basis of the conflict between individuals, families, and groups described in the novel. This manner of thinking contrasts sharply with the traditional theory that explains the tragedy of the northeasterners as a combination of the rigors of nature (principally the droughts), religious conditioning, and total dependence upon the will of God as the dominant forces. In the same way the existence of prostitution in the cities is seen as the result of unemployment and social inequality rather than as a consequence of predestination. Social problems are not consigned to the supernatural but are brought into practical focus by means of realistic documentation.

The psychological and introspective novel has suffered from the heritage of realism-naturalism, especially in the works of a great number of incompetent writers whose primary concern is the portrayal of exaggerated characters with pathetic or crude personalities. Perhaps no other literature in the world has as many pathological characters as does the Brazilian literature. Outlandish isolated situations supplant the narrative of customs and peculiarities of nature. In the better psychological and introspective novels of the modernist movement one finds moderation and sobriety which yield greater subtlety and expressiveness (a legacy of Machado de Assis), a more tightly constructed prose, and more sophisticated imagery. In the former category one can cite writings of Ciro dos Anjos, for example his books *O amanuense belmiro* (10) and *Abdias* (9), and Gracilano Ramos's work *Angústia* (82). In the latter category one finds authors such as Cornélio Penna and his books *Fronteira* (72), *Dois romances de Nico Horta* (71), and *Repouso* (73).

The tendency to use dramatic situations to describe pathological characters or states of anxiety was prolonged even after World War II while a documentary style was still used with a mechanical explanation of abnormal or unnatural symptoms. Subsequent Brazilian writers were influenced by psychoanalysis, which had already influenced a great many writers around the world. The element of mystery, fear, and the fantastic is treated in a book by Lygia Fagundes Teles called *Praia viva* (112). The use of psychoanalysis is well exhibited in two books by Mário Donato, *Presença de Anita* (26) and *Madrugada sem Deus* (25), and more recently by Roberto Freire, who abandoned his profession as a psychoanalyst and devoted his life to literature and the theater, in 1965 publishing his *Cleo e Daniel* (33).

After World War II the Brazilian social novel experienced a minor change. Especially in the stories about the backland, it became less emphatic in its content and stylistically more rigid, that is to say, less spontaneous. A good example of this tendency is Mário Palméiro's *Vila dos cofins* (70). The work shows the political tradition in the backlands but without a great deal of superficial complexity. In the same year Heberto Sales published *Cascalho* (108), in which he wrote of the search for precious metals in the interior of the country. In 1959 Hernâni Donato, in his book *Selva trágica* (24), examined the inhumane cases of slavery in the southern part of Mato Grosso. Indeed it is important to mention José Cândido de Carvalho, who became well known in 1964 with his work *O coronel e o lobisomen* (17), vividly portraying the typical character of the rural areas. Finally, Maria Alice Barroso with her work *Um nome para matar* (13) won the Walmap Award in 1967. She narrates the political fights that take place in the state of Rio de Janeiro, giving special emphasis to the struggle for power between the young and the old in a predominantly rural setting.

The urban social novel is naturally influenced by new methods of communication, and although it tends to follow a documentary style, it is often patterned on the journalistic manner of presenting conditions in an industrialized, capitalistic city. The books of Esdras do Nascimento (from *Solidão em família* [64] in 1963 to *Engenharia do casamento* [63] in 1968) and of Macedo Miranda (especially *O rosto de papel* [59], 1969) illustrate the strength of this tendency.

The social documentaries and personal diagnoses continue to inspire artistic work and to reinforce a revolutionary position in Brazilian fiction. The renovating attitudes have often been mistaken for overt challenges to political stability and the prevailing moral values. But as a rule, the literary language, the artistic form, and the structural composition have remained the same. No formal outcry of anger has come down upon the writers, even those who shouted loudest for a definite promise of a reorganization of the entire social structure.

At the same time there continues the literary mimicry which has never been completely erased in Brazil. The spirit of renovation was used purely as a demonstration of the knowledge of the latest techniques in other countries, principally European and the United States. From these developed a certain awkward awareness based on journalistic synthesis of the work of Sigmund Freud, James Joyce, Franz Kafka, Marcel Proust, William Faulkner, Ernest Hemingway, Jean Paul Satre, Michel Butor, and Truman Capote. Through these authors the Brazilians acquired their ideas of psychoanalysis, super-realism, existentialism, the nouveau roman, and all of the new modes of expression used by foreign writers. Originality, however, mainly consisted of being up to date with the new styles and the transitory issues on the international scene. Occasionally Brazilians will break into polemics about who should be given credit for introducing the new European or American *dernier cri*.

Just after World War II the process of Brazilian industrialization fostered the development of new, dynamic internal centers of literature. As a consequence of the intense urbanization there exists a great polarity between the forces of localism and cosmopolitanism. So, in part, the spirit of imitation of the works of foreigners, the colonial inferiority complex, unfortunately prolongs the nationalistic tradition of a constant preoccupation to exalt the man, nature, and wealth of the nation without any attempt at rationalizing this exaltation or without using intrinsically literary means. The regional idioms, peculiarities of folklore, and customs of a technologically developing society are mobilized in order to reveal the provincial inspiration of the Brazilian and to demonstrate a national spirit, loyalty to a nation that sees itself with a rural perspective and a limited horizon.

Among the authors of great importance during the modernist period we must mention the intellectual and cosmopolitan José Geraldo Vieira. Originally a physician in Rio de Janeiro with a very extensive background, he published in the early 1940s a book of international flavor under the title *A quadragésima porta* (123). In 1928 Mário de Andrade, also a leader in the renovation movement, published *Macunaíma* (8), in which he creates "the hero without character," a symbol of the Brazilian without his own identity in a heterogeneous society in transition. This work is truly a mark of the nationalistic spirit of literary writing in Brazil. A great student of Brazilian folklore, Mário de Andrade, manages to bring together the linguistic flavors of all the sociocultural areas of the country. In *Macunaíma* he takes his characters through different time spans and locations with great linguistic ease. Still, there continues a Brazilian nativist tendency that started in the nineteenth century with the political liberation from Portugal in 1822. This tendency was exemplified in literary publications in an attempt to point up the nationalistic characteristics and to give them the eloquent, romantic expression of the times. Indian lore became the symbol for the artistic production of the nativist temper: the Indians were the indigenous owners of the land and the true spirit of Brazil. Neither the white man who brought the other European colonizers nor the subjugated and enslaved black man could reflect the spirit of liberty that the writers jealously cultivated.

After World War II the Indian-nationalist cult experienced only a few high moments. One was a novel by the essayist, playwright, and novelist M. Cavalcânti Proença entitled *Manuscrito holandês ou a peleja do Caboclo Mitavaí com o Monstro Macobeba* (80). The author accentuates stylistic Indianism and supports it with an extensive knowledge of the peculiarities of the language. The main purpose of the novel is the exploration of the national essence. The extensive title and description has its roots in popular pamphlets, sometimes called "cheap literature." It reflects the Iberian tradition in which the picaresque novels and the satirical novels of medieval chivalry utilized long titles and chapter headings explaining as much of the content as possible. This same method was used in the important chronicles of the Portuguese voyages of the fifteenth and sixteenth centuries as well as in the Gongorist literature of the seventeenth century. Jorge Amado, in his most recent works, overuses the comic aspects of this method, as seen readily in his *Gabriela, carvo e canela* (7). M. Cavalcânte Proença can be considered a follower of Mário de Andrade; he is the author of one of the best works about the leader of modernism. In his *Roteiro de Macunaíma* (81), he made a meticulous investigation of the underlying Indian mythology in the symbolism of the book.

The nationalist tendency in Brazilian fiction has not always been revolutionary as the majority of the writers would have preferred. Once the novelists ingenuously adorned their work with picturesque, pathetic, sentimental, and anecdotal elements with which they supposed they would be able to please foreign critics. This idea was especially prominent in the regional literature. The great difficulty that the regional writers faced was their formal accommodation. But their decision to return to the Brazilian and to give special emphasis to national themes was simply not enough; it was not even sufficient to create an independent mode of literary expression. From the formal point of view, Brazilians did not try to arrive at any conclusion of their own. There was no agitation, not even an attempt to break the natural domination of foreign influences. Nevertheless, the international experience has been useful in contemporary Brazilian literature to the extent that it was adapted to the national mood and to internal demands and circumstances.

The writer, in effect, is a revolutionary when his social role conflicts with the expectations of a complacent society, a society that is subjected to a rigorously controlled social existence. Such a writer proposes a battle, an alternative, a reform, and his job becomes that of a dynamic challenger. He must conceive of and communicate a new reality, establish a system of linguistic relationships, and invent a world of specific tensions. In this way he demonstrates his originality and gains his autonomy.

In Brazil today some writers have begun to conceive of language not merely as an instrument to represent an objective reality whose content is simply presented and criticized. Language is no longer a link between subjectivity and objectivity; a literary language has appeared to transmit its own innate reality. The artistic revolution, however, is not designed simply to change views of society, the individual, nature, and the dramatic situations of life. It also has necessarily created a relation between its own created reality and the means of literary expression. Along these lines of Brazilian innovation one should mention Guimarães Rosa, Murilo Rubião, and Clarice Lispector.

After World War II, Brazilians experienced a gradual change in the literary tradition. The narrative style was abandoned to make room for works with the spectacular gesture or revolutionary act. This movement was led by a group anxious to establish itself. The documentary tendency still continued in order to describe life in the backlands, but emphasis was placed on society rather than on nature or divine predestination. An important contribution is the book *Irmão Juazeiro* (36), by Francisco Julião, the organizer of the famous peasant leagues in the Northeast.

The work of this group presents a much more careful literary style with less flowery speech and a more refined aesthetic (the influence of Guimarães Rosa is obvious in this respect). The documentary tendency in the novels about the city yields an urban treatise-document. The result is no longer a simple chronicle of misfortune aimed at bourgeois society. The motivation has appeared to be that of examining social pathology, for example, prostitution and the dissolution of the bourgeois family in the large cities. Orígenes Lessa describes, with rare felicity, the episode of a strike in a brothel, in his book *A noite sem homem* (40), in which he narrates the customs and language of this area of social relations. Esdras do Nascimento describes the raw life of the semimarginal youths who live in one of Rio's most populous areas, Copacabana. His first book was called *Solidão em família* (64); the second, *Engenharia do casamento* (63).

The political events of 1964[1] produced a "literature of protest" which was especially noticeable in the theater. While novels of Carlos Hector Cony, Antônio Calado, Macedo Miranda, and various others were becoming popular the psychological novel was abandoned little by little. With few exceptions, the common man begins to emerge, demonstrating acts of cowardice and heroism as conditioned by certain circumstances and special moments. One sees also the abandonment of society's biased reflexes toward the individual who now becomes a psychologically eccentric but picturesque character in the novel. He thus passes from trivial shallowness to normal common daily life. Also in the modernist tradition, some authors strike out against the pathetic characterizations and the excess of flowery speech in the novel. They prefer to describe the peasants as being repelled by the local condition of life *(Vidas sêcas* [83] by Gracilano Ramos is the best example) and to relate the bitter life of a small bourgeois bureaucrat *(O amanuense belmiro* [10] by Ciro dos Anjos is an excellent model).

We should not fail to note the emergence of concern by the Brazilian novelist in developing and enlarging the scope of the novel. Here we should give particular attention to the works of Guimarães Rosa and Clarice Lispector. They both are noted short-story writers as well as novelists. In the last few years they have been the most respected of the Brazilian fiction writers. Both Murilo Rubião and Breno Accioly gained much fame after World War II and have remained excellent short-story writers because of their novelty of expression. Since 1960 the number of short-story writers has grown tremendously with an emphasis on a new, refined style. Perhaps the short story, given its dimensions, has attracted a great majority of

1. In March, 1964, the Brazilian military overthrew civilian President João Goulart. The military has controlled the country, through a series of presidents, since that time.

fiction writers largely because of the influence of rapid means of communication in this day and age. With some authors the short story has been transformed into a microcosmic unity. Yet in terms of style the short story continues to be the best attempt at a renovation of Brazilian literary efforts.

The search for the everyday man in casual everyday situations has been very prominent in the recent novel and short story of Brazil as in the rest of the world. In reality the new and direct spatial elaboration in painting and the interesting temporal space solutions in movie productions have demanded a rethinking of the idea of perspective in the writing of fiction. The novel, too, must be liberated from ingrained perspectives and from the congested mass of space and time in order to explore human destiny as determined by a specific situation. Thus literature will develop as an artifact of the natural aesthetics rather than a manifestation of social or biological agitation. The fiction writer has begun to spend more time investigating the fundamental mystery of life and different facets of existence by means of an indirect observation of motivation. At the same time, one finds a closer approximation between the narrator and the narration; the literary language no longer constitutes simply an instrument of communication, a means, but instead is transformed into an object itself. Certain "literary" elements in painting and the movies have been impossible to categorize, especially when they have succeeded in freeing themselves from common modes of conceptualization. They have assumed an essence all of their own. Fiction writing, which demands a more distinctive style, has experienced some "feedback" from this tendency. For example, Geraldo Ferraz in his novel *Doramundo* (32) narrates the sexual dramas of a small city which decides to import prostitutes in order to relieve social tensions. The plot is a type of detective story in which a couple, completely enveloped in true love, dominates the entire scene. However, this couple is condemned by society, since the woman is already married to another man. Yet ironically they enjoy the only honest relationship in the city. (Teodora, or simply Dora, becomes deeply involved with Paimundo, or simply Mundo. *Doramundo*=hard world.)

The increased valuation of the literary text, as a universal tendency, coincides with a natural propensity of Brazilian psychology, aestheticism. We believe that this is one of the aspects that indicates most strongly the enormous potential for the novel in the Brazilian tradition. The thematic complexity, structure, syntax, and vocabulary adjust marvelously to the Brazilian temperament. This explains the tremendous success of the works of Guimarães Rosa, a definite landmark in Brazilian fiction of the postwar period. Since the publication of his first book, a collection of short stories (*Sagarana* [104], 1946), and through his last book *(Tutaméia* [105], 1967), he has been a point of reference in our literature. He has been the subject of one of the most copious critical bibliographies of the country and has received bitter criticism by some fiction writers who do not appreciate his role as a link between universal tendencies and the national variations of those tendencies.

Indeed, the progress and the diffusion of new means of communication in prose fiction has meant an increase in the potential of literary expression. This implies the added aesthetic value of the language; and in spite of Brazil's past tradition, it was readily accepted within the country. We have already spoken of the Brazilian "baroque spirit," the surprising psychology and the lack of compatibility to a rigid structure. The popular music and sports activities, high points of improvisation, attest to the flexible character of the national psychology. All in all, this is the ornamental mark of our artistic work and of the popular artifacts. Some authors insist that aestheticism is the special way of being of the Brazilian man, a man who contemplates the world as a stage and life as a performance, so that no act of nobility nor any unworthy gesture, no merit, action, or noteworthy intention should pass unnoticed. In this way the common Brazilian prefers the externalization of feeling and has little respect for less explicit human qualities.

In the field of literature, it is necessary to note the great influence of the sacred orators, especially Father Antônio Vierra.[2] The fastidious and baroque style was repeated in the twentieth century, especially in the works of Rui Barbosa,[3] an orator of great verbal and symbolic orchestration during the first Brazilian republic. It was the most complete representation of the small bourgeois middle class that, at a critical juncture in the evolution of Brazil, sought to emerge from the domination of the rural aristocracy. The frondescent and emphatic style became a part of the written Brazilian tradition: Euclides da

2. Vieira, a seventeenth-century Jesuit priest, delivered impassioned sermons against the evils of Indian slavery in colonial Brazil.

3. Rui Barbosa, one of the framers of the Brazilian republic in 1889 and the founder of the Civilian party, represented his country at the second Hague Conference, where he eloquently voiced the demands for the rights of weak nations.

Cunha, Coelho Neto, José de Alencar, Monteiro Lobato, and Oswald de Andrade constitute some of the best examples worthy of consideration.

One can see a definite tendency among Brazilians to give literary importance to works in the social sciences, principally in history, sociology, and anthropology. Thus some of the most important works in the Brazilian culture are *Um estadista do império* (62) by Joaquim Nabuco, *Os sertões* (23) by Euclides da Cunha, *Populações meridionais do Brasil* (122) by Oliveira Vianna, *Casa grande e senzala* (34) by Gilberto Freyre, and *Raízes do Brasil* (35) by Sergio Buarque de Holanda. According to the sociologist and critic Antônio Cândido (16), literature in Brazil has been "more than philosophy and humanities, the central phenomenon of life .of the spirit." The forementioned works are frequently objects of literary appraisal in addition to being interpretations of the different periods of Brazilian history and society.

Aestheticism, however, as a national inclination of the Brazilian, facilitated the literary refinement of modern works of fiction and stimulated experimentation. In general, the experimental works are well received by the literary critics. The presumption that these works are good and original dominates the thinking of some people.

### THE NOVEL AND THE SHORT STORY

Brazilian fiction in the postwar period was helped along by the opportunities opened by expressionism, which, to a certain degree, opposes the interest of the simple documentary. Expressionism carries with it the ability to awaken the senses by external and internal impressions. It limits itself to offering subjective thoughts and feeling about the subject present in the speculative conscience. The expressionist artist refuses to narrate what occurred or what he saw, but emphasizes what affected him.

One of the great moments in the effective use of language in Brazilian literature occurred with the work of Clarice Lispector (46, 47, 48, 49, 50, 51, 52, 53), whose first piece was published in 1944. Novelist of the subtlety of the soul, of the microcosm of human behavior, observer of emotional states, she renovated the psychological novel in Brazil. With her great skill in giving distinction to a simple gesture, a state of mind, or an everyday occurrence, she treats human essence in detail through small openings. Her short stories "Alguns contos" and "Laços de família" together constitute masterpieces of the genre. "Mistério de S. Cristovão" has become one of the most outstanding works of its kind in Brazilian literature.

But her efforts in the short story have by no means detracted from her novels, which offer great continuity in their subjectivity and subtlety of abstraction. *A paixão segundo G. H.* (52) and *Uma aprendizagem ou o livro dos prazeres* (47), for example, reveal a profound intimacy, deeply shaped by syntactical and psychological nuances. In her first works Clarice Lispector achieved more than what we would call an action novel. *A cidade sitiada* (48), for example, studies the modification of a suburb which has been subjected to such urban necessities and technical innovations as machines, asphalt, and the expulsion of animals. The meaning of the modification is reflected in the psychology of the central character.

The characters of Clarice Lispector suffer more than they impel. One notes a certain moroseness in the narrative, especially in her largest novel, *A maçã no escuro* (51). The central dramatic situation revolves around a criminal (Martim) who is attempting to flee from the consequences of his crime and to find himself, to find some explanation and some objective in life, and to reincorporate himself in the world as a changed man. In his complex of guilt and desire slowly coming to the forefront from fear of being punished, he encounters Vitória, an apparently strong and aggressive woman. Little by little she lets down her defenses and reveals a tormented soul, corroded by failure. She lives on an abandoned plantation with Ermelinda, a fragile character, a delicate heart, always in fear of death, and easy prey for men (Martim). Throughout these episodes there is a world of suggestion. The repetitious phrases of Clarice Lispector create an obsessive picture of each character. One notes, a sententious style in the attempt of each character to define the imponderable.

In *A maçã no escuro* one sees the destruction of the notion of space, so that objects serve the function of emotional significance. Being a novel of characters, the possible dynamics are internalized and translated into a rich language of surprises and twists. The characters endure the drama of expression. They attempt to say things that they are incapable of saying. The protagonists invent new vocabularies and new sentences. Vitória, in the act of revealing her secret, becomes hoarse. Martim, in order to overcome the gloomy situation in whch he finds himself, must come up with a definite word, a word capable of dominating, illuminating, and clarifying the others. Finally he discovers that the most important thing is to live and that the hand can reach out and understand the apple in the dark, without action, without verbs, without words.

Another novelist of great importance, as we have already indicated, was Guimarães Rosa (101, 102, 103, 104, 105). Rare is the Brazilian author who has enjoyed as many of the fruits of notoriety as the author of *Grande Sertão: Veredas* (102). His work has been the target of countless analyses, thoroughly investigating its sociological aspects, its literary attributes, and its linguistic peculiarities. It has been the subject of innumerable dissertations. It constitutes a confluence of universal mythology with national mythology, a rigorous endeavor to renovate the Brazilian short novel, presenting the articulation of new symbols and an elevated experiment in innovations at the level of language and word usage.

Many interpreters have encountered in Guimarães Rosa's chief work—*Grande Sertão: Veredas*—a synthesis of epic elements, a fusion of values from the medieval novels of chivalry, a reelaboration of the Faustian drama, exceeding the epitome of the great Western myths. At the same time, the work projects itself within the context of national tradition, when, during the retaking of the *sertão*, it shows in relief one of the Brazilian dualities, the antagonism between coast and interior first explored by Euclides da Cunha in his famous book *Os Sertoes* in 1902.

Guimarães Rosa considered in a special way the dynamic character of the landless peasants, who, having neither interest nor hope in working the land of others, chose to organize themselves and live as nomadic tribes, in opposition to the laws of the nation but obedient to the rigid ethic principles predominant within the group. The ethics are those of *cangaço*, the interminable battle for a hypothetical power, beyond time and space. Their greatest activity of subsistence was attack; their search for power and prestige in that restricted region constituted war. The novelette reflects the passion for the unknown that always stimulated the author and yielded his religious imbuement and profound mysticism. The epic axis is completed by a fertile imagination, a great knowledge of the landscape, a profound animism. Added to this is an intense psychological subtlety capable of marking the individuality of each character. The result is a work of great Dionysic vibration, which enhances the aesthetic feature that one finds in this Brazilian writer. An impressive aspect in Guimarães Rosa is the rigor of the details encrusted in an assemblage of monumental dimensions.

One notes, in the works of Guimarães Rosa, perfect coexistence of magical thought with logical thought, resulting in a highly metaphorical and referential language. One of the features of his prose is the enriching emphasis that deforms or re-creates language. The exaltation of the soul leads to a certain type of expressionism. Analyzing his work, one finds the origin of his linguistic creation in the lyrical process, that is, in the subject-object fusion that, in turn, leads to the identification between the narrator and the narrative (84). One may add to this the vast extent of the subconscious in Guimarães Rosa, a source of some of the mystery in his fiction. The magic and the symbolism appear esoteric to many ordinary readers, especially when his expression molds itself into a collective subconscious. Through his magical realism he is capable of transmuting the motives of daily life in symbols of fantasy and myth. In the narrative prose of Guimarães Rosa, more than in any other Brazilian writer, one finds that the work of verbal art is a multistratified reality, subjected to a structurization involving a number of harmonious themes.

The Brazilian novelette reached two high points in 1956, *Doramundo* (32) by Geral Ferraz, already mentioned, and *O encontro marcado* (107) by Fernando Sabino. The latter sought to pin down the psychology of a group of young people and resulted in one of the most successful publishing ventures in recent times. Sabino describes an immature, agitated, insecure generation that gives excessive value to the ornamental and literary aspects of life. The characters are morally decadent; they marry, they separate, they change in status, but they continue to view life as one would a child's game. In their own way they represent the Brazilian "aestheticism."

Fernando Sabino is a fascinating analyst who dedicates himself to dramatic or picturesque commentary about daily Brazilian life. He is widely read in newspapers and magazines. His journalistic background has influenced his fiction, which is constructed of small episodes and articulated collections of "chronicles." Many times the parts show independence of composition, although they function perfectly together in a romanesque structure. *O encontro marcado*, of urban orientation, contains some elements common to our everyday fiction: the instability of the characters, moral disaster, sexual excitation and failure, ornamental intellectualism, the impossibility of intersubjective exchange of experiences, etc.

In 1961, Autran Dourado launched *A barca dos homens* (27), which successfully combines the principles of the novelette of action with those of the novelette of characters. The book is dominated by internal monologue. It is based on a variety of human feelings: the existential uneasiness and dramatic situations which constitute an all-encompassing means of expression. *A barca dos homens* is one of the best Brazilian novels of the postwar period. The author made use, principally, of the literary progress made in the short story. He had published in 1957 *Nova historias em grupos de três* (28), the book which marked his presence in Brazilian literature. Writing short stories in modern language, he tried to deepen his awareness of the human essence. He always showed a preference for the psychological novel. In the construction of *A barca dos homens,* avoiding the extravagant plot, he preferred to employ autonomous parts, pictures complete in themselves yet interlinked by the general plot. He repeated in a certain way the technique of Fernando Sabino, but with greater complexity. Later, in 1964, he published a short Flaubertine novel, *Uma vida em segredo* (30), an account of the reactions of a primitive, unprotected character, Biela, who is unable to absorb certain values of civilization as he moves from the country to the city. Biela's elemental psychology is projected simply in an uncomplicated plot. A lyrical note, properly proportioned, sustains the literary dimension of the novel.

Autran Dourado's most recent novel, *Opera dos mortos* (29), re-creates an archaic social picture. He describes the static material elements with an almost naturalistic exactitude (the landscape, the affluence of a small city of the interior, an aristocratic family which changes little from generation to generation). An external element, José Feliciano, is introduced into this sleeping and stagnant society, bringing a new dynamism affecting especially the principal character, Rosalina. All of the romanesque tension, the climax, so to speak, results from the encounter of the principal character of the narrative, adjusted to her social framework, with the external element, who interferes with the system of established values, awakening potentialities until then asleep. The climax having passed, the system does not return to its former equilibrium. On the other hand, the transformations introduced are not conclusive. Certainly, only the relationship between the principal element of the plot and the protagonists involved by their dramatic situation is unalterably changed.

Actually, the characters of Autran Dourado are heard more than seen. Interior monologue constitutes the principal means of developing the protagonists. The main character, who takes an antogonistic attitude toward society, gradually suffers a division of personality: there is one everyday, traditional Rosalina on one hand, and on the other, a Rosalina of the night who gives herself up to intoxication and sexual pleasures. A battle between education and the instincts, between the conscious and the subconscious, ensues.

Macedo Miranda, a short-story writer, is now trying to produce a cyclic work that he projects for twelve volumes. His most recent book, the seventh of the group, is *O rosto de papel* (59). It deals with the psychological and moral disintegration of a journalist unsuited for professional life and torn by frustration. It is basically an antiheroic novel, a type very popular in contemporary Brazilian literature. We have, indeed, a generation of novelists of the outcasts and the failures, and thus Macedo Miranda, like innumerable Brazilian novelists, reinforces the substance of that type of modern fiction, depicting decadence, uncontrollable sensualism, the sharp and fragmented perception of phenomena, free intellectualism, the exciting game of life, the lack of objectivity, lyricism, the cult of chance, brutality, and stifled political protest.

The modernist spirit, added to contemporary tendencies in literature and to social change in Brazil, has sustained a wave of experimentalism in Brazilian fiction. Maria Alice Barroso, for example, in 1960 gave us the novel *História de um casamento* (12), in which she tried something more than the parallel monologue of Chekhov: she searched for simultaneous monologue, the representation, side by side, of two consciences. She worked out in this way the fragmentation of the text, in order to offer a constellation of data united by the main plot. Nelida Piñon in 1961 submitted to criticism her *Guia-mapa de Gabriel Arcanjo* (77), an attempt at the subjection of language to the conflict of love. Her experimentation continues in *Madeira feita cruz* (78), in which myth dominates reason and the force of the subconscious conditions existence. Experimentalism takes another emphasis with Campos de Carvalho, author of *Vaca do nariz sutil* (18), a work of imaginative composition, surrealist, and written in hallucinated prose. In speaking of "chronicles of the absurd," one must mention Hermann José Reipert's *Travessa do elefante sem número* (96). The work reflects the convulsed inner world of a neurotic. In the words of one of his critics, the author tried to fuse the "roughness of the language" of Graciliano Ramos with the "phantasmal ambience" of Cornélio Pena (67).

Postwar Brazilian regionalism was well expressed in the work of

Dalcídio Jurandir, known as the novelist of the Amazon. Joining the currents of documentation and of personal testimony, he gives an original picture of the island of Marajó. He feels himself motivated by social problems and projects them in books like *Marajó* (38), *Linha do parque* (37), and *Três casas e um rio* (39). As previously indicated, the fiction that portrays life in the rural areas also concerns itself with the problems of language. One notes a new perspective on traditional motives of Brazilian narrative in the work of Odylo Costa Filho, *A faca e o rio* (22), for example. Economy of means, verbal plundering, also is observed in Assis Brasil's *Beira rio beira vida* (15).

Social drama of the marginality of the great city of São Paulo is depicted by João Antônio in his book *Malgueta, Perus e Bacanaço* (11). This novel captures the speech of the scoundrels, the slang of the *bas-fonds*, as well as the dominant ethics of that border zone of the metropolis.

In the area of the psychological novel, other names may be recalled. Antônio Olavo Pereira creates an introspective novel of good literary quality, dealing particularly with family tragedy. The author of *Contramão* (74), *Marcoré* (76), and *Fio de prumo* (75), he may be considered a novelist of the crisis of conscience. Geraldo Mello Mourão, a poet and fictionist, places himself among the innovators of the Brazilian novel. Writing in a prose heavy with ardent lyricism and philosophical meditation, he published *O valente de espadas* (61) in 1960 and *Dossiê da destruição* (60) in 1966. Sex, religious unrest, and criticism of bourgeois values feed the prose of novelist Carlos Hetor Cony. His characters are the afflicted and the marginal people. His novels are nourished on wild language and contain elements of the detective story to hold the reader's attention. He is the author of several works, including *O ventre* (21), *Antes, o verão* (19), and *Pessac: A travessia* (20).

Mário Garcia de Paiva, novelist of existential anguish, was the first Brazilian novelist to use the city of Brasilia as a setting. *Luana* (68) is a book which the grandeur of human ability (the new capital) contrasts with the fragility of human passions. The failures of domestic life receive an intense coloring in the novel *Ontem* (69), in which Mário Garcia de Paiva again shows himself to be an assured writer and extremely objective in elaborating the small details of human conduct. With Manoel Lobato's *Mentira dos limpos* (54), we have the drama of the troubled conscience. The protagonist, a neurotic, reveals great dissatisfaction with the social, political, and family situation to which he is subjected. Educated in a puritanical community, tried for a crime of opinion, interned in a sanitorium, distrusting the intentions of those around him, feeling insecure about the conduct of his wife, he ends up in a great erotic adventure, seeking his identity.

Novels of action supported by personal experience and good poetic prose are found in the work of Moacir C. Lopes, sailor turned writer. His *A ostra e o vento* (56) and *Cais, saudade em pedra* (55) are documentary and lyrical. Although Lopes is not a great stylistic innovator, he must be placed among the good Brazilian novelists of the postwar period.

Some modernist fiction writers have also cultivated the Brazilian historical novel. Jorge Amado and Erico Veríssimo are notable examples. Presently one notes an interesting experiment, *Judeu Nuquim* (6), by Octâvio Mello Alvarenga, a work deserving the Walnap Award. It relates the history of a Jew persecuted by the Holy Office of the Inquisition in Bahia. He flees to Minas Gerais, a province still in its formative stage in the seventeenth century and one which will reach its height in the eighteenth century with a civilization nurtured by the discovery of gold. Contemporary "history," principally the separation of the upper bourgeoisie of São Paulo, is reflected in the work of Maria de Lourdes Teixeira, in *Rua Augusta* (111). This book shows the emptiness of that elite, left to intemperance and ostentation. In addition, she published *O pátio dãs donzelas* (110), treating the same subject but with a new theme dealing with girls who seek meaning in life through sex and frivolity.

The crisis of the novel, manifested throughout the postwar world, contributed in a way to an improved short story. The fight against the Rocambolesque and cyclopean plot contributed to the exhaustion of stereotyped characters and conditioned a new point of view for the fiction writer. Dramatic situations of short duration and psychologies adapted to the exigencies of the moment of emotional intensity were preferred. Beyond this, the taste for verbal solutions was perfected and the art of fiction became more "literary." These tendencies helped make the Brazilian short story more susceptible to experimentation and the medium of greatest innovation.

By 1941, Mário Neme (65, 66) was already trying to communicate a new style. His was an anecdotal, ingenious fiction in a language above all colloquial. With much humor he successfully paraphrased the archaic style in relating the episodes of daily life. Subsequently, however, he abandoned the field of literature to pursue the study of anthropology.

In 1944 the first volume of Breno Accioly's (1, 2, 3, 4, 5) short stories appeared. A writer from Alagoas, with a degree in medicine, he made his debut at the age of twenty-three with a surprising book. He created exceptional characters with a tormented inner life touching upon insanity. The critic Tristão de Atâide, writing about *João Urso*, recorded: "We in Brazil have never before seen so well expressed that terrible land of transition between the light of perception and the other light of insanity." The literary quality of his following volumes did not always attain such a high level.

In 1946 Murilo Rubião achieved a true revolution in the conception of the short story with the book *O ex-mágico* (106). This work is one of the most successful manifestations of magical realism in our prose fiction. A writer of great poetic strength, Rubião instills a meaningful essence in all beings in order to deepen the perspective of the human soul. He differs from Kafka in that he contemplates the smallest actions and intentions with innocent and fascinated eyes. His symbols and myths emanate from the depths of unassuming infancy and cover, with illusion and fantasy, impotent destiny, frustration, and the path to death.

The common man, freed of insanity but always in a dramatic climate, victimizied by entangled situations, appears in the short stories of various important postwar authors. We mention, for example, Ricardo Ramos (86, 87, 88, 89, 90, 91) and Samuel Rawet (92, 93, 94, 95). Both are representative of literary excellence. Both make use of a carefully chosen vocabulary and purity of language. These concerns are carried to the extreme in the works of Ildeu Brandão, who, after years of scanty publication (but always of good quality) in 1968 gave the public the collection entitled *Um míope no zoo* (14).

The regional short story merits special consideration in Bernardo Elis's *Veranico de janeiro* (31), winner of the José Lins do Rêgo Award given by the Livraria José Olympio Editôra. Rural relationships are analyzed through social conflicts, with little importance given to traditional theses and ancedotes. Drawing upon his own experience and studies of his cultural area (the environment of Goiaz, western Brazil), Bernardo Elis accurately portrays the local customs and the characteristic speech of the region without neglecting universal literary values.

Psychological investigation, which assumes special characteristics in the works of Lygia Fagundes Teles and Breno Accioly, reaches new levels of cruelty, revolt, and sadism in the short stories of Otto Lara Resende (97, 98, 99, 100), especially those brought together under the title *Bôca do Inferno*. The author explores the rebellion of the child against his elders, particularly against parental authority. The children in his short stories become thieves, murderers, sadists. There is an incestuous basis for the pleasure with which the young ones beat down the adults and attack their values.

In 1959 two refreshing short-story writers appeared on the Brazilian scene, José J. Veiga (119, 120, 121) and Dalton Trevisan (113, 114, 115, 116, 117, 118). The former, born in Goiaz and raised in Rio de Janeiro, invented a new language for the legends of the interior which he recounted or imagined. His stories attack the core of human destiny, always leaving an eliptical suspension for the readers. His expression is highly metaphorical and the stories are often in the form of parables. He is a notable writer, withdrawn in modesty and little accustomed to the task of promoting his own works. Dalton Trevisan concerned himself with the society of his own city, Curitiba, in the state of Paraná. He wrote surprising short stories and distributed them among his friends. He edited them at his own cost until he was discovered by the Brazilian public and by critics, who lavished praise. In 1951 he published a novel, *Sonata ao luar,* without national repercussions. His short stories constitute microcosms of narrative experience. Brief, synthetic, constrained, they say a good deal in little space. They depict the marginality of Curitiba and portray frustrated, unhappy men, the eternal victims of sexual compulsions. Strong anguish dominates his fiction.

In 1961, story writer Ivan Angelo published in Belo Horizonte his *Duas faces* and immediately emerged as a great star. Using a polished language, he created the impression of spontaneity with his rhythm and volume of information. His style was colloquial, tense, elaborate, and sought out the trauma of the subconscious. The short story "Homen sofrendo no quarte" best reflects this experiment. It was Angelo's last work. Another isolated experiment was that of Nelso Coelho, who wrote *O inventor de Deus* (São Paulo, 1962). Well within expressionistic lines, the author tries to capture the dimensions of oriental philosophy, through his particular way of placing the human being in the cosmos.

In 1963 the Brazilian literary community was surprised by Rubem

Fonseca's *Os prisioneiros*. The literary environment was by then saturated with fiction of the internal life, slow verbal pace, and descriptions of the environment. The reading public wanted dynamism, action, rapid expression, conflict of characters. They found all of this in Rubem Fonseca's *Os prisioneiros*. The same attributes reasserted themselves even more solidly in his next book, *A coleira do cão*, published in 1965. Few fiction writers are capable of describing life in the great cities as truly a "tragic jungle," in which one encounters fatal, irreversible traps daily. Failure is the general rule but the will to survive, innate in humans, makes the characters singularly careless, easy prisoners of their own unknown impotence. The descriptions of Rubem Fonseca are marked by impressive realism; they are supported by language induced by each experience in such a way that the vocabulary, rigorously chosen, sustains the narrative. Since the short stories of Rubem Fonseca are ones of action, the author arms the dramatic situation with rapid events. The dialogues, the monologues, the descriptions of scenes and objects—all are functional, all lead to the climax and to an inevitable situation. His characters are almost always presented in a world of various alternatives. With the plot securely constructed and the dramatic circumstances adeptly prepared, one clearly observes the irreversible and the inexorable. Rubem Fonseca created one of the most valid experiments of the modern Brazilian short story.

One of the most important of the new generation of Brazilian fiction writers, Osman Lins (41, 42, 43, 44, 45) began in 1966 with the book *Nove, novena,* a landmark in the evolution of the Brazilian short story. Novelist, essayist, and writer of short stories, Lins captured the essence of his experience in that volume and achieved a rare efficiency in the creation of a new narrative. Producing a short story of action, he gave a new dimension to the design of characters and personalities. The plot evolves around various centers. Each vital focal point has its own corresponding linguistic universe. Even in such an ambitious project, Osman Lins succeeded in giving harmony and structure to each composition. "Perdidos e achados," for example, constitutes a masterpiece of the genre. The same is true of "Retábulo de Santa Joana Carolina." The author created his own verbal tempo. He frequently delves into the roots of words, into the biological rudiments of man, into the revelation of communication through symbols of literature, linguistics, and anthropology. He searches for the fundamental mysteries of existence and challenges them: the origin of the cosmos, the destiny of man.

Luiz Vilela made an auspicious debut in 1967 with *Tremor de terra* (125), the book which won him the Fundação do Distrito Federal Award. His short stories carry profound philosophical significance; they apprehend the mutilated man's inability to communicate with himself. Beings do not transmit their essence, they suffer and destroy themselves. The word becomes an imperfect and deceptive vehicle. Having won a prize in a second national short-story contest, sponsored by the state government of Paraná, Luiz Vilela has published another work, *No bar* (124).

To complete this brief history of postwar Brazilian fiction, the novel *Quarup* by Antônio Calado deserves special mention. Calado, a journalist who had experienced some modest success with earlier novels, completed *Quarup* in 1967. This book constitutes still another demonstration of Brazilian aestheticism; a complex work, it combines tradition and revolution, and provides both anthropological and linguistic contributions. The plot summarizes the life of a priest who, in a climate of Dionysic sensuality, breaks with secular sexual restraints. Later, yielding to his instincts, he embraces a political cause and enlists himself in revolutionary battle. *Quarup* continually confronts man with society in a dialectic antagonism.

(Translated by James Riordan)

# BIBLIOGRAPHY

1. Accioly, Breno. *Os Cata-ventos*. Rio de Janeiro, 1962.
2. ———. *Cogumelos*. Rio de Janeiro, 1955.
3. ———. *Dunas*. Rio de Janeiro, 1955.
4. ———. *João Urso*. Rio de Janeiro, 1944.
5. ———. *Maria Pudim*. Rio de Janeiro, 1955.
6. Alvarenga, Octãvio Mello. *Judeu Nuquim*. Rio de Janeiro, 1967.
7. Amado, Jorge. *Gabriela, carvo e canela*. Lisbon, 1966.
8. Andrade, Mário de. *Macunaíma*. São Paulo, 1962. First published in 1928.
9. Anjos, Ciro dos. *Abdias*. Rio de Janeiro, 1965.
10. ———. *O amanuense belmiro*. Rio de Janeiro, 1966.
11. Antônio, João. *Malagueta, Perus e Bacanaço*. Rio de Janeiro, 1963.
12. Barroso, Maria Alice. *História de um casamento*. Rio de Janeiro, 1960.
13. ———. *Um nome para matar*. Rio de Janeiro, 1967.
14. Brandão, Ildeu. *Um míope no zoo*. Belo Horizonte, Braz., 1968.
15. Brasil, Assis. *Beiro rio beira vida*. Rio de Janeiro, 1965.
16. Cândido, Antônio. *Literatura e Sociedade*. São Paulo, 1967.
17. Carvalho, José Cândido de. *O coronel e o lobisomem*. Rio de Janeiro, 1965.
18. Carvalho, Walter Campos de. *Vaca do nariz sutil*. Rio de Janeiro, 1961.
19. Cony, Carlos Heitor. *Antes, o verão*. Rio de Janeiro, 1967.
20. ———. *Pessac: A travessia,* Rio de Janeiro, 1967.
21. ———. *O ventre*. Rio de Janeiro, 1965.
22. Costa Filho, Odylo. *A faca e o rio*. Rio de Janeiro, 1965.
23. Cunha, Euclides da. *Os sertões*. Rio de Janeiro, 1956. First published in 1902.
24. Donato, Hernâni. *Selva trágica*. São Paulo, 1959.
25. Donato, Mário. *Madrugáda sem Deus*. Rio de Janeiro, 1954.
26. ———. *Presença de Anita*. Rio de Janeiro, 1948.
27. Dourado, Waldomiro Autran. *A barca dos homens*. Rio de Janeiro, 1961.
28. ———. *Nove histórias em grupos de três*. Rio de Janeiro, 1957.
29. ———. *Opera dos mortos*. Rio de Janeiro, 1967.
30. ———. *Uma vida em segredo*. Rio de Janeiro, 1964.
31. Elis, Bernardo. [B. E. Fleury de Campos Curado.] *Veranico de janeiro*. Rio de Janeiro, 1966.
32. Ferraz, Geraldo. *Doramundo*. Santos, Braz., 1956.

33. Freire, Roberto. *Cleo e Daniel.* São Paulo, 1965.
34. Freyre, Gilberto. *Casa grande e senzala.* Rio de Janeiro, 1964.
35. Holanda, Sergio Buarque de. *Raízes do Brasil.* Brasília, 1963.
36. Julião, Francisco. *Irmão Juazeiro.* Rio de Janeiro, 1960.
37. Jurandir, Dalcídio. *Linha do parque.* Rio de Janeiro, 1958.
38. ———. *Marajó.* Rio de Janeiro, 1947.
39. ———. *Três casas e um rio.* São Paulo, 1958.
40. Lessa, Orígenes. *A noite sem homem.* Rio de Janeiro, 1968.
41. Lins, Osman. *O fiel e a pedra.* Rio de Janeiro, 1961.
42. ———. *Os gestos.* Rio de Janeiro, 1957.
43. ———. *Guerra sem testemunhas (o escritor, sua condiçao e realidade social).* São Paulo, 1969.
44. ———. *Nove, novena.* São Paulo, 1966.
45. ———. *O visitante.* Rio de Janeiro, 1955.
46. Lispector, Clarice. *Alguns contos.* Rio de Janeiro, 1952.
47. ———. *Uma aprendizagem ou o livro dos prazeres.* Rio de Janeiro, 1969.
48. ———. *A cidade sitiada.* Rio de Janeiro, 1949.
49. ———. *A legião estrangeira.* Rio de Janeiro, 1964.
50. ———. *O lustre.* Rio de Janeiro, 1946.
51. ———. *A maca no escuro.* Rio de Janeiro, 1961.
52. ———. *A paixão segundo G.H.* Rio de Janeiro, 1968.
53. ———. *Perto do coração selvagem.* Rio de Janeiro, 1944.
54. Lobato, Manoel. *Mentira dos limpos.* Belo Horizonte, Braz., 1967.
55. Lopes, Moacir C. *Cais, saudade em pedra.* Rio de Janeiro, 1963.
56. ———. *A ostra e o vento.* Rio de Janeiro, 1964.
57. Martins, Wilson. "Brazilian Literature: The Task of the Next Twenty Years." In *Portugal and Brazil in Transition,* ed. by Raymound S. Sayers, pp. 12–13. Minneapolis, Minn., 1968.
58. ———. *O Modernismo.* São Paulo, 1965.
59. Miranda, Macedo. *O rosto de papel.* Rio de Janeiro, 1969.
60. Mourão, Geraldo Mello. *Dossiê da destruição.* Rio de Janeiro, 1966.
61. ———. *O valete de espadas.* Rio de Janeiro, 1960.
62. Nabuco, Joachim. *Um estadista do império.* São Paulo, 1949.
63. Nascimento, Esdras do. *Engenharia do casamento.* Rio de Janeiro, 1968.
64. ———. *Solidão em família.* Rio de Janeiro, 1963.
65. Neme, Mario. *Donana Sofredora.* São Paulo, 1941.
66. ———. *Mulher que sabe Latim.* São Paulo, 1944.

67. Nemes, Cassiano. "Bimbo na Travessa do Elefante." *Correio Braziliense,* April 20, 1968.
68. Paiva, Mário Garcia de. *Luana.* São Paulo, 1962.
69. ———. *Ontem.* Belo Horizonte, Braz., 1966.
70. Palméiro, Mário de Ascenção. *Vila dos cofins.* Rio de Janeiro, 1956.
71. Penna, Cornélio. *Dois romances de Nico Horta.* Rio de Janeiro, 1939.
72. ———. *Fronteira.* Rio de Janeiro, 1935.
73. ———. *Repouso.* Rio de Janeiro, 1948.
74. Pereira, Antônio Olavo. *Contramão.* Rio de Janeiro, 1950.
75. ———. *Fio de prumo.* Rio de Janeiro, 1965.
76. ———. *Marcoré.* Rio de Janeiro, 1965.
77. Piñon, Nelida. *Guia-mapa de Gabriel Arcanjo.* Rio de Janeiro, 1961.
78. ———. *Madeira feita cruz.* Rio de  Janeiro, 1963.
79. Preminger, Alex. *Encyclopedia of Poetry and Poetics.* Princeton, N.J., 1965.
80. Proença, M. Cavalcânti. *Manuscrito holandês ou a pelaja do Caboclo Mitavai com o Monstro Macobeba.* Rio de Janeiro, 1959.
81. ———. *Roteiro de Macunaima.* São Paulo, 1955.
82. Ramos, Gracilano. *Angústia.* São Paulo, 1964.
83. ———. *Vidas sêcas.* São Paulo, 1966.
84. Ramos, Maria Luiza. *Fenomenologia la obra literaria.* São Paulo, 1969.
85. Ramos, Pericles Eugênio da Silva. *Poesia Moderna.* São Paulo, 1967.
86. Ramos, Ricardo. *Os caminhantes de Santa Luzia.* São Paulo, 1959.
87. ———. *Os desertos.* São Paulo, 1961.
88. ———. *Memoria de setembro.* Rio de Janeiro, 1968.
89. ———. *Rua deserta.* Rio de Janeiro, 1963.
90. ———. *Tempo de Espera.* Rio de Janeiro, 1954.
91. ———. *Terno de Reis.* Rio de Janeiro, 1957.
92. Rawet, Samuel. *Abama.* Rio de Janeiro, 1964.
93. ———. *Contos do imigrante.* Rio de Janeiro, 1956.
94. ———. *Diálogo.* Rio de Janeiro, 1963.
95. ———. *Os sete sonhos.* Rio de Janeiro, 1967.
96. Reipert, Hermann José. *Travessa do elefante sem número.* São Paulo, 1962.
97. Resende, Otto Lara. *Bôca do Inferno.* Rio de Janeiro, 1957.
98. ———. *O braço direito.* Rio de Janeiro, 1962.
99. ———. *O lado humano.* Rio de Janeiro, 1952.
100. ———. *O retrato na gaveta.* Rio de Janeiro, 1962.

101. Rosa, Guimarães. *Corpo de Bailo*. Rio de Janeiro, 1956.
102. ———. *Grande Sertão: Veredas*. Rio de Janeiro, 1956.
103. ———. *Primeiras Estórias*. Rio de Janeiro, 1962.
104. ———. *Sagarana*. Rio de Janeiro, 1946.
105. ———. *Tutaméia*. Rio de Janeiro, 1967.
106. Rubião, Murilo. *O ex-mágico*. Rio de Janeiro, 1946.
107. Sabino, Fernando. *O encontro marcado*. Rio de Janeiro, 1963.
108. Sales, Heberto. *Cascalho*. Rio de Janeiro, 1967.
109. Solt, Mary Ellen. *Concrete Poetry: A World View*. Bloomington, Ind., 1968.
110. Teixeira, Maria de Lourdes. *O pátio dãs donzelas*. São Paulo, 1969.
111. ———. *Rua Augusta*. São Paulo, 1962.
112. Teles, Lygia Fagundes. *Praia Viva*. São Paulo, 1943.
113. Trevisan, Dalton. *Cemitério dos Elefantes*. Rio de Janeiro, 1964.
114. ———. *Desastre lo amor*. Rio de Janeiro, 1968.
115. ———. *Morte na praça*. Rio de Janeiro, 1964.
116. ———. *Novelas nada exemplares*. Rio de Janeiro, 1959.
117. ———. *Sonata ao luar*. Rio de Janeiro, 1951.
118. ———. *O Vampiro de Curitiba*. Rio de Janeiro, 1965.
119. Veiga, José J. *Os cavalinhos de Platiplanto*. Rio de Janeiro, 1959.
120. ———. *A hora dos ruminantes*. Rio de Janeiro, 1966.
121. ———. *A maquina extraviada*. Rio de Janeiro, 1968.
122. Vianna, Francisco José de Oliveira. *Populações meridionais do Brasil*. Rio de Janeiro, 1952.
123. Vieria, José Geraldo. *A quadragésima porta*. Pôrta Alegre, Braz., 1943.
124. Vilela, Luiz. *No bar*. Rio de Janeiro, 1969.
125. ———. *Tremor de terra*. Belo Horizonte, Braz., 1967.
126. Williams, Emmete. *An Anthology of Concrete Poetry*. New York, 1967.

# BRAZILIAN POETRY

*Wilson Martins*

The generations of Brazilian poets that have emerged since 1945 have been confronted, above all else, by the awesome task of eliminating that gigantic corpse of modernism.[1] In terms of literary history and of poetic schools, two different techniques were employed successively in trying to get rid of it. First, between 1945 and 1955, without ever formulating any expressed credo, the new poets attempted to prolong the exclusively aesthetic tendencies of modernism but rejected its sociological and nationalistic aspects. They sought to recapture the formal regularity that free verse and the even freer poem had discredited since 1922. It was not unreasonable that these writers, at first for lack of anything better, should accept the name of neomodernists, an epithet suggested for the whole school by Alceu Amoroso Lima (b. 1893). Perhaps sensing, however, that there was something anachronistic in these efforts to resurrect the modernist aesthetic (efforts which were characterized by an intransigent rejection of the more characteristic half of modernism), and failing to discover in their own art some sufficiently remarkable and distinctive trait, these poets resolved to pass into history with the name of the Generation of '45. The idea is credited to Domingos Carvalho da Silva (b. 1915), one of the representative poets of that group, who in the First Paulista Congress of Poetry in 1948 specified that the new poetry was pristine, exact, constant, clearly distinct from what the masters of 1922 had practiced. Actually, expecting the technical rigor, or rather, the "technical-mindedness," which distinguished it from the poetry of '22, where rather a "subject-mindedness" was predominant, the poetry of '45, to judge by a few poems of Carvalho da Silva, was not as far removed as one would think from some of the modernist trends presaged in the *Paulicéia desvairada* (1) of Mário de Andrade.

Still, the ideal of the Generation of '45 was to create a poetry stripped of all rhetoric and of all sociological and historical connotations; even a certain hermeticism was not altogether displeasing to them, although allied, paradoxically, to what Péricles Eugênio da Silva Ramos (b. 1919) calls a "clarity of expression" (15). The truth is

---

1. On the nature and chronology of Brazilian modernism, see the study by Wilson Martins (7.)

287

that the poets of '45 were seen and read as universalistic aesthetes, as ascetics in the particular intransigency with which they sought to overcome any rhetorical impulses. At the same time they could not resist experimenting once again with abandoned forms of traditional poetry.

At his literary debut in 1944, Lêdo Ivo (b. 1924) was hailed as the first great poet of the new generation, not only because he announced a return to rhyme and the sonnet, but also, unexpectedly, because he reintroduced to Brazilian poetry that romantic passion which the modernists had scorned and which other poets of '45 sought to contain within the bounds of classical expression. Lêdo Ivo rejected neither sentiment nor even sentimentality itself, and his images are closer to traditional Brazilian sensibilities than to the intellectualized "translations" which in general distinguish the poetry of '45. In his subsequent poetic evolution, on the one hand he separates himself more and more from modernism, which he has begun to criticize severely, and on the other hand he welcomes without restraint the romantic tendencies of his own temperament. He becomes the Childe Harold of the new Brazilian romanticism, and so it is not odd that in 1962, for the new edition of his first four books, he chose to use the famous title of Alvares de Azevedo (1831–52), *Uma lira dos vinte anos* (5).

After ten years of activity, the poets of '45, having triumphed without conquest, were reduced to a small group of aesthetes who tended to dwell on the style of the poem rather than on the message of poetry. The most representative authors have been gathered by Péricles Eugênio da Silva Ramos into his excellent anthology *Poesia moderna* (15) and include, in addition to those already mentioned, Mauro Mota (b. 1912), Bueno de Rivera (b. 1914), José Paulo Moreira da Fonseca (b. 1922), Geir Campos (b. 1924), and Thiago de Melo (b. 1926). João Cabral de Melo Neto, who in one sense is the most important poet of that generation, will be treated below, because in another sense he extends beyond the chronological and aesthetic limits of the Generation of '45. Notwithstanding the personal success of one or more of its members, the Generation of '45 did not offer a satisfactory response to the problems it raised by contributing to the demise of modernism; something new had to be tried.

The new movement—concrete poetry—was formed by the *Noigandres* group in São Paulo in 1952. Its most eminent theoreticians and its best-known poets have been two brothers, Haroldo (b. 1929)

and Augusto (b. 1931) de Campos, and Décio Pignatari (b. 1927); they
are the triumvirate of concrete poetry, which they affirm and reaffirm
as a Brazilian invention and an "export poetry," since it might have
inspired the appearance of similar movements in Switzerland and
Sweden in 1953, in Austria in 1955, in Germany and Japan in 1957,
in France in 1962, and in other countries. In the United States, e. e.
cummings and Ezra Pound are the two sources of that trend, although,
in Mary Ellen Solt's words, "it would be an exaggeration to speak of
a concrete poetry movement in the United States" (16). Solt's study
and Alex Preminger's *Encyclopedia of Poetry and Poetics* (14) seem to
attribute priority to the Swiss poets and, more precisely, to Eugen
Gomringer; yet Solt concedes that the 1955 meeting of Décio Pignatari
with Max Bill in Ulm "can be taken as the beginning of the international movement of concrete poetry." These questions of individual
precedence do not have much importance, as either Filippo Tommaso
Marinetti's *Parole in libertà* (1912) or Guillaume Apollinaire's *Calli-
grammes* (1918), can be pointed to as the original precursor of the
idea of concretism. Let us remember, for example, that Carlo Bellolí,
avowedly affiliated with Italian futurism, was even writing and publishing concrete poems in 1943.

It is equally certain that the Brazilian concrete poets were, from
the start, outstanding in their efforts to create, before the actual composition of the poems, a complete credo, which for some time determined their basic theoretical principles.[2] Ultra-aestheticism was
destined to replace the rather moderate aestheticizing tendencies of
the Generation of '45. However, once the first moments of surprise
and curiosity had passed, these exclusively formal poems, conceived
expressly for the purpose of encapsuling rather indirect messages, and
in the majority of cases containing no message at all, soon revealed
themselves to be as uninteresting to their poets as they were to the
readers. Thus, as I have had the opportunity to mention elsewhere:

> The same Concretists decided to outdo themselves: they proposed
> in 1961 a return to "content-ism" *(conteudismo)* in the Congress on
> Literary Criticism and History held in Assis, Brazil. Incidentally, the
> return was never realized, and later on, they proposed a return to a
> poetry founded on the theory of communication or "semiotics," with
> the aim of developing printing and industrial design as a form of

---

2. See the famous 1957 manifesto in Wilson Martins, "Brazilian Literature:
The Task of the Next Twenty Years" (6).

language, according to Décio Pignatari. From 1961 on, concrete poets face definitely the "engagement" question. What issued—social and political concrete poetry—was chiefly based on Mayakovsky: "There is no revolutionary art without revolutionary form." Today there are diversified trends and tendencies within the group, some worrying more about semantics and permutational features of the language (Augusto and Haroldo de Campos, the latter also interested in prose problems), some turned to the creation of new languages— even before and/or beyond the word—in poetry as well as in prose, as far as a text can be so divided. [6]

Actually, there has been, since the beginnings of concrete poetry, a latent tendency toward "engagement" and political debate; concrete poetry itself being in other countries an exclusively aestheticizing movement, it was, from the outset of the very idea of its creation in Brazil, an instrument for the rejection of bourgeois society and its values. However, the "participatory phase" of Brazilian concrete poetry ended up being even more disenchanting and frustrated than its purely aesthetic phase had been. The final image of the whole movement is that of the "verbi-voco-visual" poems, invented as typographical objects.

Like a true *Chapelle litteraire,* the concrete group soon transformed itself into a religion and even had its own heretics (the first auto-da-fé occurred in 1962 with the exclusion of Mário Chamie) in the same way as concrete poetry itself had been, to a certain extent, a heretical deviation from tendencies first made manifest in the work of Ferreira Gullar (b. 1930), whose volume of poetry *A luta corporal* (4) might justly mark the point of transition between the Generation of '45 and the concrete movement. Mário Chamie (b. 1933), with the publication of his *Lavra lavra* (3), launched praxis poetry, a movement which has been characterized, as much as concrete poetry, by successive and repetitious publication of literary manifestos. Its credo continues to be expressed in the review called *Praxis,* begun in 1962, the same year in which the anthologies of the concrete poets, called *Noigandres,* were supplanted by the review called *Invençao.* What is the praxis poem? According to Mário Chamie's "didactic manifesto," it is one that aesthetically organizes and sets up a situated reality, following the conditions of action: the act of composing, the area surveyed in the composition, and the act of consuming.

It is perhaps interesting to cite Péricles Eugênio da Silva Ramos's comments on one such work:

This Praxis poem is, in traditional terminology, a *labyrinth* in terms of its verses, which can be read in the first strophe from left to right, from right to left, from top to bottom or from bottom to top; each segment can be read together with what follows it in the line, or with what comes below it and so on. The last strophe is also labyrinthian, just as the first, in terms of the blocks of words but not in terms of the isolated words. The quatrain and the two distichs in the middle are also readable from top to bottom or from bottom to top. Use is made of rhymes, assonance, paronomasia, and of anti-meres . . . . The stylistic resources are therefore traditional; the innovation lies in the systematic rigidity with which the words are combined, the poem producing itself as an artifact. [15]

In the midst of the furor of opposing schools, one poet went on patiently constructing his compositions without affiliating himself with any movement. He thus assured the continuity of literary tradi-tions and poetic forms which renew themselves. That poet, João Cabral de Melo Neto (b. 1920), was considered the poet of the Gen-eration of '45 who most closely approximated the masters of 1922 and who exerted the most appreciable influence upon the very young. He is accepted simultaneously by the concrete and the praxis poets, while becoming the true successor to Carlos Drummond de Andrade and Manuel Bandeira, that is to say, the creator of a poetry which is modern without being modernist, concrete, or praxist. The poetry from *O Engenheiro* was received, in 1945, as the emblematical work of the Generation of '45; it is an abstract and cerebral kind of poetry, divested of all suspect charm, hostile to the adjective and to the orna-mental.

However, Cabral de Melo Neto's evolution through the years surprised his first admirers; although he continued to practice a poetry that was laconic and austere, he quickly passed from hermeticism to communication, from aestheticism to participation, from the abstract to the concrete, and from the universal to the regional. *O cão sem plumas* (8), *O rio ou Relação da viagem que faz o Capibaribe de sua nascente à cidade do Recife* (12), *Quaderna* (11), *Terceira feira* (13) and *A educação pela pedra* (9) mark the stages of these transforma-tions. João Cabral de Melo Neto seemingly seeks to maintain the equilibrium between what can be viewed as his "social thinking," such as appears in *O rio* and *Morte e vida severina* (10) and the inven-tion of a pure poetry, often expressed in the form of a "poetry of things," as in the work of Francis Ponge.

Of all the poets discussed, Cabral de Melo Neto is the only one who gives the impression of going forward: the successive theoretical metamorphoses of the concrete poets have been just so many confessions of frustration; the Generation of '45 is already considered a fad of the past, a historical phenomenon; the praxis movement has not opened the way to the promised transformation; Mário Chamie has in fact abandoned praxis for the more recent developments in *Indústria*. With the passing of Manuel Bandeira in 1968 the last patriarch of the heroic times of modernism is gone; Carlos Drummond de Andrade, who has been the great poet of the second generation, is now at the memoirs age and stage; Jorge de Lima (1893–1953) and Augusto Frederico Schmidt (1906–65) are, for the while, in limbo and have ceased to be the subjects of criticism; yet they are still not seen clearly as subjects of literary history. Still, the influence of Cabral de Melo Neto has not turned into Cabralism and, as I see it, the youngest poets look upon him as a great poet with modern sensibilities and extraordinary qualities of craftsmanship rather than as a model to imitate or an influence to adhere to, in the appropriate sense of the word. He is the great solitary figure of modern Brazilian poetry, which has, moreover, completely lost the gregarious and fraternizing instinct that characterized the literary generations from 1916 to 1945.

Truthfully, the most common sentiment, although it is rarely expressed by the critics of contemporary Brazilian poetry, is of its temporary passing through a period of depression and emptiness: the most active wander in search of new and surprising formulas; the most conservative repeat the formulas which have been handed down by their predecessors. It is perhaps the very concept of what poetry is that has no clarity in their minds; to a people who tend to be lyric and passionate, the poem that is excessively "literary" has the effect of a cold and brittle object in the household, ornamental but void of affection, and lacking any significance whatsoever in the history of the family.

(Translated by Thomas Colchie)

# BIBLIOGRAPHY

1. Andrade, Mário de. *Pauacéia desvairada*. São Paulo, 1922.
2. Azevedo, Manuel Antonio Alvares de. *Obras*. 8th ed. 2 vols. Rio de Janeiro, 1942.
3. Chamie, Mário. *Lavra lavra*. São Paulo, 1962.
4. Ferreira, Gullar [pseud. for José Ribamar Ferreira]. *A luta corporal*. Rio de Janeiro, 1954.
5. Ivo, Lêdo. *Uma lira dos vinte anos*. Rio de Janeiro, 1962.
6. Martins, Wilson. "Brazilian Literature: The Task for the Next Twenty Years." In *Portugal and Brazil in Transition*, ed. by Raymond Sayers. Minneapolis, Minn., 1968.
7. ———. *O modernismo*. São Paulo, 1965.
8. Melo Neto, João Cabral de. *O cão sem plumas*. Rio de Janeiro, 1950.
9. ———. *A educação pela pedra*. Rio de Janeiro, 1966.
10. ———. *Morte e vida severina*. Rio de Janeiro, 1955.
11. ———. *Quaderna*. Rio de Janeiro, 1960.
12. ———. *O rio ou Relação da viagem que faz o Capibaribe de sua nascente à cidade do Recife*. Rio de Janeiro, 1954.
13. ———. *Terceira feira*. Rio de Janeiro, 1961.
14. Preminger, Alex. *Encyclopedia of Poetry and Poetics*. Princeton, N.J., 1967.
15. Ramos, Péricles Eugênio da Silva. *Poesia moderna*. São Paulo, 1967.
16. Solt, Ellen. *Concrete Poetry: A World View*. Bloomington, Ind., 1967.
17. Williams, Emmete. *An Anthology of Concrete Poetry*. New York, 1967.

*Part Four*

# GEOGRAPHIC AND ECONOMIC SCHOLARSHIP

# 4. GEOGRAPHIC AND ECONOMIC SCHOLARSHIP

Geography, as a profession, has not participated fully in the development process of Latin America, according to Professors Dickinson and Crist. They indicate that in spite of the fact that there has been a growing concern for the participation of geographers in policy planning and in various aspects of social and economic developmental projects in the last twenty-five years, they have not yet shared the major responsibility of implementing the plans. However, worthy efforts have been made, both at the academic level and in field work. Geographers, according to the authors, benefited from the sudden official concern in Latin America after Castro's victory in Cuba. Institutional and individual grants for research have been important incentives to young scholars in geography. For example, in 1967 the Organization for Tropical Studies created a special field course in Latin America that affords graduate students the opportunity to become familiar with the American tropics. Nevertheless, many professional schools do not have the "international dimension" necessary for the optimum use of scientific knowledge.

In the field of economic integration, the scholarship has been mainly normative and has encouraged the development of economic integration. Professor Carnoy surveys thoroughly the scholarly contributors that support and question the concept of customs union. He also evaluates both attitudes and the interaction between the United States and the integrationists in Latin America. One point that seems to be of paramount importance, especially in the writings published by the Economic Commission for Latin America (ECLA), is the need for "equitable distribution of industrialization and growth," in order to assure the maximum benefits to all the participating countries. The author underlines the works of Sidney Dell, Victor Urquidi, and Raymond F. Mikesell as most outstanding in analyzing the various arguments for specific measures leading to the common market in Latin America. The book *Latin American Integration,* edited by Miguel Wionczek, is an important collection of essays addressed to pursue this study to its ultimate possibilities. Professor Carnoy's article demonstrates the variety of opinions, often passionate, concerning a complex idea which has political as well as economic overtones.

297

# GEOGRAPHERS IN THE DEVELOPMENT PROCESS

*Joshua C. Dickinson III and Raymond E. Crist*

## I

A growing interest in the American tropics is found among the biological, agricultural, and social sciences. The great complexity of the tropical ecosystem, its productivity and diverse flora and fauna, is only now attracting biologists. The midlatitude agriculturist has suddenly been called upon to help tropical nations produce badly needed basic foods. With the exception of intensive production of export crops such as sugar cane, coffee, and bananas, the modern agriculturist has heretofore played a minor role in the tropics.

The economist is looking more closely at the tropical countries to determine where his macroeconomic theories ran afoul of non-Western value systems. Geographers, anthropologists, sociologists, and political scientists are examining the intricately related cultural processes that influence man's receptivity to new ideas, his economic motivations, and his relationship to the land. The tropical disease specialist, the general practitioner, and the nutritionist find challenges which no longer exist in most developed countries.

Hunger is not only a problem localized among a mass of isolated peasants or in a ghetto. Where there is hunger, its causes and effects can be found everywhere in the land and throughout the fabric of society. The effects are physically and, most tragically, mentally debilitating. The political implications are global in scale. At present, lack of economic development and hunger are more common among nations in the tropics than among those in higher latitudes.

This dichotomy in development rates has occurred mainly since the Industrial Revolution. The food crisis is largely a result of population growth caused by disease control during this century. The cultural, economic, locational, and environmental factors which limit development and food production are interrelated and must be so treated if balanced development is to take place.

The proximity and seriousness of the crisis are subject to considerable controversy. The results achieved with new rice and wheat varieties in Asia have been outstanding, but the optimism voiced by

299

the Agency for International Development (AID) in late 1968 concerning self-sufficiency in food in the immediate future is not justified from the perspective of the yet unsolved problems of potential plant disease, transport, storage and marketing, protein deficiency, lack of purchasing power, and unchecked population growth.

A markedly different viewpoint is voiced by the Paddocks in their book, Famine 1975 (24). They claim that the crisis is here and mass starvation is inevitable. The President's Science Advisory Committee takes a cautiously optimistic position based on the condition that all developed nations embark now on a massive research and development program in the food-deficient countries (35).

Efforts to avert a world food crisis by AID, international organizations, foundations, philanthropies such as CARE, private enterprise, and the countries themselves, have not averted the world food crisis, but only cushioned and delayed its impact. Among the reasons for limited success to date are that

1. The total effort by the developed countries has been inadequate, both in relation to the magnitude of the problem and to the financial and technological resources at their disposal
2. The agribusiness community—the manufacturers and sellers of fertilizers, chemicals, machinery, feed, and seed—has not been aggressive in seeking or creating markets in the tropics
3. Basic knowledge concerning the soil, climate, plants and management systems required for the tropics is inadequate
4. Existing knowledge developed by social science research has not been applied in agricultural development because there is little communication between the agricultural and social scientists either within institutions or in the field
5. U.S. domestic problems, concern about Vietnam, residual isolationism, and general ignorance about the rest of the world has led to ambivalent grass-roots support of development agencies
6. The recipient countries generally lack effective research, educational, and development institutions, particularly in agriculture, limiting their capacity to make use of new technology (20)
7. The socially and politically dominant elements in many countries prefer the status quo to development, or, where control of government is in a state of violent flux, the necessary stable infrastructure cannot be maintained
8. Efforts to control human fertility have been effective with relatively few people.

The future of Latin American studies and indeed the entire United States commitment to development abroad is being questioned and attacked. Geography was among the disciplines to benefit from the burst of official concern for Latin America that followed Castro's takeover in Cuba. This concern also set the stage for the Alliance for Progress, the Peace Corps, and the funding of internationally oriented research and teaching. For the Latin Americanist, the post-Castro surfeit of broad-spectrum research support has largely passed. Congress is looking critically at the budgets of such traditional sources of fellowships as the Department of Health, Education, and Welfare. The Fulbright program has been drastically cut back. The International Education Act remains little more than a vague hope in the near future. The foundations have cut back their level of support to the area study programs in universities and are funding only institutional projects that have mission-oriented goals. Much support in the social sciences is going to domestic urban programs.

Foreign aid appropriations were cut back drastically in 1968. The State Department's Agency for International Development is under fire from both the traditional conservative and the liberal concerned about domestic problems. Even the universities most strongly committed to development are critical of AID's methods, though not its purpose. AID has contracted the service of professional school faculty without the institution itself becoming involved. Hence, feedback into the school's curriculum and basic research program has been disappointingly small. Because of poor intra-institutional communications with professional school colleagues, geographers and other social scientists have been twice removed from the overseas effort in Latin America.

A blue ribbon task force of the Association of State Universities and Land Grant Colleges made several recommendations that would augment and enrich the total university's involvement in development assistance. Among these are, first, provision for exploration in depth by teams of university personnel and the development of appropriate long-range strategy (acceptable to the host country, relevant to the U.S. university's academic program, and consistent with the funding agency) prior to university commitment to participate; and second, replacement of the present "buyer-seller" type of contract used by AID in its relationships with universities, which has demonstrated itself to be seriously less than adequate as an instrument to further this partnership, by a variety of longer term grants and project agreements (17).

The philosophy espoused in the report is particularly relevant because of the subsequent appointment of two of the committee members to high policy-making positions, one as secretary of agriculture and the other as administrator of AID.

The food problem, with its complex interrelationships of environmental, social, historical, and political facets, requires a multidisciplinary solution. To date, the brunt of the effort to produce more food has been borne by the midlatitude agriculturist. The productivity of American agriculture is a tribute to the know-how generated by the land grant college and disseminated by the extension agent among his *own* people. With this magnificent example at hand, it was thought that a simple transfer of technology could be effected. However, the "know-how show-how" concept has not worked well. Often the technology has proved to be inappropriate in the alien cultural setting and inapplicable in the tropical environment. Incipient recognition has taken place of the need for special training of overseas workers and close cooperation of the social scientist if assistance is to be effective.

George M. Foster has been one of the most outspoken champions of social science involvement in the development process. In his *Traditional Cultures and the Impact of Technological Change,* he indicates how anthropologists, geographers, and other social scientists could make valuable contributions to rational development (13). He describes the role of the social scientist working not only in an alien cultural setting but also in an equally alien team framework with its complement of administrators, technicians, and scientists of different persuasions and professional values.

Human resources for development work in the social sciences are both more abundant and better trained than ever in the past. Many graduate students in the social sciences and humanities were drawn into Latin American language and area studies by the National Defense Education Act fellowships and related programs since 1960. While financial considerations may have been an initial attraction for many students, the vast majority have become dedicated Latin American scholars. The NDEA fellowships in Portuguese have led to a particularly marked increase in Brazilian studies.

Returning Peace Corps volunteers are both a numerically significant and a particularly valuable element in Latin American studies programs. By virtue of their experience they help create and demand a more dynamic and realistic atmosphere in the classroom. Some, without previous academic background, enter graduate programs in development-oriented studies such as agricultural economics. These fields are frequently chosen because of the volunteer's continuing interest in serving abroad and his desire for applicable training.

Institutional and individual grants for research have reinforced the fellowship program by the strengthening of faculty competence in the Latin American area. The total result has been the creation of a large cadre of young scholars in geography and in other disciplines who could man effective interdisciplinary research and development efforts.

Interdisciplinary, or more recently, multidisciplinary research has become an extremely popular, though ambiguous, term in academic and governmental parlance. In practice, the term encompasses two types of research. The type usually envisioned by planners and administrators involves a concentrated effort by several scientists, each working on an aspect of a well-defined problem. More common, either by design or through the degeneration of the first type is, independent research by several scientists loosely linked in time and place. Facilities such as a ship or a field laboratory, a computer or data bank, or field transportation combined with research funds bring together representatives of various disciplines. Achievement of individual goals is of primary importance, with the seeking of correlations and achievement of overall project goals decidedly secondary. While a project fielding a loose confederation of scientists is not conducive to production of a crisp, complete report, a bomb, or a new rice variety, it does have some advantages. Frequently the only way to assemble first-class scientists of unlike temperament and interests in a regional study is to minimize the imposition of predetermined goals. The unexpected results of independent inquiry into a topic or region may be of considerable value, particularly when the results are later correlated.

This latter type of research will probably continue to be called "interdisciplinary" for lack of a more appropriate term. To achieve a coherent approximation of the original aim of the project is a difficult, often thankless, and sometimes impossible job. Some geographers are best suited by training to the role of integrating the results of diverse research efforts. Intellectual satisfaction derives from discovering relationships which yield a holistic result of value as a contribution to knowledge or to more rational development recommendations.

In addition to the role as an academic catalyst, the geographer may also serve as contributing specialist or as an overall coordinator and administrator. The specialist role is probably the more coveted, but not necessarily the role in which the most valuable contributions can be made. The coordinator role is one assumed by scientists of undifferentiated callings. Personal leadership ability, recognized genius for integration, success in unrelated endeavors, and seniority are factors which may be considered in selection of a project leader. The above attributes are equally influential if a geographer should be selected. Many geographers, by virtue of their academic preparation, are trained in the integration of the findings of other disciplines.

In contrast, those in highly technical disciplines have sharply focused professional interests and tend to view the broad problems of development within the narrow context of their specialty. However, geographers have not sought, nor have they been selectively courted, to assume leadership roles in interdisciplinary research or development projects. They have worked alone, usually in advance of, peripheral to, independent of, or following major developmental activities.

The academic geographer has before him the opportunity and challenge to make a significant professional contribution to the development process in Latin America. A strong regional interest in this hemisphere marked by a fine sense of history and an ecological perspective based on field observation has afforded geography a firm benchmark for predictive and applied work. The coming generation of research geographers can be particularly effective if they adapt the expertise and techniques of modern urban and economic geography in North America to the cultural setting and data framework of Latin America.

## II

James Parsons has provided an excellent summary of published research in geography dealing with Latin America before 1963 (30). The accompanying selected bibliography is particularly useful both as a topical reference and as a means of gauging the scope and evolution of research in that area of the world since Humboldt.

In research on development there has been a rich variety of scholarly contributions. Thorough and incisive studies have been made of government projects and colonization by cohesive ethnic minorities (2, 12, 18, 33, 34).

Studies of human migration and settlement have been vigorously pursued by Raymond Crist, especially during the past two decades. In order to understand motivations, basic investigation of man's incumbency in his present habitat have been made, and the factors that operate to push him from it, as well as the factors that pull him to his new home, have been carefully noted. Crist, as well as a number of his students, has carried out studies in the proper weighting of the roles of cultural and physical factors in the penetration of the hot, humid sectors of the Americas, from Mexico to Paraguay (3, 4, 5, 8, 9, 15, 31).

Changes in the landscape due to human presence through time and the accelerating environmental modification associated with modern development are discussed in *Man's Role in Changing the Face of the Earth* (28). Geographers were major contributors to this symposium and point out the pressing need for study of side effects as an essential adjunct to development planning in Latin America and elsewhere. Early efforts to predict the development potential of the tropics, notably by Huntington and by Gourou in the earlier editions of his *The Tropical World* (14) had a strong negative and deterministic influence on both public and scientific attitudes toward the tropics.

Needed now are predictive development studies to complement analyses of completed projects, and critiques of schemes in which the course of action is irrevocably determined. Few geographers have been actually engaged in direct policy planning, or in interdisciplinary and mission-oriented research, training, or project execution. The geographer has exhibited a predilection for projects that are academically intriguing, but often not developmentally or socially relevant. Research related to dynamically evolving situations is not timely. Social science journal articles often appear two years after the actual research, and monographs of books often far later (13). This is not overly disturbing to the writer or his scholarly peers, but results in the findings being dated, from a potentially interested project director's point of view.

Several geographers have participated actively in development or related studies. Possibly the most intimately involved has been Dr. Rafael Pico, who was president of the Puerto Rican Planning Commission from 1942 to 1955. Under his guidance, planning techniques which had evolved on the mainland were adapted to the island and its capital, San Juan (26). Dr. Pico's geographical background, coupled with political acumen, provided an opportunity to implement ideas which is generally not open to the alien academic geographer in Latin America.

Raymond Crist's monograph on the Cauca Valley of Colombia was based on research supported in part by the Institute of Tropical Agriculture in Puerto Rico and sponsored by the Ministry of Agriculture of the Cauca Valley (7). This work was subsequently drawn upon heavily by those organizing the Corporación Valle Caucana (Cauca Valley Corporation.)

Richard P. Momsen, Jr., has participated in two international and interdisciplinary research and planning projects in the capacity of a geographer and administrative coordinator (22). One project was the location and evaluation of potential sites for Brazil's inland capital, Brasilia. The other was a comprehensive survey of the Guayas Basin in Ecuador to determine areas for potential settlement and development.

In Guatemala, Dr. Arthur Burt developed a project in which geographers and their students worked with the General Directorate of Public Works and other agencies in joint research, inventory, and planning projects throughout the country (16, 21). The experience gained in such a binational project is invaluable whether concrete results are immediately apparent or not.

The Center for Tropical Agriculture of the University of Florida has partially bridged the on-campus gap by sponsoring geographic research on topics related to agricultural systems in Latin America. The center was responsible for conducting the agricultural ecology phase of a major bioenvironmental feasibility study of proposed sea-level canal routes in the Darien of Panama and the Rio Atrato region in Colombia. Two M.A. theses, a dissertation, and a reconnaissance report resulted which described the agricultural systems employed by the four major cultural groups on the two proposed routes (11, 25, 27, 32). Field research by two doctoral candidates was completed during 1969 on cattle production and marketing as part of a research project on livestock production in the wet/dry tropics. While the social scientist has not worked side by side with the agricultural scientist to form a truly interdisciplinary team in the aforementioned projects, nevertheless efforts overlapped time and place sufficiently to yield complementary results.

The Center for Tropical Agriculture is sponsoring a research project in the humid Caribbean lowlands of Guatemala. The purpose of the project has been to learn more of the environment and man in order to utilize more effectively the high biological productivity of the humid tropics. Headquarters have been located at Murcielago on Lake Izabal on a five-thousand-acre site served by an airstrip. The lake is thirty miles long and fifteen miles wide and is connected to the Caribbean by a navigable river which gives those working at the research site access to a large area for investigations of the humid tropical environment. Funding and facilities have provided a flexible framework for individual research with a sharp regional focus. A concept of man's occupance of the region over time has been gained by pollen analysis of sediment cores reaching back more than three thousand years, archeological excavation of preconquest and early Spanish sites, study of historic accounts and documents dealing with the area, and investigation of the current population by a cultural anthropologist and geographer with a background in nutrition.

Detailed studies of the environment have been made by the climatologists, soil scientists, botanists, and zoologists. Microclimatic data was gathered in different types of vegetation and at various levels above the ground. These data are being combined with soil analyses in the study of productivity, nutrient uptake, and species composition of various vegetation types and successions (10).

Theo Hill's tropical grassland study is another example of an interdisciplinary and interinstitutional project in which a specific environmental type in the tropics was studied from many points of view, both cultural and physical (19).

Training in geography related to Latin America has three basic functions: first, to prepare geographers competent to carry out original research and to participate as full-fledged professionals in development work; second, to join with other disciplines in the social sciences and the professional schools in providing methodological and area training for students preparing for careers in international work; third, but no less important, to develop, in concert with the other social sciences, undergraduate curricula designed to create an awareness and understanding of other cultures and places.

The primary concern of the profession is to train students for teaching, research, and service in geography. To be effective in the tropics, both in the academic sphere and in planning and guiding the change of man-land relations, requires specialized, intensive preparation. The student must be well versed in the philosophic concepts of geography, in knowledge of the processes governing the spatial distribution of physical and cultural phenomena. It is from the ability to integrate and synthesize data from diverse sources that geography draws its strength as a discipline. Knowledge of the most sophisticated methodology is needed for geographic research and for communication with workers in other fields. A strong systematic speciality in areas such as tropical agriculture, ecology, economics, or climatology would give the geographer the tools needed to conduct valuable, timely research while gaining traditional competency through field experience. Training in botany and forestry in addition to geography afforded Joseph Tosi a unique background for his very useful ecological study of Peru (29).

One of the most significant developments in the training of geographers for Latin American work has been the incorporation in 1967 of a geography field course in the curriculum offered by the Organization for Tropical Studies. Through this medium, graduate students receive a brief, but thorough, initial exposure to the cultural landscape of the American tropics. An inescapable appreciation of the problems and delights of field work is gained which is impossible to convey in the classroom. In addition to faculty-guided field work and seminars, the student is able to test his training on a short research project of his own choosing. The opportunity to exchange ideas with students from a diverse cross section of American geography is particularly valuable.

OTS is a consortium currently numbering some twenty-five institutions, engaged in graduate training and research in the tropics. The primary focus of the program has been to foster and support study of the tropical environment. The basic course has been "Tropical Biology: An Ecological Approach." In addition, other specialized courses have been added in botany, entomology, geography, forestry, agriculture, and marine biology (23).

The professional schools, such as agriculture, engineering, and medicine, generally lack an international dimension in their curricula although they are the most heavily involved in technical assistance within the academic community. Most scientists leave the campus with little or no knowledge of the language, culture, or physical environment in which they may spend several years and many thousands of dollars. Because of their strong technical orientation, the professional schools have not sought help from the social sciences in briefing faculty and training students so that they might be more effective abroad (1). On the other hand, the social sciences have not been quick to design up-to-date courses that would be useful to the agronomist or engineer. As universities develop long-term commitments to assist on particular classes of problems over a wide area, it will be possible to design supporting social science curricula based on related research.

A major problem facing AID in gaining legislative support for its programs has been the lack of constituency. Neither the voters nor their elected representatives are fully aware of the grave problems in developing countries and their implications for the security, economic well-being, and reputation of the United States. The International Education Act, for which funds were never appropriated, was to have been a major vehicle for broad area-studies programs at the undergraduate level. Current cultural and regional courses in geography could fit into the area-studies framework. Modifications would be needed to focus on relevant aspects of other cultural environments.

The effort devoted by geographers to Latin America over the last two and a half decades has not been wasted. They have contributed substantially to the breadth and depth of our store of knowledge about the total environmental and cultural ecology of the Americas. The veteran geographers bring the invaluable yardstick of long experience, and their younger colleagues offer new tools and techniques, which together can assure the profession a vital role in the massive development effort which must come in the decade of the seventies.

Application of geography in Latin American development should concern us all. Geographers need to achieve a balance between academic enquiry and professional application. Satisfactions are inherent in guiding as well as analyzing change in Latin America.

As a profession, geography has remained peripheral to the development process. The assumption of a more activist role in reconnaissance, data integration, projection, planning, and program execution will not be easy. Some of the luxuries of unfettered individual research will have to be forgone at times. It may be salutary to his profession if the geographer has to prove the efficacy of his unique approach to problems, indeed his very raison d'être, both to the entrenched elements of other social science disciplines and to the skeptical technician and administrator.

# BIBLIOGRAPHY

1. *Agricultural Development Council Newsletter* 20 (May 1968).

2. Augelli, John P. "Cultural and Economic Changes of Bastos, a Japanese Colony on Brazil's Paulista Frontier." *Annals, Association of American Geographers* 48, no. 1 (March 1958).

3. Crist, Raymond. "Along the Llanos-Andes Border in Venezuela—Then and Now." *Geographical Review* 46, no. 1 (January 1956): 187–208.

4. ———. "Along the Llanos-Andes Border in Zamora, Venezuela." *Geographical Review* 22, no. 3 (July 1932): 411–22.

5. ———. "Bolivia, Land of Contrasts." *American Journal of Economy and Sociology* 5 (1945): 297–325.

6. ———. "Bolivians Trek Eastward." *Americas* 15, no. 4 (1963): 33–38.

7. ———. *The Cauca Valley, Colombia: Land Tenure and Land Use.* Baltimore, 1952.

8. ———. "A Cultural Traverse across the Eastern and Central Cordilleras of Colombia." *Bulletin of Pan American Union* 76 (1942): 132–44.

9. ———. "Go East, Young Man." *Americas* 13 no. 6 (1967): 6–9.

10. ———. *Human Geography and Neighboring Disciplines.* Chicago, forthcoming.

11. Dickinson, Joshua C. III. Route 25 Reconnaissance (Colombia) and Agricultural Ecology in Uala (Panama)." In *Bioenvironmental and Radiological Safety Feasibility Studies, Atlantic-Pacific Interoceanic Canal Agricultural Ecology.* Final Report, vol. 3, pp. 41–52. Gainesville, Fla., 1968.

12. Dozier, Craig L. "Mexico's Transformed Northwest: The Yaqui, Mayo and Fuerte Examples." *Geographical Review* 53, no. 4 (October 1968).

13. Foster, George M. *Traditional Cultures and the Impact of Technological Change.* New York, 1962.

14. Gourou, Pierre. *The Tropical World.* London, 1958.

15. Hegen, Edmund E. *Highways into the Upper Amazon Basin.* Gainesville, Fla., 1966.

16. Hoy, Don R. "Geographer's Role in Development Planning in Guatemala." *Professional Geographer* 20, no. 5 (September 1969): 333–36.

17. *International Development Assistance: A Statement by the Task Force on International Developmental Assistance and International Education.* National Association of State Universities and Land Grant Colleges, 1969.

18. Masing, Ulf. "Foreign Agricultural Colonies in Costa Rica: An Analysis of Foreign Colonization in a Tropical Environment." Ph.D. dissertation, University of Florida, 1964.

310

19. McGill University Savanna Research Project. Various technical reports and publishing accomplished under U.S. Office of Naval Research, Geography Branch Contract no. Nonr-3855(00).

20. McPherson, W. W., ed. *Economic Development of Tropical Agriculture.* Gainesville, Fla., 1968.

21. Minkel, Clarence W. "A Bi-National Experiment in the Urban Geography and planning of Guatemala." *Pennsylvania Geographer* 4, no. 3 (November 1966).

22. Momsen, Richard P., Jr. "The Role of the Geographer in Development Surveys, with Examples from the South American Tropics." *Professional Geographer* 17, no. 1 (January 1965): 1–3.

23. Organization for Tropical Studies, Inc. *A Program of Activities for 1968–1969.*

24. Paddock, William, and Paul Paddock. *Famine 1975.* Boston, 1967.

25. Paganini, Louis A. "Agricultural Systems of the Chucunaque-Turia Basin, Darien, Panama." Ph.D. dissertation, University of Florida, in preparation.

26. Pico, Rafael. "La estrategia de la planificación en Puerto Rico." *Revista de la Sociedad Interamericana de Planificación* 2, no. 7 (September 1968).

27. Smith, Vernon R. "Rural Economic Activity in the La Palma Area of Panama: An Analysis of Three Ethnic Groups." Master's thesis, University of Florida, 1967.

28. Thomas, William L., Jr., ed. *Man's Role in Changing the Face of the Earth.* Chicago, 1956.

29. Tosi, Joseph A., Jr. "Zonas de vida natural en el Perú." *Boletín Técnico* (Instituto Interamericano de Ciencias Agrícolas de la OEA, Project 39), no. 5 (1960).

30. Wagley, Charles, ed. *Social Science Research on Latin America.* New York, 1964.

31. Wesche, Rolf J. "The Settler Wedge of the Upper Putamayo River." Ph.D. dissertation, University of Florida, 1967.

32. Williams, Jerry R. "The Human Ecology of Mulatupu, San Blas: Caribbean Gateway to a Proposed Sea-Level Canal." Master's thesis, University of Florida, 1967.

33. Winnie, W. W., Jr. "The Papaloapan Project: An Experiment in Tropical Agriculture." *Economic Geography* 34, no. 1 (January 1958).

34. Winsberg, Morton D. "Jewish Agricultural Colonization in Argentina." *Geographical Review* 54, no. 4 (October 1964): 487–501.

35. *The World Food Problem: A Report of the President's Science Advisory Committee's Panel on the World Food Supply.* Vol. 1. Washington, D.C., 1967.

# ECONOMIC INTEGRATION

## *Martin Carnoy*

The literature of Latin American integration forms an important part of the intellectual battleground between Latin American reformers and the elites of the developed world. The reformers reacted to the theory of international trade in the late 1940s and early 1950s in much the same way that their economies reacted to the temporary collapse of the international economic system twenty years earlier. They realized that since the doctrines of traditional theory do not serve the less developed world, then traditional theory itself is a rationalizing device of existing inequalities, and conflicts directly with Latin American development aims. It therefore became intellectually necessary to attack developed-country concepts of the international exchange of goods and the distribution of income, and to pose alternatives which would increase, rather than diminish, the Latin American share of world output. The major focus of the reformers became the economic integration of the region.

Much of the literature on integration, then, tends to be normative—its aim is to justify economic integration, to mobilize intellectual and political groups behind the integration movement, and to find the most rapid road to increased regional trade. The strength of this type of analysis is its motion and direction. Treaties *were* signed.[1] Largely through the discussions which surrounded the establishment of economic unions in Central America and the larger economies of Latin America, the traditional theory of customs union *was* revised and made dynamic to fit the political reality of growth objectives in the "third world." These are important and permanent results. However, the great weakness of the normative approach is that it yields almost no information on its own past effectiveness and the probability of its future effectiveness. Nine years after the treaties that established

---

1. The General Treaty for Central America Economic Integration (Treaty of Managua) was signed by El Salvador, Guatemala, Honduras, and Nicaragua in December, 1960. Costa Rica signed the treaty in July, 1962. The Montevideo Treaty was signed in February 1960 by seven countries—Argentina, Brazil, Chile, Mexico, Paraguay, Peru and Uruguay. Shortly afterwards, Colombia and Ecuador subscribed to its provisions. The treaty established the Latin American Free Trade Association (LAFTA). Both treaties went into effect in June, 1961, and LAFTA was subsequently and recently joined by Bolivia and Venezuela.

these unions were signed, little more is known about the process of integration in less developed countries—as opposed to the reason for it—than was known in the 1950s. Lack of information has led to the avoidance of important decisions or to ineffective resolutions and policies. In the present body of research there are few empirical foundations available for these decisions.

Besides the elements of intellectual style and purpose, the literature has a distinct temporal pattern. As a previous survey points out (41), research in this field closely follows the evolution of integration itself. Before the institutionalization of the integration process, the literature concentrated on the rationalization of integration as an important and positive force in Latin American development. After the treaties were signed, a great deal of descriptive work emerged which also attempted to analyze the rationale behind the provisions. Once the Central American Common Market (CACM) and the Latin American Free Trade Association (LAFTA) had been operating for a few years, studies of their effect were undertaken; in some cases, the authors began to investigate the causes of effectiveness or ineffectiveness.

The purpose of this review is to present the most significant contributions to the subject of Latin American economic integration. The bibliography at the end of the paper includes a number of studies not reviewed, but which may be of interest to the reader. The review concentrates on four topics of research: (a) the "background" literature, which establishes the challenge to existing theory and develops the concepts for Latin American customs unions; (b) the "discussion" literature which analyzes the challenge and concepts evolving from (a); (c) the empirical literature, which attempts to measure the relationships discussed in (a) and (b); and (d) the literature which analyzes the relation between the United States and the Latin American integration movement.

## THE BACKGROUND LITERATURE

Although the 1949 *Economic Survey of Latin America* (49) only mentions economic integration in passing, it is an essential piece of reading for those interested in the integration issue. The first part of the *Survey* presents the arguments and empirical justification for the Economic Commission for Latin America's (ECLA) attack on the traditional theory of trade. The discussion attempts to show why Latin America—and by implication, all less developed countries (LDCs)—

must industrialize and protect its industrial sector from foreign competition. This discussion forms the basis of all ECLA literature on trade, including the liberalization of trade among Latin American countries.

Beginning in 1949 as well, ECLA published a series of documents which propose the rationale and eventually the ground rules for the integration of the region (49–59). The analysis contained in these documents is based on two assumptions: first, "industrialization is an inevitable feature of economic development," and second, "a reasonable measure of protection is generally indispensable for industrialization" (52). These assumptions result from the grim prospects for primary exports and the constraints imposed by basing development on such exports. The analysis argues that while industrialization is essential to development, it becomes increasingly difficult to substitute domestic production for imports once the stage of light manufacturing is passed; markets for capital equipment and large consumer durables are too small in any single Latin American economy to make the production of these goods even reasonably competitive with imports. In the case of capital and equipment, the high price of domestic production is especially harmful to further development because capital goods enter into both light industry and agriculture as inputs. The case for industrialization and for development rests on the constraints imposed by a decrease in traditional exports relative to imports. Increasing the rate of growth in this model, therefore, requires an increase in exports, achieved by exporting manufactures, or a decrease in imports, achieved by shifting the unit of account from the individual country to the region and increasing regional trade relative to trade with the outside world. In both ways, the balance-of-payments problem which has shackled further industrialization (and therefore the rate of growth) is greatly reduced. Economic integration is, for ECLA, the primary way out of the balance-of-payments dilemma; with larger markets and eventually reduced imports from outside the region, Latin America can overcome the obstacles which face the development process.

Another theme that runs through the ECLA studies is that lowering or eliminating tariffs is not enough to increase regional trade. Not only do nontariff obstacles such as historical tradition and poor transportation impede intra–Latin American trade, but the equitable distribution of industrialization and growth are essential elements of economic union among these countries. Market forces can be expected to polarize points of growth in the region with free trade, so regional planning is necessary to assure that the benefits of integration accrue to all members. This is the "reciprocity" principle. The principle is interpreted in a number of ways. In *The Latin American Common Market* (53), for example, it is suggested that there may be imbalances in growth, but the "advantages and disadvantages accruing to each country from the common market should not be judged from differences between the individual rate of development of each member country with respect to that of the others. The real yardstick is the difference that each country could attain inside and outside the common market, respectively" (53). Economic planning as proposed by ECLA is also a reaction to the unplanned protectionism which has characterized Latin America since the 1930s. Industrialization has been carried out without much regard for the relative cost of various import substitutions or for the most effective means to produce a given product.[2] One of the recommendations made by ECLA, which fulfills both the distribution requirement and the effectiveness of import substitution, is the "complementarity agreement," under which various components of a product are manufactured in different countries and the final product is assembled in each country. These principles and recommendations were incorporated into reports which outlined the structure of a regional market and a multilateral payments system (53). The bases for the common market place special accent on assurances for less developed countries in the region, including a provision for temporary import restrictions if those countries undergo persistent disequilibrium in their balance of payments with the rest of the region.

At the same time that ECLA was promoting the economic integration of the entire region, the Commission was also involved in helping to create the Central American Common Market (51). Despite the differences in levels of development among the CACM members, there is no specific reciprocity provision in the Managua Treaty which corresponds to those in the Treaty of Montevideo (56); however, the Central American agreement includes an Agreement on the Regime for Central American Integration Industries which defines those industries whose minimum capacity requires the whole Central American

---

2. For example, there are a multiplicity of automobile and tractor factories in Argentina and Brazil, none of which is operating nearly at Western European output levels. Because of product differentiation and extremely high tariffs, even very inefficient producers can continue to exist.

Market as "integration industries." Provisions were made to promote an equitable geographic distribution of new industrial plants in those industries, thus creating, in effect, a reciprocity arrangement.

Although ECLA continued to produce studies after the treaties were signed, its next significant contribution came as LAFTA began to flounder. In early 1965, the dissatisfaction of the reformers with the progress of LAFTA prompted a letter from the president of Chile, Eduardo Frei, to Raul Prebisch, José Antonia Mayobre, Felipe Herrera, and Carlos Sanz de Santa María, four of the leading "técnicos" and reformers in Latin America. The letter called for a Latin American Common Market (LACM) and the replacement of the Treaty of Montevideo with a new instrument which would assure the rapid attainment of economic integration among Latin American countries. The letter, the answer from the four, and the proposals of ECLA for a LACM are reproduced in *Hacia la integración acelerada de América Latina* (23). These efforts resulted in the Declaration of the Presidents of America at Punta del Este in April, 1967.[3]

## THE DISCUSSION LITERATURE

As the negotiations for CACM and LAFTA moved into an advance stage in the late 1950s, some of the economists closely involved with the ECLA efforts began writing accounts of the integration movement—its origins, its raison d'être, and the meaning of the reciprocity arrangements and other provisions. The main purpose of these articles and books is to inform and substantiate, the latter to readers raised on the dicta of free trade and the traditional theory. Since the writers have, in a sense, a vested interest in the success of Latin American economic union, their analysis is limited to interpreting the various aspects of integration proposals, and to assess the obstacles which face the realization of economic union. The first of these studies, published in 1959 and 1960 by the Centro de Estudios Monetarios Latinoamericanos (CEMLA) were written by Sidney Dell (16) and Victor Urquidi (63). Both books summarize the ECLA arguments for customs union among LDCs. Both review the proposals that had been put forth at that time for the formation of common markets. Urquidi's approach tends to be more historical, and Dell's somewhat more subject oriented, since each chapter is a lecture given at CEMLA. Because of his Euro-

---

3. The Punta del Este meeting is discussed below in the context of U.S. relations with Latin American integration.

pean experience, Dell also discusses the lessons of the European Economic Community (EEC) and how they apply to Latin American integration. Both authors pay considerable attention to the problem of less developed countries in a Latin American union, to the principle of reciprocity, and to the contrast between the different aims of customs unions among developed countries (to increase the efficiency of existing industries) and among less developed countries (to permit the creation of new industries).

Dell raises one important point that Urquidi only mentions in passing: how much more likely is the success of small contiguous groups of countries than of a large, disparate economic union? Dell argues against such smaller unions despite the higher probability in such groups of finding opportunities for regional specialization. He argues for the global approach because he fears that once these subregional groupings are formed, it will be very difficult to supersede them with regional economic cooperation.

But neither writer analyzes the political bases for such cooperation. In the late 1950s and early 1960s, all the major countries of Latin America had "reformist," elected governments which were sympathetic to the idea of regional cooperation. Clearly, the extent of the market depends on the willingness of the member governments to cooperate with other members. As became obvious later on, the more global the market, the more likely that one of the members would beget an unfavorable political situation and stall the entire movement. Urquidi sees the principle, but does not analyze its implication for the probable success of either CACM or LAFTA:

> The Latin American free trade area and, ultimately, the common market, will only progress if the member countries are capable of submitting their national interests—which should never be neglected— to the interests of the region as a whole; and to do this by negotiation and mutual confidence, because eventually the interests of the region will coincide with the interest of the individual countries. [62, p. 116]

After the signings of the integration treaties, a number of studies appeared which cover more or less the same ground as the Dell and Urquidi books. Each, of course, has its own points to make, and with the passage of time, there is more information to present to the uninformed reader. Dell himself produced another book in 1963, *Trade Blocs and Common Markets* (17), which deals with a number of customs unions besides CACM and LAFTA. He repeats the arguments of his earlier work for unions among less developed countries, but adds considerable criticism of United States' trade practices, arguing that protection of U.S. domestic, agricultural and industrial interests has forced the LDCs to produce for themselves. He also discusses Latin America's fear that foreign private enterprise will use Latin American integration for its own ends, a theme which he continues in his next book, *A Latin American Common Market?* (15). Since the book was written in 1965, however, Dell has the opportunity to analyze some of the posttreaty problems of the two Latin American markets. In his view, "the absence of an agreed program of joint development has thus been a major factor—perhaps the most important factor of all—in slowing down the process of tariff-cutting within LAFTA." He further suggests that "what LAFTA countries need most is to eliminate their mutual tariffs not so much on existing trade, but on the industrial goods they import from developed countries" (15). In general, he comes down hard for "deliberate and rationally determined planning," since market forces will tend to concentrate development in richer areas, bypassing poorer areas. He also points out, in the context of the CACM, that much of manufacturing growth in the CACM consists of assembly. The danger of unplanned industrial development such as the increase in assembly plants is that it may increase external vulnerability without adding much to growth. He advocates integration industries in CACM, criticizing the Interamerican Bank and the U.S. Agency for International Development (AID) for refusing to let their funds be used for these industries. The most interesting chapters in the book, however, treat the problems of transportation in LAFTA and the role of foreign private enterprise. These problems are closely intertwined with U.S.–Latin American relations, and Dell is critical of the political performance of the United States in both.

Raymond Mikesell is another non–Latin American who was intimately involved with the formation of the LAFTA. In Albert Hirschman's collection of essays, *Latin American Issues* (38), Mikesell reviews the role of ECLA in promoting economic union, and discusses the issues confronting union with a more pessimistic view than either Dell or Urquidi. Mikesell does not hide his dislike of many of the provisions of the Montevideo Treaty, especially the absence of across-the-board tariff cuts and the principle of reciprocity, both of which he believes will "constitute a very serious limitation on the expansion of trade among the members of LAFTA, and probably an insuperable barrier to the eventual achievement of a free trade area" (38). He also criticizes the absence of provision for market competition within the area:

> This is certainly in line with ECLA's negative attitude toward competition in favor of regulation, planning and government operation, but it is firmly rooted in the attitudes and practices of most Latin American governments. The concept of competition is certainly not a respected one in Latin America. . . . On the other hand, there is recognition of a need for greater complementarity between the industrial sectors of individual Latin American countries. . . . If complementarity is to be achieved by means of private agreements, which would amount to international cartel arrangements, such agreements either will need to be subject to a high degree of governmental control or they are likely to be in opposition to consumer and general public interest. [38, pp. 141–42]

Mikesell is critical of other provisions as well, especially the escape clauses provided by the treaty, which he regards as yet another means to avoid achieving free trade within the region. Altogether, he would probably put the blame for the slowness of tariff-cutting not on the absence of planning (Dell), but on the lack of willingness of the signing countries to enter into free trade competition in the first place. The ECLA model, however, assumes that Latin American countries *should not* enter into destructive competition with each other. As Urquidi points out in his rebuttal of Mikesell, "to throw the doors wide open to the extent of imposing drastic readjustments on a particular country would be self-defeating" (61). In the ECLA view, as upheld by Dell's statement about "new industries," which produce the goods currently imported from developed countries, the purpose of integration is not to make existing production more efficient, but to permit the continuation of the industrialization process. The critical issue is whether such partial integration is at all possible, even though it seems politically more feasible. Mikesell's assessment of the Montevideo Treaty made in 1960 turned out to be a much better predictor of the future of LAFTA than the more optimistic view of Urquidi. Countries have been using the escape clauses frequently, they have not been willing to subject current production to tariff cuts, and the two complementarity agreements now functioning are essentially cartel arrangements. Conversely, Mikesell's insistence on private investment versus public, and "competition" versus "monopoly," as Urquidi says, is largely paying homage to developed-country concepts and dilutes the strength of his valid criticisms.

The largest collection of writings on integration outside of ECLA and Sidney Dell is a book edited by Miguel Wionczek, *Latin American Economic Integration* (67). It contains nineteen essays, including two by Wionczek himself, and selections by Dell, Balassa, Linder, Prebisch, Mikesell, Herrera, Triffin, Garcia Reynoso, and others. Wionczek's first article, "Requisites for Viable Integration," launches a passionate attack on the developed-country view of the requirements for customs unions, and defines the very different theoretical basis of Latin American integration. He goes on to draft a brief outline of the conditions that an integration program should meet in less developed regions in order to avoid a predestined failure. Wionczek agrees in essence with Dell that planning is crucial to such an endeavor, and that the "concept of reciprocity has to be a broader one and might well comprise four essential aspects of integration: balance of payments; overall growth; industrialization; and the relative level of development" (67). Wionczek also begins to define those groups in Latin America who are prointegration, and those who are against the movement. Unfortunately, his terms of definition cast them in "good-guy" and "bad-guy" categories rather than attempting to analyze the ecopolitical structure in which integration efforts must operate.

The three theoretical essays by Bela Balassa, Staffan Linder, and Hiroshi Kitamura (67) should be put together with an excellent article by Keith Griffin and Ricardo French-Davis (21) to familiarize the reader with the discussion relating traditional to dynamic trade theory. These papers formalize the earlier ECLA discussion and summarize the evolution of dynamic theory. There are a number of other theoretical pieces which do not refer directly to Latin America, but grew out of the controversy between the LDCs' and the developed countries' concepts of customs union. Bela Balassa has made several contributions to this literature (2, 3, 4). Tibor Scitovsky, in his evaluation of the European Common Market (46), suggests that the most important effect of liberalizing trade in Europe is not the welfare gains from increased specialization or economies of scale, but an increased rate of investment which results from the risk-spreading influence of larger markets. Cooper and Massell (14) describe the social welfare function of LDCs not only in terms of the rate of per capita income growth, but the rate of industrialization as well. LDCs will give up a certain amount of overall growth in the short run in order to have an industrial sector and the modernity that that sector implies.

The second set of essays in Wionczek (67), which take up most of the collection, deal with LAFTA. They are, on the whole, quite disappointing if the reader has read the ECLA literature, one of Dell's books, or Urquidi. None of the articles except Barry Siegal's and Gonzalez del Valle's says anything that is not said more effectively or clearly either by someone else or by the author himself in some other piece. Dell repeats Dell, Prebisch repeats Prebisch, Mikesell is still concerned about competition, and this time applies his concerns to the external financing of integration. He supports, for example, the withholding of funds from the Central American Bank for Economic Integration (CABEI) for use in "integration industries"—the potential monopolies of CACM—and he recommends that similar restrictions should be put on external financing for LAFTA projects. Enrique Angulo's piece on transportation problems is in the same genre as Dell's chapter on the same subject. The interested reader can pursue either one for a good background to the problem. Neither, however, compares to Robert Brown's study (7) reviewed below.

The two best articles in this section of Wionczek's book, and the best article of the following section on Central American integration, all have to do with payments systems. There are two issues in the payments system problem: the first is the conflict with the International Monetary Fund (IMF), which is against Latin American clearing arrangements because it believes that such arrangements slow down the movement toward currency convertibility, and that with currency convertibility, payments unions are not necessary. ECLA argues that even if the clearing house does tend to slow currency convertibility, it will increase trade among Latin American countries. Siegal comments:

> Indeed, the recent debates between ECLA, on the one hand, and United States officials and the IMF, on the other, are very reminiscent of the classic controversies that arose in the 19th century between protection-minded young republics, such as the United States, and free-trade-oriented industrialized countries, such as Great Britain. [67, p. 241]

The second issue is more complex: Should the clearing house give credits to those with overall trade deficits or to those with regional trade deficits? Siegal summarizes the pros and cons of both these issues, as well as compromise proposals advanced by Mikesell and Triffin.[4] Triffin presents the Triffin proposals in his contribution to

---

4. These proposals were advanced at CEMLA's seventh operational meeting and are published in *Cooperación financiera en Américan Latina.*

Wionczek's book (67), but a much better English version of these proposals is to be found in the *Journal of Common Market Studies* (48). The latter piece has the added advantage of placing some expected magnitudes on the proposals, even though these figures are only presented for the Caribbean rim and Central America. The González del Valle paper in Wionczek (67) analyzes the effect of multilateral payments in Central America. It shows that between 1961 and 1963, an increasing percentage of total settlements in Central American trade were represented by multilateral clearances (44 percent increasing to 74 percent) while dollar payments fell to only 16 percent of total settlements. Also, the automatic credits provided for in the multilateral arrangement are quite small in relation to total settlements. The analysis is brought up to date in another article by the same author in *Journal of Common Market Studies* (20).

Before moving on to the empirical literature, two other studies should be mentioned. The first is by Felipe Herrera (26) and it contains, in its first chapter, an excellent statement of the political idealism of the technocratic reformers:

> It would seem that our peoples, distressed by misery, surrounded by an inferiority complex that is accentuated by observing the progress achieved in other regions, would have lost faith in their creative capacity. Latin America must carry out the gest of its political unity, not only because through it she can give content and effectiveness to economic integration and the common welfare that is expected from integration, but, besides, because that collective fulfillment will bring with it the creation of dynamic spiritual forces that will allow us to consolidate the belief in our cultural values and avoid that the expressions of this continent be only a copy of foreign concepts. [26, pp. 32–33, my translation]

The second work is a paper by Carlos Díaz-Alejandro on the Andean Group (19). It evaluates the economic rationale for the subregion and its prospects. The Andean countries (Bolivia, Chile, Colombia, Ecuador, Peru, and Venezuela) formed this group in August, 1966, as a reaction to the difficulties encountered by LAFTA. Their governments are generally more progressive than those of Argentina and Brazil (the group, of course, includes its own military government, in Peru, since 1968), and the economies are somewhat more homogeneous than the entire LAFTA. Díaz argues that the potential trade-creative effects of an Andean common market are large, provided that tariffs are reduced on already established "vegetative" activities. Although the dynamic effects may be more important in the long run, he stresses that these activities are no longer infants, and that they are ready to face Latin American competition and are *almost* ready to face world markets. Thus Díaz disagrees with Dell's view that integration should take place only in the dynamic sector, even though limiting it to the dynamic sector may be politically easier.

## The Empirical Literature

There are an increasing number of studies which move away from the attempt to justify Latin American integration or explain it, and begin to measure the changes which have resulted from integration or the relationships which may affect its course. Some of the articles which belong here have been included in the previous two sections. For example, the 1949 *Economic Survey*, section B of *The Latin American Common Market*, and the Triffin and González del Valle articles all make empirical contributions to the literature.

The first comprehensive attempt to determine the effect of integration on trade in LAFTA is *Latin American Trade Patterns* (1). Because its publication came only a few years after the Montevideo Treaty went into effect, the study can only suggest a methodology for measuring changes in trade patterns. The most useful tables are those which break down intra-LAFTA (including Bolivian and Venezuelan) trade into various types of products and product groupings (primary, intermediate, and manufactured) by country and by year between 1959 and 1963. By combining these tables with similar ones for more recent years it would be possible to measure the effect of tariff versus nontariff effects on trade.

Little is known about the actual level of tariffs in Latin America, especially since we may be interested in the level of "effective" tariffs (the tariff on value added) rather than "nominal" tariffs (the tariff on total value). Research is being conducted now at the International Bank for Reconstruction and Development (World Bank) under the direction of Bela Balassa which aims at measuring effective tariffs in several Latin American countries. Nominal tariff levels are available from a study by Santiago Macario (34). Macario shows that the average level of nominal tariffs is extremely high in Argentina, Brazil, and Chile relative to tariff levels in developed countries and even other Latin American countries. He contends that these high tariffs are a major cause of the slow rates of growth in these countries in recent years—there has been overprotection of many industries which has resulted in a pernicious tax on exports and domestic agricultural production. His analysis suffers from not accounting for nontariff barriers, such as quotas, which are used in place of tariffs by countries like Mexico. Therefore, Macario does not show how Mexico's protection compares with that of the other large economies in Latin America. On the other hand, it could be argued that the large income from tourism makes Mexico a special case and Macario's conclusions would still hold even if Mexico protection were also high. The article is important because it implies that, at least for countries like Argentina, Brazil, and Chile, there may still be considerable room for improvement of their balance-of-payments position and continued industrialization and development from merely rationalizing the tariff structure. If this rationalization results in a lowering of production costs in manufacturing, and the developed countries lower their own tariffs against LDC manufactures (29), the larger, more advanced LDCs might expand their manufacturing sectors without entering into economic union with each other. Of course, they would then be subject to economic fluctuations in the developed world, much as they were in the 1930s, so the benefits and possibilities of this alternative to integration have to be weighed against the dynamic effect implied by the added risk of producing for non–Latin American markets.

A similar lack of knowledge faces policy makers when they deal with the effects of economies of scale. Although the scale variable is vital to the whole discussion of Latin American integration, its magnitude in the Latin American context has been approximated for only a few industries. Ana M. Martirena de Mantel (35) estimates the cost function for the steel industry in Latin America, David Kendrick (30) develops a dynamic linear programming model and estimates cost functions for steel production in Brazil in order to find the optimum location for that industry in Brazil, and Vietorisz and Manne (64) use process analysis and linear programming to show the variation of cost of producing nitrogenous fertilizers at various locations in Latin America. Carnoy (9), in conjunction with a number of Latin American economic institutes, builds on the Vietorisz and Manne model to approximate the welfare gains to the region of producing six product groups in Latin America on a regional scale rather than importing, and of producing on a regional scale rather than on a national scale. The results of the Carnoy study are interesting because they show that the welfare gains are considerably greater than those found for the EEC. The difference is due to the potential effects of economies of scale in a Latin American market. Although the results of all scale studies are only approximate, since production does not presently take place in most industries in Latin American countries over the whole range of production possibilities, they do indicate that in many such industries, regional production could make Latin American costs competitive with developed-country exports.

The Brown study (7) analyzes transport problems in South America. He finds that the attention of LAFTA members since 1961 has been focused largely on devising a draft convention designed to develop a Latin American merchant fleet instead of solving the more important problem of improving the area's transport service. His data show that per mile shipping rates in southern South America and along the West Coast compare favorably with per mile rates between Europe and South America and between the United States and the region; however, the rates between Caribbean ports and both the West and East Coasts are relatively very high. Furthermore, port costs in Latin America are also very high and harmful to trade. Brown cites the need for frequent and regular service between LAFTA countries, and to achieve this, he recommends multilateral cargo reserves for liner ships following fixed schedules and charging published rates.

All of the empirical studies reviewed here have dealt with specific problems such as economies of scale, trade patterns, or transport. There are two important empirical works on Central America which are more general in scope and attempt to measure the total effect of the common market on the rate of growth in that region. Hansen's recent study (24) is an extensive review of the first five years of the CACM. Together with Castillo's more historical orientation (10) and Nye's study (42), it provides a rather complete analysis of the background, achievements, and problems of the Central American integration movement. Hansen points out that despite the fact that most of the increase in growth rate in the region in the early 1960s can be explained by a rapid increase in traditional exports to the developed world, the CACM has had an important effect on the rate of industrialization in the region and the type of products produced. Between 1960 and 1965, there was a threefold increase in the percent of total Central American trade that went to Central America, a fivefold increase in the absolute quantity of manufactured goods traded, and a fall in traditional manufacturing as a percentage of total manufacturing from 87 percent in 1960 to 82 percent in 1964 through the creation of new industries, primarily chemicals. But the CACM faces serious problems: much of the industrial growth has been in assembly industries; thus, the value-added component of these industries is small and results in making foreign exchange for imports even more essential to the functioning of the economy. Hansen also argues that assembly industries do not exploit the natural-resource base of the area. Furthermore, higher post-CACM protection levels are taxing agricultural production, and there is little coordination of industrialization in the region. The principle of reciprocity, designed to help industrialize Honduras and Nicaragua and built into the Managua Treaty through the Regime of Integrated Industries, has not worked because of opposition from the U.S. and the Interamerican Development Bank. These problems can probably be overcome by the technocrats; however, Hansen is not as sure that CACM technocrats can cope with the unequal distribution of income and wealth—primarily agricultural land—in the region. Neither can the political structure in the member countries continue to be ignored. Despite his careful economic analysis of the effects of union, however, and his recognition of political and social problems as they relate to economic development. Hansen gives us little insight into the changes provoked in these noneconomic variables by the CACM.

Donald McClelland's paper (36) conflicts with Hansen's statement that the increase in exports to the world explains the entire increase in growth rates in CACM during its first years. McClelland explains that the effect of CACM has centered on the manufacturing sector, and the contribution of intra–Central American trade to growth is a function of the multiplier effect of manufacturing growth on the rest of the economy. He concludes that with a "minimum normal" growth of 5 percent for manufacturing, a 4 percent for the whole economy, a 0.2 export multiplier and a 0.5 manufacturing multiplier, 4 percent of the 7 percent rate of growth in Central America from mid–1962 to 1965 is due to minimum normal growth, 2 percent to the increased growth of exports, and about 1 percent to CACM.

There are several good papers which, unlike those of the technocrats, try to come to grips with the political and social variables influencing integration. Haas and Schmitter (22) attempt to fit LAFTA negotiations and difficulties into a model of "politicized economic integration." The intervening variables which "politicize" economic concerns at the regional level are strangely similar to the conditions set down for economic union by traditional trade theory. Nevertheless, the model is used effectively to analyze regional interest groups and the style of LAFTA negotiations. The authors conclude that

> thinking about industrialization and economic development continues to focus on national rather than regional perspectives; hence preferential margins in favor of LAFTA trade and discriminating against traditional outlets and suppliers have simply not found consistent favor. One of the reasons for this style of negotiation is surely to be found in the particularistic and diffuse nature of many Latin American business practices and in their influence in government circles, as opposed to the efforts of cohesive groups of manufacturers accustomed to hard bargaining with government officials along functionally specific lines, as in Western Europe and the United States. [22, p. 21]

Haas and Schmitter also feel that the "técnicos" have failed to get the private sector behind integration because they have failed "in developing a viable decision-making style that would make LAFTA's institutions into dynamic promoters of regional integration." According to the authors, this is due in part to the diverse loyalty of the tecnicos, and their resultant lack of concentration on LAFTA. There are few, if any, democratic forces in the region which will come to the automatic assistance of the integration process; therefore, the tecnicos, if they are to succeed, must not only agree on a plan of action, they must articulate more effectively to national decision makers. The politicians must then "lend their power to an institutional breakthrough as a result of which the dynamic industrial entrepreneur can play the role in which the tecnicos have cast him" (22).

Teubal (47) is even more pessimistic than Haas and Schmitter. He characterizes the ECLA tecnicos as most in accord with reformist governments, and integration as depending on the existence of such governments in Latin America. He states that the group that ECLA has in mind to push for integration are the "national bourgeoisies" of member countries, but he does not believe the national bourgeoisies in Latin America are capable of assuming the role that explicitly or implicitly is assigned to it by ECLA, since they are connected largely with the traditional manufacturing sector and hence see their immediate interests in conflict with the interests of manufacturing sectors in other countries. Heavy industry, which should be much more responsive to integration, is largely in the hands of foreigners. In addition, reformist governments depend on especially favorable economic conditions, and so usually do not last long. The present Brazil and Argentine governments represent the reaction to popular reformism and are ultranationalistic. They are currently encouraging the expansion of industry on a national scale through liberal rationalization of tariffs, an indirect alternative to regional integration and planning.

## THE RELATION BETWEEN THE UNITED STATES AND LATIN AMERICAN INTEGRATION

The role of the United States in one or another aspect of Latin American integration has already been referred to a number of times in this review. Although the U.S. did not take a formal part in integration until the preparation for the Presidents' Meeting at Punta del Este in April, 1967, it has played an important informal role in integration attempts during the entire postwar period. The U.S. has intervened directly in two aspects of integration: as a number of authors have pointed out, among them Hansen and Mikesell, the Agency for International Development has withheld funds to CABEI that would be used to finance integration industries in CACM, and this has had an important and detrimental effect on the reciprocity arrangements in CACM. U.S. shipping interests working through the State Department have threatened to impose sanctions against Latin American countries which reserved cargo for Latin American ships—this despite the fact that the U.S. government reserves cargo for U.S. shippers in all international loans or grants.

The U.S. position on Latin American integration as expressed at Punta del Este is still that integration must not interfere with competition in the region, and that any common market arrangement must provide "reasonably low" external tariffs to competition from outside the region. The United States continues to push for the promotion of foreign private investment in any integrated region, also in the name of competition and the access to markets. These views are in direct conflict with the reformist ideas of regional planning of the ECLA, and the possible need for increased protection to promote further industrialization. Foreign investment, while recognized as an important means of transferring technology and of increasing the rate of investment, is feared by Latin Americans because of its great power, and cannot be accepted by them as the primary dynamic force in the LACM. During the preparations for the Presidents' Meeting, the Latin American view came into direct conflict with the U.S. view on both foreign investment and trade. Latin Americans saw the opportunity to press the U.S. on lowering developed-country tariff barriers to LDC primary and manufactured goods. The U.S. was and is not willing to do this unilaterally, and, in sharp contrast to the agreements reached among developed countries in the Kennedy round, the issue of tariff preferences for LDC goods remains completely suspended.

There are a number of recent studies which form the general background to U.S.–Latin American relations. All have a distinct point of view, however, and so no single book should be read alone. Robert Burr's *Our Troubled Hemisphere* (8), for example, while seeming to be well balanced, concludes that Latin America should be more independent, but it should be modeled on U.S. concepts of democracy and capitalism. It is in the interest of the United States for Latin America to grow rapidly, because, by growing rapidly, the kind of system which is compatible with U.S. interests will be preserved. Burr does not question whether independence and growth in Latin America are at all compatible with U.S. concepts of democracy and capitalism. Robert Heilbroner discusses these possible fallacies in U.S. concepts of "third world" development in his article "Counterrevolutionary America" (25).

The best discussion of various current views of Latin American integration in the United States is presented in the *Hearings on Latin American Development and Western Hemisphere Trade* (60). The *Hearings* cover a range of reports and testimony from U.S. businessmen, U.S. government officials, intellectuals, and Latin American reformers, such as Felipe Herrera. It is probably also worthwhile to read the opinion on integration of the "enlightened" business community as represented by the Committee for Economic Development's *Cooperation for Progress in Latin America* (12) and *Regional Integration and the Trade of Latin America* (13). These can be compared to the ECLA view of integration, which, it should be clear, is a reformist solution to Latin American problems, and is hardly radical or revolutionary.

The literature on foreign private investment in a LACM is directed at the very real problem of foreign-firm domination of the future market. A good expression of the Latin American view of the foreign investor can be found in Raymond Vernon's *How Latin America Views the U.S. Investor* (66), and there is a short summary of the problem of foreign investment in LAFTA and CACM in Dell's study of the common market (15). The most extensive treatment of foreign investment in LAFTA is a series of studies recently published by the Interamerican Development Bank (5). While most of the studies are specifically interested in multinational investment and how efficient it is in distributing growth and mobilizing capital, Paul Rosenstein-Rodan's essay presents an excellent summary of the arguments for and against foreign private investment. He discusses multinational investments in this context, and he concludes that economic integration requires multinational enterprises. In the EEC, the European enterprise was not created, and U.S.-based international firms have largely taken over its function.

# BIBLIOGRAPHY

1. Baerresen, Donald W., et al. *Latin American Trade Patterns*. Washington, D.C., 1965.

2. Balassa, Bela. *El desarrollo económico y la integración*. Mexico, 1965.

3. ———. The Theory of Economic Integration. London, 1961.

4. ———. "Toward a Theory of Economic Integration." *Kyklos* 14, no. 1 (1968): 1–17.

5. Banco Interamericano de Desarrollo. *Las inversiones multinacionales en el desarrollo y la integración de América Latina*. Washington, D.C., 1968.

6. Botero, Rodrigo. *La comunidad económica caribe andina*. Bogota, 1967.

7. Brown, Robert T. *Transport and the Economic Integration of South America*. Washington, D.C., 1966.

8. Burr, Robert. *Our Troubled Hemisphere*. Washington, D.C., 1967.

9. Carnoy, Martin. "A Welfare Analysis of Latin American Economic Union: Six Industry Studies." Paper presented at the Conference on the Economic Integration of Latin America, May 9–11, 1968, Stanford, California. Mimeographed.

10. Castillo, Carlos M. *Growth and Integration in Central America*. New York, 1966.

11. Centro de Estudios Monetarios Latinoamericanos. "VII reunión operativa, relatorias." *Técnicas Financieras* (Mexico) 4, no. 1 (September–October 1962): 3–14.

12. Committee for Economic Development. *Cooperation for Progress in Latin America*. New York, 1961.

13. ———. Regional Integration and the Trade of Latin America. (Supplementary paper no. 22.) New York, 1968.

14. Cooper, C. A., and B. F. Massell. "Toward a General Theory of Customs Unions for Developing Countries." *Journal of Political Economy* 73, no. 5 (October 1965): 460–76.

15. Dell, Sidney. *A Latin American Common Market?* New York, 1966.

16. ———. Problemas de un mercado común en América Latina. Mexico City, 1959.

17. ———. Trade Blocs and Common Markets. New York, 1963.

18. Development and Resources Corporation. *Multinational Investment Programs and Latin American Integration*. New York, 1966.

19. Díaz-Alejandro, Carlos F. "The Andean Group in the Integration Process of Latin America." Paper presented at the Conference on the Economic Integration of Latin America, May 9–11, 1968, Stanford, California. Mimeographed.

20. González del Valle, Jorge. "Monetary Integration in Central America: Achievements and Expectations." *Journal of Common Market Studies* (Oxford) 5, no. 1 (September 1966): 13–25.

21. Griffin, Keith, and Ricardo French-Davis. "Customs Unions and Latin American Integration." *Journal of Common Market Studies* 4 (October 1965): 1–21.

22. Haas, Ernst B., and Philippe C. Schmitter. *The Politics of Economics in Latin American Regionalism.* Denver, 1965.

23. *Hacia la integración acelerada de América Latina.* Mexico City, 1965.

24. Hansen, Roger D. *Central America: Regional Integration and Economic Development.* Washington, D.C., 1967.

25. Heilbroner, Robert. "Counterrevolutionary America." *Commentary,* April 1967, pp. 31–38.

26. Herrera, Felipe. *América Latina integrada.* Buenos Aires, 1964.

27. ———. "Inter-American Development Bank and Latin American Integration." *Journal of Common Market Studies* (Oxford) 5, no. 2 (December 1966): 172–80.

28. Hoselitz, Bert F. "Economic Development in Central America." *Weltwirtschaftliches Archiv* (Jena) 76 (1956): 267–308.

29. Johnson, Harry G. *Economic Policies toward Less Developed Countries.* Washington, D.C., 1967.

30. Kendrick, David. *Programming Investment in the Process Industries.* Cambridge, Mass., 1967.

31. Labastida, Horacio. "Aspectos sociales de la integración económica." *El Trimestre Económico* (Mexico) 32, no. 125 (January–March 1965): 70–88.

32. Little, I. M. D. "Regional International Companies as an Approach to Economic Integration." *Journal of Common Market Studies* (Oxford) 5, no. 2 (December 1966): 181–86.

33. Lower, Milton D. "Economic Integration in Latin America: A Dynamic Assessment." In *Some Aspects of Latin American Trade Policies,* pp. 1–30. Austin, Tex., 1964.

34. Macario, Santiago. "Protectionism and Industrialization in Latin America." *Economic Bulletin for Latin America* 9, no. 1 (March 1964): 61–101.

35. Martirena de Mantel, Ana M. "Integración y economías de escala." *El Trimestre Económico* (Mexico) 31, no. 123 (July–September 1964): 412–22.

36. McClelland, Donald. *The Common Market's Contribution to Central American Economic Integration: A First Approximation.* Paper presented at the Conference on the Economic Integration of Latin America, May 9–11, 1968, Stanford, California. Mimeographed.

37. Mikesell, Raymond F. *Liberalization of Inter–Latin American Trade.* Washington, D.C., 1957.

38. ———. "The Movement towards Regional Trading Groups in Latin America." In *Latin American Issues: Essays and Comments,* ed. by Albert O. Hirschman, pp. 125–51. New York, 1961.

39. Mills, Joseph C. "La política de desarrollo y los convenios regionales de comercio: El caso de América Latina." *El Trimestre Económico* (Mexico) 30, no. 119 (July–September 1963): 382–96.

40. Moscoso, Teodoro. *United States–Latin American Relations.* Oakland, Calif., 1965.

41. Navarrete, Jorge E. "Latin American Economic Integration: A Survey of Recent Literature." *Journal of Common Market Studies* (Oxford) 4, no. 2 (December 1965): 168–77.

42. Nye, Joseph S. *Central American Regional Integration.* New York, 1967.

43. Perloff, Harvey S., and Romula Almeida. "Regional Economic Integration in the Development of Latin America." *Economía Latinoamericana* (Pan American Union) 1, no. 2 (November 1963): 150–80.

44. Pincus, Joseph. *The Central American Common Market.* Mexico City, 1962.

45. Sammons, Robert L. "Proposals for a Common Market in Latin America." In *Public Policy, 1959–60: A Yearbook,* by Harvard University Graduate School of Public Administration. Cambridge, Mass., 1960.

46. Scitovsky, Tibor. *Economic Theory and Western European Integration.* London, 1958.

47. Teubal, Miguel. "El fracaso de la integración económica latinoamericana." *Desarrollo Económico* (Buenos Aires) 8, no. 29 (April–June 1968): 61–93.

48. Triffin, Robert. "International Monetary Arrangements, Capital Markets and Economic Integration in Latin America." *Journal of Common Market Studies* (Oxford) 4, no. 1 (Oct. 1965): 70–104.

49. United Nations, Economic Commission for Latin America. *Economic Survey of Latin America.* New York, 1949.

50. ———. *Foreign Private Investments in the Latin American Free-Trade Area.* New York, 1961.

51. ———. *La integración económica de América Central: Su evolución y perspectivas.* New York, 1956.

52. ———. *International Cooperation in a Latin American Development Policy.* New York, 1954.

53. ———. *The Latin American Common Market.* New York, 1959.

54. ———. *The Latin American Movement towards Multilateral Economic Cooperation.* New York, 1961.